India's Late, Late Industrial Revolution

There is a paradox at the heart of the Indian economy. Indian business-men and traders are highly industrious and ingenious people, yet for many years Indian industry was sluggish and slow to develop. One of the major factors in this sluggish development was the command and control regime known as the License Raj. This regime has gradually been removed and, after two decades of reform, India is now awakening from its slumber and is experiencing a late, late industrial revolution. This important new book catalogues and explains this revolution through a combination of rigorous analysis and entertaining anecdotes about India's entrepreneurs, Indian firms' strategies, and the changing role of government in Indian industry. This analysis shows that there is a strong case for a manufacturing focus so that India can replicate the success stories of Asian countries such as Japan, South Korea, and China.

SUMIT K. MAJUMDAR is Professor of Technology Strategy in the School of Management, University of Texas at Dallas, Richardson. Intimately familiar with Indian industry, he has observed India's industrial trans-formation, from a closed backward economy to one rapidly becoming one of the world's major powers, from an inimitable historical as well as a contemporary perspective. He maintains deep ties with and regularly visits India to engage in interactions with entrepreneurs and policymakers from all of India's industrial sectors. His interest areas are competition policy, entrepreneurship, political economy, regulation, and technology strategy. He has published extensively in the academic and popular presses and has edited the two-volume *Handbook of Telecommunications Economics*.

Advance praise for *India's Late, Late Industrial Revolution*

In the spate of literature that is being published on India's economic growth, Sumit Majumdar's book can claim several special distinctions. First, it squarely focuses its attention on entrepreneurship, a central element in any capitalist growth story. He does not confine his attention to the so-called business Maharajahs but deals with the phenomenon of what he calls "democratization of entrepreneurship." Second, while arguing that the so-called economic reforms gave these small entrepreneurs their head, he does not take the side of those who regard all earlier state action as only inhibiting India's growth. He points out, for example, that nationalization of banking with its attendant broadening of the circle of borrowers from banks helped entrepreneurs in their ventures. Majumdar also does not blink in recognizing that the business practices of many entrepreneurs could be quite dubious, but for him that is an essential part of capitalist growth. I hope that both proponents and opponents of economic liberalization will read this book.

Amiya Bagchi
Institute of Development Studies, Kolkata

Professor Majumdar's book comes when the Government of India is framing a new policy, stressing the importance of accelerating manufacturing activity. The author has come to the same conclusion, with the backing of an enormous amount of well-researched data. Very timely and well worth reading.

R. C. Bhargava
Chairman, Maruti Suzuki

With an engaging mixture of anecdote and analysis, Sumit Majumdar identifies the democratised entrepreneurship that is at the heart of India's current economic revolution, and expounds and explains the historical context in which this has occurred. This important book should encourage Indians from all backgrounds to transform their lives.

B. R. (Tom) Tomlinson
Professor Emeritus, SOAS, University of London

India's Late, Late Industrial Revolution

Democratizing Entrepreneurship

SUMIT K. MAJUMDAR

CAMBRIDGE
UNIVERSITY PRESS

CAMBRIDGE
UNIVERSITY PRESS

Shaftesbury Road, Cambridge CB2 8EA, United Kingdom

One Liberty Plaza, 20th Floor, New York, NY 10006, USA

477 Williamstown Road, Port Melbourne, VIC 3207, Australia

314–321, 3rd Floor, Plot 3, Splendor Forum, Jasola District Centre, New Delhi – 110025, India

103 Penang Road, #05–06/07, Visioncrest Commercial, Singapore 238467

Cambridge University Press is part of Cambridge University Press & Assessment, a department of the University of Cambridge.

We share the University's mission to contribute to society through the pursuit of education, learning and research at the highest international levels of excellence.

www.cambridge.org
Information on this title: www.cambridge.org/9781107015005

© Sumit K. Majumdar 2012

First published 2012

A catalogue record for this publication is available from the British Library

Library of Congress Cataloging-in-Publication data
Majumdar, Sumit Kumar.
    India's late, late industrial revolution : democratizing entrepreneurship /
    Sumit K. Majumdar.
        p. cm.
    Includes bibliographical references and index.
    ISBN 978-1-107-01500-5 (hbk.) – ISBN 978-1-107-62286-9 (pbk.)
    1. Industrialization–India.   2. Entrepreneurship–India.   3. Industrial
    policy–India. I. Title.
    HC435.3.M355 2012
    338.0954–dc23
    2012001944

ISBN   978-1-107-01500-5   Hardback
ISBN   978-1-107-62286-9   Paperback

*This book is dedicated to the memories of
two remarkable individuals*

*Anil Kumar Majumdar
and
Coimbatore Krishnarao Prahalad*

Contents

Figures

Tables

Acknowledgments

In writing this book, I have had the benefits of numerous conversations with many senior Indian businessmen, civil servants, and professionals who have handled industry-related issues. These individuals were: Messrs. P. Baijal, V. Balachandran, R. B. Barman, S. Bhattacharya, P. Braganza, the late A. Das, the late B. G. Deshmukh, R. Goswami, A. Gulabchand, B. Jalan, the late P. D. Kasbekar, F. C. Kohli, M. S. Krishnamoorthy, V. Krishnan, A. Lahiri, A. Maira, A. D. Moddie, S. Mukherji, A. K. Nag, P. Pandian, D. N. Prasad, the late V. G. Rajadhyaksha, the late N. Raghunathan, Y. V. Reddy, D. Sakhuja, S. Sanyal, the late K. K. Sen, N. K. Sengupta, K. V. Seshadri and A. Sonde. They provided detailed insights into many aspects of Indian industry.

Messrs. L. Mansingh, G. Owen, S. Rajgopal and S. Ramamoorthi were policy experts who generously shared their insights and provided detailed manuscript comments. Professors A. K. Bagchi, P. K. Bardhan, R. Chatterjee, R. Deb, V. Jacob, A. Rasheed and R. Ramamurti deserve considerable approbation for detailed manuscript comments. R. Bhattarai and V. Trivedi, former students at the University of Texas at Dallas, helped me collect materials. Many thanks are due to my editor at Cambridge University Press, Dr. C. Harrison, for support of the project and the copy editor Annie Jackson for processing of the manuscript. Thanks are due to anonymous referees for important comments.

Throughout the book I use the measure of lakhs (100,000) and crores (10 million) in dealing with numerical quantities of rupees (₹); the spelling is Americanized; and older place names such as Bombay, Calcutta, Madras, and Poona, are retained in place of the new names such as Mumbai, Kolkata, Chennai, and Pune.

Preface

The Maharaj and the saffron

I met my first payroll when I was 19 years old. There was a convention, in the hostel in Bombay for commerce, law, and science students that I stayed in as an undergraduate student, that a final-year commerce student or a postgraduate law or science student would become the Mess Secretary for each of the four messes that provided meals to residents. In my final year, it was not a case of me volunteering to become the Mess Secretary. It was a case of when on parade the entire line stepping back and leaving me stranded ahead. Thus, I, as a non-vegetarian Bengali, found myself the Mess Secretary of a Gujarati vegetarian mess. The Gujarati messes had a person of Gujarati origin designated as the Maharaj. He was the chief chef, the business manager and the major-domo. As the operations boss, he had hired a number of Maharashtrian helpers. These were supernumerary peasants, from the Konkan region of Maharashtra, whose family plots could not sustain their existence. They came to Bombay searching for work. Thus, in the course of my Mess Secretary tenure, I entertained several requests for an extra day off because a person had to go home to Konkan to lend a hand in harvesting the crops. But, it is not these sons of the Konkan soil that the story is about.

I took over the Mess at a time when inflation was 25 percent per annum in India. These circumstances explain why the parade line stepped back at duty allocation time. No one wanted to be perpetually accused of raising the prices of meals by his peers. Anyway, I had to meet payroll every week. I had to have adequate revenues. I had to control costs in a draconian way. My first task was to sit with the Maharaj, an astute businessman if ever there was one, and go through the economics of feeding about a hundred people twice daily. I discovered that there were certain very cheap vegetables peculiar to the Gujarati palate. These were *alvi, fansi, valor, tinda,* and *looni.* When cooked as vegetables on their own, they were hardly edible. As a snobbish Bengali, I would have called them weeds. But I had made a major discovery. When chopped up, appropriately spiced, mixed with potatoes and fried, these weeds made superb vegetable cutlets. Cutlets were a product innovation, and a value-added item, as far as my Mess clients were concerned. Thus, hordes flocked to eat my meals. I offered value-added products. My costs went down, as did my prices. More individuals wanted to join my Mess. The Mess on the floor below, with a traditional menu, went out of business. My costs and prices went down even more, as I took over its clients. I had discovered the secrets and benefits of product innovation and scale economies, though I did not know it then.

This preface is not my story. It is the story of the Maharaj. Initially, the Maharaj was quite put out at my purchase of cheap vegetables, as his peculations were affected. But he soon realized that we were buying more in volume, and he kept his mouth absolutely shut. At the end of the year, when it was time to hand over, before we all went our separate ways, I decided to have a big feast. My Mess was flush with funds. I had generated large surpluses, even though inflation in India was raging. The Maharaj and I decided we would offer our clients, as the *pièce de résistance*, unlimited amounts of dry fruit shrikhand. Shrikhand is a rich, full-fat, milk-based sweet in which expensive dry fruits, such as almonds, cashew nuts, pistachio nuts, and raisins, can be added. To top it all off, saffron is also added to make the dish fit for the gods. One can consume, at most, a very small amount of such a rich food. Since my clients were impecunious and hungry students, they could eat well, some of them exceedingly well; but even they could not consume more than three or four small helpings of shrikhand. After that, a two- to three-hour nap was mandatory.

This is where the story of Indian business and industry comes in. Carried away by a wealth endowment effect, and a feel-good factor, from having created a liquid Mess, I had rashly told the Maharaj we would have only the very best. He would prepare the tastiest shrikhand he had ever made. His face was absolutely non-committal. We went through what we needed, and decided on the quantities of items required and to be ordered. When it came to the saffron, I had suggested that we would need to order a kilogram of it. His face showed an element of surprise, but he quickly masked it. Yes, he said, I was absolutely right. A kilogram of saffron was what we needed, and that was what he would order straight away along with the other items. So, the order was placed with the Sahakari Bhandar, a giant department and provisions store, not far away, which catered to our needs.

Two days later I received a telephone call. It was the General Manager of the Sahakari Bhandar. I had never met or spoken to this august functionary, and had no need to. The Maharaj normally dealt with individuals several layers below. The General Manager was himself on the telephone because he was surprised, shocked would be more apposite, to receive such a large order for saffron. He explained to me that the quantity might not be available in all of Bombay. If we insisted, he would acquire it in little bits from every source in Bombay and surrounding regions to meet our order. He was curious to know what was it that we had in mind, what grand orgy was it that was being planned, because saffron was normally ordered and consumed in grams, and not in kilograms. A kilogram of saffron would be extremely expensive. When I described to him our special feast, he said that for the numbers planned we needed two to five grams at most; but, if we were scared of running short, he would supply us ten grams of saffron. A kilogram of saffron was enough to flavor two helpings of that dish for the entire population of the locality within a mile's radius of the hostel, say 50,000 persons. As I have since discovered, at my local Indian grocery store, one acquires just a sliver or two of saffron for one's culinary needs.

I then realized that the Maharaj, knowing my ignorance, had allowed me to go ahead with the order quantity because with the surplus 995 grams, or thereabouts, of the remaining saffron, he would have control over, he could then set himself up as a saffron trader and would make a small fortune. This was my first, shall we say humbling, experience that led to a realization of the ingenuity and drive of the Indian businessman, who would utilize all opportunities available.

When I was doing my postgraduate degree, at the Jamnalal Bajaj Institute of Management Studies, in our second year we had to develop a detailed business idea and a project plan. To seek out what industry we had to develop a business plan for, we were referred to the *Guidelines for Industries*. This was the Indian entrepreneurs' bible, as well as the bane of their lives, published annually by the Ministry of Industrial Development. We discovered that whatever industry we chose, almost all such industries were impossible to enter into for entrepreneurial new ventures because capacity limits for firms in that industry had been reached. Government had dictated that only so much capacity in a sector could be installed, and firms had either installed that capacity or had acquired the licenses to do so.

In 1977, the Indian electorate had acted in overwhelmingly removing from power the draconian Indira Gandhi government that had imposed a state of emergency on India. An issue that had started nagging me as a student then was, why was India, the world's largest functioning democracy, an impossible place to engage in industry and business for a citizen of this democratic nation? We now know thanks, *inter alia*, to Seymour Martin Lipset and Robert Barro, that economic growth rates are higher in a democracy than under different political systems, such as a dictatorship.[1] Of course, what comes first, democracy or prosperity, is an open-ended issue. Alexis de Tocqueville had written: "I do not know if one can cite a single manufacturing and commercial nation from the Tyrians to the Florentines and English, that has also not been free. Therefore a close tie and a necessary relation exists between those two things: freedom and industry."[2] In India, the democratic political system came first, India having followed a domestic policy of inclusion,[3] and economic growth, along with industrial growth, followed later.[4] Thus, the democratization of enterprise came well after India had become a democratic republic.

If Indian businessmen were innately entrepreneurial, commercially insightful, and highly ingenious persons, as the Maharaj demonstrated, why was there this paradox in India's industrial performance? Why was Indian industry backward? Why was Indian industry primitive in its methods, as I discovered later when I started working in Calcutta and directly observed Indian factories? Even later, when I started working in Britain, and observed some of Britain's declining factories, for example in the E14 postal district of London, which is now the financial district in the Docklands, the primitiveness of Indian industry, and the paradoxes of her economic performance, were exacerbated. The questions then became, when would the command and control regime, known as the *License Raj*, go away? When would the Indian economy awaken from the sleep of Rip Van Winkle; and what would happen after these occurred?

This book is a story of modern Indian enterprise that attempts to answer the questions articulated above. The intent is to evaluate India's industrial resurgence phenomenon over the last two decades. The data indicate that India is engaged in her own unique industrial revolution.

The timing is very late. As a result, the catch-up may be problematic. Based on research that I have carried out over several years on India's industrial performance, analysis of secondary data, interviews with policy makers and managers, and anecdotes, I explore the contours of India's late, late industrial revolution and evaluate some of its drivers. I draw straightforward conclusions, having attempted a close penetration of complex facts, a plethora of material, and a "blooming, buzzing confusion," to conceptually understand the structure of Indian industry. Within the chapters, as relevant, I narrate anecdotes so that lay readers, as well as academics, may get a sense of the ground realities of Indian business and industry, yesterday and today, albeit based on my limited experiences.

The book is an interdisciplinary analytical narrative. It connects and combines materials related to economic growth, economic history, industrial organization, and management strategy. My approach to the analysis is pragmatic and limited. Endemic income inequalities, gender issues,[5] farmers' suicides, corruption, and poverty are major concerns in India. I do not stray into these topics, which are the mainstay of the development economics literature. There are many providing us with the necessary frameworks to assess poverty reduction approaches. I focus on industrial growth. By doing so, one retains unity among the related issues. Also, a number of poverty reduction issues can be dealt with after entrepreneurs' growth drives have created the funds for a corpus of necessary resources available for amelioration. This is one view of fostering development in the literature.[6]

While I hope that the story of Indian industry is compelling, targeted at a general audience, a specialized academic may find materials in the book to be of use. Eric Hobsbawm has remarked on the trade-offs between prose and numbers. An excess of the latter makes a book unreadable.[7] Similarly, economic historian Jonathan Hughes had said it was worth "bearing in mind that 'straight' history bores many readers and that unembellished economic analysis tends to mystify most."[8] Hence, a mixture of approaches is necessary. The topic demands facts. I have provided adequate data such that the book contains the necessary statistics. I have done this in spite of the risk that parts of the book, say, those dealing with the production growth of items such as caustic soda, may resemble excerpts of a five-year plan document, released by the State Planning Bureau of the People's Democratic Republic of Zabardastan. Partha Chatterjee had written

that: "History writing ... relies on the power of the rhetoric to produce the effect of truth."[9] Thus, I have used rhetoric, in places, to make
certain points.

I call India's industrial resurgence a late, late industrial revolution,
though the number of autonomous technological innovations triggering this change is small. An industrial revolution implies the application of scientific and technological knowledge and empirical processes
to production.[10] It does not matter where such knowledge evolved.
Initial levels of industrial growth may be the consequences of firms'
responses to market-opening incentives and demand. As time passes,
growth will be driven by a number of unique autonomous endogenous innovations. Many of the technological functionalities that Indian
firms use have been adopted from others' examples. This approach is
legitimate, and used by other Asian countries, though numerous business-model innovations in India now exist. Really, one should classify
this on-going transformation as India's late, late industrialization. But
there is no point in splitting hairs. The fundamental transformation in
India has been in the altered role of the state. Whether by design or
accident, and more due to the latter, its role as the dictator-in-chief to
India's entrepreneurs has been simply washed away by the giant tsunami waves of autonomous entrepreneurship that have engulfed the
nation.

There has been a transfer of power in India. A civil servant friend
I have known since childhood described to me the contemporary
role of civil servants like him and his colleagues as being enterprise
facilitation. That is a very good thing. Government in India needs to
be smart government. Whether that is happening or not is a pressing concern. But dealing with quality of governance is beyond this
book's scope. Unlike the late industrialization programs of Japan,
Taiwan, South Korea,[11] and now China, where the government has
played a major guiding role, in contemporary India such a role for the
state does not exist.[12] Entrepreneurs have fully taken over. In a fully
democratic manner, anyone can set up any business, of any scale, in
any industry, anywhere in India. Just as all adult Indians have the
right to vote, all Indians have the right to establish an enterprise.
Equality of entrepreneurship opportunity defines modern India. This
democratization of entrepreneurship is the real revolution. Hence,
India's industrialization story deserves the sobriquet of a late, late
revolution.[13]

Since we are dealing in an entrepreneur-led Indian industrial revolution, albeit after a fashion, as described in Chapter 1, a logical structure for the book suggests we should understand details of the original industrial revolutions (Chapter 2), and India's role in those episodes. Considerable details are provided as background materials, and it is important to appreciate the contours of all of these industrialization episodes. A little-publicized fact is India's major role in triggering the original British industrial revolution in the eighteenth century. It was India's wealth, based on her land revenues and success in textile manufacturing, which provided Britain with the incentives and the finances to implement the first industrial revolution.[14] Till the industrial revolution, Indian textiles had been the world's largest manufacturing export.[15] A large proportion of the funds to set British industrialization in motion came from India. The British industrialization episode is the source of subsequent industrial growth experiences for the world's economies.

This book is about the present and the future of India's industry. I delve into India's economic history to bring the past in as an important context for the future. To cite social historian Keith Thomas, history "enhances our self-consciousness, enables us to see ourselves in perspective, and helps us toward that greater freedom and understanding which comes from self-knowledge";[16] consequently, India's own past business and industrial history (Chapters 3 and 4) merits some description. I do not go into the de-industrialization thesis, as the topic has been covered by others. A chapter evaluates the past experiences of India's Asian sisters, such as Japan, Taiwan and South Korea, to understand their late industrialization nuances, as these were contemporaneous with India's twentieth-century industrial experiences (Chapter 5). Again, considerable details are provided, as the experiences and examples of the various countries are salient for an appreciation of the way Indian industry may evolve.

India's contemporary entrepreneurship democratization is 20 years old, though it builds on past policy foundations. The issues of why it happened, why, unlike Western Europe and later East Asia, India did not succeed in the 1950s and 1960s in government-led industrialization, and the consequences of India's contemporary entrepreneur-led industrialization in transforming her economic landscape form the heart of the book (Chapters 6 and 7). The latter of the two chapters (Chapter 7) contains the data reflecting the occurrence of the waves of tsunami constituting autonomous Indian entrepreneurship. There are many debates on India's growth and inclusiveness. India's growth has been a story of information technology and the services sector in public perception. Such a view short-changes other sectors. The share of the services sector in India's national income has risen. Chapter 8 contains a discussion of the role of the services sector in India. It summarizes analysis evaluating service sector productivity, the first to be so reported. The services sector in India engages in inefficiently producing commodities with the means of commodities. Such inefficiencies are rising. This is unsustainable. No theory suggests that service sector growth alone can lead to economic development. The services sector has generated growth and inflation, but not jobs and productivity. Chapters 6, 7, and 8 collectively help assess whether India's contemporary industrialization phenomenon is future-proof, or something too little and too late.

I follow up with a discussion on the role of the manufacturing functionality in past industrialization epochs, and why manufacturing is fundamental for the present (Chapter 9), even though industry's share in national income has been stagnant. The growth and development of an economy are propelled by innovation and technical change. These are reflected by the manufacturing function adding value to raw materials.[17] Industrial manufacturing-driven resource accretions for the economy, based on value addition, have major connotations for wealth creation and poverty reduction. Jagdish Bhagwati had written that "It is necessary to argue forcefully that efficiency and growth are important, indeed given our immense poverty the most important, instruments for alleviating poverty."[18] When the industrial revolution first commenced in Britain, in the eighteenth century, "the central problem of the age was how to feed and clothe and employ generations of children outnumbering by far those of any other time."[19] This problem was solved by wealth creation. Thomas Ashton wrote that "She [Britain] was delivered, not by her rulers, but by those who, seeking no doubt their own narrow ends, had the wit and resource to devise new instruments of production and new methods of administering industry."[20] This sentiment was echoed by Phyllis Deane, who stated that "It is now almost an axiom of the theory of economic development that the route to affluence lies by way of an industrial revolution."[21] Those governing in Britain also possessed wits. Eric Hobsbawm has written that "the right conditions were present in Britain ... since private profit and economic development had become accepted as the supreme objects of government policy."[22]

Wealth creation and poverty reduction are two sides of the same coin. Wealth creation implies a positive attitude, based on an additive motivation. Poverty reduction implies dealing with a negative condition, based on an amelioration dispensation. Industrialization is a value-additive process preceding amelioration, since it generates the resources that eventually improve the lot of people. If a central problem in India is poverty, then the creation of wealth, through this late, late industrial revolution, can lead to the amelioration of India's poverty.[23] The late Chidambaram Subramanian had written that "there are no rewards for caution in economic development. On the contrary, the economic history of nations has nowhere recorded a penalty for boldness."[24] If a central concern in India is development, then bold risk-taking by her entrepreneurs in manufacturing can foster development.

Numerous theoretical reasons suggest that manufacturing should be the driver of development. India's manufacturing future matters enormously. Many possibilities exist for Indian industry to achieve global manufacturing stardom. Many necessary conditions are also required to take India's late, late industrial revolution forward, so that she is a pre-eminent manufacturing nation. She has to produce or perish. India is a heterogeneous economy, and I cannot even think of all the possibilities that will lead to the crystallization of this global stardom contingency, let alone cover the details, since the issues are so complex. The late Morris D. Morris stated that "To date no one, not even D. R. Gadgil in his seminal survey, 'The Industrial Evolution of India,'[25] has been able to capture the relationship of the individual parts to the whole of the economic system."[26] I pass on this challenge. I let it be carried forward for future scholarship. I cover some key dimensions of industrialization (Chapter 10) which, in my opinion, are necessary; but, in themselves, these are hardly sufficient. The normative elements within the sections of the chapter highlight certain aspects of industrialization that can make India's experiences unique.

1 | Vent for growth

Outside-the-box thinking

India has, seemingly and finally, embarked on her late, late industrial revolution. This has occurred more than two centuries after Britain launched hers, and a century after Japan commenced the industrialization process. She is several decades behind Japan, South Korea, and China, three other important Asian economies, in this industrializing and economic growth catch-up process. But it is better to have commenced the process now than never to have commenced it at all. In every decade, an ideal business and economic model is proclaimed and held up as exemplary. Thus, the central planning model of Soviet industrialization and the American New Deal in the 1930s, the indicative planning model of the French variety in the 1960s, the German co-determination model in the 1970s, and the Japanese *kanban* system of the 1980s were given approbation.[1] South Korea's late industrialization model was the exemplar of the 1990s, and the Chinese model of the 2000s was to be the workshop of the world. Can India's model of a late, late industrial revolution define the contours of business and economic discourse in the 2010s and beyond?

The answer to this question depends very much on India's entrepreneurs. In this respect, my niece Dr. Aindri Raychaudhuri, popularly known as Mikku, who is a very successful young infertility specialist in Calcutta, described an interesting entrepreneurship case to me. Now renamed Kolkata, it was once Rudyard Kipling's "city of dreadful night." For many now, Calcutta is the city of joy. It was then, and it still is now, one of India's largest and most vibrant cities. It has also emerged as the medical hub for eastern India. Mikku runs one of Calcutta's thriving in-vitro fertilization (IVF) clinics. An IVF baby is a test-tube baby, and an IVF therapy program is used for couples who have not been able to conceive naturally. In Western societies, many couples engaged in same-sex relationships or marriages also use IVF to

start a family of their own, since the natural processes of human biological reproduction are denied to them. The Calcutta IVF market may
be somewhat socially different from that of the West at this point.

While the first test-tube baby was born in Calcutta in October 1978,
just three months after the world's first test-tube baby was born in
Britain, IVF therapy has only recently taken off in India.[2] In-vitro fertilization is not cheap. A rise in discretionary incomes, that has accompanied India's burgeoning economic growth, has made available the
large sums of money that couples may require for IVF therapy if their
natural attempts to have a family have failed.[3] While past business
growth in the IVF sector may have lagged behind the technology of
assisted reproduction, today the IVF sector displays boom symptoms.
Such booms are accompanied by numerous individual entrepreneurial experiments and bets on ideas, to solve problems that may exist
for consumers and in the market, in the context of a growing awareness of opportunities.[4] India's IVF sector is no exception.[5] The term
manufacturing may apply, in a broad sense, and also in a polemic
philosophical way, to the IVF sector. Yet, the IVF saga may reflect the
emergent entrepreneurial contours of India's late, late twenty-first century industrial revolution.

The details recounted so far are standard. They apply to the formal
element of India's IVF sector. Much of the elements of the formal IVF
sector mimic those of formal sectors in other countries. But the real
story is not the formal sector story. As with other sectors of the Indian
economy, there is a large informal component in the IVF sector of
India. The informal sector co-exists with the formal sector in a mutual
symbiosis. This informal sector displays ingenuity and enterprise in
equal or greater measure than that of the formal sector. This aspect of
the IVF story provides the backdrop for the evocative tale of India's
new entrepreneurial revolution.

Mikku shared with me several details of how a typical IVF center
works. Mikku's center, and other IVF centers, are reliant on the supply of eggs and sperm from donors. These donors' eggs and sperm are
stored for future use. These are the raw material resources required
for an IVF center to operate successfully. The supply chain of an IVF
center is based on the procurement of egg and sperm supplies from
donors.[6] In the case of Calcutta women, a monthly egg donation,
for those willing to do so, enables them to currently earn ₹30,000
on each occasion. In the case of men, many monthly donations are

feasible. Every donation nets Calcutta's male donors ₹1,000 per operational visit.

One of Mikku's most reliable egg suppliers is an enterprising woman from the urban working class of Calcutta, named Sumangala.[7] Originally from Purnea, in Bihar, a backward district of India, she is married, in her early thirties, and has a small child. Sumangala has had some school education, but no college education. She came as a donor to Mikku's clinic some years ago and, thereafter, consistently donated month after month. Of late, she has stopped donating her eggs because she wishes to conceive again. Her claim to fame has been her ingenuity in altering the contours of Mikku's resource supply chain for donor eggs. Sumangala has organized several women, at last count numbering over 15, to become egg donors. She directs them to Mikku's center where they donate eggs. These are women mostly in their early to mid twenties; some are in their early thirties. They are in the prime of biological life, and good donors. These women are from the urban working class or the urban lower middle class of Calcutta. Many have had severely impoverished rural backgrounds. Some have been disenfranchised Calcutta slum dwellers, who have typically provided the grist for Western movie-makers to make films depicting India's poverty.

These donor women would never have heard of the egg donation possibilities at Calcutta's IVF centers were it not for Sumangala. They are a part of Sumangala's informal egg donation network. For every donation that they make Sumangala receives ₹5,000 as her fee. The women then receive ₹25,000 each. In Calcutta, wages are relatively much lower than in Bombay or Delhi. These women may have been earning about ₹8,000 to 10,000 a month, at most. They have been able to supplement their monthly incomes by a large magnitude without major risk to their well-being. In the process, their donations may bring eventual joy to a childless couple. What of Sumangala? In addition to her existing income from her full-time day job elsewhere, in a good month when she is herself a donor, and say 15 of her current women also donate, she earns over ₹100,000 a month. That is the salary of a professor at Calcutta or Jadavpur University or the Indian Institute of Technology or of a very senior civil servant. Her ingenuity has enabled Sumangala to reach an income level compatible with a very comfortable middle-class lifestyle in one of India's largest cities.

Sumangala has since expanded her supply chain operations to supply several other IVF clinics in Calcutta. Her informal network of

potential donor women is growing every day and not only keeps
Mikku's IVF center in eggs, but several other IVF centers in Calcutta
are now assured of a steady and reliable supply of a key resource
for their therapeutic needs. For the IVF clinics, a random process
of egg availability has been replaced by a certain continuity of flow.
This is important in the management of their business model. For
the relatively impoverished women who supply this resource flow,
Sumangala has enabled them to improve their economic lot in life.
Sumangala's activities reflect the burgeoning informal entrepreneurship that co-exists, with its own ecology and structure, side by side
with formal sector industrial businesses in India. Though she lacks
a formal college education, Sumangala's informal segment entrepreneurial activities have changed the supply chain contours for an IVF
center's key resources. Such entrepreneurship, of which there are
many examples, is an important element of India's late, late industrial revolution.

The story is incomplete. Another of Mikku's suppliers, this time
of sperm, is a young man named Onkar Mahalingam.[8] Popularly
known as OM to his friends and colleagues, he is single and in his
late twenties. He is a flight attendant, based out of Calcutta, for one
of India's new private airlines. OM is originally from Golmalpur, in
Karnataka state; a search for better opportunities brought him to
Calcutta as a student over a decade ago. In his free time, of which he
has large chunks, since his schedule of flying permits him to accumulate these holiday blocks, OM is a sperm donor. When in Calcutta, his
first daily task is to visit Mikku's center to make a sperm donation.
After the event, he pockets ₹1,000 for his exertions. If OM has a free
month, and is not flying, his earnings from daily sperm donations
amount to over ₹25,000. This sum is almost as much as his monthly
flight attendant's salary from the airline. OM's combined monthly
income of over ₹50,000 is a sum he never believed, as a teenager
in Golmalpur, was within his reach. Given OM's seminal contribution to the resource base of Mikku's IVF center in Calcutta, he may
well account for the paternal genes of a large number of babies conceived, albeit in a Petri dish, in twenty-first century Calcutta. He may
be a latter-day Genghis Khan. It is outside-the-box thinking by OM
that has enabled him to turn a liquidity contingency into a financial
opportunity.

In addition to the large sums being invested by companies and private investors, many non-traditional persons have turned to entrepreneurship. Because there have have been no precedents, given sector novelty, they have generated, whether by accident or design, new business models. Similarly, it is the informal sector organizational ability, displayed by the likes of Sumangala in subtly altering the IVF raw material supply chain, which epitomizes contemporary autonomous Indian entrepreneurial activity, with important spillovers into the social sector. By weaving other women closely into the fabric of her informal social network, Sumangala has also enabled once-disenfranchised women to engage in commercial activities within India's economy in a way they would never have thought possible. The rewards for these women are considerable, for what is relatively low risk. Such financial rewards can enable them to make considerable enhancements in the various parameters of daily living and impact the qualities of their lives. Such financial outcomes function to enhance both personal autonomy and national economic growth.

Enterprising ventures are also the norm in the large corporate sector. Over the space of a few days, in the second week of February 2011, four announcements relating to Indian businesses were made. The first dealt with a multinational company, manufacturing consumer products, investing in India. The giant Japanese electronics corporation, Panasonic, was to start production from a newly established manufacturing facility at Jhajjar in Haryana in three months' time. The company had originally set a target to go on-stream in 2012. The economic boom in India persuaded it to advance the launch date for the manufacturing of home appliances, such as refrigerators, air conditioners, and washing machines. Simultaneously, it was to double its Indian workforce to 20,000 by 2012, and to make a total investment of ₹1,000 crores to set up Indian research and development and manufacturing facilities.[9]

Second, India's oil and gas giant, Indian Oil Corporation, a state-owned firm, commenced production from a naphtha cracker plant at Panipat in Haryana that had been established for ₹14,000 crores. This cracker unit became the largest industrial complex in the state of Haryana, and it would produce feed for downstream polymer units. This was a case of a state-owned enterprise investing in very large-scale industrial facilities.[10] Third, in a role reversal, the Anglo-Dutch oil and gas giant, Royal Dutch Shell, sold its Stanlow refinery in Britain, and the entire inventory of crude oil and refined products located there, to an Indian oil and gas firm, Essar Energy, for US$1.3 billion. This was a case of a recently started Indian private oil and gas company, already possessing substantial resources, acquiring significant assets and businesses abroad.[11] Fourth, an Indian pharmaceutical company, Venus Remedies, set up 20 years ago by a former practicing chartered accountant, announced plans to enter the specialty oncology segment. It created a new dedicated business unit, with a product basket of 21 products in injection form, for fighting various types of cancer. The goal of the business unit was to offer affordable medicines to the mass market of India.[12] Collectively, the examples given, just the tip of the iceberg since numerous similar episodes exist, highlight contemporary autonomous entrepreneurial activity.

India's unique industrial revolution

An industrial revolution implies major quantitative performance transitions, as well as qualitative transitions in undertaking economic activity. An increase in the production of goods and services is accompanied by an upsurge in the consumption of items, and a production revolution is also accompanied by a consumption revolution.[13] The data on India's industrial production suggest that a major quantitative wealth creation process is in progress. These data provide a general overview of the transition. In the last 30 years, between 1980 and 2010, the overall index of industrial production has risen from 100, for the base year 1980–81, to over 720 by 2009–10. Figure 1.1 graphically displays the annual growth in the index of industrial production from 1980 onwards. In the three decades, of the 1980s, 1990s and 2000s, the index of industrial production has grown at 7.5 percent, 6.4 percent and 7.5 respectively. In the latest year for which data are available, 2009–10, the index has risen at 11 percent over the previous year. The annual growth rates are presented in Table A1.

Additional details support the thesis. When the index of industrial production is decomposed into its constituent parts, the trends are even more evocative of a late, late industrial revolution. The index comprises separate components for basic goods, capital goods, intermediate goods, consumer durables, and consumer non-durables. The two important enhancements of industrial production have been in the capital goods and consumer durables segments. These trends are clear from figure 1.2. In the capital goods segment,[14] between 1980

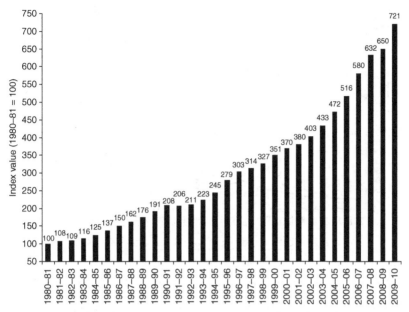

Figure 1.1. Index of industrial production in India: 1980–81 to 2009–10.

Source: Derived from Table 28 of the Reserve Bank of India Database on the Indian Economy.

and 2010 the index of industrial production has risen from 100, for the base year of 1980–81, to 1,339 by 2009–10. Growth of production in the capital goods segment indicates the long-term investment intentions of the business community. The index of production for the consumer durables segment has risen from 100, for the base year 1980–81, to 1,941 by 2009–10. This is an important segment to gauge consumer sentiments. Typically, the population of a country enjoying economic progress would invest in consumer durables as discretionary items. Such expenditures would be incurred after other important needs were met. The growth in the output of this particular segment reflects the economic growth of India as a whole, after economic liberalization has led to the increased production of goods and services available for consumption.[15] A consumer revolution is in progress. A consumer revolution reflects changes in the experiences of India's population, just as the industrial revolution in Britain, as an epochal event in the lives of her population, changed the patterns of consumption

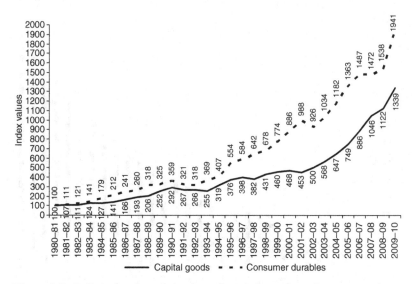

Figure 1.2. Indices for the production of capital goods and consumer durables: 1980–81 to 2009–10.

Source: Derived from Table 28 of the Reserve Bank of India Database on the Indian Economy.

and habits as rising disposable incomes and a growing supply of inexpensive goods and equity permitted less fortunate people to consume what the elites had been consuming.[16]

In the producer and consumer goods segments, there have been 13-fold and 19-fold increases in output in the course of the last three decades. These segments of Indian industry reflect important producer and consumer sentiments respectively. By any standards, these are substantial growth rates. When coupled with a median age of India's population of 24 years, compared to 34 years for China, 37 years for the United States and 40 years for Europe, the consumption experiences of participants in India's economy can dominate the logic of world markets. India's youth population will be the largest in the world. Given a lack of purchasing power relative to the West, the Indian market can provide the inducements, and economies of scale necessary for tailored innovation and product development of low-cost items to be sold cheaply around the world. The development of Tata's Nano car, to be sold at about $2,000, heralds this phenomenon.[17] The other segments constituting industrial output in India have not lagged behind in displaying growth. The basic goods segment index has grown from 100, for the base year 1980–81, to 622 by 2009–10. The intermediates goods segment index has grown from 100, for the base year 1980–81, to 556 by 2009–10, while the basic consumer non-durables segment index has grown from 100, for the base year 1980–81, to 488 by 2009–10. While the broad growth trend for capital goods and consumer durables is brought out in figure 1.2, Table 1.1 provides details of the growth trends by decade.

Allied to major institutional changes, there has been a change in the entrepreneurial culture of India. There are little local difficulties;[18] nevertheless, entrepreneurs have propelled significant investments into agricultural, manufacturing, service, and knowledge sector activities. These have interacted to boost India's economic growth, and this economic growth performance has been substantially driven by the performance of India's manufacturing and service industries. Such growth is unsurprising. Indians have been an enterprising people for over 4,500 years. Research on the economic prehistory of India, on the Indus Valley Civilization, shows a pattern of trade, domestic and global, entrepreneurship and organization, at that time second to none. Till the British arrival on India's governance scene, in 1757, India was a dominant economy. India was not only the world's leading manufacturing country, but there was a large commercial sector, with a sophisticated structure of markets and credit, manned by a skilful commercial class supported by a competent class of service-providers.[19]

In relation to the industrial revolution, which started in the mid eighteenth century, in 1750 India's share of world manufacturing was over 25 percent.[20] At that time, the share of China in world manufacturing was 33 percent, that of the United Kingdom 2 percent, and that of the United States a tenth of a percent! Then, the first industrial revolution occurred. India did not participate. She was a mute bystander to the world's most fundamental economic transformation. Her relative share of total world manufacturing shrank rapidly, simply because the West's output was rising more swiftly. By 1860, India's share of world manufacturing was down to 8.6 percent, while that of the United Kingdom was 20 percent and that of the United States almost 15 percent. By 1900, India's share of world

Table 1.1. *Annual percentage growth in the constituent components of the index of industrial production*

	Overall index of industrial production	Basic goods index	Capital goods index	Intermediate goods index	Consumer durables index	Consumer non-durables index
Annual percentage growth in the 1980s	7.46	7.99	10.96	6.05	14.23	5.43
Annual percentage growth in the 1990s	6.36	6.17	6.74	6.68	9.65	4.18
Annual percentage growth in the 2000s	7.50	5.58	11.50	5.77	9.98	7.46
Annual percentage growth in 2009–10	10.92	7.18	19.34	13.64	26.23	1.32

Source: Reserve Bank of India Database on the Indian Economy, Table 30, and author's calculations; computations expressed in percentages based on data at factor cost and in constant rupees.

manufacturing was less than 2 percent, that of the United Kingdom was almost 19 percent, and that of the United States was almost 24 percent. Also, the size of the economy declined in absolute terms due to de-industrialization.[21]

India's markets were penetrated by the cheaper and better products of the Lancashire textile factories. After 1813, when the East India Company's trade monopoly ended, imports of cotton fabrics into India rose from 1 million yards in 1814 to 51 million yards in 1830 and to 995 million yards by 1870. In this process, traditional domestic producers were wiped out.[22] By 1900, India's share of world manufacturing share was less than 2 percent. Conversely, Britain, with a share of world manufacturing of less than 2 percent in 1750, had a world manufacturing share of 20 percent in 1900. Measured relative to Britain in 1900 as 100, India's per capita industrialization in 1900 could be depicted with a value of 1. In 1750, Britain's position, relative to herself in 1900, could be depicted with a value of 10. India's position in 1750, relative to Britain's position in 1750 could be depicted with a value of 7. In 1750, Britain and India were almost equally matched as economies. Hence, over the course of a century and a half, India's economic decline was precipitous.

By the turn of the twentieth century, India's position had declined to nothing. Then, some industrial development by domestic entrepreneurs and foreign capital commenced. Yet, manufacturing industries, organized on a large scale, employed a trivial proportion of industrial workers. The large-scale manufacturing sector accounted for 5 percent of industrial employment in British India in 1891. This increased to 11 percent by 1938. The large-scale manufacturing sector, nevertheless, did give rise to cities such as Calcutta and Bombay. The manufacturing sector shaped urban labor markets, encouraged the growth of infrastructure, such as railways, ports, laws, insurance companies, banks, and technical schools, and influenced the modernization of trade and other financial services.[23] Till independence in 1947, however, nothing much happened by way of industrialization to raise per capita incomes of India's population by any order of magnitude. Pre-independence manufacturing sector investments, and other sector investments, did not lead to growth. Per capita income growth was stagnant from 1900 to 1946. Estimates show a compound growth rate of real national income of 0.7 percent in the last half century of colonial rule in India.[24]

In the years since independence, Indian economic growth has been much faster than in the colonial period. After independence, India's industrialization took off. But, it spluttered to a halt in the mid 1960s and there was stagnation for a decade and a half.[25] As summarized into four half-decade periods, between 1961 and 1965, the average annual industrial growth rate was 9 percent, but slipped to 3.7 percent between 1966 and 1970 and to 3.6 percent between 1971 and 1975. Between 1975 and 1980, the average annual industrial growth rate recovered to 4.8 percent. Clearly, Indian industry was stagnant.[26] Fernand Braudel wrote, in the early 1960s, "What is interesting is that the economy is taking off. After Japan, and not far behind China, India is becoming one of Asia's great industrial powers."[27] He was premature in his good wishes for India by half a century!

Some speculation has taken place as to the reasons for this lack of attention to industry and to manufacturing. Profits were not well thought of in Asia as a whole, and particularly in India.[28] To seek them was to be selfish. To base plans upon profits as the primary goal was to subordinate the necessities of the people to the haggling of markets.[29] Lloyd Rudolph and Susanne Rudolph wrote, "Until the mid seventies, modern capitalists in India had to contend with preindustrial cultural prejudices and postindustrial ideological doctrines that picture them, on the one hand, as heartless moneylenders and, on the other, as antisocial profiteers."[30] Profits are an expression of the difference between the real resources required to produce any particular thing and the real resources people are prepared to pay in order to get it. Yet, profit was a bad word in India.

A reawakening of the industrial spirit, with which is associated a restoration of the upward trajectory in the numbers depicting industrial growth, started in 1991. This is what the broad facts about industrial production growth indicate. The big picture is positive. It is evocative of an economy no longer just taxiing along the runway, but using its powerful, high-thrust industrial engines and entrepreneurial afterburners to take off. Since the early 1990s, there has been take-off in industrial growth and entrepreneurship. Indian grassroots capitalism in the agricultural, manufacturing, and services sectors is substantial. Individuals have set up numerous new ventures, based on diverse business models. The world is Indian firms' oyster. Global operations are treated as a matter of course.

A definition of an entrepreneur is that of a person looking for market opportunities to mobilize resources for organizing production, so that there may be a profitable outcome.[31] Today, profit is no longer a bad word. The mobilization and utilization of resources to earn profit are vital. Such profits can be used to reduce prices, increase wages, or be consumed by the entrepreneur. All these actions directly raise the standard of living of individuals, as well as the gross product of the nation.[32] If the statistics of enhanced production values of various items are reviewed, then India's growth represents the harnessing of the substantial search, mobilization, and organization talents of her entrepreneurs to venture forth in the search for profits. Along with a quantitative increase in production volumes, there is simultaneous development of an advanced system of banks and credit facilities.

For policy makers in the realm of diplomacy, the rise of India promises to change post-Cold War geopolitics, with the rise being of a magnitude attracting the term tectonic.[33] Changes in the quality and quantity of human capital can engender this shift of underlying plate-structures holding up Indian economy and society, as there is expansion of and changes in the quality of the educational system. Entrepreneurs demand more and better-quality employees. These better-quality employees are no longer subservient. They are assertive in their role in Indian society and in India's role in the world. These factors have changed the political economy of doing business in India, as well as the way India does business in the world.

There is the development of new constellations and conurbations of cities or towns near manufacturing centers. Thus, we are witnessing the transformation of Gurgaon, an impoverished, hot, sandy, sleepy little town, full of camel carts, on the edge of the Thar Desert, into a global business hub, attracting hundreds of Indians back from the United States to live and work there. Similarly, Poona, now called Pune, once the butt of lowbrow music-hall jokes in Britain, and a base for retired army colonels, is a vibrant educational, cultural, information technology and business destination. Lufthansa has operated a business-class-only service between Munich and Poona, a concept once unthinkable, as several German companies have located there. Poona also contains, within its precincts, over one hundred MBA-degree colleges. The manufacturing works of Tata Motors, Bharat Forge, and Volkswagen are located in Poona.

These facts suggest key transformations in progress. These transformations have to be evaluated against the backdrop of India's industrial history. This history is massive. All economies, societies, and their histories evolve. Therefore, there are ebbs and flows, and rise and fall, and then there may be a rise again. India's economy fell from a position of pre-eminence. It is rising again in relative global standing. India, along with China, can drive the trajectory of future growth in the world economy, since such a large population base was available to no other developed nation when they achieved their growth. This is an unprecedented situation in human history.[34] Behind this rise is a question relating to the psychological character of this rise. Is it simply a revival, and hence reactionary to past impoverishment? Or is it regeneration and a revolutionary transformation, so that a new milieu is defined?[35]

Associated with this question is the concern of whether the Indian economy is really taking off? The development economist Walt Rostow put forward three necessary conditions for an economy to take off. These conditions are: that there has to be a rise in the rate of productive investment from 5 percent or less to over 10 percent of the national income; there has to exist or emerge an institutional framework that exploits impulses for economic expansion by engendering entrepreneurship; and there has to occur the development of one or more substantial manufacturing sectors, with a high rate of growth in production, which can sustain economic growth.[36]

Is the Indian economy meeting Walt Rostow's take-off requirements? If so, what are the contours of this process? What has happened to account for it? What can Indian firms do to regain the position India once held in the world economy in 1750? These are some of the issues dealt with in this book. The book evaluates India's industrial growth and entrepreneurship story over the course of the last six decades, but particularly for the last 20 years. The core themes dealt with are how has entrepreneurship been affected by policies related to industry, how have the institutional changes put through in 1991 led to a transformation of the industrial and entrepreneurial landscapes of India, and what explains the resurgence in India's industrial growth and entrepreneurship performance. Simply put, what drives, what explains and what constrains India's late, late industrial revolution?

Recent growth performance in India

India's economic growth, fuelled by an entrepreneurship boom and industrialization in the last decade and a half, has been impressive. The real growth rates of gross domestic product averaged 3.5 percent in the 1950s, 4 percent in the 1960s, 2.9 percent in the 1970s and 5.6 percent in the 1980s. Now, it is over 8 percent per annum. The "Hindu Rate of Growth" malady, in which the growth rate stagnated at 3.5 percent for a decade or more, has been cured. Some call it a miracle. That is going a bit too far. Some may have considered it to be pre-ordained destiny, given India's history and collection of dynamic people. In a country of 1.2 billion persons, applying a rate of just 1 percent for those classified as dynamic and enterprising yields 12 million Sumangalas. Actually, the number of such people is much more.

What is the backdrop? As is now well known, in the early 1990s, a fundamental institutional transformation in the environment for business took place in India. At that time, licensing regulations were completely overhauled, and free entry was permitted for businesses to operate in almost all sectors of the Indian economy. The Secretariat of Industrial Approvals (SIA), in the Department of Industrial Development, was renamed the Secretariat of Industrial Assistance. The Directorate General of Technical Development (DGTD) was abolished, and the department was renamed the Department of Industrial Policy and Promotion.

One can be cynical about relabeling activities, which the bureaucracy engages in, changing the word *Approvals* to *Assistance*. But these changes were more than skin deep. They were an institutional discontinuity, representing a major break with the past. They involved jettisoning ingrained mental models among the civil servants operating the regulatory system. The changes have led to a transformation of India's industrial economy.[37] India's rate of growth averaged 5.7 percent in the 1990s, the last decade of the old millennium. It has averaged 7 percent in the 2000s, as depicted in figure 1.3. In the 2000s, India's income growth rate has been double what it was 60 years ago. India has overcome its "Hindu Rate of Growth" malady, and such growth can be a confidence multiplier. Confidence can lead to greater income, which then leads to greater confidence, and so on.[38] Yet, the current rate of growth may not be enough to close the per capita

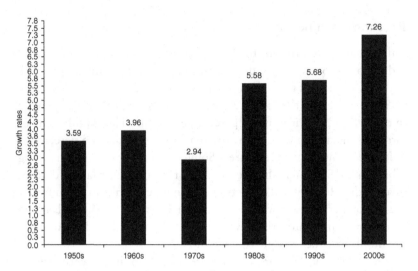

Figure 1.3. Average growth rates in India's national income over six decades.
Source: Derived from Table 224 of the Reserve Bank of India Database on the Indian Economy.

income gap with the United States, Japan, or South Korea. For that, current growth rates have to double.

India's gross domestic product growth rates, given in Table A2, in the first decade of the new millennium have been 1.8 times the growth rate of the 1960s, which was 3.9 percent per annum. This was the decade when Britain was basking in the so-called white heat of the technological revolution. India's rate of growth is now 2.4 times that of the 1970s, which was at 2.9 percent per annum, the decade when South Korea began getting its act together to commence its ascent to global economic dominance. In these two critical decades, India was a laggard. That is now history. In the 1980s and 1990s, India's growth rates were respectable. Nevertheless, in the latter part of the 2000s, India's growth rates have touched almost 10 percent in three of the five latter years of the decade. She may become an economic legend. But it is as yet only a potential.

A spur to this performance has been growth in the activities of firms, enterprises such as Mikku's IVF center, and industries, influenced by the institutional changes put in place over 20 years ago. Today's aggregate picture also reflects the activities of millions of individuals engaged in providing services, such as OM and Sumangala, as well as of numerous manufacturing businesses. There is demand for advanced distribution and transportation infrastructures. These lead to the development of advanced logistics facilities. Risking a debate with potentially deep political, psychological, theological, and sociological connotations, one can suggest that Mikku runs a manufacturing sector business. She helps produce babies to order. Entrepreneurial activities have led to a structural transformation in the logistics facilities and supply chain of raw materials for her IVF business facility. In the last 60 years, the Indian industrial economy has emerged as a heterogeneous entrepreneurial economy in which small firms, large corporations in the private sector promoted and managed by private industrialists, firms owned by foreign investors, and firms owned by government and run by public sector professional executives, co-exist. Not only do these firms co-exist, sometimes the private sector firms lead the race, and sometimes the public sector firms are in front. Yet one feature, dynamic enterprise, is common to all forms of business in India.

An example highlights these phenomena. I took a morning train journey from Bombay to Poona last year. The route goes over the Western Ghats. The entire journey was like being in a shopping mall. Until we reached Nerul, in the coastal plains, staff of the Indian Railways Catering and Tourism Corporation (IRCTC) sold breakfast in the train. At Karjat, where the flatlands end and the hills commence, local entrepreneurs entered the compartments to sell their wares. These Karjat entrepreneurs sold *batata wadas*, or potato fritters. The train watering-stop, thereafter, was Jumrung. At this stage, the Karjat entrepreneurs exited and a new group came into to sell passengers South Indian snacks, cosmetics, stationery and *Lonavala chikki*, a nutty nougat confectionery. Until Thakurwadi, these Jumrung traders sold their wares. Then, at Thakurwadi, in the high hills, a family group of tribal women, consisting of a grandmother, a mother, a young daughter, and the family puppy, entered the train. They sold local fruits and peanuts till Monkey Hill. At Monkey Hill, the all-female tribal family business group, and dog, exited the train, and new entrepreneurs entered to tempt us with jelly beans and chocolate. Till Khandala, where the Deccan plateau starts, these Monkey Hill businessmen carried out their transactions. Then, they too exited. All the while, the IRCTC staff had been going up and down the train selling omelettes, sandwiches, and vegetable cutlets.

Not only were passengers able to purchase items from the staff of
one of India's largest formal sector employers, the Indian Railways,
because IRCTC is a state-owned enterprise, operated by the Ministry
of Railways, but they could acquire items sold by hill tribal people
surviving at the margins of existence in the Western Ghats, the family that sold their humble food items gathered from forest floors. All
Indian trains carry important persons called the travelling ticket exam-
iner (TTE). In the Western Ghats' hills, as elsewhere in India, there is
another TTE breed, the *"ticketless travelling entrepreneur."* I will not
comment on the rights and wrongs of the situation because some will
argue, perhaps legitimately, that Indian train passengers should not be
held hostage to the commercial motivations of various hawkers. The
example highlights the mutual co-existence among the great variety of
entrepreneurs flourishing in India within the same market space.

Industry in the second half of the twentieth century

To provide the background for India's late, late industrialization, it
is useful to cover the complex pantheon of the political economy of
India's industrial development in the second half of the twentieth century. Much has been written. I will deal here with the essential points.
Later, more details will be provided. In 1945, just before independence,
overall industrial growth was low. In important areas, growth, relative
to pre-war performance, had been high. The Second World War had a
positive impact on the growth of some capital goods.[39] With the war
at an end, it was back to business as usual for Indian firms. In the summer of 1945, the industrialists G. D. Birla and J. R. D. Tata led a delegation to Britain and the United States. Agreements were concluded
between Birla Brothers and the Nuffield Organisation in Britain to set
up Hindustan Motors and make Morris cars in India,[40] and between
Tata Sons and Imperial Chemical Industries. India's independence formalized Indian firms' domination of the Indian economy. With independence in 1947, the ability of foreign firms to tweak the levers of
power diminished. Indian industrialists, however, were not sure as to
the emerging political economy environment. It seemed that the government of free India did not fully favor private enterprise.

Such attitudes also prevailed in the intelligentsia. Professor D. R.
Gadgil, one of India's most distinguished industrial economists, had
remarked that "Private enterprise is ... far from being free enterprise,"

since Indian entrepreneurs were anxious to avoid competition after independence.[41] Also, the Prime Minister Jawaharlal Nehru had reasoned that a civilized nation like Britain had behaved savagely in India because imperialism and capitalism were inextricably linked together. India, for the British, was an investment to be held on to at all cost. Thus, all civilized behavior could be set aside if imperialist and capitalist interests were threatened. Hence, to Jawaharlal Nehru, imperialism was an evil that dehumanized man. The equation of imperialism and capitalism in Nehru's mind led to the development of his later antipathy to free enterprise.[42]

During the Second World War, with the backing of the then Governor General of India, Field Marshal Archibald Wavell, whose role in the politics of India in the period leading up to independence was substantial,[43] a group of Indian businessmen, economists, and public servants issued a document called *A Brief Memorandum Outlining a Plan of Economic Development for India*, in 1944. This document set out a vision for India's post-war reconstruction. This so-called Bombay Plan was to be financed in part by drawing down India's extensive accumulated sterling balances. The plan envisioned the doubling of India's per capita income, the tripling of national income, the increase of industrial output by five times, the doubling of farm production, and extensive improvements in housing, education, transportation, communication, health, and sanitation facilities.

The principal intellectual architect and draftsman of the document was Ardeshir Dalal, a former Indian Civil Service (ICS) officer, who was the Managing Director of the Tata Iron and Steel Company. The other group members were five businessmen, G. D. Birla from Calcutta, Kasturbhai Lalbhai from Ahmedabad, Lala Shri Ram from Delhi, J. R. D. Tata and Purshotamdas Thakurdas, both from Bombay, and two professional advisers in economics, Dr. John Mathai and A. D. Shroff. The Bombay Plan document recognized the symbiotic role that government and private businesses could play in India's future industrial development.[44] The Bombay Plan was a short cut to a strong, prosperous, and industrialized India through the heightening of national purpose, confidence, and solidarity.[45] Private sector firms accepted the important regulatory role for the state, and that the state would actively participate in industrial development.[46]

It was natural that the denizens of Indian industry suggest a strong role for the state in India's industrial development. Relationships are always important for business. Relationships between business, government, and political parties mattered a great deal then in India, as they matter several decades later. The Bombay Plan proposed key roles for the state in Indian industrialization not only in providing the infrastructure, but also in operating the heavy industries such as steel and machine building which the nascent private sector could not. These would be industries that led to the building of other industries. The government could use its advantageous position to acquire substantial capital amounts, particularly from the foreign capital markets and agencies, necessary to implement large-scale projects. To use a phrase invented by Prime Minister Jawaharlal Nehru, the public sector enterprises were to be the *"temples of modern India"* that would ensure the conditions for successful take-off into industrialization.

A perusal of the list of the top 47 Indian companies in the world for 2009 shows that of the companies, ranked by revenue in $ billion, listed in the top ten are four private sector Indian companies and six public sector Indian companies. These 47 companies figure in the *Fortune* list of top 200 global firms. The list is in Table A3. Incidentally, the list does not include either Arcelor-Mittal or Vedanta Resources because these companies are British. The four largest Indian private sector companies are Reliance Industries, Tata Steel, ICICI Bank, and Hindalco Industries. Other important Indian private sector companies are Tata Motors, Larsen & Toubro, and Bharti Airtel. The seven largest India public sector companies are Indian Oil Corporation, Bharat Petroleum, Hindustan Petroleum, Oil and Natural Gas Corporation, State Bank of India, National Thermal Power Corporation, and the Steel Authority of India Limited. The mixed economy visualized over 60 years ago has come to fruition.

That the industrial economy of India has been exceedingly dynamic over the last 50 years or so is also brought out by the transition of firms from the list of the top business groups of India in 1965. Many have gone on from positions of absolute dominance to destitution and death. The Monopolies Inquiry Commission of 1964, headed by Justice Kulada Charan Dasgupta, ICS, had listed the top 75 business groups in India as of the mid 1960s. The list of these groups is given in Table A4. In the top ten of this larger list were, in asset size order, the Tata group, the Birla group, the Martin Burn group, the Bangur group, the Associated Cement Companies (ACC) group, the Thapar group, the Sahu Jain group, the Bird Heilgers group, the J.

K. Singhania group, and the Soorajmull Nagarmull group.[47] Almost half a century later, only two of the older business groups participate in Indian industry. These are the Tata group and the Birla group. The other groups have dropped out of reckoning or have died. Darwinian competition has taken a substantial toll on firms in India. Conversely, in the 2009 list of the largest 47 Indian companies are firms such as Reliance Industries, Bharti Airtel, and Housing Development Finance Company. These companies, in the mid 1960s, had not even been conceptualized as likely businesses to bring global approbation for India in the twenty-first century.

Little details supporting the big picture

Do Walt Rostow's requirements for a growth take-off find data support? Do the little details support the big picture? First, I show the broad patterns of savings and investment in the Indian economy over a period of six decades. Based on macroeconomic data, as collated by the Reserve Bank of India, I calculated the ratio of gross domestic capital formation to the gross domestic product. Figure 1.4 displays a chart for the ratio of capital formation over time, and as can be seen from the 1950s to the 2000s its progress has been akin to that of a mountain-climber ascending from the foothills of the Himalayas to Mount Everest. The ratio has always been more than the magical level of 10 percent that Walt Rostow suggested was the *de minimis* requirement for a take-off, and in the 2000s the ratio had reached an average value of 32 percent. In the last few years of the 2000s decade for which data are available, the ratio has been in the high 30 percent range. The ratio has more than doubled between the 1950s and the 2000s. Indians as a nation save and invest comprehensively. At least two of Walt Rostow's conditions – a rise, preferably a doubling, in the rate of productive investment relative to national income, and the existence of an appropriate institutional framework – are met. Whether the third necessary condition, that there exist one or more substantial manufacturing sectors with a high rate of growth, is met has to be empirically evaluated.

Further facts support an industrial growth and economic performance story. I use three sets of industry level data to provide support for the thesis of a late, late industrial revolution. The first set of data relate to the production of certain items in Indian industry over the

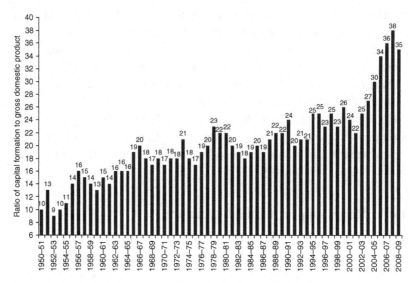

Figure 1.4. Capital formation ratio in India from 1950 to 2008.

Source: Derived from Table 224 of the Reserve Bank of India Database on the Indian Economy.

period 1981–82 to 2009–10. The data coverage is annual. Growth statistics for specific items are shown in Table 1.2.[48] The growth in the production of the listed items has been considerable in each of the three decades.[49] In the almost three decades, between 1981–82 and 2009–10, there has been a doubling of production of the items listed. In the case of capital goods, the magnitude of production increases for items have ranged between 28 times for automobile ancillaries to 200 times for heavy structures. Since this item, heavy structures, is an input for the construction of buildings, equipments, and plant used for the manufacture of other consumer and industrial products, the enhanced production of heavy structures is a function of the derived demand from other growing segments of Indian manufacturing industry.

After the fundamental transformation of the business environment, which occurred in the early 1990s, the production data for the decade of the 1990s or 2000s reflect an important industrial transformation under way. These data support the aggregate trends captured by the index of industrial production. Recollect that, between 1980 and 2010,

Table 1.2. *Growth in the production of specific industrial items between 1981–82 and 2009–10*

	Increase over entire period	Overall growth	Growth in the 1980s	Growth in the 1990s	Growth in the 2000s
	(Times)	(Percent)	(Percent)	(Percent)	(Percent)
Electricity	6.24	6.78	9.01	6.97	4.82
Steel	8.49	8.37	4.39	12.73	7.20
Fertilizers	3.96	5.35	10.10	5.45	1.44
Cement	9.53	8.48	10.07	8.39	7.31
Forgings	2.20	7.97	15.60	8.57	1.27
Sulphuric acid	3.22	4.61	5.18	5.73	3.05
Caustic soda	3.41	4.77	5.71	4.58	4.21
Heavy structures	214.54	59.85	28.88	136.50	7.97
Automobile ancillaries	27.82	13.78	13.54	17.93	9.81
Ship repairs	59.67	21.94	34.19	12.30	21.78
Boilers	37.35	15.20	13.63	4.10	27.55
Petroleum products	5.28	6.33	7.29	5.31	6.57
Beer	3.27	5.66	3.50	7.32	5.72
Phones	8.86	13.27	19.94	18.82	2.38
Watches	2.34	4.66	9.42	1.87	3.63

Source: Reserve Bank of India Database on the Indian Economy, Table 24, and author's calculations.

the index of industrial production for capital goods rose from 100, for the base year of 1980–81, to 1,339 by 2009–10. Thus, a growth of 28 times in the production volume of automotive ancillaries, a growth of 60 times in the production volume of ships and ship repairs, and a growth of 37 times in the production volume of boilers are items contributing to the capital goods sector's growth performance.

The recent availability of alternate data on India's production of various items, released by the Department of Industrial Policy and Promotion of the Ministry of Commerce and Industry, for a considerably longer period of time, permits an assessment of the late, late industrialization thesis. The data relates to production output volumes for each of the years 1950–51, 1960–61, 1970–71, 1980–81, 1990–91, 2000–01 and 2006–07. The second data set also contains production details for a number of consumer items that are used daily by India's people. Some of these items are cars, bicycles, and electric lamps, and consumption items such as tea, coffee, and cooking oil. In 1950–51, a few years after independence, India produced just 1 million tons of steel. By 2006–07, she was producing over 50 million tons of steel. In 1950–51, India produced 8,000 cars. By 2006–07 she was annually producing 1,500,000 cars. In 1950–51, India produced no two-wheeled motorized transport items, such as motorcycles or scooters, at all. By 2006–07, she was producing 8,500,000 units annually. In 1950–51, India produced just 200,000 tons of petroleum products. By 2006–07, she was producing over 135,000,000 tons of petroleum products annually.

I have suggested that the reforms of the early 1990s transformed the business environment and made production of many items attractive. It is worth evaluating the items which have recorded a five-fold increase in production since the 1980s, when the business environment was very different. The items which have recorded a greater than five-fold increase in output in 2006–07 over their output levels in 1980–81 are steel, commercial vehicles, cars, two-wheeled transport units, cement, petroleum products, and sugar. Steel and cement are basic goods that help build the physical infrastructure of a nation. Commercial vehicles, cars, two-wheeled transport units, and petroleum products enhance national mobility. They are energy transmission and transformation items. Sugar is an important food energy source in a country that does not consume substantial quantities of animal fat. Its role in the Indian diet is vital. Hence, these production data, denoting considerable output increases, reflect the coming of age of Indian industry. These trends are clear from the data in Table 1.3.

Yet, will these growth rates in industrial production be revolutionary enough? Eric Hobsbawm has documented British industrial growth in the nineteenth century, the period in which the industrial revolution took roost. These industrial growth rates were much lower than the industrial growth rates India currently enjoys. Hobsbawm's figures show that while the United Kingdom experienced high industrial growth through the nineteenth century, it never exceeded 4.4 percent

Table 1.3. *Production statistics of selected items between 1950–51 and 2006–07*

	Units	Years							Production increase by 2006–07	
		1950–51	1960–61	1970–71	1980–81	1990–91	2000–01	2006–07	Number of times relative to 1980–81	Number of times relative to 1950–51
Coal	million tons	32	55	76	119	226	333	462	3.88	14
Steel	million tons	1	2	5	7	14	31	50	7.38	50
Aluminum	million tons	4	19	169	199	451	620	719	3.61	180
Automobiles	thousands	17	55	88	121	366	784	2,066	17.06	125
Commercial vehicles	thousands	9	28	41	72	146	152	520	7.25	60
Cars	thousands	8	27	47	49	221	632	1,546	31.29	196
Two–wheeled units	thousands	0	1	97	447	1,843	3,756	8,436	18.86	9,374*
Diesel engines	thousands	6	43	65	174	158	306	461	2.65	84
Bicycles	thousands	99	1,063	2,042	4,189	7,084	14,975	10,598	2.53	107
Transformers	million Kva.	0	1	8	20	37	71	71	3.66	357
Motors	million HP	0	1	3	4	6	6	12	3.02	124

Table 1.3. (*cont.*)

	Units	Years							Production increase by 2006–07	
		1950–51	1960–61	1970–71	1980–81	1990–91	2000–01	2006–07	Number of times relative to 1980–81	Number of times relative to 1950–51
Lamps	million	15	44	119	198	274	449	471	2.38	31
Paper	thousand tons	116	349	755	1,149	2,088	3,090	4,139	3.60	36
Cement	thousand tons	300	800	1,400	1,900	4,900	9,900	15,500	8.32	57
Petroleum	million tons	0.2	6	17	24	48	96	136	5.63	678
Mill cotton yarn	million kg	533	788	929	1,067	1,510	2,267	2,824	2.65	5
Sugar	thousand tons	1,134	3,029	3,740	5,148	12,047	18,510	28,199	5.48	25
Tea	million kg	277	318	423	568	705	827	949	1.67	3
Coffee	thousand tons	21	54	71	139	170	313	254	1.83	12
Cooking oils	thousand tons	155	355	558	753	850	1,445	1,286	1.71	8

* Relative to production levels in 1960–61

Source: Government of India, *Handbook of Industrial Policy and Statistics* (New Delhi: Department of Industrial Policy and Promotion, Ministry of Commerce and Industry, 2009), Table 3.16, 76 and 78; and author's calculations.

per year. In the early decades, between 1800 and 1850, the average annual industrial growth rates in Britain were 2.3 percent, 3.7 percent, 4.4 percent, 3.6 percent and 3.8 percent in each decade. Between 1850 and 1900, the average industrial growth rates in each decade were 2.7 percent, 3.3 percent, 2.1 percent, 1.7 percent and 1.8 percent.[50] According to the late Angus Maddison, the year 1820 is taken as the point of take-off.[51] Based on Eric Hobsbawm's data, if the index of British industrial production 1820 is pegged at 100, then by 1850 the industrial production index would have been 202. By 1870 the industrial production index would be 360. India's industrial growth rates have been three times larger in magnitude than Britain's industrial growth rates in the nineteenth century. In the 30 years between 1980 and 2010, the index of industrial production in India has increased seven times, as figure 1.2 shows. Based on current growth, India can easily become a major industrial power.

The size and scale of India's industrial growth rates overshadow those achieved during the industrial revolutions in Britain, Germany, and the United States, by an order of magnitude. India's growth rates are comparable to the industrial growth rates achieved by other Asian countries, such as Japan, South Korea, and Taiwan, during their late industrialization. At her current industrial growth rates, India could replicate the British and American phenomena. Might this happen? The following discussion, relating to entrepreneurial expectations, helps address this important issue.

The third set of data relates to entrepreneurs' investment intentions. With the abolition of industrial licensing in 1991, domestic firms making investment have had to simply notify the Department of Industrial Policy and Promotion of the Ministry of Commerce and Industry of their intentions. In a few cases, firms have to seek an industrial license, though they can do so voluntarily in all cases. The item of some note is the death of the *License Raj*. As figure 1.5 shows, industrial licensing has been an important part of India's economic history. By 2008, the number of licenses issued had come down to 12 from a peak of 1,845 licenses that were issued in 1960.[52] This was only to be expected.

The data on entrepreneurs' investment intentions are filed and collated by the Department of Industrial Policy and Promotion. Their release provides further credence to the late, late industrial revolution thesis. The data that are available for examination relate to entrepreneurs' investment intentions for all of the years between 1991 and

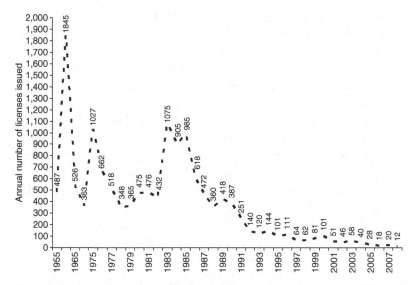

Figure 1.5. Annual number of industrial licenses issued between 1955 and 2008.

Source: Government of India, *Handbook of Industrial Policy and Statistics* (New Delhi: Department of Industrial Policy and Promotion, Ministry of Commerce and Industry, 2009), Table 5.6.

2008. In that period, as a whole, an average of 4,000 investment intention filings were made annually, for an average annual aggregate investment amounting to over ₹275 crores. The average investment amount per intent was ₹64 crores. These projects were expected to generate, in aggregate, over 900,000 annual jobs, with each project employing an average of 220 persons. Table 1.4 provides the details of the entrepreneurs' intentions. Have India's entrepreneurs displayed a bigger appetite for risks? In the 17 years between 1991 and 2008, the quantum of proposed investments, as depicted by investment intentions filings, has risen 23 times. Proposed employment has risen three times.

Specifically, the quantum of capital investment per application has risen 17 times. This suggests a decline in entrepreneurial risk aversion among Indian industrialists. Indian entrepreneurs have acquired progressively bigger risk appetites. Similarly, the quantum of employment per investment filing has risen twice, suggesting considerable job creation willingness by Indian industrialists. This is in spite of the fact

Table 1.4. *Entrepreneurs' investment intentions in India*

Year	Number of intents filed	Proposed investment (rupees crores)	Average investment per intent (rupees crores)	Proposed total employment	Average employment per intent	Capital labor ratio (rupees crores per employee)
1991	3,048	76,310	25	769,000	252	0.10
1992	4,860	115,872	24	923,000	190	0.13
1993	4,456	63,976	14	703,000	158	0.09
1994	4,664	88,771	19	829,000	178	0.11
1995	6,502	125,509	19	1,140,000	175	0.11
1996	4,825	73,278	15	696,000	144	0.11
1997	3,873	52,379	14	522,000	135	0.10
1998	2,889	57,389	20	521,000	180	0.11
1999	2,948	128,892	44	477,000	162	0.27
2000	3,058	72,332	24	411,000	134	0.18
2001	2,981	91,234	31	809,000	271	0.11
2002	3,172	91,291	29	380,000	120	0.24
2003	3,875	118,612	31	833,000	215	0.14
2004	5,118	267,069	52	1,898,000	371	0.14
2005	6,203	353,956	57	1,271,000	205	0.28
2006	6,260	588,271	94	2,100,000	335	0.28
2007	3,725	827,500	222	1,342,000	360	0.62
2008	4,184	1,782,723	426	2,199,000	526	0.81
Average for the period	4,258	276,409	64	990,167	228	0.22
Ratio of 2008 data to 1991 data	1.37 times	23.36 times	17.02 times	2.86 times	2.08 times	8.17 times

Source: Government of India, *Handbook of Industrial Policy and Statistics* (New Delhi: Department of Industrial Policy and Promotion, Ministry of Commerce and Industry, 2009), Table 5.1, 105.

that labor laws in India are considered draconian. Now, whether this is genuine, or simply a myth that has percolated into policy analysts' consciousness after being in circulation for years, bears examining. The real truth may be that Indian labor markets are not inflexible. This conjecture needs verification. A change in the scale of the unit of production, and the basis on which the unit can compete, is under way. Significantly, industries have become heavier users of both capital and labor.[53]

As a firm moves up the ladder of comparative advantage, the ratio of capital usage to labor usage increases. A firm moves into more capital-intensive areas of production.[54] Hence, a transition from lighter to heavier industry involves a transition from firms competing on the basis of cheap labor to firms competing on the basis of capabilities embodied in machinery and capital equipment. To operate capital equipment requires the use of better quality human capital. This is borne out by the use of more capital measured in rupee of capital investment made per unit of labor, over the 19-year period. Second, there is greater employment per intent. These dual facts signal that Indian firms are ascending the ladder of comparative advantage. With India's overpopulation, there was plenty of cheap labor. It may have been cheaper to hire people than to invest in capital equipment.[55] But high labor usage per unit of capital does not lead to industrial productivity and an industrial revolution. Capital intensity of production is an extremely important driver of productivity, and of an industrial revolution. The transformation of the labor usage amount, per each crore of Rupees of capital invested, suggests that the fundamental technological change phenomenon, the substitution of labor by capital, is in progress in India. For each crore of Rupees invested, there were just over ten persons employed in 1991. By 2008, for each crore of Rupees invested, there was one person employed.

Is there a transition under way in Indian industrialists' psyche? Gurcharan Das has noted that the adult Indian male personality has a weak sense of the self. He is uncomfortable making major decisions on his own. He needs the support of authority figures.[56] Of course, there was precedent for this outcome. Gunnar Myrdal had remarked that, in India, no major and few minor business decisions could be taken without prior permission of administrative authorities, or at the risk of subsequent government disapproval.[57] Perhaps the breakdown of the *License Raj* has led to the resurgence of Indian entrepreneurs' self-confidence. The renaming of the Secretariat of Industrial Approvals

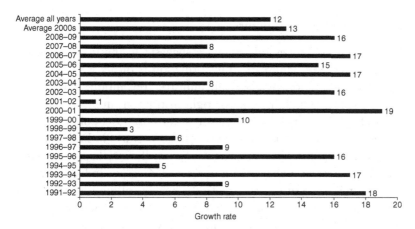

Figure 1.6. Growth of exports by Indian firms.

Source: Derived from Table 128 of the Reserve Bank of India Database on the Indian Economy.

has taken away the necessity for seeking an external authority figure's approbation, and transferred the onus of decision-making on to entrepreneurs' shoulders. Indian industry has entered the age of autonomous thinking.

After a process of learning necessary for industrialization of once-backward countries,[58] such as India, India's industrial entrepreneurs have emerged as those who by 2008 have been willing to invest ₹1,782,723 crores in industry relative to the ₹76,310 crores of 1991. They are also willing to provide employment to over 2.2 million people, relative to just over 750,000 people 19 years earlier. This 23-fold increase in investments and threefold increase in employment symbolize order-of-magnitude enhancements in Indian entrepreneurs' self-confidence. The increasing scale of entrepreneurial decisions taken represents the willing participation of many in India's late, late industrial revolution.

The book is not oriented to foreign trade, investment, or globalization issues since the subjects demand separate books. Yet, a review of India's export growth in the last two decades is instructive. An unwillingness to engage with the world has been replaced by an export optimism, itself a sign of changes in attitudes. Figure 1.6 displays the annual growth in the real value of India's exports between 1991–92 and 2008–09. In some years, there has been double-digit growth. In the overall period, the annual real rate of growth has been 12 percent. In the 2000s, such annual growth has been 13 percent.

Insights from the big picture

What conclusions does this evidence suggest? In the manufacturing sector, an industry landscape transformation is on its way. Can this transformation represent a late, late industrial revolution? If an industrial revolution implies having the right institutions in place, then the data so far provide a broad overview that the post-1991 policy changes have led to a transformation of productive structures in Indian industry. A step back into history is useful. The late B. K. Nehru, ICS, wrote that "the Industrial Policy Resolution of 1956 ... put Indian industry into a complete strait-jacket ... with the benefits of hindsight it seems totally absurd that a country wanting to develop its industry should prescribe for its establishment conditions which were guaranteed to strangle it."[59] The release of the silken cords around entrepreneurs' necks has led to substantial cardio-thoracic revival.

The late American social scientist John P. Lewis wrote that virtually every Western social scientist who arrived in India would exclaim over the wonderful crackle of concepts and insights to be found in New Delhi. These would be packaged always in the superb Indian ability to articulate.[60] In the 1950s and 1960s, a considerable debate, perhaps a sharp confrontation, occurred between the Bombay and Calcutta schools of thought on an appropriate theory of economic development for India. The insights generated had far-reaching consequences for Indian industry. The Bombay school was driven by business, commercial, and industrial interests, while the Calcutta school was driven by academic, technical, and welfare interests, but both schools contained seasoned professionals of each genre.

Compared to Britain, where the post-war planning effort was devoid of technocratic insights, and directed by a group of humanist amateurs who were well versed in the bureaucratic minutiae and political mores and infighting of Whitehall,[61] Indian planning started out with a much more robust set of capable technocratic planners and policy makers. The Bombay team protagonists were Professors C. N. Vakil and P. R. Brahmananda, of Bombay University.[62] Their view was that India lacked financial capital but had plenty of cheap human capital on hand. They argued that the only way to increase investment without inflation was to make sure that there was sufficient supply of mass consumer goods. That meant prioritizing investment in consumer goods industries.[63] There was substantial disguised rural unemployment. This could be ameliorated by using unemployed persons productively in businesses deploying relatively little capital. Such surplus labor could produce wage goods. These were consumer products meant for immediate mass consumption. These low capital businesses would yield quick output and attract entrepreneurial entry. The now-employed surplus labor would consume goods with the wages earned in production. The Bombay strategy would lead to investments in rural infrastructure, agriculture-based industries, and the manufacture of simple consumer items.[64]

The Calcutta school of thought was propounded by Professor Prasanta Chandra Mahalanobis, of the Indian Statistical Institute. Professor Mahalanobis was a Cambridge-educated physicist turned statistician turned economic planner. He played a more important role in India's national economic planning than professional economists did. His views prevailed over all others.[65] During the 1950s, influential intellectuals in the Planning Commission were not economists but ICS officers, S. V. Ramamurti,[66] Tarlok Singh, and Edward Penderel Moon. The late E. P. Moon had been impressed by Soviet heavy industrialization, and strongly proposed that approach to India's industrialization.[67]

The core of the Calcutta school strategy was a move towards capital-intensive and heavy industrialization, led by the public sector, to build the key industries and control the commanding heights of a new modern industrial economy for India.[68] The private sector would play a complementary role in the mixed economy.[69] The Calcutta school was based on the setting-up of very large plants, in substantial state-owned enterprises, in sectors such as steel and heavy machinery. These capital-intensive facilities, employing few people, would deliver low returns over long gestation periods. But they would be used for the purposes of building machines that built other machines. Without these other machines, the output of the important capital goods sector, downstream industries could not be set up. Certain types of big industry were treated as basic because they made possible the emergence of other industrial enterprises, whether basic or not. The approach represented a means for the government to influence the speed and direction of economic growth.[70]

John P. Lewis had written that there was opposition to the capital-intensive state enterprise model, but it came from two unusual sources. The first was a small group of independence-movement veterans, rural reformers, ascetics, and intellectuals. They, as the legatees of a pure Gandhian economy, were committed to the idea of a self-sufficient individual village economy as the appropriate base for the regeneration of India. Giant plants, full of machinery, were anathema to these individuals. Such a landscape simply did not belong in their collection of mental pictures of India. The more sophisticated neo-Gandhians were led by the redoubtable Jayprakash Narayan, an American-educated social scientist. Jayprakash Narayan had realized that their ideal was inconsistent with the efficient scale on which modern industry needed to be conducted even after extensively adapting modern technology to Indian conditions. The more sophisticated neo-Gandhians were willing to permit modern industrial processes. There was also a very small group of extreme laissez-faire oriented persons, most notably Professor B. R. Shenoy, who denied the legitimacy of any centrally conceived and directed development effort.[71]

The neo-Gandhians and laissez-faire oriented persons were articulate. In diversity-tolerant India, both got a good hearing.[72] The neo-Gandhians, in fact, had an affectionate and deferential audience as they offered Indian intellectuals and men of affairs a vicarious asceticism appeasing a traditional cultural strain. But the neo-Gandhians, and the laissez-faire group were cast inescapably in the role of respected crackpots, unlikely to win practicing converts.[73] The neo-Gandhian crackpots also exasperated Pandit Jawaharlal Nehru, who summed up by saying that "An abyss separates those whose psychology is turned towards the future from those who lean towards the past."[74] On the Mahatma, he had stated that "For him, those who wished to serve the masses should not concern themselves with raising the standard of living as with lowering themselves, leveling themselves, so to speak, with the masses and mixing with them on an equal footing. That, for him, was true democracy."[75]

In the absence of serious opposition, the Calcutta vision won the day in the 1950s and 1960s. But the end result was a shortage of consumer goods and heavy inflation. Unfortunately, there were other serious economic consequences, as the policy framework led to economic inefficiencies and resource misallocations, while the cumulative effect of these policies became a growth obstacle.[76] Arguably, two of the builders of modern India were Mahatma Gandhi and M. Visvesvaraya. The seeds of such Bombay versus Calcutta controversies are also found in the diametrically opposite views of the two important builders of modern India, as revealed by their correspondence. Mahatma Gandhi's motto was "industrialize and perish," while M. Visvesvaraya's was "industrialize or perish," and in the 1930s Mahatma Gandhi had written to M. Visvesvaraya that "in India, at any rate for generations to come, we shall not be able to make much use of mechanical power for solving the problem of the ever growing poverty of the masses."[77]

M. Visvesvaraya replied:

You say we hold perhaps diametrically opposite views. You are for developing village industries and I favor both heavy industries and village industries. To the extent that you propose to advance village industries, I am at one with you. I can never persuade myself to take up a hostile attitude towards any constructive work, from any quarter ... I am in favor of heavy industries because heavy industries will save the money that is going out of the country in large sums every year; heavy industries are required to provide the local manufactures of machinery and equipment required by our railways and for defence forces and heavy industries are required also for supplying machinery and tools for the village industries themselves. I recommend more extended use of mechanical power because it produces results for the country much more rapidly than human power. The object is to get food and commodities required by our people for a decent standard of living as speedily as possible.[78]

Fortunately, there is no longer any controversy between Bombay and Calcutta schools of thought. India, as a whole, has emerged as a nation in M. Visvesvaraya's vision. Indian industry is presently ideology free. Pragmatism and native entrepreneurial spirit have won the day. Straightforward conclusions emerge. There has been an output explosion in the consumer goods segment. This is a win for the Bombay view, as many smaller enterprises, some of them employing surplus rural labor, have set up shop to provide consumer goods. Next, there has been an output explosion in the capital goods segment. This is a win for the Calcutta approach, as many businesses and industries that can beget other businesses and industries have emerged. Then the data indicate that there is a capital-for-labor substitution under way in Indian industry. The importance of this key technological change phenomenon cannot be downplayed. Such a technology diffusion effect is an extremely important industrialization contingency. It is a signal that India could become a manufacturing nation. That outcome will affect the future course of India's late, late industrial revolution.

The ground realities of behavior by firms and entrepreneurs back up the evidence presented. What conclusions are suggested? India is fertile ground for consumer goods and heavy industry; her firms are globalizing, a major issue not dealt with; and emergent technology entrepreneurship may change the nature of Indian markets. India's industrial growth story is being driven by a variety of entrepreneurs and firms. These are informal-sector entrepreneurs, private enterprises, state-owned enterprises, and multinational corporations. Some Indian firms have the wherewithal to become seriously large global corporations. Many large-scale business expansion announcements are made every day in India. It is the concatenation of such dynamic investment and entrepreneurial activities that will sustain and drive forward India's industrial progress. Because I have framed the story of India's industrial progression as a late, late industrial revolution, it is useful to understand what the original industrial revolutions were all about. The next chapter describes the brief history of industrial revolutions over the course of the last 250 years: what were they, what made them happen, why did they happen where they did, and what were their consequences for various economies, particularly India?

2 | *Industrial revolutions*

Origins

Economic history includes three groups of events called revolutions. In the eighteenth century, the first industrial revolution occurred. At the end of the nineteenth and beginning of the twentieth century, the introduction of electric power and the internal combustion engine led to a second industrial revolution. Advances in computing, electronics, data storage, and communications networks have led to an information and knowledge revolution. The impact of each revolution has been massive. In many cases, aftershocks continue centuries later. Modern societies have emerged because of the systematic application of scientific knowledge for productive uses. The late Nobel laureate Simon Kuznets had remarked that "The epochal innovation that distinguishes the modern economic epoch is the extended application of science to problems of economic production."[1]

The industrial revolution commences with world leadership in productivity and technology for the past six centuries, initially provided by the region that is the north of Italy and the Flanders region of Belgium. These regions, where the renaissance generally took place after the Middle Ages, played the leading role in the global economy from 1400 to 1600. Then the Netherlands led from 1600 to 1820. After 1820, there were two global technology leaders. The United Kingdom had the highest levels of economic attainment, from 1820 to 1890. Thereafter, the United States took over. In the twentieth century, the leader set the stage for others. It was accepted that the United States was the twentieth-century leader.[2]

Carlo Cipolla had asked the important questions as to why were the Europeans not only able to force their way through to the Spice Islands, but also gain control of all the major sea routes and establish overseas empires? What allowed the Europeans to accomplish the dramatic and sudden transition from a state of insecurity to that of bold and aggressive expansion?[3] Why did the "Vasco da Gama era," which had critical effects on India, come into being?[4] The success of Europe during the Renaissance period was based on technological change, and resource substitution effects. Seagoing galleys' oarsmen were substituted by sails. Wind power took over from manpower. Guns substituted for warriors. Gunpowder substituted for swords. These led to the exchange of human energy for inanimate power. By using sailing ships carrying guns, the Europeans accomplished an energy transformation by breaking the bottleneck inherent in human energy use.[5] European maritime expansion was one factor paving the way for the industrial revolution.[6]

The fundamental transformation in human economic circumstances occurred in the late eighteenth century. Around 1780, the steam engine further substituted inanimate for animate sources of power. The steam engine was first used for pumping water out of coal mines. It later replaced water power in driving machinery.[7] A vast new source of energy was opened up. Heat conversion led to the use of new machines, with major consequences of introducing such machinery.[8] Thereafter, new techniques for making iron, by replacing charcoal with coke in iron ore smelting, and a new process for refining pig iron, increased supply and lowered the price of wrought iron. By 1788, there were 59 blast furnaces using coke in the British iron industry. Iron was smelted in blast furnaces with constant blast pressure and rolled mechanically.[9] The products of these mills became the building blocks of the industrial revolution.[10]

The primary consequence of introducing such machinery was the origin of the factory system, the division of labor, and major increases in productivity. By the final decades of the eighteenth century, the British had burst through the labor barrier in textiles.[11] In the textile industry, with which the industrial revolution is associated, by 1820 a worker operating several looms, originally invented by Edmund Cartwright, driven by power, produced 20 times the output of a manual worker. A single railway engine could transport goods requiring several hundred horses. This functionality led to the origin of the term horsepower.[12] These productivity increases, primarily in textiles, in turn stimulated demand for more machines, raw materials, iron, shipping, and communications.[13]

The use of steam-powered engines also removed a binding constraint on human mobility since the invention of wheeled chariots by the Sumerians. For over 4,000 years, till the mid eighteenth century, the average speed achieved by wheeled carriages was between four and five miles per hour. Hence, a limited distance was covered in a day. Speed of land travel increased between five and ten times on trains. In sea travel, the steamships could cross the Atlantic in one tenth the time that the fastest sailing ship could achieve. These increases engendered political unification, as well as market coverage, since land that was ten times larger in linear dimensions, and a hundred times larger in area, could be brought within the range of prompt communications from headquarters.[14] The industrial revolution in Britain expanded national wealth and purchasing power. These constantly outweighed the rise in population.[15] Similarly, the use of machines led to average real wages rising between 15 and 25 percent in the years 1818 to 1850, and by 80 percent in the next 50 years. This wages growth led to rising demand for food and other consumer goods, with the steam ships and railways bringing the North American agricultural surplus to be distributed in Britain.[16]

In the mid to late eighteenth century, agriculture and the textile industry formed the basis of both European and non-European economies. In India and China there were many traders, textile producers, and craftsmen. The differences in per capita income were not enormous. Hence, the shares of India and China in global output were substantial. The industrial revolution changed the balance of world economic progress. The British share of total world manufacturing continued to rise, as it became the first industrial nation. As other European nations and the United States adopted the industrialization model, their shares of global manufacturing and per capita incomes rose steadily.[17]

In creating modern industry, inanimate sources of power transcended human biological limitations. The course of an industrial transformation had certain characteristics. These were: the introduction of energy sources via fossil fuels use, the extensive use of mechanically powered machinery, and the widespread use of materials not occurring in nature. These factors interacted to expand output, with the process of output expansion depending on the capture and use of transient energy. The greater the number of mechanical means a system possessed for the recapture, use, and passing around of energy before its discharge from the system, the larger were the cumulative consequences of the energy utilized. Such a process led to the emergence of the scale effect in industry.[18]

Thus, the British rate of productivity growth in the first half of the nineteenth century became thrice the rate observed for the first half of the eighteenth century. In the second half of the eighteenth century, the rate of growth had been twice what it was in the preceding period.[19] In an industrial economy the role of agriculture diminished, but agricultural productivity increased greatly. Because of industrialization, the structural transformations led to the rise of the mining, manufacturing, and construction sectors.[20] The significant technological improvements involved the use of machinery and mechanical power to perform tasks done slowly by human or animal power, or not done at all. This period in British industry witnessed the application of mechanically powered machinery in the textile industries, James Watt's invention of the steam engine, and the development of the factory system of production.[21]

Why did the industrial revolution happen? The application of science to industry is the distinguishing characteristic of modern industry.[22] Given interactions in human history, there were important and significant relationships between the scientific revolution and the industrial revolution.[23] One of the important historians of the industrial revolution, Thomas Ashton, wrote that the changes were not just industrial, but also social and intellectual. Along with industrial changes, there were commercial, financial, agricultural, and political changes. The intellectual changes were fundamental because they allowed the other changes to occur.[24]

What were these intellectual changes? Key individuals in human history, such as Nicolaus Copernicus, Galileo Galilei, René Descartes, and Isaac Newton, via their scientific achievements, had reinforced ideas in circulation about the practical possibilities of harnessing nature's forces. The science of mechanics, in all its branches, became central to generating industrially usable knowledge.[25] Between the scientific ideas that became established in human knowledge about nature, beginning with Copernicus in 1543, and culminating with Newton in 1687, several other intellectual, ideological, and utilitarian ideas arose within the matrices of knowledge systems.[26] In 1660, Francis Bacon had influenced the founding of the Royal Society for Improving Natural Knowledge in Britain. From then onwards, methods of science such as observation and experiment were applied for utilitarian purposes.[27]

As discoveries occur, the scale of their occurrence expands and changes human consciousness.[28] Within scientific discovery efforts, the processes of adapting, assimilating, transforming and general borrowing take place.[29] Intellectual ideas and resources are routinely borrowed.[30] Thus, by 1750 the same scientific knowledge was available in all major languages but its utilization varied substantially.[31] In Britain, prior to the eighteenth century, technology was based on handicrafts, and production had been slow.[32] In the late eighteenth century, the application of scientific knowledge and experimental forms of inquiry into the making of goods, the moving of heavy objects, whether by coal or water, and the creation of new power technologies transformed human productivity.[33] By the second half of the nineteenth century, the flowering of chemical and electrical science theories then provided the foundations for new processes and new industries.[34]

India's role in motivating the industrial revolution

Technology application is an expression of human responses to a changing environment, so that new situations may be met with new ideas, and new actions are generated.[35] What might have been the political economy motivations for the industrial revolution? Every scholar of the industrial revolution, whether Thomas Ashton, Fernand Braudel, Rondo Cameron, Phyllis Deane, Eric Hobsbawm, Paul Kennedy, Geoffrey Owen, Nathan Rosenberg, or Walt Rostow, has agreed that the first industry significantly affected was the cotton textile industry. Eric Hobsbawm had explicitly remarked that: "whoever says industrial revolution says cotton."[36] The first major increases in output growth and productivity were noted in this industry. Between the 1750s and 1830s, the mechanization of spinning in Britain increased productivity in the sector by over 300 times. The cotton industry led industrial change in general, created industrial regions, and led to the development of the factory form of production, an organization type which changed the basis of society forever.[37] The textile industry continued as the mainstay of the industrial revolution till the mid nineteenth century, when the railways took over as the driving force.[38] Profits from the textiles sector financed heavy industrialization and railway building.[39]

The technical problem of mechanization in the cotton industry had been the imbalance between the efficiency of spinning and weaving. The spinning wheel was much less productive than the handloom, speeded up by the flying shuttle (invented by John Kay), and could not supply weavers fast enough. Three inventions changed the picture. James Hargreaves' 1764 spinning jenny enabled a single spinner to spin multiple threads at once. Richard Arkwright's 1768 water frame used the idea of spinning by combining rollers and spindles. A fusion of the two machines led to the creation of the mule, developed by Samuel Crompton, to which steam power was applied.[40] James Hargreaves' and Richard Arkwright's innovations established factory production.[41] Subsequently, cotton masters began to build functional factories. By the early nineteenth century, they had lengthened the working day by illuminating their factories with gas. They also bleached and dyed textiles by recent inventions of chemistry, a science which came of age in the late eighteenth century.[42] The impact of the cotton industry extended well beyond its own market environment. While the industry did not directly stimulate the heavy capital goods industries of coal, iron, and steel, it stimulated urbanization as workers clustered in factory towns. This general urbanization provided a stimulus for coal in the eighteenth and early nineteenth centuries.[43]

While the growth of the textile industry slowed down in the middle of the nineteenth century, a textile industrialization age of crisis indirectly led to breakthroughs for coal, steel, and iron, as alternative growth drivers were sought. These were the staple items for railway construction. Between 1830 and 1850, over 6,000 miles of railways were opened in Britain. The two periods, between 1835 and 1837 and between 1845 and 1847, characterized the second phase of the British industrial revolution, when the focus shifted to railways. The railways were largely responsible for the doubling of British iron output between the mid 1830s and the mid 1840s.[44] The railways were revolutionary because they affected ordinary citizens' lives.[45]

The industrial revolution in Britain being the first such revolution, it cannot be explained in terms of imitative behavior leading to the adoption of more advanced techniques, since these techniques were first invented during the revolution, nor to the import of capital or the impact of an already industrialized world economy.[46] Could there be some other reason, along with the interplay of science and technology, which motivated the search for alternatives? India had resounding success as a textile manufacturing nation, in a non-mechanized way, by the seventeenth century. She had made major inroads into British and European markets. A substitution of imports motive proved to be the critical economic trigger for the industrial revolution.[47] Businessmen search for ways to reduce costs, as items become more expensive. Technological innovations are sought, to reduce costs. Capital, embodying the latest technology, becomes the important factor of production.[48] Replacement of Indian imports, which created a trade deficit, motivated the search for a technological breakthrough in Britain.

By the year AD 600, Indian cotton had been introduced to Iraq. It then spread to Syria, Cyprus, Sicily, Tunisia, Morocco, Spain, and Egypt.[49] From 1670 onwards, imports of cotton textiles from India had become widespread in Europe. The only pure cotton industry known in Europe at that time was that of India. By the end of the seventeenth century, Indian textiles were a major force in European markets,[50] leading to continuous trade deficits in Britain.[51] Its products, called calicoes,[52] the term originating from the name of the port town Calicut,[53] were imported by the Eastern trading companies. The sales of popular Indian textile items were bitterly opposed by European manufacturers of wool, linen, and silk.[54] In Britain, the Calico Act had been passed in 1701 to ban Indian imports. Its failure led to a second Calico Act in 1721 banning all textile imports.[55] Indian textiles' quality provided a major challenge to European manufacturers, because of the fineness of muslins from Bengal and the brilliant colors and patterns of other cloths.[56] Abbé Raynal remarked in 1777 that "If Saxony and other countries of Europe make up fine China; if Valencia manufactures Pekins superior to those of China; if Switzerland imitates the muslins and worked calicoes of Bengal; if England and France print linens with great elegance; if so many stuffs, formerly unknown in our climates, now employ our best artists, are we not indebted to India for all these advantages?"[57]

In his economic growth theories survey, Walt Rostow included a description from the eighteenth century of the impact on French women of Indian calico textile items: "fruit defendu, les toiles deviennent la passion de toutes les filles d'Eve françaises" ("forbidden fruit, cotton cloth became the passion of every French daughter of Eve").[58] The taste for printed calicoes spread rapidly in Europe, especially in Britain and France. The authorities in France tried various measures, such as confiscation, imprisonment, and fines, but no measures worked. A Paris merchant, based in the rue des Bourdonnais, named Brillon de Jouy, even offered to pay 500 *livres* to anyone willing "to strip in the street any woman wearing Indian fabrics." If this was thought too extreme, he invited citizens to "dress up streetwalkers in

Indian fabrics."[59] The satirist Daniel Defoe had also mocked the fashion of the day for Indian clothing. In an article in the *Weekly Review*, he wrote:

Such is the power of a mode as we saw persons of our quality dressed in Indian carpets, which but a few years before their chambermaids would have though too ordinary for them; the chints were advanced from lying upon their floor to their backs, from the footcloths to the petticoats; and even the Queen herself at this time was pleased to appear in China and Japan, I mean China silks and calico. Nor was this all, but it crept into our houses and bedchambers; curtains, cushions, chairs and at last beds themselves were nothing but calicoes and Indian stuffs.[60]

The demand for Indian cotton cloth was so much that it was estimated half the French population wore cotton as opposed to the locally available linen or wool. The French had resorted to duties, and other inhibitions on imports, to protect their domestic industry, but finally in 1757 reduced their tariffs. The quality of Indian goods set off a chain reaction, via a demonstration effect, to reproduce goods of similar quality, at low cost, and enjoy the profits.[61] This provided incentives to develop machinery to produce fine textiles that clumsy European hands could not produce, though hand-weaving methods had long been used in India. A major spur to the industrial revolution in Britain was the motive to substitute Indian imports by domestic manufactures. Richard Arkwright's machines could not spin cloth as fine as Bengal muslin. Samuel Crompton's machine finally achieved the production quality of Bengal hand-woven cloth.[62] There was also a cost motivation, based on an explicit capital for labor substitution,[63] since wages in Europe were six or more times higher than wages in India.[64]

What was the impact on India of British industrialization via the textiles sector? The Indian export trade in textiles had accounted for almost 2 percent of national income in Moghul India.[65] The early nineteenth-century era of cheap textiles from Lancashire effectively destroyed the Indian export trade in textiles, simply because the Indian items were no longer cost competitive.[66] By the first half of the nineteenth century, Lancashire had progressed swiftly, and Britain replaced India as the largest supplier of cotton goods to the rest of the world. The domestic market for yarn and cloth in India then fell into British hands.[67] Effectively, for three quarters of a century, the industrial revolution in textiles led to the domination by the Lancashire firms of global and India's domestic trade.[68]

The tables started turning in the late nineteenth century, when India adopted industrial practices and revived Indian cotton production via the use of mechanized spinning and weaving. The modern Indian cotton textile industry was born in 1854, when the first cotton mill powered by steam in Asia, established by Cowasjee N. Davar, became operational in Bombay. Yet, by 1865 there were only ten cotton mills. Expansion occurred in the 1870s, with 47 cotton mills in operation by 1875, and 79 cotton mills by 1883.[69] By then, however, mercantile exploitation of the Indian economy had been under way for over a century by the British. First, between 1757 and 1813, when it lost its trading monopoly, the East India Company used the revenues it collected on behalf of the Moghuls earlier, and then themselves, to buy goods in India for sale in England. In other words, the revenues of India provided the East India Company with capital for their trading operations. These revenues were euphemistically called the "investment" of the Company in India.[70]

After 1813, and the loss of the East India Company's trading monopoly, the industrial revolution generated a new economic relationship between India and Britain. Between 1813 and 1858, when the governance of India passed from the hands of the Company to the Crown, the pattern of activity changed to one of free trade whereby India became the market for Lancashire products,[71] while she supplied the raw materials to Britain for processing.[72] Arnold Pacey wrote:

After 1803, however, the arrogance of conquest was reinforced by the rapid development of British industry. This means that Indian techniques which a few years ago earlier seemed remarkable could now be equaled at much lower cost by British factories. India was then made to appear rather primitive, and the idea grew that its proper role was to provide raw materials for western industry, including raw cotton and indigo dye, and to function as a market for British goods.[73]

After 1813, imports of cotton fabrics into India rose from a million yards in 1814, to 51 million yards in 1830, and to 995 million yards by 1870. This drove out the traditional domestic producers and in the process led to India's de-industrialization.[74]

Britain and the industrial revolution

Why in Britain? Why not elsewhere? From the middle of the seventeenth century, British science had come wrapped in an ideology encouraging material and commercial gain.[75] In Britain, many networks linked scientists with businessmen.[76] Scientists were heroes, with exploits popularized in newspapers and journals. Science became a belief system yielding power over nature. Initially in Britain, and then gradually throughout Western Europe, the population learned about science in schools and lecture halls, and picked up its contents from general textbooks. In Britain, science integrated differently with the social environment. By 1750, people approached the productive process through an implicit mechanical lens by visualizing it as something to be mastered by machines.[77] On an abstract level, the process was conceptualized in terms of weights, motion, the principles of force and inertia. Copernicus had argued that the sun lay in the center of the universe. In the next generation, Johannes Kepler established the laws of planetary motion, while Galileo had discovered the keys to the local motion of earth-bound bodies. In the 1660s, Robert Boyle perfected an air pump that convincingly displayed the presence of vacuum, and discovered the laws of gases. Isaac Newton demonstrated the law of universal gravitation, thereby proving the importance of Kepler's planetary laws and elaborating on the mechanics of Galileo.[78] One can now easily see how tying together the ideas of Galileo, Kepler, Newton, and Boyle would have led to the subsequent invention of the steam engine.

Next, take the case of Jean Desagulier, a Huguenot refugee in Britain who was a lecturer and official experimenter for the Royal Society. He had authored a book in 1744 on mechanical knowledge titled *A Course of Experimental Philosophy*. This text, while discussing the steam engine, contains the first instance when anyone writing, in any language, spelled out the critical insight that mechanization undertaken by engineers could enhance the profit of entrepreneurs by reducing labor costs. By the middle of the eighteenth century, a materialist ideology of commercial development was linked in the minds of entrepreneurs with mechanical applications, and writings of people such as Desagulier appealed directly to them. British science, in the form of Newtonian mechanics, it is suggested, directly fostered industrialization.[79] Margaret Jacob states that "there was one common element that would prove immensely germane to the mechanization of the manufacturing and transportation systems: the belief that science and technology could control nature and that creativity in both was desirable."[80]

While workers could be brutalized, when viewed in these terms, manufacturing costs were reduced by the use of machinery instead of people, thus increasing profits.[81] By the end of the eighteenth century, capital and ingenuity had promoted industrial progress for reasons that had much to do with scientific and commercial cultures.[82] By 1800, a British mechanical vision had synthesized nature with a moral economy of prosperity. The scientific innovations that abounded were applied to practical matters by scientists.[83] The pervasive new scientific learning fueled British entrepreneurs' imaginations as to how to make profits.[84] It led to the creation of the technology entrepreneurs' class.[85] Industrial entrepreneurs either possessed technical skills, or hired people who did. They needed to assimilate applied scientific knowledge along with business skills.[86]

Sharing a common vocabulary of technology, engineers and entrepreneurs, such as Mathew Boulton and James Watt, could talk the same mechanical talk, were able to visualize the physical world in its mechanical and commercial terms, and align their common interests into partnerships.[87] The impact of this alignment had permanent effects on the evolution of the world's economy. In Britain itself, the advance of the industrial revolution by 1820 had attracted attention. Economists even formulated a law, known as Say's Law, named after Jean-Baptiste Say, which stated that supply created its own demand. A useful modern statement on Say's Law is by the historian Fernand Braudel, who said:

Another, more logical way to put the same thing is that the production of any good which will sooner or later be in supply on the market, has already led, in the very process, to a distribution of money: the raw materials have had to be paid for, the costs of transport found, and the workers given their wages. Once this money has been distributed, its normal function is to reappear, sooner or later, in the form of a demand or if one prefers, a purchase. Supply makes an appointment with itself.[88]

The economic impact of the industrial revolution is best assessed by reviewing patterns of British industrial growth in the nineteenth century. In this period, Britain experienced relatively high industrial growth. The growth rates touched almost 48 percent, over the decade between 1820 and 1830. A slowdown took it to 37 percent over the decade between 1830 and 1840, and to 39 percent over the decade between 1840 and 1850. Thereafter, it slowed down considerably.[89] But the manufacturing revolution had triggered Say's Law!

The American experience with industrialization

The American experience has been fundamental to global industrialization. The phenomenon of growth in cotton, electricity, and cars is history. America, however, is the home of mass production of machinery. Advances in mass production, particularly of the Colt revolver, the Winchester rifle, the clock, and the sewing machine, and the use of the assembly line, initially in Chicago and Cincinnati slaughterhouses, and then in mass producing cars, originated in America.[90] Yet, America's industrial revolution, along with that of Germany, came after that of Britain. What were its contours? What lessons can be learnt from these experiences? Industrialization in the United States and in Germany was characterized by scale and scope economies. These were based on unique designs for production and distribution organizations. Nevertheless, these innovations came much later, in the latter half of the nineteenth century, when Britain had been an industrial power for a century.

What was the American position when the first industrial revolution was under way in Britain in the late eighteenth century? The United States did not have a great reputation for scientific originality, because many of the fundamental discoveries had originated in Europe in the fifteenth and sixteenth centuries. At the time of the American Revolution, the American economic position was so backward that it was felt that the fledgling republic could not play a role in the affairs of nations. Enthusiastic imitation had to be the norm. The Americans had to beg, borrow, and steal ideas in order to commence industrialization, but inventors and innovators such as Eli Whitney and Thomas Edison transformed America and the world.[91]

In 1790, America had a population of 4 million compared to Britain's 14 million people, the economy was based on farming, and just about 6 percent of the population lived in urban areas. Also, one in six persons was a slave.[92] By the late 1790s, Britain was supplying

80 percent of American imports while taking half its exports.[93] The money system was chaotic, with promissory notes or bills of exchange being more valuable. There were no decent circulating mediums of exchange. In 1789, in the provisional state of Tennessee, it was proposed that the Governor be paid 1,000 deerskins annually; the Chief Justice and the Attorney General were to receive 500 deerskins, the County Clerk was to receive 300 beaver skins a year, the members of the General Assembly were to receive a daily allowance of three raccoon skins and a justice of the peace could charge one muskrat skin for signing a warrant.[94]

In a backward economic and social milieu, the importance of Eli Whitney's invention is out of all proportion to subsequent inventions that emerged from the United States. Eli Whitney was the son of a small New England manufacturer who made nails, and had been sent to Yale. Finding little employment in the region, after graduation, Eli Whitney went to Georgia as a private tutor. Finding conditions unwelcoming, he stayed on briefly in South Carolina where he happened to notice the large amounts of labor required to harvest rice, then a staple item in American trade. In social gatherings, he had heard that if a machine could be found to clean cotton, which was the other staple export item, it would be of great consequence. While the cotton being grown in the Caribbean to supply Britain was the long staple kind, the type grown in the American South was the short staple variety. Since tobacco and rice were the key trade items, there could be major impact of developing the cotton sector; however, cleaning the short staple variety cotton was difficult.

Eli Whitney's development of a simple cotton harvesting and cleaning machine, called the cotton gin, in 1793 revolutionized American cotton growing. In 1791, cotton exports were 189,000 pounds, but fell to 138,000 pounds a year later. By 1793, it had grown to 487,000 pounds, to 1,601,000 pounds in 1794 and to 6,276,000 pounds in 1795. By 1800, about 18 million pounds of cotton were being exported from America.[95] This was the biggest breakthrough in production scale that the world has ever seen to occur in less than a decade. Cotton at that time was the basis for the world's largest industry, textiles. The United States played an increasingly vital role in the British industrial revolution by providing the raw cotton, enabling Britain to become the world's loom. The United States eventually supplied Britain with 75 percent of its cotton. By 1860, Britain consumed half the world's cotton supply. It had 3,000 factories, using 400,000 powerlooms and employed 500,000 people in cotton textiles.[96]

The simplicity of Eli Whitney's gin was in its original use of standardized parts. This made it possible to rapidly mass manufacture the machines and diffuse them through the relevant parts of the country. Eli Whitney is one of the founders of the mass production approach; one of those, according to Jonathan Hughes, of "American genius that put the system of standardized output and interchangeable parts to work for the good of mankind."[97] This production approach soon had impact elsewhere. The spillover effect was that many British firms in the metalworking industries adopted the American system of manufacture by making standard machinery products from interchangeable components.[98] In the 1850s Britain was the industrial leader; by the end of the nineteenth century the United States had overtaken Britain. This facet of relative performance is also apparent from the slowdown in British industrial growth in the latter part of nineteenth century. By the final decades of the nineteenth century, British industrial growth rates were between 1.7 and 1.8 percent per annum.[99]

The growth of American manufacturing after the Eli Whitney era led to a change in economic processes. This was the substitution of capital for labor in the American economy. Differences in resource endowments, and demand conditions, materially affected the economic development of a country. They influenced the type of product characteristics and manufacturing processes to be used.[100] An abundance of natural resources meant it was rational to use approaches intensive in natural resources consumption, rather than less freely available labor and capital equipment. Thus, America became an early pioneer in the development of machinery for woodworking, because of an abundant supply of resources from the forests.[101]

In America, farmland was plentiful and bountiful. This attracted people to work on the land as farmers. Labor, especially trained labor for manufacturing units, was in very short supply. America was a dynamic society built on settlers. It was one in which labor was more mobile relative to Britain. Opportunities for self-employment were greater. Restrictions on personal freedom, which factory apprenticeships entailed, were unacceptable. Wages were high, so as to retain men in manufacturing plants. High wages, however, meant uncompetitive products. Thus, substitution of capital for labor enhanced the capital-to-labor ratio in firms.[102] Firms replaced a more expensive factor of production by a cheaper factor. As labor became more expensive, it was replaced by capital, which embodied the current technology in vogue, as a factor of production.[103]

Firms combined the quantities of labor and capital which maximized profits, the motivation being to maximize the cost reductions by substituting capital and technology for labor where feasible. Therefore, technology substituted for labor inputs. Consequently, American manufacturers looked for manufacturing methods that economized on the use of craft skills, as principally embodied in human beings, which was the expensive labor factor of production, and used greater proportions of machinery. The manufacturing processes to do so involved greater standardization.[104] At the Crystal Palace exhibition in Hyde Park, London, in 1851, the British coined the phrase "American system of manufactures" because of the distinctiveness of American products. These referred to goods which were produced by specialized machines, were standardized, and used interchangeable parts.[105] This standardization approach had evolved in United States government armories, such as the Springfield Arsenal in Massachusetts, for the production of small arms.[106] It was then taken up by the manufacturers of items such as bicycles, sewing machines, typewriters, and other products for which there was a large and homogenous demand.[107]

Behind standardization was the prior development of a capital goods sector. In the early economic history of the United States, the capital goods sector primarily dealt with metal forming and metal shaping. There were learning centers where metal-working skills were developed, and then transferred to the production of a sequence of standardized products. The commonality of production processes was diffused across a range of industries, so that there was mutual learning across industries. Production processes for items such as firearms, clocks and watches, agricultural machinery, hardware, sewing machines, typewriters, office machinery, bicycles, and automobiles had similarities and common features.[108] Such similarities engendered knowledge spillovers. These steps would lead to the generation of manufacturing efficiencies across the production systems for the entire range of items required for daily human activities.

On October 21, 1879, Thomas Edison took a piece of cotton thread, put it in a mold and carbonized it in a furnace. He had been experimenting for some time to develop a long-lasting filament for an incandescent lamp. He put the carbonized filament in a glass container, removed the air in the container and passed electricity generated from a small dynamo into the container. The filament lit up and stayed lit for over 12 hours.[109] Thus, the electric light bulb was born, and soon thereafter the electric power industry. Thomas Edison had been trying for some time to develop a working light bulb but his previous attempts to make the filament stay alight for any length of time had failed.

The broad principles behind electricity and electric lighting were already known. In 1801, Humphrey Davy had demonstrated carbon arc lighting, in 1831 Michael Faraday had invented the dynamo to convert mechanical power to electric power, and by the 1860s Joseph Swan held a British patent for incandescent lighting.[110] Thomas Edison's breakthrough in 1879 had come because he had visualized the overall system of incandescent lighting incorporating the glass container with a vacuum and the filament to which an electric current had to be applied. The broader industrial system involved wiring, switches, meters, a power plant, and light bulbs, so that homes, factories, businesses, and other users of electricity could utilize it for lighting and other purposes. It was this same system-visualization which led to the modern power industry. By the end of the 1880s, Thomas Edison had laid the foundations of Consolidated Edison and General Electric, two corporations which are still major economic influences today.[111]

The growth of the electrical industry in the United States rested on organizational skills involving the construction of an integrated system for generating, transmitting, and distributing electricity and the recognition that once the system was in place there was a mass market waiting to be tapped.[112] The new electrical energy source not only transformed the mechanical processes of production within factories and created a new form of urban transportation, but also revolutionized the making of many metals and chemicals.[113] The economic consequences of electrification were high. The average cost of each lamp had fallen from 70 cents in 1881 to 31 cents in 1884. By 1888, there were 185 electricity stations in the center of towns supplying 386,000 lamps, and 1,281 dispersed stations supplying 344,000 lamps. The United States Census of 1880 had listed 40 electrical establishments employing fewer than 900 workers. By 1890, there were 189 electrical establishments listed employing 46,000 workers. Power stations in 1890 employed 2,000 staff, and by 1902 there were 3,620 power stations employing 30,000 staff.[114]

No less compelling than the achievements of Eli Whitney and Thomas Edison were the achievements of Henry Ford. His greatest triumph, and that of the American system, was the mass-produced automobile. American entrepreneurs were good at taking inventions made elsewhere, like the internal combustion engine, and adapting them to local conditions.[115] As innovators, they could put together separate components that others had originated and devise a system that would transform economic life. Henry Ford changed the American economy by making the automobile ubiquitous.[116] The automobile turned the static mechanical energy available in a stationary engine dynamic by putting wheels on that engine. It made human beings more productive by replacing the energy of several horses. It made transportation more efficient. The multiplier effect of such efficiencies on national output was massive and inestimable.

The automobile (the term includes cars, trucks, and buses) changed American topography. It transformed the landscape by creating suburbs. Cities in America spread out in all directions. They still continue to do so. In many parts of the country, the ratio of automobiles to people is greater than 100 percent. It is believed that the area of southern California designated the Greater Los Angeles Area contains many more automobiles than people. In my town of current temporary residence, Dallas, the entire metropolitan region covers an area 80 miles in distance in its north–south axis and 90 miles in distance in its east–west axis. The area has more motorway miles than contemporary Great Britain. In this area, there are more automobiles than people. The sociological impact of such changes was substantial. New shopping centers, malls, and an entire urban culture based on the automobile were created. This was in diametric opposition to the urban street culture of Europe, where street life and a café society were the norm in cities. The automobile revolutionized the transport of goods. It created a whole multi-billion dollar ecosystem of industries devoted to its production and maintenance.

A bigger impact was on human welfare. The automobile offered particularity. Anyone owning a car could decide when to start and finish a journey, and where that journey was to be. The route from place A to place B could be self-chosen, subject to available roads. The journey could be made alone or with others. The choice of speed, subject to institutional constraints, was discretionary. An individual would no longer be isolated if one possessed a car and could set out on a journey.[117] The automobile expanded human choice and freedom in critical welfare-enhancing ways that have yet to reach their limits. The ubiquity of the automobile was apparent in the United States by the start of the First World War. It was only in the 1950s, after the Second World War, that European countries accepted personal cars as a necessity. It is in the first decade of the twenty-first century that the automobile is coming into its own in China and India.

Where does Henry Ford fit? Apparently, the years of his greatest success, between 1903 and 1926, were the years in which the national income of the United States grew at 10 percent per annum, but that is a coincidence. Henry Ford was not an inventor, but his ability to translate his vision of making what was then a rich man's toy available for everyone had an influence on economy and society beyond what the statistical correlations imply. The instrument Henry Ford used, the Ford Model T, made the automobile an item of mass production and consumption. His methods for attaining mass production have become a legend. The Model T was designed as a light and strong but also a powerful and efficient automobile. Most of all, it was cheap. Originally planned to be priced at $850, it was sold only in black color. Henry Ford also decided to manufacture just one model of car.[118] These simple strategies revolutionized production economics. Anyone could own a car, and be on equal terms with other car owners. The Model T made automobiles classless. It commenced the market democratization era by democratizing transportation.

What would further revolutionize the manufacturing sector for ever was the introduction of the assembly line in the Model T's manufacturing process. The work moved to the worker. The large River Rouge plant in Detroit was fully vertically integrated. Ore would come in at one end, be processed into metal, have components bought from outside added, and then emerge as a finished car. This approach may upset make-or-buy purists who will wish to examine the marginal costs and benefits of integration. But at that time this approach worked wonders. In conjunction with fundamental redesign of the materials handling process, such that a tributary of parts flowed into the river that was the assembly line,[119] the process of assembly line manufacturing enhanced productivity substantially, in conjunction with Henry Ford's $5 per day wages strategy of 1914, which he had called "efficiency engineering."[120] The assembly line was a successful innovation that was copied in all industries and all countries wherever feasible.

The impact of the assembly line can be measured by output. In 1909, the first year, 10,600 Model T cars were made. By 1926, when the model was withdrawn, 15 million Model T cars had been made. By the time the scale efficiencies had percolated through the system, the costs had dropped rapidly. The most basic utility version of the Model T could be purchased for $250.[121] At peak production, one Model T came off the assembly line every 15 seconds, although usually it was one every 45 seconds. Till 1926, half the cars made and sold in the United States were Fords. The output increase of over 150 times was due to the introduction of the assembly line. This took scale economies' exploitation to their logical conclusion.[122]

Eli Whitney had belonged to the first industrial revolution era. Thomas Edison and Henry Ford are the originators of mass manufacturing and production approaches that matured during the second industrial revolution. Their lessons became widespread. In many industries, expansion of output could occur by adding more machines and workers, but would not increase costs linearly.[123] Now costs would rise incrementally. In the 1880s and 1890s, new technologies of mass production brought about the second industrial revolution. This further enhanced capital–labor substitution in the American economy. In the process, America also commenced the steps towards becoming a knowledge economy.

The democratization of invention

The interplay of scientific and technological thoughts led to the initial launch of the industrial revolution. Its commercial propagation, initially via the cotton textile industry, had economic motivations as drivers. The potential textiles market to be accessed was large. India had earlier shown that it could be captured. While these intellectual and economic processes were at play, institutional changes promoted the use of technological innovations to further humanity's material progress.[124] These institutional changes have been described as important non-economic factors that led Europe to escape from poverty.[125] The first is the role of government policies in the late eighteenth and nineteenth centuries. The first set of such policies related to the decentralization and secularization of commerce. By the middle of the nineteenth century, the United States, and several other European countries had given enterprises rights that were a grant of authority to make a number of decisions that earlier were made by political or religious authorities.[126]

The second set of policies led to economic freedom to undertake commercial activities free from political interference. The relaxation of political control over the commercial and economic sphere took several forms. Individuals were authorized to form enterprises with few political restrictions. These enterprises could acquire goods and hold them for resale at a profit, again with hardly any restrictions. Then enterprises were authorized to add activities and to switch from one line of activity to another that seemed more promising with no restrictions.[127] The third set of policies led to property rights' inalienability. While the assets of a business enterprise, and its profits as accumulated from its activities, could be taxed, its property came to be regarded as immune from arbitrary seizure or expropriation by political authorities.[128] The placing of systematic limits on the exactions of the government increased commercial security and gave protection to entrepreneurs' expectations. Contractual arrangements began to be enforceable by courts. These replaced a "might is right" syndrome, whereby force or status could be used as the enforcement device. Hence, uncertainties as to what dispute resolution mechanisms might yield were reduced.[129]

The property rights innovations led to the democratization of invention. The emergence of the patent system, by 1700, to protect private property in knowledge, has been given considerable prominence as an institutional factor that set the stage for the industrial revolution in Britain.[130] Subsequent analyses have borne this out. An evaluation of the connection between the patent system and inventive activities during the British industrial revolution found that the British patent system had stimulated inventors' efforts. In addition, a class of professional inventors, who would generate patents to gain financially, via their sale or licensing, arose. While small in size in that period, patenting activities led to the development of technology markets.[131]

Similar phenomena were taking place across the Atlantic. The framers of the United States Constitution were familiar with British precedents and provided for economic inducements to be enshrined in the Constitution. Accordingly, an intellectual property clause, providing for the patent and copyright systems, appears in the very first Article of the Constitution, whereby Congress was instructed to "promote the Progress of Science and useful Arts, by securing for limited Times to

Authors and Inventors the exclusive Right to their respective Writings and Discoveries."[132] A result of such efforts was the world's first modern patent institution with low costs of filing and relatively rapid development of mechanisms for enforcement. These factors encouraged the Americans to be enthusiastic about establishing claims to intellectual property. By 1810, the United States had far surpassed Britain in per capita patenting.[133] The United States patent system was cheap, with costs being 5 percent of patenting costs in Britain. It included an examination system, by technical examiners, facilitating the use of patents as general assets to be sold, licensed, or given as loan collateral. This feature became important, since technologically creative individuals without money to exploit inventions directly could still engage in discoveries.[134]

These developments were central to patenting growth, as they motivated individuals with relatively modest amounts of skills and capital to invent. This led to the rapid growth in inventive activity in the United States during the early nineteenth century, which coincided with a substantial broadening of the segments of the population participating in the process of patenting. The United States patent system extended property rights in technology to a wide section of the population. Invention became a democratic activity in the United States throughout the century. Though individuals who had studied at institutions of higher learning were among many well-known inventors, the growth in patenting during the beginning of American industrialization was marked by a disproportionate increase in invention by ordinary citizens, sometimes with little formal schooling, operating with common skills and knowledge, rather than by elite with specialized and technical expertise or extensive financial resources.[135]

This process of democratization of invention was grounded in the access to economic opportunities available in an environment where enterprises operated on a small-scale, markets were rapidly expanding, and the barriers to entry were modest. An extension of property rights in technology to the general population meant that persons of humble origins were, by design, well represented among the inventors of the United States.[136] These circumstances made it easier for the United States economy to realize major increases in invention and productivity growth, once conditions raised the private returns to inventive activity and encouraged an allocation of individual resources in that direction.

The democratization of markets

Important drivers of American productivity were scale and scope economies. These arose from organizational innovations. In several industries, expansion of output came about because of a critical change
in the ratio of capital to labor. This would occur by improving and
rearranging inputs, by using new or improved machinery, by reorient-
ing production processes, by integrating several intermediary processes
required to make a product within a single facility, and by increasing
the application of energy.[137] Hence, there was a systemic reorganization of production toward commonalities and volume. In capital intensive industries, new processes of production were invented or existing
ones improved.[138] In the capital goods sector, the functionalities were
utilized for the manufacturing of complex light, standardized machinery items through the fabrication and assembly of interchangeable
parts, and for the production of industrial machinery and chemicals
by a series of interrelated mechanical and chemical processes. In many
such high capital-using industries, investments in new facilities further increased the ratio of capital to labor. Production units achieved
greater economies of scale. The cost per unit dropped more quickly as
the volume of materials being processed increased.

These cost advantages, however, could not be fully realized unless a
continuous flow of materials through the plant ensured capacity utilization. Thus, two decisive factors in determining scale and volume
economies were the rated volumetric capacity of the plant, and the
throughput, which was the amount actually processed within a spe-
cified time period. In industries using large amounts of capital, the
throughput needed to maintain minimum efficient scale required care-
ful attention not only to flows through the processes of production,
but also to the flows of inputs from suppliers and the flows of outputs
to intermediaries and final users. Hence, along with scale economy
considerations, materials acquisition and handling assumed importance.[139] Because of scale and scope economies, at the end of the nineteenth century a petroleum producer could reorganize the processes of
production by shutting down some refineries, reshaping others, building new ones, and coordinating the flow of materials through refineries and to consumers.[140]

The increasing scale of manufacturing operations also brought with
it the need for well-trained and technically competent managers.[141]

As production volumes rose, and expensive investments were made in high output machinery, informal arrangements were inadequate. Tighter discipline and closer supervision were needed. In the 1890s, Frederick Winslow Taylor, a production engineer at a leading steel company, was brought in to work out new ways of organizing and motivating shop-floor employees in order to ensure that machinery was used productively.

Simultaneously, in the second industrial revolution, the Germans began to exploit economies of scope. The large German chemical plants produced hundreds of dyes and pharmaceuticals from the same set of raw materials, and the same set of intermediate chemical compounds. Bayer, Hoechst, and BASF are still famous names today. They were the initial companies to exploit the cost advantages of scale and then scope, and reduced the per-kilogram price of a new synthetic dye by about 90 percent between 1869 and 1886. A new dye or pharmaceutical added little to the production cost, and product additions permitted a reduction in the unit cost of other products.[142]

The second industrial revolution led to the origins of industries such as tobacco processing, grain processing, and the production of alcoholic beverages, sugar, vegetable oil, and other foods. It transformed oil refining and the manufacturing of steel, copper, aluminum, glass, abrasives, and other materials. It created new chemical industries that produced synthetic dyes, synthetic fibers, and fertilizers. It led to the development of light machinery for sewing and agricultural and office uses, and to the development of heavier machinery items such as elevators and refrigerating units.[143] The use of manufacturing practices,[144] such as the mass production method of fabricating and assembling fully interchangeable parts, adopted during the second industrial revolution, appropriate business organizations,[145] and the scale and scope economies that these practices engendered, had a significant impact on the world economy in the twentieth century. These practices directly led to giant-scale production. They shaped consumer demand, eventually leading to the creation of markets in novel products. They created new activities, such as home sewing, and changed the nature of consumption.[146]

What did manufacturing economies of scale and scope do to market structure? The use of telegraphs helped integrate markets and bring about a change in activity coordination. Prior to the American Civil War, general merchants had been the important determinants of market demand, as the principal United States economic activity was trading. Merchants aggregated demand. Merchants were general traders with a diverse range of activities. Demand satisfaction was based on craft production. As a result, specialization in manufacturing was low and inefficiencies high. Manufacturing economies of scale and scope led to production specialization. Then, manufacturing economies of scale and scope led to distribution economies of scale and scope, and the development of professional management because of the need to coordinate different aspects of the value chain. In sum, the manufacturing and distribution economies of scale and scope led to the integration of markets, expansion of demand, a retail revolution, and the origins of professional management.

By the late nineteenth century, the first and second industrial revolutions had changed the transportation sector. By the 1870s, in the United States particularly, railways, telegraph, steamship, and cable systems operated as a cohesive transportation and communication network. Because of integrated communications, materials could flow in and finished goods be moved out at high speed and in high volume. These led to major changes in distribution practices. A review of the development of railways in the nineteenth century is useful. By the middle of the nineteenth century, when the United States started building railways, Britain was at its peak of railway construction. Thereafter, the growth of railways in the United States, elsewhere in Europe, and in the Americas, particularly in Canada and Argentina, was substantial. These railway developments had a major impact on the nature of world trade, as farmers from the North American prairies, the South American pampas, and the south Russian steppes starting exporting agricultural items to the world.[147]

On the mass consumer products side, again in the United States, new volume wholesalers and new mass retailers evolved. These were department stores, catalog and mail-order stores, and chain stores. The numerous and widespread location of the stores meant that goods were available widely. If a customer could not go to buy the goods, they would come to her via mail.[148] Wholesalers and retailers came into being after the transportation and communication networks made possible high-volume and high-speed shipments.[149] The merchandisers, wholesalers, and retailers also exploited economies of scale and scope generated by the second industrial revolution. The core activity of a volume distributor was buying. The coordination of the flow of purchased items through facilities became important, and the turn-over of goods processed was to mass distributors what throughput had been to those engaged in mass production. The greater this vol-ume, the lower the unit costs were.[150] Low unit costs of items, their widespread availability, and the retail revolution engendered the dem-ocratization of markets.

This process of market democratization first occurred in the United States. By 1913, it was the largest economy in the world. It produced over 33 percent of the world's industrial output, which was just under the combined total output for Germany, Great Britain, and France put together. In 1929, the United States produced over 42 percent of the total world output.[151] The United States steel production rose by 25 percent between 1913 and 1920, while steel production in the rest of the world fell by 33 percent.[152] In general, the industrial revolu-tion had been accompanied by a consumer revolution, as there was a large and rapid increase in the consumption of consumer goods. Such consumer revolutions had occurred in Britain and Europe by the second half of the eighteenth and the nineteenth centuries.[153] The scale of the American industrial revolution engendered such an exten-sive low-cost democratization of markets that a consumer revolution became axiomatic.

In the twentieth century, after the Second World War, substantial industrial growth occurred in the developed countries. For a gener-ation, these countries accounted for 75 percent of global production and 80 percent of manufacturing exports. There were also smaller industrial revolutions elsewhere in Europe, such as in Spain and Finland. Agrarian countries such as Bulgaria and Romania acquired large industrial sectors. In the developing world, many countries were newly industrialized.[154] Luxury items became necessities. Take the refrigerator, the home washing machine, and the telephone. In 1971, there were 270 million telephones in the world, mostly in North America and Western Europe.[155] Today, there are 2 billion telephone connections, mostly in China and India. The prime driver of this phe-nomenon has been wireless technology, its widespread diffusion, and the capital intensity of processes.[156] Such capital intensities are a sur-rogate for knowledge embodiment.

Scientific research has found practical applications. These applica-tions have transformed the activities of daily living, not just in rich countries but also in poor ones. Good Indian examples are the impact of the radio, the television, the green revolution in agriculture, and now mobile phones. The operations of Engel's law, by which the poorer spent a greater proportion of their income on basic necessities, has been shrinking, as people have more to spend on other items that matter.[157] By engaging the largest possible number of human beings in enjoying the fruits of technology-led growth, the industrial revolutions have led to the democratization of markets.

India's non-participation and its consequences

India was an important industrial power at the beginning of the industrial revolution.[158] At that time, the primary global industry was cotton textiles. In that sector, India was the world leader. She is not now one in any sector. India did not participate in the industrial revolutions. Why she did not participate is a big question. One can take a simplistic but system-oriented view that suggests a lack of overall agricultural development led to the continuation of rural poverty, and the lack of a robust market with adequate purchasing power. Economic conditions were not conducive. Additionally, there was inadequate human capital development through lack of scientific training and education. The basic human capital skills to permit participation in an industrial revolution, driven by science and technology, were lacking. Even if finances were forthcoming, the institutional structure supportive, and entrepreneurs willing to take the risks, which they might not have had inclinations for, there was inadequate human capital to support involvement.

The consequences of industrial revolutions are the democratization of invention and then, as some of these inventions succeed, the democratization of markets. The impact on national incomes is the measure of these effects of an industrial revolution. Indian industrialization seriously started only after independence in 1947. The late Nobel laureate Octavio Paz had written that "A recurrent theme of Indian history is the clash of civilizations."[159] The late C. S. Venkatachar expressed India's historical and psychological dilemma thus: "In the days of her nationalism India rejected the idea of westernization under an alien agency. After independence she decided against the continuance of traditional forms of her society and the closed cultural circuit which it implied, by opting for vigorous modernization."[160] Modernization of the economy and society, along successful Western lines, started only after independence.

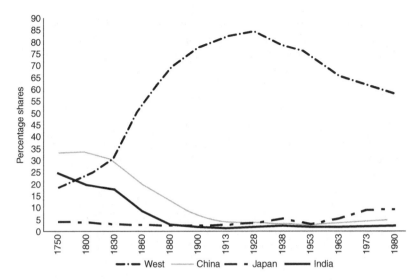

Figure 2.1. Share of manufacturing in the world economy of various countries from 1750 to 1980.

Source: Table A5.

Paul Bairoch[161] and Paul Kennedy[162] documented the changing shares of countries in world manufacturing output. I have provided details from Paul Kennedy's work in another chapter. The details of Paul Bairoch's numbers are provided in Table A5. In this chapter, based on the documentation by Bairoch, I discuss the changing shares of Western economies, China, Japan, and India in world manufacturing output from 1750 to 1850. Some countries' details are displayed in figure 2.1. The figure shows that both China and India slipped and fell from pole positions, after 1750 and till 1980. Since then, China has picked herself up. What is apparent is how the two industrial revolutions changed the relative position of the West by the middle of the twentieth century, how engaging in such a process changed the fortunes of Japan, after engaging in the process, especially during and after the Second World War, assumed a leading position in global manufacturing.

What did not participating in the industrial revolution mean for India? I used data that were generated by the late Angus Maddison to address this issue. The data generated relate to per capita income

Table 2.1. *Relative per capita incomes from 1820 to 1989 with India's income in 1820 as the base case benchmark*

	1820	1890	1950	1989
Germany	184	339	672	2,807
India	100	106	102	223
Japan	124	172	331	3,130
United Kingdom	296	690	1,153	2,759
United States	249	633	1,756	3,731
Base case benchmark: India in 1820 = 100				

Source: Calculated from the data in Angus Maddison, Explaining the Economic Performance of Nations, in W. J. Baumol, R. R. Nelson and E. N. Wolff (eds.), *Convergence of Productivity: Cross-National Studies and Historical Evidence* (New York: Oxford University Press, 1994), Table 2–1, 22–23.

levels for a variety of countries from 1820, when the first industrial revolution was on its way, till 1989.[163] I take a sample of the countries that were used, and convert all per capita income levels to a benchmark case of Indian income in 1820. The use of this period permits an assessment of where India was in 1820, and where she had come by 1989. By then, the first and second industrial revolutions had their impact. The year 1989 also precedes the appearance of South Korea and, latterly, China as major industrial countries. It precedes the information and communications technology revolution, in so far as it has had an impact on India. The indices computed are given in Table 2.1. The countries compared are Germany, Japan, the United Kingdom, and the United States. Germany is a large manufacturing economy, and participated in the second industrial revolution. Japan was a late starter, but has achieved miracles; the United Kingdom has had a very long relationship with India; and the United States is the twentieth-century exemplar.

In 1820, India's per capita income, while the lowest because of the size of its population, was large in absolute terms relative to the other countries. By 1820, the first industrial revolution had kicked in and the United Kingdom's per capita income figure was 296 relative to India's figure of 100. Japan, however, was a small and feudal agrarian economy, and its per capita income figure was 124. By 1820, the cotton boom had occurred in the United States, and its per capita income figure was 249, but on an extremely small population base. The industrial revolution changed everything. By 1890, India's per capita income had reached an index value of 106, while the United Kingdom and United States per capita incomes were 690 and 633 respectively. Japan was still just commencing its own industrialization, but it had reached a per capita income index value of 172 in 1890.

In 1950, after the world wars and independence, India's per capita income index value had taken a drop to 102, relative to 1890. It was just 2 percent more than in 1820.[164] By then, Germany, having industrialized in the late nineteenth century, had charged ahead, the United Kingdom income index value was ten times that of India, and the United States was the leader of the pack. In 1989, two years before the fundamental reforms in India were implemented, India's per capita income index was 223. It had more than doubled since she became a republic in 1950. By then, the others' incomes had leapt ahead. Germany and the United Kingdom were relative laggards compared to the United States and Japan. They too displayed per capita incomes that were at least ten times larger than India's in 1989, and over 20 times larger than India's in 1820.

The important countries to be compared with are Japan and the United States. Let me take the United States first. Like India, the United States is physically large, ethnically heterogeneous, has been colonized by the British and is a pluralist democracy. While the United States was just twice as well off as India in 1820, at that time though on a trivially small population base, in 1989 she was at least 15 times richer relative to India in 1989, and over 30 times richer in 1989 relative to India in 1820. By 1989, her population had also increased massively. An important factor has been the industrial revolutions that the United States has engendered and participated in. The United States is an important role model for India today.

Next, let us take Japan. Like India, she is an Asian country. She came to industrialization very late. As I will discuss in Chapter 5, Japan is the first case of late industrialization and catching-up in the twentieth century. She participated in her own industrial revolution. Therefore, Japan is an important role model for India today. Between 1950 and 1989, after suffering ravages in the Second World War, Japan has increased her relative per capita income index to a figure of 3,130 relative to India in 1820. Japan is now over 30 times better off than

India was then. Relative to herself in 1950, she has increased her per capita income ten times. Relative to India in 1989, Japan was about 15 times better off. At that time, she was also 25 times richer than she had been in 1820, using Indian income of 1820 as the base case. Yet, in 1890 she was scarcely better off than India in absolute terms. Today, Japan's per capita income matches that of the United States. The lesson for India from the Japanese example is straightforward. Late industrializing nations can rapidly catch up with the rest if the appropriate lessons from successful participants in the industrial revolutions are followed.

Leaders start suffering from atherosclerosis. Witness the falling behind of Germany and the United Kingdom, relative to Japan, by 1989. Late industrializing nations can become leaders by leapfrogging over extant leaders by adopting appropriate strategies. There are many learning options available to India based on the American, Japanese, South Korean, and Taiwanese experiences. The issue is can the Indian elephant play leapfrog? Entrepreneurship and commercial and manufacturing activities in India have long histories, stretching back to the dawn of modern civilization. To understand modern Indian industry, it is important to know the history. The next two chapters deal with India's industrial past. In the real sector, however, path dependencies matter greatly because attitudes and approaches persist, even if insidiously, while bricks and mortar perish with the ravages of time. The path dependencies of India's industrial past may generate the psychological impulses propelling her economic future.

3 | *Aspects of Indian enterprise history*

Commerce and industry in ancient India

This history of India's entrepreneurial activity goes back to the dawn of civilization. India has been a commercialized country for over 4,500 years. Unlike in the United States, in which there was no industrialization at all prior to the eighteenth century, India had been an industrialized country thousands of years ago as well. Then there was a hiatus and only in the last 150 years or so has India resumed the path of industrialization. The story of the evolution of Indian enterprise is fascinating, since the time-paths of this particular process reflect the ebbs and flows of generic human civilization in one land mass.

In the 1870s, when Major General Alexander Cunningham, the Archaeological Surveyor to the Government of India,[1] published details of the first Harappan seal, which had been discovered at an ancient site in Harappa in what is now the Pakistan part of Punjab, the world become aware of what might potentially be India's past. Not until the early 1920s, when archeologists Daya Ram Sahni and Madho Sarup Vats discovered the city of Harappa, and Rakhal Das Banerjee discovered the city of Mohenjo Daro in Sind, both on the banks of the Indus, were the secret of India's past civilization finally revealed. The then Director General of the Archaeological Survey of India, John Marshall, stated that: "India ... must henceforth be recognized ... as one of the most important areas where civilizing processes were initiated and developed."[2]

Since then, the secrets of India's past have been revealed in detail. The Indus Valley Civilization, as evidenced by the Mohenjo Daro, Harappan and related finds, such as at Lothal, have been classified as dating back, at least, to 2500 BC. In the Indus Valley the rich alluvium soil was ideal for agriculture. The land produced plenty of surplus food, which allowed many persons to withdraw from food production, leave the land, and become urban dwellers. They then occupied themselves with craft, trade, religion, and politics.[3] This development of commercial and political cultures led to the development of institutions. An aspect of such institutional development was the emergence of standardization. Standardization has been referred to as a process by which the United States became a great manufacturing power at the end of the nineteenth century. This process had been discovered over 4,000 years before that.

The enforcement of standards led to the stabilization and homogenization of the cultural and economic practices of the Indus Valley Civilization. The level of conformity required was rigid and comprehensive. From pottery vessels, stamp seals, the script, the dimensions of bricks, the system of weights and measures, and norms for urban planning, absolute uniformity was maintained throughout the Indus Valley Civilization area for many centuries.[4] Trade and industry were regulated by standardizing weights and measures, and the diffusion of systematic production techniques. Bricks were made everywhere to only one ratio; the width would be twice the height and the length twice the width. There were three standard sizes. The most common dimension was 30 centimeters by 15 centimeters by 7.5 centimeters.[5]

The Indus people cultivated crops such as wheat and barley and grew pulses, sesame, linseed, several fruits, and cotton. Several animals, such as cattle, buffaloes, goats, sheep, domestic fowl, pigs, donkeys, and elephants, were domesticated.[6] Production of agricultural as well as industrial items was for trade and not just domestic consumption. There were large craft industries where the output exceeded local needs and was meant for export. Commercial production was organized in the Indus Valley Civilization by concentrating different trades and manufacturing activities in different city zones and encouraging specialization,[7] highlighting the fact that spatial and agglomeration economies, a concept popular today, had been conceptualized and related policies implemented 4,500 years ago.

A bead factory has been excavated at Lothal, an Indus Valley Civilization trading station in Gujarat, and an industrial area for copper working has been found in Harappa.[8] Indus Valley Civilization craft products were traded in Sumeria and Mesopotamia. Mesopotamia and the Indus Valley Civilization were the literate and urbanized societies of ancient times, representing the zenith of the Bronze Age. Mesopotamia was also agriculturally rich, as befits a river valley civilization. It had large quantities of grain, oil, and woolen textiles to offer.[9] The trade contact between the Indus and Sumerian civilizations were of ancient origin and by the 2370 BC to 2100 BC period was well established. It continued to be active until about the second quarter of the second millennium BC.

The Indus Valley Civilization centers of business were involved in maritime trade with centers of business in Mesopotamia through the sea lanes of the Persian Gulf. The commodities imported by Sumeria and Mesopotamia included timber, copper, carnelian, gold dust, lapis lazuli, and birds such as peacocks.[10] Also, a group of Indus Valley Civilization traders had settled in Sumer, as Indus-style engraved seals and other artifacts have been found there. One seal has the imprint of coarse cloth on its back. Thus, cotton was a major item of export from India. Wild cotton had been domesticated by the Indus Valley Civilization, and Indian weavers' and dyers' skills were quickly in demand from the neighboring civilization.[11] The Indus Valley Civilization traders used land and sea routes for trade. They carried on extensive overland trade through Baluchistan, using caravans of pack oxen or donkeys. Clay models of ox carts are common finds at Indus Valley archeological sites. These prehistoric Indus carts were heavy and lumbering vehicles, with solid wheels and a wheelbase of a meter. They resemble the ox carts found in the Sind region in the twenty-first century![12]

For river and sea transport, the traders of the Indus Valley Civilization used sailing ships. If shipbuilding and naval construction is to be taken as a major industrial activity, then the ancient Indus Valley Civilization was, by the standards of the day, a very advanced industrial civilization. Large harbor facilities have been discovered at Lothal, in the state of Gujarat, near Ahmedabad, where a very large dockyard and a wharf have been excavated. The Lothal dockyard had been ingeniously designed with a spillway and a locking device. It had artificial channels connecting it to a tributary of the Sabarmati, a river which flows through Ahmedabad. Several stone anchors were found in the dock basin. The wharf, constructed of brick, stretched over the entire eastern side of the town. Alongside it ran a high platform on which were located warehouses and granaries. The dockyard resembles the modern port of Rotterdam, albeit on a smaller scale, but had been built several thousand years ago.[13]

Finally, evidence has also been uncovered of technology transfer in ancient times, with Mesopotamia supplying metal and metallurgical skills to the Indus Valley Civilization, while it imported ships and shipbuilding skills. Mesopotamia had large quantities of silver and lead, and the Indus Valley Civilization was a large importer of these items. It also needed the associated metalworking skills.[14] On the other hand, a lack of good wood meant that Mesopotamia could not build large seagoing craft. The only vessels would be reed boats or dugout canoes, which would be risky and ineffective in ocean voyages. The dry and arid lands of Mesopotamia did not support forests, and there was a lack of timber.

The Indus Valley Civilization, however, possessed timber supplies. It had become expert in making boats built of planks, as the evidence of the Lothal dockyard shows. The use of wooden planks made boats larger and deeper, permitted the use of larger sails, and opened up ocean commerce. Metal tools developed with the ores available in the Persian Gulf region and Mesopotamia, and the metallurgical skills available, could be adopted by entrepreneurs of the Indus Valley Civilization. They, in turn, could use these tools to do the advanced carpentry required to build large ocean-going craft.[15] The issue of mutual technology and trade flows between countries is a concept in vogue today. Over 4,000 years ago, a mutually reinforcing process of trade and technology transfers led to the diffusion of capabilities between civilizations. The increasing use of metal enabled more efficient modes of transportation to evolve, and this process benefited both civilizations.[16]

Industry and trade in Maurya times

By 1500 BC, however, the Indus Valley Civilization had declined. During the Vedic ages, which occurred between 1500 BC and 900 BC, there was a considerable development of Indian culture.[17] The social structure of India changed, with landlords emerging as major controllers of resources. Semi-hereditary merchant classes developed because this is when the caste system emerged in its now well-known form. Trade and industry further developed along large-scale and specialized lines. There was the elaboration of a complex financial structure. This period contained the seeds of several aspects of economic and social organization still found in India.[18]

Since the sixth century BC India has been noted as having a substantial and prosperous mercantile class who grew rich on foreign trade.[19] There was limited trading contact between the Greek and the Indian civilizations, until the establishment of the Achaemenid Empire in Persia in the sixth century BC. This stretched to Greece in the west and to India in the east, and the empire brought both Greeks and Indians in contact with each other.[20] The Indian product that the Greeks consumed most was cotton cloth. Cotton weaving had begun with the Indus Valley Civilization, and had reached a high degree of refinement. Cotton cloth was a major item of trade between India and Greece. Much of the trade was carried over land routes. Indian traders were active in Iran and Mesopotamia in the sixth and fifth centuries BC. It was apocryphally noted that a tavern in southern Iraq was run by an Indian businesswoman.[21] Sea trade between these countries, via the Red Sea and Alexandria, was equally important, initially being in the hands of Indian and Arab traders.[22]

Around the first millennium BC, several navigation texts also emerged to detail the international sea routes between the Red Sea and the west coast of India. These texts also dealt with coastal shipping, so that the east coast towns of India could be described for the benefit of seafarers. Astronomer and geographer Claudius Ptolemy gave the world a detailed knowledge of the Bengal coast.[23] Subsequently, Greek traders became a part of the bustle of Indian ports. Ancient Tamil poets would sing of the good ships of the Yavanas, as the Ionian Greeks were named, that arrived at their ports bringing cool and fragrant wines and returned laden with pepper.[24]

There were extensive international trade flows between India and the Roman Empire. There was even global migration and settlements in India. Excavations by archeologists at Arikamedu near Pondicherry have revealed Roman pottery such as Arretine ware and wine amphorae from the Mediterranean. Thus, in the southern part of India, by AD 1, in the time of Augustus Caesar, there was a colony of Roman traders and settlers who played an important role in the Indian and Red Sea trade.[25] As well as the Romans, Egyptian merchants came directly to India to obtain silks, cotton, spices, and jewels. There were Arab ships engaged in the coastal trade with India, and Indian vessels involved in the coastal trade of the subcontinent.[26] As Octavio Paz remarked: "India, in contrast, was always in communications with other peoples and cultures of the Old World: first with Mesopotamia, and later with the Persians, Greeks, Kuchans, Romans, Chinese, Afghans, Mongols. The thought, religions and art of India were adopted by many Asian peoples; in turn the Indians absorbed and transformed the ideas and creations of other cultures."[27] Similar trade exchanges enriched both India and the rest of the then known world.

On the domestic front, the Mauryan Empire, which ran its course between 321 BC and 185 BC, was a formidable economic force. By the time of the Mauryan regime, agriculture had displaced a subsistence pastoral economy. Extensive tracts of virgin lands were cleared for cultivation by the state and private farmers. Trade and industry had emerged as a major field of economic activity in Mauryan times. With the spread of urbanization, and the growth in the demand for goods and services, craftsmen were ubiquitous in towns. They gradually turned into small manufacturers and gained in wealth.[28]

Mining also received special attention in Mauryan times, because of its revenue and military potential. The state ran all mines, salt pans, and pearl and conch fisheries as state monopolies. Where the mines or fisheries were difficult to run, or of uncertain profitability, they were leased to private operators. This started the concept of private and public partnerships.[29] The Mauryan state was an important economic actor. State-owned enterprises were key entities and the state itself entered the market as a dominant player, selling the output of its numerous manufacturing units and mines, the yield of its forests, the harvests of crown lands, and the produce received through tax collections. These goods were stocked in state warehouses maintained throughout the empire, and were sold directly through royal officers or through private agents.[30]

During this period, trade increased and urbanization proceeded rapidly and prosperity expanded the Indian market. The creation of road infrastructure, various amenities along the roads, and improved travel security facilitated trade. There was also a lifestyle-based economy, with a high demand for luxury goods. The gradual monetization of the economy, the standardization of weights and measures, and appropriate trade regulations substantially invigorated the market.[31] Several centuries before the arrival of Christ, the existence of domestic as well as long-distance seaborne and overland trade had given India a distinguished mercantile character.

India as a medieval economic power

Again, there is a hiatus. The story of evolution of Indian enterprise and business comes to a stop. Or, rather, there is a chasm as we do

not know much about the interregnum. Let us move several centuries ahead to the medieval period to assess India's economic vibrancy.
The nature of India's economic situation cannot be assessed without
understanding its overall structure of activity, and its political structure, since the modes of governance will have directly affected the
institutional conditions and the incentives agents will have faced.

The Indian economy was divided into three elements. There was
a world of great cities, which formed the base for external trade,
traders and financiers who moved wealth around the country in the
form of bullion and credit notes. Next, there was an intermediate
economy of mass artisan production in small country market towns.
There were also the petty traders and revenue farmers or revenue
collectors who existed in every political dispensation. Thereafter, the
main bulk of India was an internal agrarian economy.[32] This internal
agrarian economy responded to changes in other elements, since it
was affected by money supply and demand conditions. Yet it was the
core of India. It always retained a great deal of autonomy. The village
markets and local cattle fairs were spasmodically and poorly linked
to the sub-continental economy.[33] The village economies, however,
relied on the functions performed by small traders and peddlers in
the distribution of commercial goods. Thus, the structure of trade
was characterized by extreme fragmentation, multiple markets, and
price instability.[34]

To astute nineteenth-century observers, such as legal scholar Henry
Sumner Maine, India was a land of Teutonic village republics and a set
of medieval feudal kingdoms.[35] According to Maine,

the village communities are little republics, having nearly everything that
they can want within themselves, and almost independent of any foreign
relations. They seem to last where nothing lasts. Dynasty after dynasty
tumbles down; revolution succeeds to revolution; Hindoo, Patan, Mogul,
Mahratta, Sikh, English, are all masters in their turn; but the village community remains the same ... If plunder and devastation be directed against
themselves, they flee to friendly villages at a distance; but when the storm
has passed over, they return and resume their occupations ... This union of
village communities, each one forming a separate little state in itself, has, I
conceive, contributed more than any other cause to the preservation of the
people of India through all the revolutions and changes which they have
suffered, and is in a high degree conducive to their happiness, and to the
enjoyment of a great portion of freedom and independence.[36]

Analysis of India's southern cone, for the Chola period, between the ninth and thirteenth centuries shows that there was not much sign of dense economic activities based on structured markets and complementary production units.[37] Between the fourteenth and sixteenth centuries, the foundations of a mercantile economy were laid in southern India[38] as extensive population movement into the dry interior areas took place.[39] In the first half of the fifteenth century, very extensive commercial contacts between western Deccan ports and the Persian Gulf started.[40] By May 1498, when Vasco da Gama navigated the Cape of Good Hope and arrived in India, the port of Calicut, now called Kozhikode, was the center of a thriving international trade, and the communities involved included Europeans, who came overland via the countries of the Ottoman Empire, and Muslim and Jewish merchants from North Africa, Turkey, Persia, and Egypt. Vasco da Gama confirmed what the European historians had vaguely suspected or might have known, that India was capable of industrial manufacturing at a quality level surpassing the then-developed European economies.[41] India, and possibly other Asian countries, possessed important production skills and capabilities.

From Aden and Hormuz, Arab merchants carried luxury Ottoman and Mamluk goods such as copper, mercury, vermilion, coral, saffron, carpets, porcelain, tin, colored velvets, silver, raisins, opium, horses, and textiles to Calicut. Items purchased from India and locations further east were textiles, pepper, ginger, cinnamon, cardamom, tamarind, amber, clove, nutmeg, mace, sandalwood, cottons, and coconut. Italian merchants would then collect Ottoman and Indian Ocean goods from Alexandria, Beirut, Cairo, and Antioch and distribute them throughout Europe.[42] Traders and merchants based in western India engaged in large-scale wholesale dealings, with operations extending from Mocha in Yemen to China. These were stolid Hindu merchants who had the financial capability to singly buy up the entire cargo of a European ship with half an hour's bargaining and then make prompt cash payments for the stock.[43] Alexander Hamilton, a seventeenth-century sea captain, wrote about his experiences and mentioned Abdul Gafoor, a Muslim trader of Surat, who could supply 20 ships, each between 300 and 800 tons, with £10,000- to £25,000-worth of stock on his own account. After that foreign stock was sent away, he could further invest in similar quantity of stock, again on his own account, for trade in the domestic market.[44]

The model of trade and commerce was different in northern India. There were a number of small merchants and traders in the bazaar who kept the agricultural economy functioning. They also controlled trade between close localities. These groups played a role in the functioning of the revenue system as revenue farmers.[45] Then there were the great merchants with a vital political role in state finances. These were important merchants, with cultural links to the smaller merchants. They had a role as Mahajans, or great traders, who traversed several regions. The Nagar Seths were the commercial elite,[46] being given the title of "Banker to the City," for their commercial services rendered originally to the Mughal emperor Jahangir.[47]

By the middle of the seventeenth century, a very highly developed network of bills of exchange, called *hundis*, was being serviced by firms in Surat and Agra to remit large sums of money across the country. These firms attained a strong coherence across urban centers and warrior fiefdoms of the Gangetic plain, in the Maratha domains of western India and also in the emergent powers of the south such as Mysore and Hyderabad.[48] By the early eighteenth century, several large banking houses had taken over the remittance function for taxation during the Mughal regime. These large merchant corporations had highly developed bookkeeping, credit management, and treasury capabilities. Their mechanisms to collect revenues and make transfers enabled coordination of extensive trade patterns between regions. From intermediaries they also became financiers of rural production.[49] They were then able to develop political capital as financiers of regimes. The firm of Jagat Seths, in Bengal, originally set up by Marwari merchants Manikchand and Fatehchand, belonging to the Oswal caste, was one of several firms set up by people from Gujarat or Multan, or people of the Bania Aggarwal community, many of whom were from Rajasthan.

From the seventeenth century onwards, a complex and integrated mercantile system developed.[50] This supported a great Ganges–Jamuna trade route that consisted of trade in cloth and grains, and had extensive transport and banking facilities.[51] Concomitantly, several older cities declined. Cities such as Surat, Ahmedabad, Masulipatnam, and Dhaka decayed. Cities such as Delhi, Lahore, Agra, and Burhanpur shrank in size. Several important new centers established themselves. These were Lucknow, Hyderabad, Benares, Mysore, Srirangapatnam, and Bangalore, which grew rapidly. Trading cities such as Mirzapur, Kanpur, and Baroda arose to service the new trades.[52]

As the Indian economy evolved, the second-level traders and merchants tried to gather dependent agriculturists and weavers within an organization approximating the condition of laborers in textile factories. Low labor quality and low levels of technology in weaving appeared, however, to have led to a contractual system based on piecework. Nevertheless, attempts to mass produce goods would have been associated with the growth of new centers of production directed at mass regional markets. Simultaneously, rich landowners also encouraged the settlement of agricultural laborers on their lands in order to raise the revenue potential. Traders and bankers also invested in the village enterprises of Rajasthan and western India. By the first half of the eighteenth century, rural markets, called *ganjs* in north India, an example being Forbesganj, and *pettas*, an example being Royapettah, in south India, were being created. Such markets also appeared in peninsular India. These factors contributed to the long-term redevelopment of commerce in India.[53]

In the eighteenth century, Asia in general, and particularly India, remained the world's major center of artisan production. European countries were important to Asians economies because they provided the silver imports which helped Asia's great kingdoms to expand and develop. Yet, in the eighteenth century, the industrial revolution in Britain shifted the balance of power between India and Europe. The Indian and Asian economies went from being producers and exporters of artisan products to exporters of agricultural raw materials. But, prior to that, India had been a medieval economic power.

Industry and political economy before colonization

During medieval times, India had been a dominant global textile exporter. Other industries were, however, limited. Luxury metal and mineral items and textiles had been produced for sale in many towns. Benares had a thriving set of workshops that made brass and copperware for religious or domestic purposes. These circulated widely. Not much more by way of industry abounded, at least in north India.[54] The Indian artisans, however, could not fully transition to factory production. This inability to attain operational scale led to their marginalization.

But not all of India was bereft of manufacturing or industrial capabilities. One area which India retained competencies in was shipbuilding, a historical legacy spilling over from the time of the Indus
Valley Civilization. The shipbuilders of Surat, around the time that
the British arrived as traders in India in the seventeenth century, had
a production repertoire matching European processes. The Gujarati
shipbuilders could replicate British vessels in all respects, if required,
and the shipyards were capable of building vessels in the range of 500
to 1,000 tons. These vessels were world class for the times. They were
capable of sailing to China and Europe.[55]

In the south, by the late eighteenth century, the tables had turned.
In 1782, the ruler of Mysore, Haidar Ali had died and in 1783 his son
Tipu Sultan was enthroned. There was a battle for political power
between the British and the French in India, and Tipu Sultan responded
to French overtures by insisting on direct dealings with Versailles.[56]
In 1785, an embassy had left Mysore for Constantinople. The same
mission was ordered to proceed to Paris. But, delayed in Iraq, it was
superseded by a separate embassy sent direct to France in 1787. This
emissary vessel docked at Toulon in June 1788, and Tipu's 45-person
mission proceeded to Paris overland. At that time, himself in a certain
amount of trouble, Louis XVI was in no position to gratify visitors'
political or military wishes.

Tipu's other requests related to capability acquisition so as to modernize the economy. He asked for seeds of flowers and plants of various
kinds, and for technicians, workers, and doctors. When the mission left
for home at the end of the year it was accompanied by munitions experts,
gunsmiths, workers in the porcelain trade, makers of glass, watchmakers,
makers of tapestry, linen weavers, two printers of oriental languages, one
physician, one surgeon, two engineers, and two gardeners.[57] Tipu had
identified the factor which lay behind European efficiency. Trade was
important. To this end, Tipu established a state trading company, encouraged investors to invest in it and organized a network of overseas factories located around the Arabian Sea and the Persian Gulf. These were
modeled on the European trading companies, and included commercial
and military staff.[58] Command of the Malabar ports gave Mysore a ready
outlet to the sea, plus control of the outward trade in pepper and timbers,
and of inward trade in horses from the Persian Gulf.

Technology was important. Tipu sought new crops by experimenting with seeds and plants from all over Asia as well as from France.

Around his palace at Srirangapatnam, the ground was laid out for botanical experiments. He was personally responsible for introducing sericulture into Mysore. Other factories in Mysore produced sugar, paper, gunpowder, knives, and scissors. Ammunition factories at Bednur produced 20,000 muskets a year.[59] The Mysore factories also made rockets, which the British had not encountered before. The British Ordnance Office was keen on this product, and technology of rocket manufacture was transferred to the Woolwich Arsenal in 1806.[60] Clearly, there was a part of India, albeit small, that was as close to the evolving frontier of the time as might have then been possible.

The history of India in the eighteenth century is one, however, of political crises. The cumulative indigenous changes of the Indian heartland reflected commercialization of the economy, coupled with the decline of the great Mughals, especially after the death of Aurangazeb in 1707. As both Hindus and Muslims prospered in Mughal service, and traders flourished, they began to separate themselves off as stable landlords through northern India. Prosperous yeomen farmers left the Mughal fold, assisted by the several moneylenders and merchants who could provide the economic basis for doing so. Commercial growth eroded the political power of the Mughals.[61]

During the waning of the Mughal hegemony, many politically autonomous groups emerged. Military entrepreneurs farmed revenues, engaged in local trade, and built up land holdings. They were closely linked to the merchant houses noted earlier. These merchant houses and firms were vital politically, as they could mobilize large liquid capital reserves since they participated in the national trade and credit chains. All groups of persons represented indigenous capitalism forms, and derived wealth from commodity trade.[62] With the decline of the Mughals, there was further development of powerful commercial forces in the regions, and these led to the emergence of additional entrepreneurship in power and money.[63] The Marathas had emerged as a political power during the seventeenth century. They consumed large quantities of grain, cattle, and cloth from the Gangetic plain acquired by trade. Mysore state consumed large volumes of cotton, northern Deccan wool and hides, Benares sugar, and Carnatic region cloth.[64]

Then there was substantial expansion of European production and trade in the eighteenth century, and the development of aggressive capitalism. This assertiveness was expressed in the approach and policies of the European companies in India from the 1730s, and by the East India Company in 1757.[65] There was relatively little domestic resistance to the creation of commercial and then political empires.[66] The Indian entrepreneurs often emerged as a comprador commercial class. The East India Company, hence, was provided with some of the capital, knowledge, and support for its activities by this Indian commercial class. Indian capital and expertise were drawn into a partnership with alien invaders, and Indian commercial groups became uneasy or maybe even willing collaborators in creating colonial India.[67] Specifically, with respect to the opium trade, which emerged as big business after 1770, the relationships between Indian traders and British private traders produced substantial profits. The Malwa opium operations involved Gujarati and Marwari traders, operating in the hinterland, financing cultivation, and collecting the produce, and Parsi merchants in Bombay shipping the opium to China with British collaboration.[68]

Transition to British rule and de-industrialization

The economic history of Indian enterprise is inextricably tied up with that of the British after 1757. The 101 years between 1757 and 1858, and then the 89 years between 1858 and 1947 represent a dark age for India. India was a British colony, but not a British settlement. I use Sumit Sarkar's classification of the economic context.[69] These are: of a mercantilist phase between 1757 and 1813, marked by plunder and monopoly trade; a phase, between the years 1813 and 1858, when India was opened to the aftermath of the first industrial revolution and the impact of free trade; and the phase thereafter, from 1858 till 1947. In the era of direct British governance, financial and industrial capitalism took hold, and Indian industrialists and Indian financiers emerged.

The British were in India to exploit her and not develop her. Benita Parry remarks that "Colonialism was, first, last, and always an instrument of capitalism."[70] The narrative of the strategic mission changed over time from one of maximizing the profit margin to one of bringing civilization to a heathen land. An almost metaphysical obligation to rule subordinate, inferior, or less advanced peoples developed among colonialists such as the British.[71] Such a narrative was expressed in florid rhetoric, replete with boasts about the British as a governing race, with claims to a secular and divine destiny ordaining them to bring technological progress, reform of social practices, and rational government, in other words modernity, to a benighted people.[72] In this respect, journalist Mark Tully's words are important. He wrote:

At least four generations of my mother's family before me spent their working lives in India. Most of them went "home" to retire, and I can well understand why. In the first place, they were positively discouraged from "staying on." Britain ruled India but did not colonize it. The British Raj did not encourage settlers. Settlers might set a bad example and "go native," hence destroying the carefully nurtured image of the difference, and hence the superiority, of the British race. The Raj, it was thought, depended on that image of superiority to enable it to rule so many with so few.[73]

Development in India occurred accidentally, or when the political economy situation tilted the balances in Indians' favor. Such a point was expressed by administrators, such as Shankar Nath Maitra, an ICS officer, who wrote:

Whatever advance was made in the political or administrative field, there was hardly any change in the basic colonial economic pattern of the Raj till its last day. In fact it may be argued that the stagnation in economic field led to the excessive importance being given to politics and the capture of power. The administration especially in the Punjab was all for the *kisan* and all against the native *bania* but could say little against the British *bania*.[74]

The British went to India as traders in the early seventeenth century. The late historian Samuel Martin Burkc, ICS,[75] noted that by 1740 British imports from India accounted for 10 percent of the British gross domestic product.[76] By 1757, after the battle of Plassey, they had consolidated their political position so much that they became the rulers of India. With the decline of the Mughals, from 1707, the consumption capacity of the Mughal elites diminished. Nevertheless, the consumption ability of the new political entities made up for the demand decline, as did foreign demand. The Marathas, the state of Mysore, petty chieftains, revenue farmers, and yeoman farmers supplanted the Mughal court as consumers. Repression was replaced by regression. The Aurangazeb regime had been brutally fascist. There was considerable political anarchy in India after Aurangazeb's death. India was back where it had been in the twelfth century, a bundle of feudal territories with neighbors at odds with each other.[77] This permitted the British to politically dominate India from 1757.

The British had been sucked into the Indian maelstrom by the dynamic of its political economy as well as their relentless drive for profit. In this process, the collaborating native business elites played a crucial role. Via these intermediaries, British businessmen joined the entrepreneurial class of late Mughal India.[78] The British then fused military and commercial power to achieve, on a larger scale, what the Indian local rulers had aimed for in the seventeenth century, the commercialization of political power. This process was carried out by a slow and steady penetration of the lines of power and flows of traded commodities, with settlement primarily based on silver. The bullion could be used to acquire or market political power. There were threads of continuity between the political economy strategy of the rulers of colonial India before she was colonized and the political economy strategy of the East India Company.[79]

The profit margin was the main British interest in India. The East India Company was out to make money.[80] In the expansion of the western economies, profit, and hope of further profit from trade, had been important, as the attractions of spices, sugar, slaves, rubber, cotton, opium, tin, gold, and silver over centuries testified.[81] Politics and governance were a means to an end. The greed motive was uppermost at the battle of Plassey, when Clive and his acolytes visualized that Mir Jafar,[82] whom they were installing as the Nawab of Bengal in place of Siraj-ud-Daula, could lay his hands on £40 million as soon as the British placed him on the chair, and salivated that the British would get a large slice of that sum. As it turns out, this was an erroneous assumption. Nevertheless, the presents received by the British were extraordinarily generous.

Clive headed the list of beneficiaries with a present of £211,500.[83] In addition, Mir Jafar had to pay £275,000 to the army for its troubles. Clive took another cut as a revenue grant of £27,000 per annum paid to him for the rest of his life, until his suicide. When, after 13 years, a House of Commons committee investigated the goings-on in Bengal, it concluded that presents to Britons in 1757 amounted to £1,238,575, and between 1757 and 1765 sums exceeding £2 million were disbursed to individuals in bullion and jewels.[84] There is considerable justification for Tapan Raychaudhuri's statement that: "The British school child who reads in his history text book of Lord Clive's wonderful achievements should also be told that the man was a criminal by any definition."[85]

Behind the British involvement in Bengal, via Plassey, had been the growth of Bengal's industry. The rise in textiles exports from Bengal between the late seventeenth and mid eighteenth centuries, and profits to be made in the trade between India, China, and Britain, had made Calcutta important since its establishment in 1690. Bengal was the wealthiest province in Mughal India. It was surplus in rice. Its weaving industry produced a high level of output till the late eighteenth century. It had a large number of literate gentry adept in revenue management.[86] The East India Company had been aware of Bengal's productive potential, and its contribution to international trade. It was India's granary; it supplied India and the world with muslin and silk yarn; and it had abundant saltpeter. These three items made it very important for trading companies.[87] Adam Smith had noted that the economic capability of Bengal derived from an extensive home market based upon inland navigation.[88]

These facets came to the notice of the British. They developed good relationships with the banking houses of Bengal, especially the Jagat Seths, and another banker Omichand.[89] The Jagat Seths and Omichand were useful intermediaries between Clive and Mir Jafar, ensuring that Mir Jafar would not respond to British attacks at Plassey and the British would be able to win the battle against Siraj-ud-Daula. Clive's victory in 1757, installing Mir Jafar as the ruler, delivered the revenues of Bengal into the hands of the East India Company. Before Plassey, the East India Company had to pay for its goods with imported silver.[90] After Plassey, the new annual proceeds of the Bengal revenues paid for the goods acquired from Bengal and other parts of India, and bullion from external sources was not required.[91]

Earlier, British and other European traders had to regularly bring bullion into India, as Indian cotton and silk goods had a flourishing European market while Indian demand for European products like British woolens was slim. After Plassey, bullion was rarely imported by the trading companies or brought into Bengal from other parts of India in any quantity.[92] The Bengal revenues amounted to £4 million a year. Thereafter, the East India Company began to create its own state using these Bengal revenues. The "investment" that the British made in acquiring Indian goods for sale overseas was financed out of the territorial revenue amounts until 1813, when the East India Company lost its trading monopoly, and its territorial and commercial accounts were separated.[93]

The economic consequences on Indian enterprise of the battle of Plassey were severe. In 1783 the Select Committee of the House of Commons set forth the position in their Ninth Report:

A certain portion of the revenues of Bengal has been, for many years, set apart for the purchase of goods for exportation to England, and this is called the "Investment." The greatness of the Investment has been the standard by which the merit of the Company's principal servants has been too generally estimated; and this main cause of the impoverishment of India has been generally taken as a measure of its wealth and prosperity. Numerous large fleets of large ships, loaded with the most valuable commodities of the East, annually arriving in England in a constant and increasing succession, imposed upon the public eye, and naturally give rise to the opinion of the happy condition and growing opulence of a country whose surplus productions occupied so vast a space in the commercial world. The export from India seemed to imply also a reciprocal supply, by which the trading capital employed in those productions was continually strengthened and enlarged. But the payment of a tribute, and not a beneficial commerce, to that country, wore this specious and delusive appearance.[94]

The takeover by the East India Company of revenue collection and administration, first in Bengal, and then successively in the south, the Gangetic plain, and western India, led to disruption in the pattern of external trade and changed the relationships of entrepreneurs with the new state.[95] A rent extraction for over 50 years, as in Bengal, is bound to have deleterious consequences. Simultaneously, the use of harsh fiscal means, such as taxation and personal rent extraction, and corruption of the Company's servants precipitated economic decline.[96] The stories of nabobs, who returned to Britain from a career in India and purchased enormous country houses and seats in the House of Commons, are legion.[97]

Indian merchants were excluded from free trade in many valuable commodities, with such exclusions enforced by military power. After the battle of Buxar in 1764, when Mir Qasim, the successor of Mir Jafar, was removed from power, British traders became monopolists and the largest purchasers of goods. The East India Company also acquired the sole rights to revenue collection, or the *diwani* rights, in 1765. The net surplus accruing to the East India Company was about

50 percent of the revenues they collected on behalf of the Mughal emperor for the regions of Bengal, Bihar, and Orissa.[98] The change in the pattern of incomes and expenditures of the East India Company after 1757 had considerable implications for the internal economy as it started the drain of India's wealth. Nicholas Dirks writes that:

Reinvestment, in other words, was nothing other than the use of the "tribute" to support the colonial state itself. But the colonial state not only did almost nothing to invest in infrastructure or provide meaningful administrative services, for agrarian or any other purposes; it was in fact designed entirely to extract resources from India for the enrichment of the Company in particular and Britain more generally. In the end, the argument over how to interpret the economic data concerning the impact of the British presence on India hinges on whether one views the colonial state as legitimate and benevolent, or as fundamentally extractive in a way no indigenous state could be.[99]

As early as 1772, Alexander Dow, in his *History of Hindostan*, had asserted that Bengal's decline had commenced with the battle of Plassey, and that it was a direct result of foreign dominion. He calculated that Bengal lost approximately £1.5 million each year through extraction of bullion and the use of monopolies in inland trade, especially in basic commodities such as salt, betel nut, and tobacco.[100] In 1888, John Strachey, who authored a work on the finances and public works of India, explained the mechanism of wealth drain: "The Secretary of State draws bills on the Government treasury in India, and it is mainly through these bills, which are paid in India out of the public revenues, that the merchant obtains money that he requires in India, and the Secretary of State the money that he requires in England."[101] The emasculation of Bengal's textile industry was graphically described, at the turn of the twentieth century, by journalist William Digby.[102] He estimated that the population of Dacca dropped from 200,000 persons to 79,000 persons between 1787 and 1817, while exports of Dacca muslins to England, which had amounted to ₹8 million in 1787, were zero by 1817.[103]

The home charges, payable to Britain for defense and administrative services by India,[104] and private remittances, were funneled through Indian exports. The drain of wealth was expressed by India's export surplus. This surplus became vital for Britain's balance of payments in the nineteenth century. The nationalist leader Dadabhai Naoroji[105] argued that the amount drained away a huge sum which would have materially improved Indian welfare if invested in the country.[106] The historian Sarvepalli Gopal remarked that: "The British had given an impetus to the destruction of the old economy but did not permit the rise in its place of one more suited to the modern age. India was made to serve as the supplier of raw materials to Britain's new industries and as the market for her manufactured goods."[107]

In the rest of India, too, commercial considerations drove British conquest. The East India Company's conquests in the western part of the Deccan peninsula and in central India arose primarily because of its commercial needs. Since the early 1780s the Bombay cotton trade had boomed. After 1784, the Company needed ever-increasing quantities of raw cotton to sell in China to increase the quantities of tea procured from the Chinese. Control over cotton territories, in the area now called Maharashtra and Madhya Pradesh but then called the Deccan or central India, was a motivator behind the Maratha Wars. In these wars, the merchants of western India, primarily from Gujarat, who were intermediaries in the raw cotton trade between the East India Company and the rural hinterland of growers, were also financiers of the East India Company.[108] Again, the Indian commercial class had been drawn into a symbiotic relationship with foreigners in furthering the conquest of India.

A final point about the establishment of British economic and political power after 1757 is of conceptual and historical interest. A concern of contemporary innovation scholars is how the nature of financing affects innovative activities. Other than market demand, and the type and quality of institutions, does the quantity and type of financing available matter in generating innovations?[109] Therefore, did the funds available from Bengal, and then subsequently from the rest of India, finance the British industrial revolution? This line of thought had been suggested a century ago by Brooks Adams[110] and William Digby, who had noticed the close correlations between dates such as the 1757 battle of Plassey and the succeeding political events, and the subsequent emergence of innovations during the first industrial revolution. John Kay's flying shuttle was invented in 1760, James Hargreaves' spinning jenny in 1764 and Richard Arkwright's water frame in 1768.

William Digby wrote:

England's industrial supremacy owes its origin to the vast hoards of Bengal and the Karnatik being made available for her use. Had this happened

honourably and in the ordinary course of trade it would have been matter
for satisfaction. Before Plassey was fought and won, and before the stream
of treasure began to flow to England, the industries of our country were at
a very low ebb. Lancashire spinning and weaving were on a par with the
corresponding industry in India so far as machinery was concerned, but
the skill which made Indian cottons a marvel of manufacture was wholly
wanting in any of the Western nations. As with cotton so with iron; industry in Britain was at a very low ebb, alike in mining and in manufacture.
The connection between the beginning of the drain of Indian wealth to
England and the swift uprising of British industries was not casual: it was
causal.[111]

Perhaps, the closeness of the various dates is an amazing coincidence. Nevertheless, it will be enlightening to investigate, in depth, the
relationships between the financing of the first industrial revolution
innovations by the cash transfers made from India to Britain after
1757. Certainly, India as a market for British products was extremely
important. But did the Indians, or rather the loot extracted by the
British from India, finance the British industrial revolution? An estimate of the size of the financial drain from Asia has put it at 1.7 percent of Britain's gross domestic product in 1770 and at 3.5 percent
in 1800. There was equally large wealth extraction taking place from
the sugar plantations of the West Indies. When the Asian and the
West Indian financial drain amounts are added together, they come
to 86 percent of the amount of Britain's gross capital formation from
domestic savings.[112] In other words, almost half of the financial sums
available to Britain for making domestic and foreign investments came
from the colonies.

The relationship between the wealth drain from colonies and the
financing of the industrial revolution deserves detailed analysis.
Britain had gained control over India at a stage when she was developing technologies that could add value to resources. Her motives
lay in the supply by the colony of biological and mineral resources,
while she supplied the colony with manufactured value-added
products. This strategy would require both the suppression of competition in areas of Indian competence, such as shipbuilding and
textiles, and financial rent extraction.[113] The use of Indian funds to
fund innovations in Britain would, therefore, be consistent with this
strategy.

The plantation industries

The modern industrialization of India began with plantation industries such as indigo, tea, and jute. Justice Mahadev Govind Ranade, an eminent jurist and political economist, had observed that the first step in the progress of India from a purely agricultural country to a manufacturing country was due to the growth of agro-based industries, producing items such as indigo, tea, coffee, oils, sugars, beer, and tobacco. This growth was simultaneous with the growth of the jute, cotton, silk, woolen, paper and flour-milling industries. The ratio of India's manufactured to raw materials exports had become 30:70 by the end of the nineteenth century.[114] The first attempt to exploit India's natural resources, clearly for enhancing British economic well-being, came at the end of the eighteenth century when the British established indigo plantations in Bengal. The vegetable blue dye had been obtained from small indigo growers of Gujarat, but their cottage industry was extinguished by better-organized plantations in eastern India. The East India Company brought in experienced planters from the West Indies and rapidly expanded the Indian indigo output into a major industry. The industry flourished until 1897, when German chemists, during the second industrial revolution in which Germany was an important participant, developed the aniline substitute dye and destroyed the natural indigo dye market.[115]

Another item that had influenced British seeking of wealth in Bengal was tea. Tea was introduced to Britain in the second half of the seventeenth century. By the early eighteenth century it had become an article of mass consumption, along with sugar, coffee, and chocolate, and was the most important item in British trade with Asia.[116] In the eighteenth century all tea was grown in China. British demand for tea, however, was insatiable, and by 1757 it was over 3 million pounds per year. The Chinese initially accepted only silver bullion in exchange for tea. Gradually, they became interested in other Indian products such as cotton piece goods and opium.[117] To fund the British tea habit, large funds were necessary, and they were available in Bengal. It was, however, necessary for the British to diversify their sources of tea supply. As we know from the industrial organization literature, single-supply sources create hold-up problems.

In 1820 the tea bush was found growing wild in Assam but the Indian tea industry did not start until 1841, when a Dr. Campbell of the Indian Medical Service brought China tea seeds from the Kumaon region of the United Provinces, now called the state of Uttarkhand, and planted them at 6,000 feet near Darjeeling. In 25 years, there were 39 gardens covering 10,000 acres. By 1874, the Darjeeling area was producing 4 million pounds of tea a year from 113 gardens.[118] The development of tea plantations in Assam, Darjeeling, and southern India was strongly encouraged, though plantations in Assam did not commence till 1855.[119] The renewal of the East India Company charter took away its trading functions, but from then on Europeans were granted the right to own land in India. With this Charter Act of 1833, European settlement in India made possible direct control by the British over the cultivation of crops such as tea, coffee, and indigo.[120]

The growth of the tea industry in India in the second half of the nineteenth century then became phenomenal. It took place mostly in Assam, not only because of soil suitability and climate but also because large tracts of virgin land were available in upper Assam for settlement.[121] The original terms of the lease were attractive. The leases were for 99 years, a quarter of the land area was rent free in perpetuity, and the other three-quarters of the land area was rent free for 15 years. Thereafter, the rent rose slowly to peppercorn levels for the full term. Renewal was promised at moderate rates. As a result, thousands of acres were taken up by prospective planters and companies.[122]

That tea was an important business of the Raj and for the Raj, an industry intended to enhance British well-being and wealth, was revealed by the nature of relationships the industry had with the government. Tea estates varied greatly in size and conditions, but the industry projected a solid face to the world via its Indian Tea Association.[123] Under the Government of India Act of 1935, which devolved political autonomy to the provinces, the small Assam provincial legislature had 108 members. Of these, seven members of the Indian Tea Association represented European planting interests in the legislature. The Indian Tea Association group had direct representation in the central legislature in Delhi, where its representative from 1937 to 1947 was Percival Griffiths, a former ICS officer and later an important economic historian.[124]

The tea lobby clearly had substantial local political clout. The Governor of Assam kept in touch with the tea planters, and on tour stayed with the superintendent of big tea companies such as the Jorehaut Company or the Bishnauth Tea Company, rather than with

civil service district heads, or in the district circuit house.[125] The close
and symbiotic relationship between the tea industry and the local
administration was taken for granted.[126] Shankar Nath Maitra, an
ICS officer, wrote: "I was DC Cachar for two years and saw a lot of
Nobby Clark, Secretary of the Surma Valley Branch of the ITA. He
was proud of his position in the ITA and proud of his decoration
CIE. Nobby Clark once frankly told me, 'I am not a planter, I am a
diplomat,' and on occasions behaved as if he was the Government
of Assam; particularly during the war, the ITA was an *imperium in
imperio.*"[127]

The indigo plantations of India have vanished, but tea plantations
are still a vibrant and major part of India's industrial landscape. A
third plantation industry that arose at that time, and is still very much
in existence today, in reduced form, was jute. As a young professional
in Calcutta, my first forays into the world of Indian industry, in the
late 1970s, were to examine the relics of jute mills that had been taken
over by the government; some of these jute mills really did have assets
on their registers which dated back to the late 1800s. Some of these
machinery items were still in operation. In one of the sick jute mills
I visited, the mill's office areas were positively dark and Dickensian.
There were high tables and high stools for the office clerks. The asset
registers were three feet in width and two feet in height. They each
required two persons to carry them around. The size of the tables
required to fully open one of these registers can be guessed. These
registers dated back to the formation of the mills. While the content
had been updated with new assets, those who operated the accounting
system clearly had never heard of information technology. Quill pens
and ink had just been given up in favor of fountain pens!

Jute is a Bengali word. The plant is mostly grown in Bengal. It was
cultivated well before the British came to India. Its fibers provided the
ropes and cordage that other parts of the world made from hemp.
Handloom weavers also made a rough cloth from it, and it was extensively used for local needs. With general growth in world trade, in
the early nineteenth century, the export of homemade gunny bags
increased, the consignments being sent to Southeast Asia and North
America. As a cottage industry, however, jute manufacturing was inefficient and the product quality was poor. The first industrial revolution
had not come to India and Bengal had at that time no coal or other
fuel; the establishment of factories was out of the question.[128]

In 1822, flax spinners in Dundee in Scotland experimented with jute manufacturing, but the results were unsatisfactory. In 1833, the British shipped home further jute fiber to supply the flax industry in Dundee.[129] The Douglas Foundry had developed a spinning machine that could handle jute as well as flax. By 1838, considerable improvement in technical processes had taken place, and Dundee factories rapidly took to using jute in place of flax. By the middle of the nineteenth century Bengal exported large quantities of raw jute to Dundee.[130] The Crimean War interrupted the supply of flax and hemp from Russia to Britain, which led to jute permanently taking their place and transformed India's manufacture of jute from the handloom to the powerloom level. The development of the Bengal coalfields in the middle of the nineteenth century made it possible to establish jute mills in Bengal.[131]

In 1854, George Ackland entered into a partnership with Bysumber Sen and in 1855, with the aid of a Dundee jute overseer, they started the first Indian jute spinning mill, at Rishra, on the banks of the Hooghly. For a time they also carried on handweaving. In 1859, the Borneo Company introduced powerlooms for jute cloth.[132] From this stage, development was rapid. By 1873, over 1,200 powerlooms were in operation. From 1872 to 1875, 13 new mills were launched and the number of looms had trebled.[133] By 1882, there were 20 jute mills, all but two in Bengal, which employed 20,000 persons. By 1885, Calcutta was the largest exporter of jute to the United States. In 1908, 38 companies employed 184,000 Indians and 450 Scotsmen in Calcutta.[134]

One of my forays as a young professional working in a consultancy practice in Calcutta was to the Hastings Jute Mill in Rishra. I am not sure that this was the mill set up by George Ackland and Bysumber Sen but it was reputed to be one of the oldest jute mills in India. This mill was very active in the late 1970s and is still in operation today. It was one of the best jute mills I had ever come across, though I had seen only a few jute mills and could not be called an aficionado. It was clean and professionally managed. Its manufacturing facilities had been continuously updated. This gave it excellent productivity, unlike that of other jute mills that had sickened and "died."

At the Hastings Jute Mill, over 4,000 persons worked in shifts. While the clatter of machinery was immense, and clearly the concept of information and communications technologies was in someone's imagination many decades away, the Rishra scene was reminiscent of a painting by L. S. Lowry of a Manchester landscape. Of course, only later in life did I understand what a Lowry painting evoked, but in the late 1970s there was an industrial India that had continued in the same way for over a hundred years. The Hastings Jute Mill also had an immense country house dating to the late eighteenth century in its huge compound, which reputedly had been a rest and recreation getaway for Warren Hastings and his Indian ladies, and each mill covered an area of about 100 acres.

The First World War, and the demand for sandbags, which is now permanent since there is a war on all the time somewhere in the world, stimulated the manufacture of jute. By 1919, there were 76 mills. By 1940, there were 110 mills, all highly profitable. An analysis carried out in 1927 showed that of 51 jute mills quoted, no fewer than 32 had paid dividends of more than 100 percent in one or more years since 1918, while 10 mills had never paid less than 40 percent in any of those years.[135] In spite of the initial partnership between George Ackland and Bysumber Sen, the industry had been primarily in British and American hands. Indians became major participants in the sector in ever-increasing proportions in the twentieth century. In 1927, about 50 percent of the shares were in Indian hands.[136] This process intensified in the fourth decade of the twentieth century. In 1937, over 63 percent of shares in 45 jute companies surveyed were owned by Indians.[137]

The industrial revolution industries

Meanwhile, what of the industries, such as coal, iron and steel, that had been the mainstay of the first industrial revolution in Britain from the mid to late eighteenth century onwards? Let me commence with coal because it is a short story for the moment, though the principal company in contemporary India, Coal India, has just made the largest-ever initial public offering of shares in India. The coal mining sector in India dates back, at the earliest, to 1774 when John Sumner and Suetonius Heatly of the East India Company were granted permission to work on seams found in the Raniganj area of Bengal. Several seams are supposed to have been worked on. Some coal extracted was delivered to the government in 1775, but this was of low quality. Then no further attempts to work any seams of coal were made till 1814. Again, this venture was unsuccessful. Yet, sufficient interest had been aroused for other ventures to be started between 1820 and 1825.[138] Nevertheless, the growth of Indian coal mining remained sluggish for want of demand. There was the odd steam-driven jute mill, which used powerlooms, but only the introduction of steam locomotives in 1853 gave rise to serious demand for coal.[139]

In the iron and steel sector, the tables have now been turned. A company run by an Indian, the Arcelor-Mittal group, is on its way to becoming one of the world's leading iron and steel producers in the twenty-first century. The manufacture of wrought iron in India has a long history. The famous iron pillar in Delhi has resisted rusting for over 2,000 years. India had world-class manufacturing capabilities in iron and steel several centuries before the Europeans and the Americans acquired theirs. Percival Griffiths[140] noted that the Damascene swords, which were famous during the Middle Ages, were originally forged in Hyderabad.[141] Steel made in the furnaces at Konasamundram and Dimdurti, two places situated in modern-day Andhra Pradesh, attracted buyers from other parts of Asia. Manufacture of the swords from the steel was carried on in widely scattered localities. These swords set the standard for iron work. They were made in Damascus, Isfahan, and in several places in southern India.[142] Incidentally, Hyderabad is still famous today for gun metalwork.

The manufacture of iron items, certainly by traditional village methods, was well established in India in the eighteenth century. It was largely a hereditary tribal craftsmen trade.[143] While the methods used were simple, and the iron usually impure, the nature of the work suggests that the craftsmen were more highly organized than their counterparts in other industries. Apparently, from the late eighteenth century onwards, European entrepreneurs had tried to improve local iron production by splicing in isolated pieces of British technology, such as the use of smelting coal and blast furnaces.[144] The first modern exploration of iron resources was carried out in the Madras presidency in the early nineteenth century, but no practical results emerged.

A more determined attempt was made by Josiah Marshall Heath, a Madras civil servant who had become interested in the local iron workings at Salem. This is first known instance of a civil servant turning to industrial entrepreneurship, though after independence many ICS members became industrialists,[145] an administration-to-industry career transition still in progress. Encouraged by Thomas Munro, then the Governor of Madras, J. M. Heath retired from the civil service and studied the iron industry in England for four years. In 1830, with the aid of English workmen and machinery, he established an iron works at Porto Novo, a location south of Pondicherry, on the Madras coast. He became a textile manufacturer and contractor for the East India Company, so as to initially finance the iron works from the profits of his cloth dealings. While J. M. Heath was a visionary, he was not a good businessman. He lost money in both textiles and iron. Several times, the government rescued him financially. From 1850 there was less help, and by the early 1850s the works closed.[146] The company was finally wound up in the 1870s.[147]

The first modern iron works in India was the Bengal Iron Works Company of 1874 at Barakar. The company started producing iron in 1877, but closed down two years later. The Government of Bengal bought the defunct firm, operated it for a few years and then sold it to a group of British businessmen in 1889. It was renamed the Bengal Iron and Steel Company. In 1897, the government agreed to purchase 10,000 tons of iron annually for ten years at rates 5 percent below the import price. In 1910, the company got access to new supplies of iron ore and coal, and became a producer of iron products. It, however, lacked expansion potential and ceased effective production in 1925.[148] In 1918, a second iron works had been founded in Bengal by the Indian Iron and Steel Company. This was linked to the Bengal Iron Works Company via managing agents Martin Burn and Company. The Indian Iron and Steel Company began production of pig iron in the early 1920s. The two companies were amalgamated in 1936. A diversification move was made by setting up the Steel Corporation of Bengal in 1937. This plant produced steel from iron from the Indian Iron and Steel Company, and by 1945 supplied about 20 percent of the market.[149] Eventually, in the 1970s, the Indian Iron and Steel Company became sick and later defunct.

Was there no hope for heavy industrialization by Indian entrepreneurs? In an often quoted passage, an American economist, Dennis Buchanan stated:

Here was a country with all the crude elements upon which manufacturing depends, yet during more than a century, it has imported factory-made goods in large quantities and has developed only a few of the simple industries for which machinery and organization had been highly perfected in other countries. With abundant supplies of raw cotton, raw jute, easily mined coal, easily mined and exceptionally high grade iron ore; with a redundant population often starving because of lack of profitable employment, with a hoard of gold and silver second perhaps to that of no other country in the world, and with access through the British Government to a money market which was lending large quantities of capital to the entire world; with an opening under their own flag for British business leaders who were developing, both at home and in numerous new countries, all sorts of capitalistic industries; with an excellent new market within her own border and near at hand in which others were selling great quantities of manufactures, with all these advantages India, after a century, was supporting only about two percent of her population by factory industry.[150]

The next chapter sets the record straight with a recounting of several Indian accomplishments in the emergence of modern Indian industry.

4 | *The emergence of modern industry*

Entrepreneurship in the nineteenth century

In 1976, in an obscure corner of the Rajabagan dockyard of the Central Inland Water Transport Corporation, in the southern reaches of the Hugli, the river that flows through Calcutta, a huge pile of rusting junk metal was discovered. On closer inspection, it turned out to be a steam engine. It was one of the first steam engines to come to India, and it might even have been the first. It had belonged to the India General Steam Navigation Company. Prior to that, it had belonged to the Calcutta Steam Tug Association.[1] The identity of that scrap metal's original corporate owners is not important. The identity of the companies' ultimate owner is. The owner of the companies was Carr, Tagore and Company, a firm founded by Dwarkanath Tagore.

Dwarkanath Tagore, known as the Prince, has gone down in history as the grandfather of two extremely illustrious grandchildren. The older of the two, Satyendranath Tagore, was the first Indian to join the ICS in 1863. A younger grandchild, Rabindranath Tagore, was India's first Nobel laureate, winning the literature prize in 1913. Dwarkanath Tagore, however, deserves approbation as the father of modern entrepreneurship in India, in the form that we know it. His firm, dating back to the 1820s, Carr, Tagore and Company, was what we today classify as a holding company for a conglomerate of businesses. It had interests in many activities, and particularly in shipping. Dwarkanath Tagore voyaged to Britain in his own ship. Carr, Tagore and Company had also formed the Bengal Tea Association, which was the first Indian enterprise to start tea cultivation.[2]

In 1836, a company operating tugs went out of business in Calcutta. Dwarkanath Tagore purchased their steamer and set up the Calcutta Steam Tug Association. Just a month earlier he had purchased the Raniganj Colliery. This colliery had been set up by one William Jones, not to be confused with the orientalist of the same name. This William

Jones was an engineer who had arrived in Calcutta in 1800 and, after working for others for a decade, had set up a canvas manufacturing factory at Howrah. He then set up a coal mine in Raniganj, and was the first person to use steam power to drive the engines that drained the mines.[3] The mine was, however, unsuccessful and was bought by Dwarkanath Tagore. Dwarkanath Tagore subsequently bought up a number of other collieries, and his steamer business was then assured of a reliable supply of coal. This is the first known instance of an Indian business engaging in a vertical integration strategy. The steamer and the coal business, which also supplied the steamers owned by the government and a few local factories, were the basis of a large commercial empire which survived into the mid nineteenth century.

Much earlier, in 1779, a Colonel Watson had set up two large windmills, each 114 feet high, in the Watgunge area of Calcutta. Industry in India that was not based on animate energy, generated from animal or human power, is assumed to have commenced from that time. William Carey, Joshua Marshman, and William Ward have gone down in history as the first missionaries in India. They, however, also deserve a place in the industrial pantheon. At Serampore, near Calcutta, where they set up a college, there was a small industrial complex that included a type foundry, printing presses, and a paper factory. These were run on steam power, and the complex is believed to have been the first to have used steam power for any manufacturing activity in India. In the engineering activities at Serampore, guidance had been given by the engineer William Jones.[4]

Meanwhile, in the 1820s, the Bowreah Cotton Mills had been set up by British interests at Fort Gloster, a location 15 miles south of Calcutta in the Howrah district. The mill used steam power, and had brought over several British women to impart machine-spinning skills to local staff. Some of these women, apparently, moved on to easier, if less virtuous, means of livelihood![5] The Bowreah Cotton Mills closed down in 1837, and then reopened as the New Fort Gloster Mills Company. In this company, Dwarkanath Tagore was a major shareholder. By 1840, the mill was the heart of a large industrial complex that included a cotton twist yarn factory, a rum distillery, a foundry, an oil mill, and a paper mill. There were five steam engines in the complex.

Dwarkanath Tagore's and others' subsequent efforts, in the first part of the nineteenth century, led to the Indians' adoption of some of the products of the industrial revolution, and also the emergence of modern large-scale factory enterprise.[6] Institutionally, important changes had also occurred. The first Companies Act in India was passed in 1850. A second Companies Act of 1857 allowed limited liability for companies in all areas, including manufacturing, banking, and insurance.[7] Wherever large capital investment was necessary, the advantages of a limited liability joint stock company were obvious. The limited liability law introduced the era of modern business enterprises into India.[8] By 1860, several companies were registered.[9]

Meanwhile, in western India remarkable changes were under way. In the cotton business, Indians had long established a substantial business foothold. The Crimean War had been, as noted, good for the jute business. It was also good for the cotton business. What was even better for the cotton business was the American Civil War between 1861 and 1865. At one fell swoop, the Lancashire mills lost their supplies of long staple cotton from the southern part of the United States. This vacuum was immediately exploited by Indian merchants, and later British merchants based in India, who made substantial fortunes.

Transfer of capabilities between businesses is an important topic today. Yet, that is precisely what happened in nineteenth-century India. The Indian cotton trading fraternity used their finance-raising capabilities, wealth, connections, trade and market contacts, knowledge of markets, and familiarity with the business to venture into the manufacture of textiles. The experience that many prominent Indian merchants had acquired, of a range of geographies and commercial approaches, facilitated the transfer of their abilities and knowledge from foreign trade to domestic industry.[10] In Bombay and Ahmedabad, this accumulated financial, social, and knowledge capital was used to create a genuinely indigenous textile industry. Raw cotton was readily available from the hinterland that had been opened up by the railways constructed from 1853 onwards. The British showed little interest in investing in an industry which would compete with Lancashire.[11] Conversely, British trading houses found that by faster adoption of many feasible business functionalities, because of the arrival of the railways, they could beat the Indian cotton traders at their own game.[12]

The modern Indian cotton textile industry was born in 1854,[13] when a cotton mill powered by steam was established by Cowasjee N. Davar in Bombay.[14] There were 10 cotton mills by 1865. By 1875, 47 cotton mills were in operation, and 79 mills by 1883. The expansion of the

Bombay industry succeeded in replacing British yarn exports to China in the 1870s and 1880s. The products of Lancashire had dominated Indian yarn and cloth markets until the 1870s. The revival of Indian textile production led to a revival of Indian fortunes.[15] In 1880, there were 58 cotton mills, employing 40,000 persons. Most of the mills, and 80 percent of the workers, were in Bombay and Ahmedabad.[16] When difficulties arose in the China market in the 1890s, Indian mill owners responded by creating integrated spinning and weaving mills. The number of looms in Bombay doubled between 1900 and 1913.[17] The diversification into textile manufacture was by traders. In Bombay, the cotton dealers had sought a new business to diversify their capital. They found it in textile manufacture. This could smooth profits when commodity markets became volatile.[18] Yet, new investments in automatic looms were constrained by problems of labor discipline, since workers held back on effort so that investments were not lucrative for owners.[19]

Most of the pioneer cotton mills are gone. In Bombay, these belonged to groups such as Petit, Wadia, Tata, Currimbhoy, Sassoon, Khatau, Goculdas, and Thakersey. Among the British business houses were Greaves Cotton and Company, W. H. Brady and Company, and Killick Nixon. In Ahmedabad's textile industry, the prominent names were Sarabhai and Lalbhai. Today, Sanjay Lalbhai, a former classmate of mine, still runs Arvind Mills, one of India's remaining operational integrated textile mills. In Ahmedabad, the old established trading and banking groups could finance a strategy of outsourcing whereby artisans would be provided with spun yarn to weave cloth that could then be marketed by the trading groups. As a consequence of the close integration of trading, financing, and manufacture within the city, and inside family groups, the Ahmedabad textile industry grew fast between 1900 and 1913, with a distinctive profile as the supplier of high-quality cloth.[20]

Grassroots industrial entrepreneurship, or what is described as the democratization of entrepreneurship, could not occur in India in the nineteenth century. Industrial development capital was severely short, and persistently scarce in India. Investments in industry cannot happen without funds and credit. In the nineteenth century, the banks in India, implicitly supported by government, were conservative and extremely choosy with lending.[21] Given this situation, it is not surprising that the Indian pioneers in large industries came from communities that had accumulated capital in trading and banking activities. They could raise money relatively easily.

Yet, a lacuna remained. Having transferred commercial capabilities to the sector, the Indian industrialists stopped there. Technology transfer was forgotten. The development of India's textile industry was characterized as a process of relentless improvisation in the use of old machinery, the manipulation of raw materials, and the exploitation of cheap labor.[22] The Bombay industrialists were relatively slow to adopt new production technologies in the nineteenth century and stuck to an inappropriate and less productive type of spinning machinery for much longer than Japanese rivals.[23] This led the Indian textile industry to be extremely unproductive. Conversely, now that Lancashire had been bested by Bombay and Ahmedabad in textile manufacture, the British became more successful than the Indians in cotton trading. After 1870, an increasing proportion of the profits in the cotton trade went to foreign firms, while previously the greater part had been earned by Indian traders.[24] By 1875 the relative roles and importance of the British and the Indians in the Bombay textile trade had been reversed.[25]

British and other European firms took advantage of their connections with the Bombay government, which even the most well-established Indian firms could never enjoy.[26] This government circle influence flowed from the strength of firms' financial connections, as the familiarity of British traders with banking methods in London meant that they were less of a credit risk.[27] The British and Europeans had another advantage. They adapted to new technologies and new ways. When new methods of conducting long-distance trade replaced the old ways, British traders made the necessary adjustments. Reliable telegraphic communications increased the capabilities of the British to engage in the cotton trade. Since speed, promptness, and precision mattered for completing trade transactions, the British traders became more efficient. The Indian traders' consignment system became outmoded and cumbersome.[28]

The British traders also readily changed their strategic models. Prior to the establishment of the railways, cotton had reached Bombay in loose bales. This packaging was unsuitable for transit in a railway wagon. The Great Indian Peninsular Railway, now the Central Railway, the major line connecting Bombay to the cotton growing areas such as Nagpur, introduced a graduated freight rate penalizing loose cotton bales and encouraging the movement of pressed cotton.[29] The merchants who wanted to use the railways had no choice but to press cotton near where it was grown, so that it was ready for immediate export on arrival in Bombay. The Indian merchants, in Bombay and elsewhere, were slow in adopting this practice. They forfeited the inland trade to British traders. By moving inland, the British vertically integrated their operations and eliminated various middlemen.[30] This gave British firms a scale advantage.[31]

A key element in late nineteenth-century development of Indian industry was the establishment of the railway and telegraph systems. Telegraph and railway lines were laid down in India to promote resource flows and transformations, as the case of backward integration in the cotton trade reveals. Nevertheless, India's heavy engineering industry was primitive. Railway engines and telegraph equipment were manufactured abroad.[32] The Indian railway network was the fifth largest in the world by 1900. The laying of railway tracks started a chain of foreseen and unforeseen results. It provided one of the foundations of industrial enterprise.[33] The railways incurred the largest capital expenditures in nineteenth-century India. They had been rapidly built up by government bodies in the 1870s, and by private subsidized contractors in the 1860s and 1880s.[34]

But the financing was substantially tilted towards British interests.[35] The financial burden was shifted to the Indians at large through a guaranteed return system on private capital by which the companies paid a minimum sum to investors in Britain even if profits were negative. This involved the payment of £50 million by 1900.[36] The return guarantee scheme had given the government the right to purchase a line after 25 years. By the 1920s, the government owned over 67 percent of the total mileage of India's railways, plus it had a small interest in all of the railways in India.[37] Yet, extremely few superior positions in the railways were staffed by Indians. Thus, the diffusion of new skills among Indians was limited while a substantial part of the income generated through railway investments was sent overseas.[38]

Early twentieth-century tipping point

The twentieth century was a time of great change in India. These numerous changes were political, social, economic, and cultural. I will cover a few topics related to the industrial development of India, particularly some aspects of the role of indigenous entrepreneurs, in general, and Bengali entrepreneurs in particular. From the middle of the nineteenth century, a considerable number of Indian entrepreneurs had emerged in Bombay and Ahmedabad. But their absence as industrial entrepreneurs in Calcutta, the heartland of India's original flirtations with modern manufacturing, is puzzling. Denizens of Bengal had been prone to take up professions like law, medicine, academe, and politics. The ICS, too, had much more than its fair share of Bengali members. George Nathaniel Curzon was soon to turn some Bengalis into dynamic entrepreneurs.[39]

The political history of India in the twentieth century is a vast subject. Curzon's role in Indian history is a vast topic. His most unpopular measure, the partition of Bengal, has aroused significant controversy. Yet it had an important and indirect effect on India's industrial evolution. Till 1905, the administrative presidency of Bengal covered the areas now covered by Bangladesh (now a separate nation) and the modern Indian states of Bihar, Jharkhand, Orissa, and West Bengal. It had complexity and heterogeneity, in languages, religions, ethnic composition of residents, administrative problems, and levels of social development that beggared belief. All in all, it was an extraordinarily heavy charge for one lieutenant governor. To relieve the pressure, Assam and Sylhet had been converted into a chief commissioner's province in 1874. There had been a proposal by the Assam Chief Commissioner, William Ward, to take over the Chittagong and Dacca divisions and the Mymensingh district from Bengal to give the Bengal lieutenant governor relief.

In 1903, the new Bengal Lieutenant Governor, Andrew Fraser, revived the idea. He had spent a lifetime in the Central Provinces, had been Home Secretary to the Government of India, posted in Calcutta, and had just finished presiding over India's first Police Commission. Andrew Fraser, in collaboration with Herbert Risley, then Home Secretary of the Government of India, and Curzon worked together to create a plan to partition Bengal. The new plan was announced in December 1903. The Chittagong, Dacca, and Rajshahi divisions, and the districts of Hill Tippera and Malda, would be combined with Assam to create a new East Bengal and Assam province.[40] This would be a predominantly Muslim province. The rest of Bengal, along with Bihar and Orissa, would stay as it was. The partition would take effect from 1905.[41]

The reasons advanced were administrative.[42] The real reasons were political, to create dissensions between the Hindus and Muslims and divisions between the Hindu politicians of East and West Bengal. Home Secretary Risley, later to be more famous for his ethnological work, had summed it up clearly: "Bengal united is a power; Bengal divided will pull in several different ways. That is perfectly true and one of the merits of the scheme."[43] The scale of popular protest in response was beyond expectations, and the partition immediately launched a stir with no previous parallels in India. The Hindus of Bengal felt that they would be marginalized in East Bengal and Assam, as that province was mostly Muslim. In the truncated Bengal, Bihar and Orissa province, again they would be in a minority as the residents of Bihar and Orissa would outnumber them. Like the spread of wildfire, the popular responses broke away from traditional protest, became militant, and broadened into a struggle for independence.[44]

At the same time, a new mood of self-confidence had been generated in Bengal by Swami Vivekananda's growing Hindu revivalist movement. The Bengal partition could not have come at a more opportune time. The floodgates of resentment, against what was perceived as unnecessarily provocative acts, had opened. Curzon's insensitivity and arrogance, and British racial discrimination, would not be tolerated.[45] The tipping point had come. Herbert Risley's assumptions had backfired on the British. One of the protest acts was the boycott of British goods. Person after person disposed off his British-made items in bonfires, as the Swadeshi movement took ground. Swadeshi literally means "of one's own country." Henceforth, all items consumed would be made in India. The Swadeshi movement resonated with nationalist leaders' ideas as well. Two influential leaders, Dadabhai Naoroji, the originator of the drain-of-wealth theory and for some time a member of parliament in Britain for the Finsbury Central constituency, and Justice Mahadev Govind Ranade, were among the figures who advocated displacing foreign goods with those made in India.[46]

The Swadeshi movement achieved some limited impact. The Collector of Customs in Calcutta noted a 22 percent fall in the quantity of cotton piece goods, 44 percent fall in cotton twist and yarn, 11 percent fall in salt, 55 percent in cigarettes and 68 percent in boots and shoes imported.[47] The real impact of the Swadeshi movement was in the revival and development of industry in eastern India. The revivals occurred in traditional handloom, silk weaving, and artisan crafts.

Earlier, in 1904, an association had been set up by Jogesh Chandra Ghosh to raise funds for sending students abroad, usually to Japan, to get technical training. The new developments were in manufacturing, setting off the stirrings of an incipient industrialization and the rising of an industrial consciousness.[48]

In the 1905 partition of Bengal, and the subsequent Swadeshi movement, lay the seeds of the early democratization of entrepreneurship in India. The Bangalakshmi Cotton Mills was launched in August 1906 with equipment bought from an existing plant in Serampore. There was a porcelain venture, the Bengal Pottery Works, set up in 1906, as were chrome tanning, and soap, matches, and cigarette factories. In Kushtia, now in Bangladesh, the Mohini Mills had been established by Mohini Mohan Chakravarty. The entrepreneurs included a few land-holders, such as Manindra Chandra Nandy of Kasimbazar, but otherwise they were from the professional class.[49] In conjunction with the release of a nationalist spirit, thanks to the sterling efforts of Messrs. G. N. Curzon, A. H. L. Fraser, and H. H. Risley, with additional support provided by J. B. Fuller, the first decade of the twentieth century witnessed the start of India's industrialization, based on science and technology, albeit on a tiny scale.

Yet, a start had been made. The precursors of this start go back to the Indian intelligentsia becoming conscious to science. In the 1830s, the Bengal renaissance leader Rammohun Roy had written to the then governor general about the need for Indians to be instructed in mathematics, natural philosophy, chemistry, anatomy, and other sciences.[50] The Calcutta Medical College had been set up in 1835 as India's first medical school along Western lines.[51] The syllabus for the bachelor of arts examination of Calcutta University, set up in 1857, included subjects such as mathematics, hydraulics, optics, astronomy, chemistry, physiology, and geography.[52] In 1869, Mahendra Lal Sircar wrote an article calling for an institution to deliver scientific lectures accompanied by illustrative experiments. His proposed institution would combine features of the Royal Institution of Great Britain with those of the British Association for the Advancement of Science.[53] The Indian Association for the Cultivation of Science came into being in January 1876.[54] It still exists today.

The heady combination of the Swadeshi movement and the scientific temper of Calcutta had made its major impact on Praphulla Chandra Ray, India's first technology entrepreneur.[55] He believed that aptitudes for applied science ought to be combined with industrial skills and money-making pursuits. He wrote in his memoirs that Curzon was a godsend for Bengal, and not the devil incarnate, for making Bengal arise from the sleep of ages.[56] The holder of a doctorate in chemistry from the University of Edinburgh, Praphulla Chandra Ray was an experimental chemist and a distinguished scientist in his own right. More than that, he was an economic nationalist, the founder of the chemical and pharmaceutical industry in India, and an entrepreneur who had established two companies himself. These were the Bengal Chemical and Pharmaceutical Works, founded in collaboration with Jagdish Chandra Bose, another distinguished scientist, and the Bengal Immunity Company.[57]

The Bengal Chemical and Pharmaceutical Works still exists, though owned by the Government of India. It currently sits on a real estate fortune, because its factories are located in some of the most expensive urban tracts in the world, in Bombay. It manufactures items such as Aqua Ptychotis and Phenyl. These are products for alimentary canal ailments and their aftermath! The Bengal Immunity Company manufactured vaccines. Like many Indian companies, it did not keep up with the times and technology. In the late 1970s, it was taken over by government. I briefly visited the factory to review assets. It was like a step back into the nineteenth century. It was located in the oldest part of Calcutta, all cobblestones and ancient red-brick Victorian buildings.

Praphulla Chandra Ray's actions, however, led to imitation, and several other Bengali entrepreneurs started manufacturing firms in the early twentieth century in Bengal. Two of these were Calcutta Chemicals, producing soap, toothpaste, and herbal cosmetics, and Bengal Lamps making electric lightbulbs. In newspaper publishing and printing, by 1910 the Ananda Bazar Group, owned by the Sarkar family, and the Amrita Bazar Group, owned by the Ghosh family, were large businesses. Bengali entrepreneurs also had a presence in the coal industry. By the end of the First World War, N. C. Sircar managed seven collieries, and a number of other proprietary or partnership firms accounted for about 20 percent of coal output.[58]

The occurrence of a structural change in Bengali society, within the space of a decade, has been noted by distinguished Indian polymath, Professor Benoy Sarkar.[59] New institutions, such as chambers of commerce, trade associations, and unions, had emerged. Bengalis were no longer clerks or lawyers but company promoters, directors, manufacturers, importers, and exporters. Yet, there was an issue. Unlike firms in Bombay which were large, Bengali manufacturing firms were small. They had an inability to scale their operations to any meaningful size, and Benoy Sarkar felt that Bengali industry was still at a very nascent stage of evolution.[60]

At the root of this scale problem was the issue of funds. The Bengalis had not been globetrotting traders, unlike the Gujarati and Parsi businessmen who had set up manufacturing units in Bombay. Hence, they had no funds of their own to reinvest in manufacturing. Neither did they have an ethnic network, derived from trade and commerce, which would enable them to acquire necessary funds for expansion.[61] Nor did they have the commercial or the managerial capabilities to tackle business on a large scale, which the Gujaratis and Parsis, after several centuries or more of global trading, had acquired. For the Bengali entrepreneurs, there were simply no capabilities to transfer from one business domain to another. The Indian cotton traders had capabilities and wealth to leverage in manufacturing. The Bengali entrepreneurs possessed book learning, they knew all about Cicero, Thucydides, and Shakespeare, had knowledge of poetry, could instantly recite Keats, Shelley, and Wordsworth, and knew science and mathematics. To parody Gilbert and Sullivan, the Bengalis were the "very model of a modern urban intellectual." But, they did not possess the all-important cash, credit, and commercial capabilities.

In fact, two early twentieth-century documents bear this out. Between 1917 and 1919, there had been a commission, headed by Michael Sadler, looking into the affairs of Calcutta University. The commission had been impressed by the level of knowledge of Calcutta University students about science, and how applications of science could lead to industrial development and subsequent wealth. The students could also sense the gap that India faced. They were motivated by nationalist feelings.[62] The commission sensed the students' frustrations. There had also been an Indian Industrial Commission, sitting between 1916 and 1918. In evidence before this commission, there were a number of aspiring entrepreneurs from Calcutta. Their basic problem, expressed to the commission, was a lack of capital. They might get trade credit, but if the credit market worsened they borrowed from moneylenders at very high rates of interest. Hence, the potential entrepreneurs demanded an industrial bank to finance small industries. Many who

gave evidence to the commission had been to Japan. They urged that
the Japanese model of industrialization, where the state played a major
role, be adopted.[63] These ideas eventually came to fruition more than
half a century later in independent India.

A spillover of Bengali nationalism was felt in western India.
Influenced by the Swadeshi movement, the nationalist leader Bal
Gangadhar Tilak had motivated a member of his community, Antaji
Damodar Kale, and Ishwar Das Varshnei, an engineer who had been
trained at the Massachusetts Institute of Technology, to set up a glass
works, the Paisa Fund Glass Works, at Talegaon, in the Poona district,
in 1908.[64] The plant was set up by raising contributions of just one
paisa, in other words one hundredth of a rupee, from the rural population, so that everyone could participate in an industrial venture being
set up by Indians.[65] This was the birth of the democratization of financing in India. While the Bengalis could not become major industrial
entrepreneurs, the diffusion of the social movement that the Swadeshi
idea unleashed led to the creation of indigenous industrial communities elsewhere, and in Bengal among other communities. There arose
the paradox of Swadeshi. Swadeshi as a concept became a public good
with positive externalities. The Bengalis had set India on the road to
modernization of ideas, but manufacturers in Bengal from other provinces and elsewhere benefited.[66]

The spillover of ideas as a public good, with major externalities,
found application half a century later. The Swadeshi Paisa Fund model
of raising funds was followed in raising capital for the launch of industrialization in Gujarat. When Gujarat State Fertilizer Company (GSFC)
was launched in 1964, fundraising proved difficult, as Bombay's capital
market investors were skeptical of Gujarat's industrialization prowess.
Till then, Gujarat had been a backward rural state. The farmers of the
rural area where the GSFC plant was to be sited were appealed to. It
was suggested that the plant would benefit them, and their agricultural productivity, significantly. Hence, a very large number of small
farmers contributed tiny sums, but collectively a large amount, to help
establish GSFC. This episode of post-independence democratization of
financing led to the launch of Gujarat's industrial revolution.

Earlier, in the 1950s, the Amul cooperative model had turned a
typical landless laborer, with two buffaloes, into an entrepreneur by
making him a member of a primary cooperative society to which he
could sell his buffalo milk. Today, Amul is a $2 billion company, with

numerous small farmers still its owners, an iconic brand name, many retail stores, and is planning to globalize its business model. As a result of policy innovations, based on Swadeshi ideas, Gujarat is India's most industrialized state.[67] Further democratization of financing took place with the nationalization of major Indian banks, in 1969 and 1980. Loans were made available to people from all walks of life to engage in trade and entrepreneurship. This financing democratization helped entrepreneurship democratization, as numerous small businessmen entered India's economic and commercial life.[68]

Entrepreneurship in steel

While G. N. Curzon was fooling around with the boundaries of the Bengal presidency, an epochal industrial event was taking place in Bihar and Orissa, an area then within Bengal. This was the first major Indian large-scale industrialization breakthrough, based on private initiative. The sector that it happened in was iron and steel. India may not have supported a substantial number of persons through factory industry employment, and still may not do so now, but for over a century several Indian entrepreneurs have succeeded in undertaking modern industrial pursuits. The seeds of what may well become the largest global steel corporation that now owns Corus, the erstwhile British Steel, were planted over a century ago.

The Jamsetji N. Tata and the Tata Iron and Steel Company story is often told. It is worth retelling, as a story of comprador capitalism redeeming itself. Jamsetji Nusserwanji Tata's father, Nusserwanji Tata, a descendant of landowners,[69] had started out as a small cotton and opium trader with operations in China. He had been a partner of Premchand Roychand, a notorious Bombay speculator. The Parsis of Bombay had been closely associated with the British in the opium trade with China, and many substantial nineteenth-century Parsi fortunes had their origins in the trading and shipping of opium.[70] The Parsis were, however, traditionally not traders or financiers. They had been artisans, carpenters, weavers, and shipbuilders. Their entry into trade was largely a result of their contact with Europeans as suppliers of ships, especially in the eighteenth and nineteenth centuries.[71] Refugees from Persia, they had settled in Gujarat. For over a thousand years they were loyal to every dynasty in power.[72] They had followed the British from Surat to Bombay, and were now their ultra-loyalists.[73] Thereafter, the Parsis became prominent in the cotton and opium trade.[74]

The young Jamsetji N. Tata had become an extremely canny and sagacious opium trader, having learnt the business in Hong Kong, and thereafter moving on to London and Liverpool.[75] Some years after his start in his father's business, the American Civil War erupted, creating massive opportunities for cotton traders to speculate and make a fortune, as the supply of cotton from the United States had dried up and the Lancashire mills were left high and dry. J. N. Tata was dispatched to Britain to take care of the booming raw cotton supply business. The end of the American Civil War ended fortune-hunting by Bombay merchants. Many found themselves in straitened circumstances. The Tatas were one of them.[76] At this time, they were able to join a group of other merchants in a syndicate of military contractors to supply a punitive expedition that the British had launched against the Abyssinians. The punitive force was to be commanded by General Napier, of Sind notoriety, and was made up of soldiers from the Bombay Army. This military contract turned out to be very lucrative, as military contracts are, and provided the large funds for J. N. Tata to launch himself on a career as an industrialist.[77]

Having known the cotton trade, he decided to copy his other Parsi brethren who had established cotton textile mills and set up one himself. Unlike the others who had decided to base their mills in Bombay, he decided to set up the mill where the cotton supplies were and chose Nagpur, in central India, as the location for his first mill, the Empress Mill. The mill commenced operations in 1877. Initially, he had purchased cheap British equipment for his mill. When the output turned out to be of low quality, he replaced all machinery with better American plant.[78] A globetrotter, J. N. Tata had seen the world's major economies, observed what industrialization could achieve, and believed it could be reproduced in India. In 1882, he read an article by a German geologist, Ritter von Schwartz,[79] stating that the best iron ore in India was in Chanda district, at a place called Lohara.[80] Lohara was close to Nagpur, where the Empress Mill was located. Ritter von Schwartz, however, had pronounced that coal deposits available nearby at Warora were no good for coking.[81] J. N. Tata had the Warora coal examined abroad, and it was found unsuitable. The government also did not support the venture, and for ten years J. N. Tata dropped the idea.

At the turn of the twentieth century, Curzon's viceroyalty had introduced a change in the attitude of the government towards industry. Industrialists were to be regarded as patriots rather than as pirates.[82] In such an atmosphere, J. N. Tata returned to his dream of an Indian iron and steel works. On a visit to Britain, he obtained the support of the then Secretary of State for India, and later visited iron and steel centers in the United States, such as Birmingham, Cleveland, and Pittsburgh. He then consulted the leading American metallurgist, Julian Kennedy, and obtained the services of one of the best prospecting geologists, Charles Perin, whose partner C. M. Weld came to India in 1903 to start iron ore prospecting in Chanda.[83]

The district of Chanda, now renamed Chandrapur, is still an extremely backward district. In twenty-first-century Chandrapur, there are issues with Maoist insurgency, and with tigers that attack human beings whom they consider to be fair game and viable food items.[84] In the early twentieth century, conditions were infinitely worse. The lack of any viable ore supplies and logistic difficulties led to the calling-off of the prospecting venture. On this exploratory expedition, C. M. Weld had been accompanied by Dorab Tata, J. N. Tata's son, and Shapurji Saklatvala, later a member of the British House of Commons. Dorab Tata went to Nagpur to see Benjamin Robertson, Chief Secretary to Government of the Central Provinces, to tell him about their conclusion. The Chief Secretary happened to be out, so Dorab Tata drifted aimlessly into the museum opposite the Secretariat to wait. There he came across a geological map of the Central Provinces, printed in several colors. He noticed that the Durg district, near Raipur, about 140 miles from the Chanda area, was colored darkly in a hue indicating large deposits of iron.[85]

The prospectors lost no time. They did not know what lay before them, but they thought that the Durg district was worth evaluating and at once went to the spot. One morning, the American surveyor, C. M. Weld, reached the village he was looking for and found some iron smelters working with primitive furnaces. He asked them where they got their ore, and they took him to a hill about 300 feet high. Mr. Weld climbed the height and was astonished to find that his footsteps rang beneath his feet as if he were walking upon metal. That was precisely what he was doing. He had found a hill of almost solid iron.[86] These hills, of Dhalli and Rajhara, were deposits containing 67 percent iron.[87]

Nevertheless, coking coal, limestone, and water were needed for a viable iron and steel plant. Thus, Durg was out of the reckoning. It stayed out of the reckoning for another 50 years, until it became the source of iron ore for the giant Bhilai steel plant. Meanwhile, Pramatha Nath Bose, a geologist who had originally prospected the Durg iron ore deposits, and drawn the maps that Dorab Tata had seen in the Nagpur museum, informed the Tatas about a similar rich iron ore source that he had discovered in the princely state of Mayurbhanj in Orissa.[88] This was close to the Bengal coalfields, as well as to large local water sources. Thus, the giant iron and steel complex in the city that is now called Jamshedpur came to be located at Sakchi in Bihar.[89]

Yet, Dorab Tata's problems were not over. By now, it was 1907. Jamsetji Tata was dead. Capital was needed. It was not propitious to raise capital in England. Dorab Tata and his colleagues took the decision to raise the capital in India, from Indians. The financial appeal was an unqualified success. In just three weeks, the entire capital required for the initial construction requirements was raised, every bit contributed by 8,000 Indians. Later, when debentures were issued to provide working capital, the entire amount was subscribed by the Maharaja of Gwalior.[90] The Tatas had spent £35,000 in exploration. They had been planning their production profile to replace India's imports. Thus, the plant was designed to specialize in three classes of products: foundry iron castings, steel rails, and bars, as they were the simplest to produce to meet rapidly growing demand. The Tatas had major marketing advantages, since Tata Sons was one of the largest iron and steel importers, it knew the Indian market, and it had old-established offices in China and Japan, where it anticipated finding export markets for the Tata Iron and Steel Company's products.[91]

This steel project could still become the bungle in the jungle. Sakchi was in the middle of absolutely nowhere, and putting up an iron and steel complex in such a location was not easy if not impossible. Communications were difficult. The local fauna, such as tigers and elephants, which had prospered in the area for several generations, were quite put out at the gross violation of their turf and tended to display bad attitudes.[92] There were no precedents in human history for an undertaking like this. Labor had to be trained, coal was not uniformly good, scientific talent was extremely sparse, and machinery meant for German conditions did not perform to the same standards in southern Bihar. It was the wrong kind of weather.

The American specialist, Charles Perin, who had again been invited from the United States to visit India and provide advice, is supposed to have been told by Frederick Upton, the Chief Commissioner of Railways: "Do you mean to say that the Tatas propose to make steel rails to British specifications? Why, I will undertake to eat every pound of steel rail that they succeed in making."[93] One hundred years ago, on February 16, 1912, the first ingot of steel rolled on the lines of the steel plant at Sakchi. During the First World War, the Tatas exported 1,500 miles of steel rail to Mesopotamia. Dorab Tata is reported to have commented, drily, that if Frederick Upton had carried out his undertaking he would have had some slight indigestion![94]

The first half of the twentieth century

The final years of the nineteenth century, the initial years of the commencement of the twentieth century, and then the First World War turned out to have been good for Indian industry. The number of joint-stock companies in India rose from 1,340 in 1900 to 2,744 at the outbreak of the First World War. The invested capital increased from ₹34.7 crores to ₹76.6 crores.[95] After the First World War, in the 1920s a substantial influx of Indian entrepreneurship started in eastern India. This intensified in the 1930s and 1940s. It occurred across the board, in new areas and in industries where the British held sway. The new participants were Marwari, Bengali, and multinational enterprises.[96] Between 1897 and 1914, the number of industrial workers in India increased from 421,000 to 951,000. India become independent of foreign countries for the supply of sugar and cotton goods, and met her requirements for cement, iron, and steel from internal production.[97] The lacuna remaining was the dependence on imported machinery and capital goods.[98]

The Calcutta jute traders, of Marwari origin, had made substantial wartime profits. They ploughed some amounts into industry. The first Indian jute mill was set up by Ghanshyam Das Birla in Calcutta in 1922. Their speculative gains in the First World War furnished the Marwari traders such as Hukumchand, Birla, and Poddar with the risk capital to start investing in manufacturing activities.[99] There were few technological barriers to entry, as the process of converting raw jute to gunny was simple.[100] With the manufacturing foray, the Marwaris would control all aspects of the jute industry value chain. By the 1930s, there were four jute mills owned by the Marwaris in Calcutta.[101] In the next 20 years, they would end up owning more than 60 percent of the sector.

Were Calcutta's Marwaris nationalists? That is an open question. They were the first community in eastern India to make the transition to large-scale manufacturing industry. From medieval times, the Marwaris had steadily been dispersing from their original home in Rajasthan. The famous Jagat Seth bankers of Bengal were Marwaris. The Marwaris settled in new locations as moneylenders, revenue farmers, and traders. The important names of the business community were Birla, Goenka, Dalmia, Poddar, and Jalan.[102] The origins of their business activities had been as agents and indigenous bankers. The merchant groups of Marwar already dominated the land caravan trade and the high finance of northern India and eastern India in the seventeenth and eighteenth centuries. This business base enabled spillovers for the Marwaris into more modern activities.[103]

Marwari merchants had developed techniques for mobilizing capital, credit skills, and information flow management. They had developed an ability to reinterpret the context, meanings, and contingencies so as to put together business models in new ways that others might have missed.[104] These enabled them to move into Bengal, where the fields were lush and the pickings ripe. They had tried moving to Bombay – for example, G. D. Birla did start his career there – but they faced stiff competition from the Kutch, Gujarati, and Parsi traders. These regional vigorous trading groups had large resources, built on prior and current extensive global trade. In eastern India, the situation was very different. The richer Bengalis were not traders, and smaller native trading houses did not possess the organization, financial resources, credit facilities, or information networks that Marwaris possessed.[105] Thus, the Marwaris came to dominate Bengal trade.

By the end of the nineteenth century, a number of Marwari firms operated from the Barabazar area of Calcutta as traders and moneylenders. They were still a part of the scene in the late 1970s, when one could see them sitting on the floor on fat mattresses, laid out with bolsters. There was no office furniture other than a cupboard for records and a phone for doing deals. These firms had set up connections in the interior of the Bengal jute-producing areas via branches and representatives. They owned baling houses and commission agencies in major inland Bengal raw jute markets such as Sirajganj, Narayanganj,

Madaripur, and Goalundo, all now in Bangladesh.[106] They controlled the Calcutta terminal market in jute, and the wholesale market in imported cloth, pulses, and groceries.[107]

Along with the Marwaris, a number of other entrepreneurs in Calcutta had become industrialists. Karamchand Thapar was an example. Several major sugar companies were set up by Indian entrepreneurs. The largest sugar mill in India was jointly owned by the Dalmia and Sahu Jain families. The Thapar family owned collieries, but branched into the manufacture of sugar, paper, and textiles. A pioneer entrant into the engineering industry was the Bhartias in 1928, a sector entry strategy imitated by G. D. Birla when he set up the Textile Machinery Corporation (TEXMACO) in Calcutta, and the Central India Machinery Manufacturing Company (CIMMCO) in Bharatpur, in the 1940s. Similarly, Lala Shri Ram acquired the Jay Engineering Works in Calcutta in 1938 to make sewing machines and fans. After initial entry in jute and textiles, the Singhanias of Kanpur branched out into engineering, insurance, paper, and chemicals.[108]

The vibrant industrial and commercial atmosphere of Calcutta deeply influenced Praphulla Chandra Ray who, after witnessing the failure of several Swadeshi era enterprises, thought that the Mahajan *gadi*, or the moneylender's mattress on the floor, was the ideal place to acquire bazaar merchant skills.[109] In the period between 1918 and 1939, the Marwaris moved into mining, import and export trade, sugar, paper, cement, construction, and share-broking activities.[110] By then, the chemistry laboratories of Edinburgh were a distant memory to Dr. Ray. He had realized that the transformation of the Marwari community from traders to industrialists was the function of a commercial culture ingrained over generations.[111]

By 1939, firms such as Birla Brothers had interests in cotton, jute, sugar, and paper manufacturing, and began to dominate Calcutta's industry.[112] The Marwaris had evolved into a major commercial community with a high degree of capital accumulation. Till independence, however, their attitude remained that of a community of traders, owing both to their conservatism and British obstructionism.[113] For the Marwaris, cash flow maximization was achieved not by technical efficiency, conspicuously absent anyway in their operations, but by control over supply and prices.[114] The profit motive was uppermost in the minds of the Marwaris. They were interested in the profit margin, rather like the British, as opposed to industrial expansion for the sake of growth and development per se, or for a sense of fulfillment arising from a mission well accomplished.

The role that India played in the Second World War deserves massive re-appraisal, as India raised the largest volunteer army in human history. This is, however, not the place to do so. The Second World War was good for India's industries in many ways. There was the demand stimulus effect. By cutting off imports, the war forced the Indians to enhance their national industrial capabilities.[115] After Japan's entry into the war, the government felt that India should develop speedily as a major Allied supply platform.[116] There was precedence for such thinking, since the success of Tata Iron and Steel Company during the First World War had led a number of established companies, Tatas and a number of British expatriate firms among them, to consider ventures in civil and mechanical engineering in the early 1920s.[117]

Two remarkable people were responsible for the coordination of the expansion efforts, Field Marshal Claude Auchinleck, the Commander-in-Chief in India, and Chandulal Trivedi, ICS, the War Secretary. By the end of 1941, pig iron production had increased from 1.6 million tons in 1938–39 to 2.0 million tons, finished steel output went from 867,000 tons in 1939 to 1.4 million tons in 1942,[118] and factory employment went up by 31 percent between 1939 and 1942.[119] Programs were initiated to expand armament works, explosive plants, and small factories. Licenses were given to 44 firms to manufacture machine tools, lathes, drilling, shaping and planning machines, furnaces, and power blowers. Over 280 new engineering items were manufactured in India. They ranged from small tools and machine parts to heavy caliber guns and degaussing cables. There was expansion in the production of drugs, leather goods, hardware, glassware, cutlery, and optical goods. A heavy chemical industry was initiated in 1941. This resulted in the production of sulphuric acid, synthetic ammonia, caustic soda, chlorine, and bleaching powder.[120] The Second World War laid some of the foundations for India's heavy industries.

These foundations were laid in spite of an obstructionist policy emanating from London. Nabagopal Das, an ICS officer and an industrial economist with a London School of Economics doctorate, served in the central secretariat in New Delhi during the 1940s. He wrote that though India was vital for the war effort, during the closing stages of the war, British policy opposed any rapid growth of heavy industries controlled and managed by Indians. Second, war conditions had potentially adverse effects on post-war industrial development as the capital equipment of many industries were used to their limits during the war years.[121] The final transformation was political and financial. During the Second World War, the relations between India and Britain were modified for ever. The United States displaced Britain as the biggest source of India's imports. India's sterling debts were liquidated through British purchases from India. To pay for further Indian war supplies, the British ran up a massive debt and by 1945 India had accumulated sterling credit balances of £1.3 billion pounds. These would boost free India's foreign exchange reserves.[122]

Colonial enterprise exit and multinational entry

Meanwhile, what of British commercial and industrial interests? They had implicit and explicit government support for generations. There were the twin policies of free trade and financial orthodoxy that were designed to stifle government initiatives for industrial development in India, so that domestic industries would not prosper and British firms would rule the roost.[123] From the nineteenth century, the rise of Bombay's textile industry had caused acute alarm in Lancashire. Thus, periodically unfair tariff and excise policies would be adopted in India. This had been a major stimulus that accentuated nationalist consciousness.[124]

British business was based primarily in eastern India. They had a considerably smaller presence in Bombay and Madras, and virtually none in the rest of India other than in Kanpur. Industries of eastern India were influenced by the emergence of a class of managing agents run by British expatriates.[125] This represented the colonial business sector. These were not multinational firms. By the late nineteenth century, these firms were widely spread in Assam, Bengal, and Bihar, but the main base of these firms was in Calcutta. Through these managing agents, British businessmen and investors, both in India and abroad, were involved in the Indian economy.[126] In 1915, half the employment in industry was provided by managing agents' firms. They controlled 75 percent of the industrial capital in India. The individuals were also socially dominant in the expatriate community. The elite within the firms consisted of partners and assistants. As a whole, the elite group did not consist of more than 1,000 to 1,500 men, and it was as small as the ICS whom they vainly tried to rival in status.[127]

The large British managing agency firms in Calcutta were Anderson Wright, Andrew Yule and Company, Bird and Company, Heilgers and Company, later to merge and become Bird Heilgers, McLeod Russell, Dunlop Begg and Company, Jardine Henderson, Octavius Steel and Company, Shaw Wallace and Company, Gillanders Arbuthnot, Macneill and Barry, Kilburn, Kettlewell Bullen, McKinnon Mackenzie, Thomas Duff, Williamson Magor, and Duncan Brothers. These agency houses controlled tea and jute companies. There were also specialist companies engaged in tea trading. These were J. Thomas and Company, Carritt, Moran and Company, W. S. Cresswell and Company, and A. W. Figgis and Company. Several companies, such as James Finlay and Company, managed tea estates. Many agency houses, such as Gillanders Arbuthnot, Kilburn and Company, and Shaw Wallace and Company, also controlled smaller breweries, distilleries, and manufacturing firms.

There were a number of British engineering firms. These were, notably, Jessop and Company, Burn and Company, Braithwaite and Company, Braithwaite, Burn and Jessop, and Balmer Lawrie and Company. They manufactured steel structures, cranes, drums, and railway wagons in India, or were specialized firms such as the Bridge and Roof Company of India.[128] Without exception, all turned sick. They are now dead or are India's state-owned firms. These eastern India engineering firms relied to a great extent on demand from the railways. In the first two decades of the twentieth century, investments in India's railways had been high. Several of India's major railway companies, the East Indian Railway, the Bengal and Assam Railway, the Bengal and North Western Railway, and the Bengal Nagpur Railway had lines with their focal point at the Calcutta termini. Till 1875, a sum of £95 million had been invested in India's railway network. Between 1908–09 and 1914–15, an average sum of £15 million was annually invested. Between 1915–16 and 1921–22, the average annual investment was £13 million, reaching a peak of £27 million in 1919–1920.[129] For the times, these were large annual expenditures and would have had a substantial spillover effect in eastern India's engineering sector.

In the engineering sector, an exception to the sordid tale of corporate demise was Guest, Keen and Williams, a subsidiary of Guest, Keen and Nettlefolds of Britain. Several subsidiaries of foreign firms commenced manufacturing operations in India, but many did not survive the long haul in India. These were Imperial Chemical Industries, Metal Box, Dunlop and Company, and Westinghouse, Saxby and Farmer.

The breadth of engineering firms in and around Calcutta, however, created an engineering and metals ecosystem in eastern India that nurtured small Indian entrepreneurs. Many large global companies today, run by Indians and based in London, such as Lakshmi Narain Mittal's Arcelor-Mittal, Anil Aggarwal's Vedanta Resources, and Swraj Paul's Caparo Steel, have their origins in this eastern India engineering and metals ecosystem.

What role did Indian enterprises play versus the British firms? A view is that the effective competition provided by Indian enterprises after the First World War challenged the British hold on industry, weakened it in the 1930s, and destroyed it after 1945.[130] These factors led to the shrinking of British investment in India. By the 1930s, India and Ceylon received as a combined amount just over 3 percent of British capital investments overseas. In the 1920s, the proportion has been almost 25 percent.[131] Before 1914, through their relationships with district administrations, British firms could prevent Indian entrepreneurs from creating rural marketing networks from the bottom up. They were, however, incapable of imposing their own structure.[132] From the 1930s, Indian businessmen excluded the expatriates entirely from operating or financing the marketing system for agricultural produce in many parts of India, and attacked their position in the export trade as well.[133] Unlike the cotton traders in western India who had been overtaken by British traders in the use of technology, which gave these British traders a competitive advantage, the twentieth-century Marwari traders overtook the British managing agents based in eastern India in the use of modern technology. This gave them the upper hand in rapidly transmitting information.[134]

In the 1930s, the political economy of global commerce had also changed. There were tariff walls in India, and these entry barriers encouraged Indian entrepreneurs to make domestic investments. The British firms of colonial origin did not exploit these options. Indian firms invested further in consumer good industries such as sugar and cement.[135] British colonial firms had the advantages of good marketing networks, financial soundness, and bureaucratic contacts. Their failures are cultural and behavioral phenomena. Psychological explanations have to be sought for the decline of expectations, the loss of will power, and an abject failure of nerve.

The British managing agency firms, in a sense, were the descendants of the East India Company. Their mentality was that of a trader, however much they tried to put a gloss on it by calling themselves merchants. A merchant's view of the world consisted of buying in the cheapest and selling in the dearest markets.[136] Such a view ignored the long term. It was also a world-view that was over a hundred years past its sell-by date. While the British managing agencies may have had the ability to comprehend the emerging opportunities in India, many were too scared to evaluate them and diversify. Too many uncertainties would destroy the consistent and secure income streams and corporate control enjoyed by them.[137]

Also, by failing to invest, British managing agents de-industrialized the companies they controlled. Their fundamental conservatism led them to deny themselves opportunities in emerging industries, because these opportunities involved complex technologies. In these diversification efforts, they would have had to delegate authority to experts. This could lead to loss of operational and strategic control. Such attitudes were, however, not uncommon, since the story of industry in Britain in the twentieth century was also that of a peculiar destructive relationship between finance and industry.[138] Technical experts and specialists were anathema, to be regarded with suspicion as dangerous unsound persons who threatened existing prerogatives, were interested in innovation for its own sake, and were prone to making expensive mistakes.[139]

The Indian entrepreneurs who moved into the new consumer goods industries were able to use high initial profits to finance expansion into other fields such as paper, chemicals, and machine tools.[140] They could also augment their financial capital substantially. Thus, by the 1930s, the Marwari firms had become the leading stocks on the bourse, and the Marwaris became the lead insiders of the stock market. They controlled Lyons Range, as the Calcutta Stock Exchange was known since it was located at Lyons Range, a street behind Writers' Building in Calcutta. Their nineteenth-century indigenous business models continued into the late twentieth century.

An anecdote illustrates this. The head offices of the firm where I worked in Calcutta in the late 1970s were next to the official Calcutta Stock Exchange in a grand building on Lyons Range. Across the street from the official stock exchange was an unofficial stock exchange. This was sited on top of the little stalls that sold cold drinks, cigarettes, and snacks. It comprised little boxes that were four feet in height, width, and depth, double stacked on top of each other in a row. In each box sat, or rather crouched, a cross-legged, dhoti-clad person with nothing else but a phone. Each man would be making indecipherable gestures with his free hand, while at the same time shouting in an unintelligible language. The customers would be standing on the pavement in front of the stalls. The resident of each box would be doing different deals. To stand on the opposite footpath, taking extreme care not to step into the flowing detritus deposited by the various cows tethered to Writers' Building, and see these day traders in action was a wonderful sight. Modern dance has no equal. Neither does atonal music. This was kerb trading, and an extremely efficient centuries-old options and futures trading system. Again, other than the telephone, no offerings were made to gods of modern technology. I wonder how settlements were accomplished.

The metamorphosis into financiers and industrialists, and a significant hold over the Calcutta share market, endowed the Marwaris with substantial economic power.[141] The Marwari financiers could adopt a "camel with its nose in the tent" strategy.[142] During the 1920s, many British companies were undercapitalized. They needed cash to expand jute mill capacity. Marwari financiers offered loans at interest rates lower than the going interest rate on company debentures, but as collateral took blocks of jute mill shares. Through the 1920s and 1930s, as British companies were short of cash, the Marwaris continued refinancing these managing agencies, held on to the shares, got themselves on boards, and acquired the firms.[143] The Bajoria, Bangur, and Goenka jute interests were acquired this way.[144] This strategy was similar to the use of convertible debt, which came into vogue in India later. Subsequently, in the 1950s and the 1960s, their Lyons Range insider status enabled the Indian businessmen of Marwari origin to take over a succession of British managing agency firms. Many of these firms were voluntarily sold to Indians. The Khaitans of Calcutta acquired Macneill and Barry, and Williamson, Magor and Company. They then merged the two agencies to create Macneill Magor. In Calcutta's business legends, this sudden and total ownership transfer was widely held to arise out of the progressive commercial, financial, and moral bankruptcy of the firms' British owners.[145]

The position of British managing agency firms in India was challenged by British and other multinational companies setting up manufacturing operations and sales and distribution networks in India in the first half of the twentieth century. These firms invested in consumer products, such as Imperial Tobacco Company in cigarettes, Brooke

Bond in packet tea, and Glaxo in pharmaceuticals; and in intermediate products such as Imperial Chemical Industries in chemicals and Indian Oxygen Company in industrial gases. British managing agency firms in India had little expertise in these industrial items.[146] They were completely out of their depth relative to the multinational firms.

After the 1930s, there was substantial growth of multinational companies in India. The multinational firms catered to the domestic market. They had little to do with the older British managing agencies. They introduced new products to the market, and used new marketing methods. The firms set up by Indian, particularly Bengali, entrepreneurs, that had earlier prospered also suffered at the hands of the multinational companies as they too were outcompeted.[147] Omkar Goswami has stated that most of the Bengali sponsored companies' shareholders were reluctant to give up dividends.[148] Thus, there were no funds available for capital expenditures and reinvestments. Yet, most of these Indian firms specialized in technologically intensive product lines that demanded constant product development and upgrading of facilities. Funds were also required for continuous market development and advertising. Nevertheless, external funds were also not welcome, since that could lead to outsider control, and the Bengalis wanted to exclude Marwaris, at all costs, from a presence in their businesses.[149]

An anecdote reveals the dividend passion of the Bengali industrialist. Many years ago, while I was in Ann Arbor, Michigan, I was talking to a scion of a Bengali-owned firm still in existence, in the tea plantations and tea trading business. It was a successful company, as their several tea estates produced excellent Darjeeling tea, reputed to be the champagne of teas. The companies were liquid, and the family was wealthy. I offered him a cup of tea, and his response was that neither he nor any of his family members ever drank tea. Tea was where the dividends came from. Drinking tea was sacrilege. It would be like consuming the dividend coupons before they were cashed. No one drank their dividends. At least, they did not drink it as tea.

There was also considerable utilization of company resources for personal benefits. One of my assignments, when I worked in Calcutta, involved the investigation of Hindustan Pilkington Glass Works, a joint venture between a Bengali entrepreneur and Pilkington Glass Works of St. Helens, Merseyside. Over several years, the Indian partner had bled the company dry. The average ratio of cost of goods sold to sales was consistently over 100 percent, and in some years the ratio had hovered near 150 percent. The benefits enjoyed with the sums so extracted included the provision of luxurious residences for the entrepreneur's mistresses. The company's Asansol plate glass factory was state-of-the-art. Its plate glass furnace was the largest, and considered one of Asia's best. The temperature in the heart of the furnace was that of the sun. Standing on the balconies on each floor, when the furnace was at full charge, and its temperature was 3,000 degrees centigrade, made the summer of Asansol, where it was a mere 48 degrees centigrade in the shade, seem cool. The company became defunct. Other companies emerged as plate glass suppliers in India.

Cash shortages, aging products, rent extractions, and low productivity hit the Bengali companies hard. Multinational corporations competed precisely in the product areas where the Bengali firms operated, such as soap, pharmaceuticals, electrical appliances, and toothpaste. Lever Brothers of Bombay had captured a sizable segment of the Indian soap market. In light bulbs, Bengal Lamp was swamped, first by General Electric Company and then Philips. Local biscuit manufacturers like Kolay had to compete with Britannia Biscuits, and Colgate Palmolive competed against Calcutta Chemicals in the toothpaste market.[150]

The habits of multinational company sales managers in India deserve a side-mention. The late Prakash Tandon, a multinational company manager himself, had described their activities.[151] Visiting sales managers of these companies used to tour India with their boxes of samples. They were known, derisively, by a generic term of *boxwallahs*. They would arrive in Bombay at the end of the monsoon, by September end. Their daily routine would involve a large egg and bacon breakfast, followed by a visit to the market where they would consume innumerable cups of sweet tea and fizzy drinks of various hues. They would meet the distributors and the main customers for three hours or more. Then, they would gather at the Harbor Bar of the Taj Mahal Hotel with their counterparts from various companies and drink beer steadily for some time. A large lunch, with several gin and tonics, would follow. This led to a siesta. In the evening, after a short walk along the sea front, they would bathe, change clothes, and settle back at the bar for whisky and soda or gin and tonic, dinner, and then brandy. They would close the day's session with cold beer at midnight. Having done the sales grind in Bombay, they would visit Karachi, Lahore, Calcutta, and Madras in turn. As the weather warmed up, in April, they would return to Britain. What sold the products was superior product quality and orderly, planned selling methods.

Nevertheless, multinational companies were not immune to mortality woes if they fell into the hands of asset strippers. The Indian Cable Company (INCAB) was a medium-sized and well-run manufacturing firm, with plants in Poona and Jamshedpur. It changed hands when its owner, British Insulated Callender's Cables (BICC), sold it to Kashinath Tapuriah, the son-in-law of Haridas Mundhra. Haridas Mundhra had been implicated in independent India's first major corporate sector scandal, involving the Life Insurance Corporation of India, in the late 1950s. Within a few years, the Indian Cable Company had joined the ranks of extinct Indian companies.[152]

In the early years of the century, Bengali firms had pioneered Indian business. They catered to the real needs of an untapped middle-class market. Second, they did not compete with the British managing agencies. Goods such as toothpaste, herbal soap, tooth powder, talcum powder, indigestion tablets, antipyretics, analgesics, vaccines, and light bulbs were not yet manufactured in India, nor were they imported in bulk by British managing agencies.[153] The only Bengali-run businesses of those times that have survived today are C. K. Sen and Company, which makes and sells the Jabakusum brand of hair oil, Dey's Medical Stores, which makes Keo Karpin hair oil, and G. D. Pharmaceuticals, which makes Boroline, a remedy for chapped lips. Perhaps neither the Marwaris, nor the British nor the multinationals, could ever figure out the business model nuances involved for these particular products. All these items, however, are branded consumer items with a particular market in eastern India. From the 1930s, the Bengali firms' shortages of funds and a lack of modernization led to their decline. In product quality, and financially, the multinationals gained the upper hand in the Indian market. There may be some truth to Omkar Goswami's comment that "To an extent the fall can be attributed to the Bengalis' almost innate inability to run a business."[154]

Industrial policy in the early twentieth century

The state had first taken a role in India's industrialization at the turn of the twentieth century. The then Governor General, G. N. Curzon, had established a Department of Commerce and Industries

in 1905.[155] Curzon's aim was not so much India's development as
to ensure that India would be an efficient and important arms and
ammunition supply platform to support the British in their great
game in central Asia. Yet, Curzon visualized an important role for
the state, and stated:

The days are gone by when Government can disassociate itself from the
encouragement of enterprise. There used to be a sort of idea that business
was an esoteric thing, to be conducted by a narrow clique, who were alone
possessed of the oracles of wisdom, and with whom Government was hardly
supposed to be on speaking terms. That was an absurd theory at any time.
It is additionally absurd in a country like India.[156]

Nevertheless, till the outbreak of the First World War, British obstructionism from Whitehall had been considerable. Valentine Chirol stated
that British officials were jealous of Indian enterprises.[157] Whatever
initiatives were taken in India raised the ire of the British managing
agency community, led by James Mackay. A weak Secretary of State
for India, John Morley, was persuaded to provide an opinion against
any state role in Indian industrialization.[158]

At the level of provincial government, in Madras an enterprising
individual named Alfred Chatterton had been motivated by a desire
to develop indigenous industry in southern India. He had recognized
the knowledge gap that Indians would face in establishing industries,
and wrote:

The men with capital, business acumen, technical knowledge and administrative capacity, who form the backbone of industrial life in Europe and
America, are lacking and no preparation has been made to create them ...
There can only be a vigorous and healthy industrial life when it is carried
on by the people themselves – that is they must supply the capital, take the
risks, enjoy the profits, bear the losses and, above all, undertake the management and control of the many branches into which it is subdivided.[159]

On behalf of the Madras Government, in 1908 Alfred Chatterton
established model factories in areas of low technological intensity,
such as chrome tanning and aluminum ware, to provide knowledge
and support for starting industries to persons of modest means wishing to be entrepreneurs. Such were the origins of modern decentralized
industrial development in India.

In a sense, these Madras initiatives of the early twentieth century were the foundations of industrial estates, now clustered into renamed special economic zones (SEZ), and seed capital funding that are worldwide policies today. Alfred Chatterton was appointed the Director of Industrial and Technical Inquiries in Madras, though not Director of Industries. In 1910, when his position was under review at the India Office, so as to regularize the appointment and create a fully fledged Department of Industries in Madras, James MacKay, a *bête noire* of Indian businessmen and a member of the Council of India, influenced John Morley against implementing such policies. Two interventionist members of the India Council, economist and educationist Theodore Morison and Krishna Gobindo Gupta, a very distinguished former ICS officer, could not make much headway against James MacKay.

James MacKay wrote in a memo:

I think it is dangerous and likely to be a mischievous interference with private enterprise and individual initiative to ... start Government factories with the idea of educating natives and passing on these factories to native capitalists. The whole thing is economically unsound ... How can a man like Chatterton possibly teach men who all their lives have been engaged in seeking for enterprise that are likely to be remunerative? The thing is absurd ... This man Chatterton, who can have no business or practical experience of factories, [is on] a salary of £1,200 p.a. with a lot of highly paid assistants to fool about with childish factories which will never earn a sixpence. This is how money is frittered away in India ... men seeking soft billets for themselves and getting round those who are responsible for the Government ... by gulling them into silly schemes.[160]

Yet, the First World War had made it abundantly clear that India needed to be developed as a supply platform for the war effort rapidly. In 1916, an Indian Industrial Commission was appointed under Thomas Holland, former Director of the Geological Survey of India. At that time there was also an enlightened Governor General, Charles Hardinge, who had realized that economic growth might assuage emergent political ferment in India, and industrial development would be important for that strategy.[161] The Montagu-Chelmsford constitutional reforms of 1919, introducing dyarchy, made industrial development a provincial subject and took it out of the remit of the Governor General in Council. This formalized, for the time being, decentralized industrial development. The Government of India, led by Thomas Holland, convened Industries Conferences in 1920, 1921, and 1922 to which provincial directors of industries were invited, but nothing concrete happened.[162] In 1922, Thomas Holland left India to become the Rector of London's Imperial College.

Till the Second World War, and the arrival of Field Marshall Wavell as the Governor General, the state took no serious role in articulating policies for rapid industrial development of India, but was content to use the levers of tariffs as incentives. Alfred Chatterton's efforts in Madras had come to nothing. He moved on to become the Director of Industries in the princely state of Mysore, which had a more enlightened administration. Nevertheless, the Madras province had taken the lead, in southern India, in state-sponsored decentralized industrial development. Political leaders such as Chakravarthi Rajagopalachari, Chidambaram Subramanian, and Ramaswamy Venkataraman subsequently carried the torch for provincial industrial development.

By the middle of the twentieth century, a breed of professionals who would start industries on their own, and not carry with them a baggage of caste, class, or community in their entrepreneurial journey, was emerging in Madras, just as it had in Bengal at the turn of the twentieth century. There arose a cadre of small, technology-based entrepreneurs who had no family business backgrounds but were professionals.[163] This very small start, in Madras, represented an aspect of the process of entrepreneurship democratization in India. The descendants of this class have emerged as some of the technology entrepreneurs of India, especially in southern India. Chapter 7 contains details of many of these modern technology entrepreneurs of India.

5 | *Asian late industrialization*

Late industrialization and its consequences

What was happening elsewhere in Asia? What lessons may India glean from her Asian sisters' industrialization experiences? These are important questions, relating to the phenomenon of late industrialization in Asia, as India proceeds on her own industrialization trajectory. Industrialization results from a complex collection of cumulative forces acting on each other in transforming an economy from an agrarian and rural character to an urban and industrial character. A key feature of the process of industrialization is the changing composition of output and employment, away from land and agricultural pursuits.[1] The term industrial revolution refers to a series of major quantitative shifts in the trajectories of industrialization based on harnessing the fruits of certain fundamental innovations. The late industrializing countries may not have innovated themselves, at least initially. At a later stage, they may well have created new innovations that might help engender another industrial revolution.

Does late industrialization pay? A clear indication of whether it does or not comes from the evaluation of two sets of data. The late Angus Maddison, in a later work, documented the incomes of different countries stretching back to the year AD 0. The resulting aggregate statistics, of the total gross domestic product generated by each country, are of useful value in understanding where India was placed in the global rankings and where she is placed now, and in comparing her economic performance to that of other countries. The data are in Table A6. Based on these data, I developed two charts comparing, first, India to Japan, and, second, India to the United States. I commence my analysis by comparing Indian and Japanese economic performance from AD 0 to 1998, as computed in 1990 US$ values. The year 1998 was the last one for which the data were computed. These data are plotted on figure 5.1.[2]

126

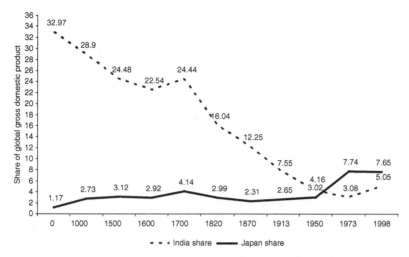

Figure 5.1. India and Japan – share of global gross domestic product, AD 0 to 1998.

Source: Table A5.

Japan is the classic case of a late industrializing country, where, till the Meiji revolution of 1868, there was a rural economy and a feudal social structure. The Tokugawa dynasty had ruled from 1603 to 1868. In 1868, when Japan started industrializing, India already possessed a nascent manufacturing sector. In the beginning, that is to say at AD 0, Japan's share in the world economy was just over 1 percent. At that time, India's share in the world economy was 33 percent. Around the time the first industrial revolution commenced, in the middle of the eighteenth century, India's share in the world economy was 25 percent. Japan's share was just over 4 percent. India had fallen badly, from its situation in the year AD 0, but still was a key player at that time. Japan was not a player at all, though its share of the world economy had quadrupled in the past 1,700 years, while India had seen its share whittled away from one third to one fourth.

Even in the early years of the twentieth century, India's share of income in the world economy was between 7 and 8 percent, though the decline in share from 1700 to 1913 had been precipitous, while Japan's share of the world economy was between 2 and 3 percent. The next two generations saw remarkable changes of fortunes for both India and Japan. In the ten years from 1954 to 1963, the Japanese real per capita gross domestic product rose at an annual average rate of 9.4 percent.[3] While in 1950 India's share of the global economy was just over 4 percent, and Japan's share of the global economy just over 3 percent, by 1973 Japan's share of the world economy had risen to almost 8 percent while India's share had dropped to 3 percent.

The next 25 years saw a lessening of the gap between India's share and Japan's share, but Japan was still ahead of India, with its share of the global economy at more than 7 percent. By 1998, India had managed to claw its way back to a share of the global economy of 5 percent. Japan's share, which in 1913 had been 33 percent of India's share, was now 50 percent more than India's share, and more than six times its share in AD 0. Many reasons can explain the variance in shares between India and Japan, but one reason is clear. Japan had embarked on a strategy of late industrialization. Japan's population was smaller too. Hence, per capita incomes would be larger in Japan then in India.

An assessment of India's position versus that of the United States has revealed the same variance, though the differences are larger and, therefore, starker. The United States embarked on the second industrial revolution from the 1870s.[4] Figure 5.2 plots the relative shares of India and the United States in the world economy between 1500 and 1998. What existed as the economy of the United States in 1500 was trivial, with good reason. Its relative share in the world economy was 0.32 percent compared to India's relative share then of over 24 percent. Even in 1870, when the second industrial revolution had commenced in the United States, India's share in the global economy was over 12 percent, compared to that of the United States at below 9 percent. By 1998, the share of the United States in the world economy was almost 22 percent while India's share was down to 5 percent. Industrialization, whether early, middle, or late, pays well in global wealth share.

This chapter deals with late industrialization, and the experiences of Japan, South Korea, and Taiwan. It is important to evaluate per capita income figures for Japan and India. Those statistics reveal the benefits of late industrialization. The late economic historian Paul Bairoch developed data on per capita gross national incomes, or gross domestic products (GDP) for several countries over a large time span.[5] Based on these data, for the years 1820 and 1989, specifically, for each year I computed the ratio of each country's per capita GDP to the per capita GDP for India. Based on these ratios, I developed a chart

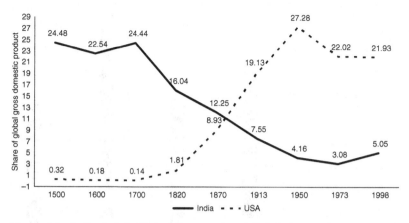

Figure 5.2. India and the United States – share of global gross domestic product, 1500 to 1998.

Source: Table A5.

relating India's per capita GDP to that of four other countries, Japan, Germany, the United States, and the United Kingdom for 1820 and 1989. These ratios are portrayed in figure 5.3. For India, for the years 1820 and 1989, relative to herself, the ratio would be 1. The discussion is based on a comparison of the Japanese case. Other countries' ratios are provided as benchmarks.

In 1820, the ratio of Japan's per capita GDP to that of India was 1.2. Recollect that, in comparison to India, Japan is physically tiny. The absolute size of its economy was also small in 1820. Hence, the ratio of 1.2 for Japan's per capita GDP relative to that of India was completely feasible. By 1989, the ratio of Japan's per capita GDP to India's per capita GDP was 14. Not only had Japan become vastly richer, in an absolute sense, but the relative position vis-à-vis India had increased by a large order of magnitude. The divergence in relative wealth between India and Japan had increased over eleven times in six generations. Similarly, the divergences in relative wealth between India and Germany had increased over six times in six generations, between India and the United States six times in six generations, and between India and the United Kingdom over four times in six generations. On a per capita basis, the consequences of late industrialization for Japan were profound.

Would there be a penalty for not catching up if others in the comparison group began leapfrogging and engaged in a process of late

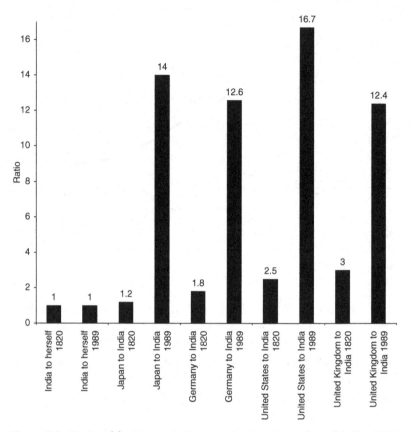

Figure 5.3. Ratio of four countries' per capita income to that of India: 1820 and 1989.

Source: Paul Bairoch, International Industrialization Levels from 1750 to 1980, *Journal of European Economic History*, 2 (1982), 268–333.

industrialization? The answer to this question comes from the data presented in Table 5.1. These data show the inter-se relative rankings of nine countries, assumed to be late industrializing nations, for the years 1913, 1950 and 1987. The GDP per capita was measured in 1980 US$, for all the years, and the countries ranked accordingly. A selection of countries is used for discussion. The details in Table 5.1 show that Argentina was ranked first in 1913, but by 1950 it had slid to second position and in 1987 was ranked fifth. Its Latin American neighbor, Brazil, could industrialize and improve its position from tenth in 1913 to sixth in 1950 and fourth in 1987. Even on the same continent,

Table 5.1. *Rise and fall in the inter-se relative rankings of selected late industrializing countries for the years 1913, 1950, and 1987*

Ranks based on per capita gross domestic product measured in 1980 United States $

Country	Rank in 1913	Rank in 1950	Rank in 1987	Change in places: 1913 and 1987	Change in places: 1950 and 1987
Argentina	1	2	5	−4	−3
Philippines	3	7	11	−8	−4
Mexico	4	5	7	−3	−2
South Korea	8	9	2	+6	+7
Indonesia	9	11	8	+1	+3
Brazil	10	6	4	+6	+2
Taiwan	11	10	1	+10	+9
China	13	14	10	+3	+4
India	14	13	14	0	−1

Source: Takashi Hikino and Alice H. Amsden, Staying Behind, Stumbling Back, Sneaking Up, Soaring Ahead: Late Industrialization in Historical Perspective, in W. J. Baumol, R. R. Nelson and E. N. Wolff (eds.), *Convergence of Productivity: Cross-National Studies and Historical Evidence* (New York: Oxford University Press, 1994), Table 11–2, 289

alternative outcomes were possible. Conversely, Taiwan, which was ranked eleventh in 1913, was ranked tenth in 1950, but by 1987 was ranked first among the countries. South Korea was ranked eighth in 1913, ninth in 1950, and by 1987 was ranked second. South Korea and Taiwan are two remarkable stories of late industrialization.

The important question is how did Taiwan become first among the countries in this analysis by 1987? The answer is by production. In many sectors, there was simply no production at all by Taiwanese firms in 1960. By 1990, just slightly over a generation later, because of industrialization Taiwan was a major global manufacturer for these items. In 1960, Taiwan produced no machine tools. In 1990, she produced 755,597 units. In 1960, the Taiwanese did not produce any televisions sets, motorcycles, telephones, radios, tape recorders, electronic calculators, integrated circuits, or electrical watches. By 1990, the production numbers were 3.7 million, 1 million, 14 million, 6 million, 8 million, 44 million, 2.7 billion and 5 million units respectively.

Such material enhancements of production were not just for consumer goods, but for capital goods as well, such as steel bars and ships. In 1960, Taiwan produced 200,528 tons of steel bars. In 1990, production was 11 million tons. In 1960, Taiwan produced 27,051 tons of shipping. In 1990, 1.2 million tons of shipping was produced. Late industrialization had a significant impact on Taiwan's economy.[6]

An initiative in Taiwan had been the setting-up of the Kaohsiung Export Processing Zone (KEPZ) in 1966. This brought foreign investment into Taiwan, and enabled small Taiwanese factories to start producing goods such as garments and radios. By the 1970s, factories in the zone employed 75,000 persons. This initiative, the first in Asia, enabled entrepreneurship democratization by permitting numerous small manufacturing enterprises to start businesses. In the 1970s, typical products made at the KEPZ were hairdryers, fishing poles, and sewing machines. In the 1980s, factories in the KEPZ made higher value items, such as cameras, microscopes, and golf clubs. Currently, semiconductor testing and packaging operations, and liquid crystal display manufacturing companies predominate. To democratize entrepreneurship, India emulated Kaohsiung's approach in developing an export processing zone. The Santa Cruz Electronics Export Processing Zone (SEEPZ) was set up in 1973, to manufacture items for the semiconductor industry and computer hardware. Businesses in these segments did not succeed. Very soon information technology services and software companies became the mainstay of SEEPZ. Thus, SEEPZ incubated India's information technology and software sector. Since then, the export processing zone (EPZ) model has been generalized to create special economic zones (SEZs), to enable cluster formation, rapid industrialization of specific areas, and to encourage entrepreneurship democratization.[7]

Reverting back to the inter-se rankings in Table 5.1, the Philippines had ranked third in 1913 and seventh in 1950. It was ranked eleventh in 1987. Clearly, countries could fall back drastically as other nations adopted a strategy of late industrialization and they did not. Indonesia had not been a late industrializing nation at all. In 1913, Indonesia was ranked ninth, eleventh in 1950, and eighth in 1987. In this pantheon of nations, India ranked fourteenth in 1913, thirteenth in 1950, and fourteenth in 1987. Very little Indian industrialization had happened. India's story was one of stagnation for most of the twentieth century. Some of the following materials deal with the Japanese late industrialization experiences. There are important lessons for India. Then, the South Korean and Taiwanese experiences will be discussed. Before that, the concept of late industrialization is described.

Definition of late industrialization

The late industrialization idea owes its popularity to Alexander Gerschenkron, who developed it to explain the emergence of once-backward states as economic powers.[8] His primary example was Germany and then Russia, from where he had emigrated. The concept has endured in explaining the emergence of many of today's modern Asian economies, such as Japan, South Korea, and Taiwan. The Asian countries' experiences are relevant in modern times, because they have achieved more than a four-fold increase in per capita incomes over a short period of two or fewer generations. In fact, the Japanese did it even more quickly, in less than one generation, between the early 1950s and early 1970s. Conversely, it took the United Kingdom, the United States, and Germany over three generations, beginning in the nineteenth century, to achieve the same level of per capita income growth.[9]

At the heart of the late industrialization concept is the idea that the industrialization trajectory depends on the relative backwardness of a country on the eve of take-off. Thus, the more backward a nation was, in relation to the others in its core group of comparative countries, the greater would be its consequent success in industrialization. By a series of eruptive spurts, a late industrializing country could transform a disadvantage into an important advantage. Also, the greater the success that such a country achieved with its industrialization, the larger would be the subsequent gap with its prior economic achievements. There would be a disruption with its past performance trends. Countries that were a distance behind the leaders would have the potential to make a larger leap, as the new technologies they would be acquiring would be possibly several generations more advanced than their existing stock of assets.

Technological differences would be a key reason why currently richer countries displayed high growth rates.[10] Now, the backward countries would be fortunate in having a larger range of available technologies to draw upon.[11] They could choose from the technologies where the developments had been particularly rapid.[12] Late industrialization also permitted a range of choices in institutional design, government policy, national economic structure, and organizational structure because of more examples to follow. These choices enabled backward countries to leapfrog existing arrangements, by designing something hybrid relevant to their local conditions.[13] By filling in the intrinsic knowledge and capabilities gap that existed, countries would be able to accelerate into a new trajectory of industrial development. Follower nations would tend to catch up faster, if they were initially more backward.[14]

There were three propellants for the new industrialization trajectory. These were operational efficiencies, scale economies, and human capital quality. A key feature of late industrialization was the emulative approach. The countries discussed, Japan, South Korea, and Taiwan, need not have innovated with respect to any of the factors driving the industrial revolution, but were adopters and assimilators of the associated functionalities. Take the case of Japan. Japan had made highly focused efforts to transfer organizational, managerial methods, production and distribution models from the West into her system. Just as the United States had imitated British technology in the first half of the nineteenth century, based on Yankee ingenuity,[15] industry in Japan adopted American practices[16] and crafted their economic organizations on the model of other successful enterprises.[17] Since knowledge is a public good,[18] as new scientific and managerial models seen to work elsewhere get known they are observed and applied elsewhere.[19] This emulation process changes human consciousness in a location far away.[20] The benefits of being a late industrializing nation using this approach were significant.

The key components of late industrialization

The initial focus in late industrialization was in the arena of firms' operations. To become world market leaders, firms from late industrializing countries needed to adopt important new production and operations management policies.[21] To propel the catch-up process at high speed, firms would have to rely on technological borrowing. A strategy of emulation of leaders would ensure that the conditions of a nation and its firms would improve significantly. The operations arena would be the strategic focus of firms competing on the basis of borrowed technology.[22] Hence, the primary learning would occur in the area of manufacturing and other operational activities by firms such that, even if the low wage cost advantage disappeared, there would be competitive advantage for firms in late industrializing nations because of other efficiencies.

During the second industrial revolution, neither Germany nor the United States industrialized by competing against Britain on the basis of low wages. German and American wages tended to exceed British wages, but both Germany and the United States were superior in efficiency compared to Britain because of manufacturing innovations that brought total costs down even if wage costs were higher.[23] Such an approach was followed by Japan early in its industrialization process. Initially, Japan did not compete versus other countries in the global market based on its expertise in iron and steel. The Japanese iron and steel industries, which were not in existence in 1868, produced 243,000 tons of iron and 255,000 tons of steel in 1913 for domestic use.[24]

The Japanese competed globally in textiles. By the 1930s, the Japanese textile industry had outpaced the British industry based in Lancashire.[25] Because growth in specific sectors was limited by the size of the small Japanese domestic market, exporting the manufactured items led Japanese manufacturers to reap scale economies and exploit the Kaldor–Verdoorn law.[26] This law suggests that a steady decline in average costs over time is driven by dynamic economies of scale. These are a function of cumulative past output and production experience. Nevertheless, such production experience will only have come from prior access to a large market, which would have triggered further investments.[27] A consequence of the Kaldor–Verdoorn law is that higher productivity generates higher growth. Textile firms were the first modern industrial enterprises in Japan.[28] The manifest Japanese economic strength in textiles led it to be the world leader in exports.[29] Actually, by the 1930s the level of Japanese wages was similar to that of Lancashire wages. Japan's superiority in textile sector performance was due to modern facilities and production processes and the organizational discipline that her firms displayed, as a consequence of the most modern managerial practices, and these enabled the textile industry to provide extremely strong competition to Britain.[30]

Britain had experienced similar pressures earlier from Germany and the United States, when these countries had embarked on the second industrial revolution in the latter half of the nineteenth century. These countries had not competed in the cotton textile sector, but in the iron and steel sector. Because Germany, and especially the United States, had changed the nature of manufacturing, among various other innovations, Britain experienced a "Made in Germany" scare in the 1880s, and the specter of an "American Invasion" in the 1890s, leading Randolph Churchill to state that the iron industry was "dead as mutton" and that the coal industry was "languishing."[31] Similarly, when South Korea and Taiwan began their late industrialization journey in the 1960s, with a foray into the textiles sector, they were lower in wage costs than Japan at that time. Yet, the facilities, processes, infrastructure, equipment and organizational discipline of the Japanese textile companies in the 1960s made it difficult for South Korean and Taiwanese textile companies to compete against the Japanese exclusively on the basis of lower wages.[32]

The Japanese experiences communicated to South Korea both the most efficient production techniques and seriousness about the manufacturing function.[33] This motivated a South Korean search for operational efficiencies, not just in the textiles sector but in all other sectors. Thus, in manufacturing firms of South Korea, there was a clear functional orientation toward production rather than toward sales or finance.[34] Specific policies assigned the best managers to the manufacturing facilities so as to improve process performance.[35] These investments would lead to the upgrading and deepening of capabilities. To become productive, capabilities were developed in three areas. The first area was in production, dealing with the skills involved in optimizing operation and output of established plants. This enabled the rapid commercialization of items based on existing frameworks. The second area was investment capability, dealing with the skills to execute new projects. The third area was innovation capability, dealing with the skills necessary to eventually create new products or processes.[36]

At least at the firm level, the initial push for efficiency came from firms investing more in new plant and equipment embodying knowledge and technology. The equipment was mostly imported. This enabled rapid knowledge acquisition, since, as Alice Amsden has remarked, "Capital goods are a major means through which both production processes and procedures are transmitted across countries."[37] As production experience, based on new and imported equipment, was gained, this process raised output per person and enhanced product quality. This, in turn, led to market expansion, both domestically and overseas.

With greater market exposure, firms become better at importing the best foreign technology or developing these domestically. Performance further increased because of process improvements, efficiencies, and quality, and set in motion a virtuous improvement cycle. In a sense, this dynamic process was a reflection of the spirit of the Kaldor–Verdoorn law, as practiced in Asia. In the late industrialization and catch-up process, the important emphasis was on large-scale production, based on capital intensive technologies, with a focus on the enhancement of the capital-to-labor ratio within firms. The enhancement of the capital-to-labor ratio, feasible in a larger firm, would speed up the rate of industrial transformation that the catch-up was expected to achieve.[38] The capital goods industries were initially targeted for the domestic market. Such industries could accumulate physical and embodied knowledge capital per person at a greater rate and faster pace. This capability acquisition process could, in turn, speed industrial growth.[39] As competencies developed, simultaneously consumer markets, especially those overseas, were targeted.

The large firm model was the model that Japan, to a large extent, and South Korea adopted. Nevertheless, there could also be an initial focus on small and medium sized firms that Taiwan based its late industrialization on. Eventually, however, to compete effectively at low cost, if a nation and her firms possessed just basic industry skills but not world-class technology skills, then firms needed to upgrade or improve their range of abilities. One key upgrading mechanism was the enhancement of a firm's scale or size of operations.[40] The issue of firm size or scale is controversial, as the benefits of scale are often thought illusory. A point has been made that the scale economies idea applies to plant size and not to firm size.[41] At the plant or factory level, scale economies lead to operational efficiency. At the firm level, scale economies lead to administrative efficiency. Scope economies also arise at the firm level. Scope economies imply the spreading of one set of costs over multiple product or service categories. They lead to the leverage of specific skills or competencies across a variety of products or services. As discussed earlier, the American industrial success was driven by the scale and scope economies that the large firms of the day engendered.

One of the often-cited examples is that of Meiji-era Japan, where, in a late industrializing economy, the conglomerates, called *zaibatsu*, led industrial growth. *Zaibatsu* firms were supposed to enjoy the benefits of scale and scope economies. There was a need for capital mobilization. Thus, *zaibatsu* attributes, such as internal financing, family wealth, family ownership, access to natural resources and to skilled labor, were beneficial. These characteristics allowed the *zaibatsu* firms to obtain equipment and technology from abroad, and employ both skilled foreigners and local Japanese staff.[42] Because the corporate organizational form was a late import into a feudal and agrarian society, there were no historical precedents holding back the introduction of new organizational forms, unlike in India where there had been a domestic way of doing business several thousand years old. Hence, Japanese corporations could begin on a large scale by a priori design, implement a complex hierarchy, adopt the latest refined tools of accounting and production, as developed in the United States and elsewhere, and adopt several organizational practices from other countries.[43]

Taiwan initially followed a small firm approach to late industrialization, as the record shows, with many small firms creating entrepreneurial clusters in the economy. Many small firms were also the first to introduce a foreign world class technology into the economy. Nevertheless, as second movers from a late industrializing nation, they needed to compete on the basis of low costs, requiring a different composition of skills, but they did not have the ability to do so. Typically, these small firms let larger Taiwanese firms take the lead in enhancing the scale of operations.[44] A lack of management skills did not permit the small firms to ramp up operations rapidly to global scale consistent with a low-cost market penetration strategy.

There were honorable exceptions, however, to this process. The most famous example is that of Taiwan Semiconductor Manufacturing Corporation, which started as a small firm in 1987.[45] By engaging in a contract manufacturing strategy for silicon chips for several years, for third parties across the world, the Taiwan Semiconductor Manufacturing Corporation benefited from substantial cumulative manufacturing volumes. Today, it has annual sales of over $13 billion. At the end of 2010, it was worth $60 billion on the stock market. Such manufacturing volumes enabled the Taiwan Semiconductor Manufacturing Corporation to eventually acquire the benefits of scale economies, and the benefits of learning arising from cumulative production. In doing so, the company created the concept of a silicon foundry. It is now one of the world leaders in the manufacture of silicon chips and semiconductors. Along with Intel and Texas Instruments, Taiwan Semiconductor Manufacturing Corporation is a world leader in the semiconductor sector today.

An important dilemma in the organization of economic and social activity is the trade-off between autonomy and control. The German sociologist Georg Simmel expressed the phenomenon as the conflict between individuality, creativity, and the subordination of the vital human spirit to a social structure.[46] The conflicts arise because of the economic necessities of efficiency, which a large-scale firm might engender, versus the psychological demands of autonomy that a small firm might allow owners to enjoy. These psychological demands celebrate individualism, cooperation, and democracy. This dichotomy has been a source of debate in the field of management for decades. Many, such as Paul Lawrence and Jay Lorsch, have highlighted the tension between differentiation and integration in organizations. The late C. K. Prahalad and Yves Doz explored the tension between global integration and local responsiveness in the context of developing international business strategies. The late Sumantra Ghoshal and Christopher Bartlett discussed the tension between autonomy and interdependence in the context of managing international business operations.[47]

In the context of the industrial structure of an economy, the tensions arise in the relationships between numerous small firms in an economy, a symptom that the economy is awash with entrepreneurship, and is booming, versus the existence of a limited number of large firms that are able to exploit scope and scale economies. The existence of a small number of large firms creates conditions for the possible generation and exercise of market power. Of course, this market power concern is also one issue that the late Joseph Schumpeter highlighted in his final seminal contributions, since large firms are the ones with the ability and cast-iron stomach to swallow the associated risks of innovation failure.[48] The large firms have the ability to efficiently coordinate and mitigate risks. Conversely, it is the small entrepreneurial firms that keep the innovation economy going. These firms are able to engender a process to generate the insights that might lead to the new combinations of resources emerging.[49]

The issue of small versus large, in relation to firm size, has never been and never will be resolved. The conclusions that are drawn for the late industrializing economies of Japan, South Korea, and Taiwan are based on relationships for small countries, with smaller populations, where an export-oriented industrialization strategy did necessitate large firm size as a required condition for industrial success. In addition, for an export-led strategy, high technology exports outpaced all others, with countries specializing in them succeeding better than others. Hence, firm size would also permit greater levels of technology acquisition. Conversely, the United States was a large country, with a large population and a large domestic market. American firms could, at one time anyway, domestically develop the capabilities to attain leading positions in world markets. Scale and scope economies were important in the making of American economic prowess in the late nineteenth century, but so was, concomitantly, the role of small firms which were central to economic life.[50]

The issue of small versus large firm size as a driver of industrial growth has been highlighted in the context of industrial structure by Michael Piore and Charles Sabel. They analyzed the forms of technological development that were in competition in the nineteenth century. These were craft production, based on machines and processes augmenting craftsmen's skills, and mass production, where the costs of making items were reduced by replacing human skill with machinery. To retain the creativity inherent in craft production, along with its associated autonomy, they suggested the approach of flexible specialization, enabling small firms to contribute as part of a bigger value chain where large firms would undertake the critical cost-reduction mass-production activities.[51]

The Indian economy is large and heterogeneous, much like that of the United States. There is now a vibrant industrial economy consisting of a multitude of firms which can exploit the large domestic market. There is, additionally, the possibility for large Indian firms to enjoy the benefits of global market opportunities. Therefore, the second feature of a late industrialization strategy, that firms were able to successfully exploit economies of scale, will warrant a reflection of the role of firm size as a component of a late industrialization strategy for a country like India. India has a dynamic entrepreneurial sector made up of numerous small firms. Many of these firms will be able to become flexible specialists, and contribute to the value-addition process undertaken by the larger firms within an industrial sector.[52]

Learning and human capital quality in late industrialization

Other than a focus on operations and scale, the interactive effect of the operations and scale factors led to learning in firms being very important in late industrialization.[53] The shop-floor changes that Japan, South Korea, and Taiwan generated might not have been the ones on which the first and second industrial revolutions could have been based. Nevertheless, for firms in a late industrializing nation, learning could inculcate a scientific and professional approach to changing the way business was managed and the thinking about the way business was conducted. An evocative statement on learning, capturing the scientific and professional approach, was made by M. Chiang, writing about China:

since we were knocked out by cannon balls, naturally we became interested in them, thinking that by learning to make them we could strike back. We could forget for the time being in whose name they had come, since for us common mortals to save our lives was more important than to save our souls. But history seems to move through very curious ways. From studying cannon balls, we came to mechanical inventions, which in turn led us to political reforms; from political reforms we began to see political theories, which led us again to the philosophies of the West. On the other hand, through mechanical invention we saw science, from which we came to understand scientific method and the scientific mind. Step by step we were led farther and farther away from the cannon ball – yet we came nearer and nearer to it.[54]

To visualize late industrialization as a process of large-scale capital investment would be wrong, since the assumption would then be that the extant technological knowledge was largely embodied in machinery and codified in blueprints and associated documents, and firms could utilize the technology simply by accessing the equipment and blueprints. This would, however, be difficult since only a small portion of the substantive knowledge needed to employ a technology would be codified. Much of such knowledge would be tacit, necessitating learning by doing.[55] Learning by doing was an important process, because of the need to move beyond learning via imitation, copying, reading, or observations. Hands-on practical experience would accrue when capability providers supported the firms in late industrializing countries via technical assistance. This process would lead to assimilation of capabilities, as opposed to mere skills acquisition.

Industrial learning has had a long history. Earlier, Germany assimilated foreign technologies. Similarly, Britain had absorbed knowledge from continental Europe, and Japan had assimilated knowledge from Britain.[56] In the British case, what was extensively borrowed was not just theoretical knowledge but also manual skills for workmen by training individuals via apprenticeship schemes.[57] Organizational learning is a capability to make operational the knowledge gained in conjunction with others. First, there is an additive effect, when an exchange of capabilities produces a new and derived capability. Second, there is a multiplicative effect, when an interaction of two or more persons results in something new. Third, there is the specialization effect, when increasing specialization of firms' resources requires cooperation as a way to mobilize complementary resources between individuals or firms.[58] Organizational and operational learning could effectively mobilize and motivate human effort under circumstances of highly constrained resources.[59] Hence, Japan and South Korea sent thousands of managers and engineers to foreign countries for training, and South Korea sent skilled shop-floor workers abroad to study from practices on the shop-floor elsewhere.[60]

Learning in firms is tacit, involving non-verbalized knowledge.[61] The tacit knowledge is internalized by workers, engineers, and managers. In general, workers, engineers, and managers have to possess good communications networks and be capable of coordinated action. It is important to retain the stock of knowledge in the firms and ensure it does not depreciate.[62] Since the core learning within firms occurs on the shop-floor, and the primary advantage that firms had was based on manufacturing competencies, worker motivation was very important so that, even if not formally educated, workers would use their intelligence, intuition, and experience.[63]

The third important dimension of late industrialization related to human capital quality. The best example comes from South Korea, where human capital enhancement policies were particularly strong and effective. As the tenor of the industrialization process changed, from the first industrial revolution to the second industrial revolution, and then to late industrialization, the identity of the key individual in each epoch also changed. In the first industrial revolution, the key man was an entrepreneur such as, say, James Watt. Then, the key man baton passed during the second industrial revolution to professional corporate managers in the United States. Finally, the key man baton was held by professional engineers in Asia during late industrialization.[64]

Based on the South Korean experiences, the late industrialization process demanded an exceptionally well-educated workforce.[65] This led to a changed composition of the staff in organizations, as the ratio of managers to production workers remained constant, but the ratio of engineers to administrative staff increased.[66] These processes flattened hierarchy, led to the diffusion of egalitarian norms throughout the organization, and to the development of a technical meritocracy. Even though the South Korean late industrialization process started because of cheap wage rates, as industrialization progressed wage rates became higher[67] so as to provide the necessary incentives for workers to meet customer deadlines, productivity targets, and quality targets. Hence, an efficiency wages model[68] was followed. This efficiency wages model was driven by the availability of a high-quality and well-educated workforce. Late industrialization success was predicated on learning. Thus, even if workers had come in with low levels of formal training, there were subsequent formal education programs for the workforce, and the apprenticeship of firms to foreign technical experts to build deep capabilities in organizational processes.[69] These practices changed human capital quality.

Similar policies had been followed by Japan, where the acquisition of scientific expertise was regarded as important from the outset by the government of the Meiji era, which took power in 1868 and lasted till 1912.[70] In 1918, there were five universities and 104 high schools in Japan. A decade later, there were 40 universities and 184 high schools, and in 1945 there were 48 universities and 342 high schools.[71] In 1974, 1.59 million Japanese undergraduate students were enrolled at national, public, or private universities. Of these, 21 percent, or 330,000 Japanese students, were studying engineering. Of the 46,000 advanced students, 33 percent were engineering students.[72]

An outcome of a national investment in engineering students, and overall national human capital quality, was the development of the key shipbuilding industry, which Japan dominated for several decades. This control of the world shipbuilding market was due to Japan's success in making improvements in welding techniques. Until this occurred, it was possible to build tankers of only about 50,000 deadweight tons. With the new welding techniques, it became possible to produce completely welded vessels of up to 500,000 deadweight tons.

At the same time, improvements in engines enabled these giant vessels to travel at high speeds. Michio Morishima has observed that "When a group-oriented society such as Japan has a total command of modern technology it can easily release a menacing productive energy, at times so great that it can be suicidal."[73] Clearly, high-quality education and proper organization could transform a nation positively, though a penchant for collective self-destruction would have to be monitored and controlled!

The case of Samsung in the global microwave market

The behavior of firms in late industrializing economies generates lessons for others to emulate. Let us take Samsung and its success in the global microwave industry. This represents a classis case of starting last and coming first, by an application of the principles that have so far been enunciated. In the late 1970s, the worldwide microwave oven industry was controlled by American and Japanese companies. South Korean companies had no presence in it at all. There was no domestic market in South Korea for microwave ovens. South Korea was a poor country.[74] Microwaves were not affordable.

In this milieu, in the mid 1970s, the electronics and appliances division of Samsung decided to enter the microwave oven business, in spite of not having a product. A Samsung vice president had visited the United States and become intrigued by microwave ovens. On returning home, his first thought was: Can we export microwave ovens if we make them? At that time, Samsung had no experience or skills in making microwave ovens.[75] A small laboratory was set up, and microwave ovens from other companies were taken apart. After a year of 80 hour per week intensive product development, the first oven blew up and the insides melted. There was another year of rebuilding, readjusting, and redesign. There were additional failures. Nevertheless, the example of Japan danced before the South Korean product developers' eyes.

The Japanese had harvested a windfall when the world market for microwave ovens leapt from 600,000 units to 2 million units per year. Today, of course, that world market size is close to 50 million units or more annually. The growth in urbanization and construction in China and India alone generates a substantial demand. After perseverance, the South Korean engineers were able to make an oven. It was a crude item that actually worked. In spite of the oven not being up to world market standards, the division was given the manufacturing green light because Samsung's pre-eminent objective was production.[76] By the middle of 1979, the world market was 5 million ovens. Samsung was able to make about two ovens per day. In spite of a lack of orders, Samsung continued with production. Having asked the question of where customer value would come from, they simultaneously targeted quality and cost as attributes to yield maximum value in the market. Samsung's managers and South Korean policy makers realized that the country's low-cost wage advantage would soon run out. Then, what was the source of advantage? The answer was that corporate and national advantage came from manufacturing capability.

After small initial orders, of a few hundred ovens, from Panama, the American retail giant J. C. Penney placed an order for Samsung microwaves, though only for a few thousand, to be marketed under the J. C. Penney label. This contract manufacturing gave the Samsung microwave operations enough volume to attain learning economies. The exposure to another market also forced Samsung to retool the production lines, so that the final oven met customer tastes in the United States. Conversely, United States firms would ship a product made to American tastes and standards overseas and expect customer to buy it.[77] Simultaneously, by keeping delivery dates sacrosanct, Samsung enforced discipline in implementation so as to turn a primitive craft-style assembly room into a modern efficient factory.[78] The original J. C. Penney order had yielded a satisfied customer, and more orders. By 1981, Samsung was making 100,000 ovens annually. But, this was still a tiny percentage of the world market. At this stage, Samsung evaluated their cost structure, found it was high and began scouting to make all components themselves. The leading American manufacturer of the magnetron, the heart of a microwave oven, Amperex Corporation, was going out of business in the United States due to Japanese competition. Samsung transplanted the entire Amperex plant to South Korea to make ovens to ship back to American customers.[79]

All the time, Samsung had been putting together the largest pool of engineers in South Korea. The structure of plant operations was that for every 500 workers, there were 150 engineers and 10 managers. A similar-sized typical American plant might have 350 workers, 50 engineers and 75 managers. The Samsung investment was in workers and engineers. That is where the manufacturing capabilities resided and where learning took place. Such an approach enhanced egalitarianism and a sense of pride, and created a technology talent meritocracy. By 1983, the leading American manufacturer, GE, was finding Japanese competitive pressures too much to bear and began scouting for production outsourcing. Eventually, though skeptical, they had no option but to place a contract with Samsung on cost grounds. By 1989, Samsung had become one of the world's largest mass manufacturers of microwave ovens, manufacturing over 4 million units annually. Samsung had attained world scale. It had expanded a factory producing a few prototypes to one containing several mass-production lines.

When consultants compared Samsung's and GE's costs structures they were staggered. The typical oven cost GE $218 to make. Of this, $8 was direct labor cost and $30 was for overheads. GE's material handling costs per oven was $4 and central management costs were $10. Thus, management costs were $52 per oven.[80] The typical oven cost Samsung $155 to make; $0.63 was direct labor cost and $0.73 was for overheads. Samsung's material handling costs per oven was $0.12 and central management costs were $0.02. Thus, Samsung's management costs were $1.50 per oven. Eventually, by 1985 GE stopped the production of all microwave ovens. Henceforth, all its GE branded products were outsourced from South Korea. Samsung became the world's largest manufacturer of microwave ovens in its own name as well as for others.

The classic conclusion is that there is no production and no productivity associated with physical factors of production, such as raw materials and machines, unless there is also human skill, ingenuity, and competence applied. Within the black box of a firm is the manufacturing black box. Within that manufacturing black box is the black box of human capital competencies. Human ingenuity and skills are tacit. These elements were assumed to be the missing link in creating economic wealth by early writers on political economy, such as John Stuart Mill, Charles Babbage, and Alfred Marshall. For John Stuart Mill, a primary productiveness factor was the skill and knowledge of laborers or of those who directed their labor. The cooperation and combined actions of labor were important.[81] For Charles Babbage, the implementation of improved techniques and processes was important.[82] Alfred Marshall laid emphasis on industrial training, use of machinery, and economies of scale.[83] These basic, almost banal, lessons were applied by Samsung.

For countries such as India, the simple lessons from firm strategy, in late industrialization, still hold good a generation later. A focus on operations and scale, engendering learning, a focus on creating a talent pool of engineers and workers, and the creation of a technology meritocracy, are fundamental. A strategy of market capture, via original equipment manufacturing (OEM) for outside buyers, acquiring total business capabilities, and then going for own label production to spread the Samsung brand name, meant sequencing the activity of production first and then sales would follow. This example is still valid. Say's law still applies in the twenty-first century. Supply creates its own demand.

The role of the state in late industrialization

There was also commensurate involvement of the state in late industrialization. Whether it was late industrialization based on small firms or large firms, the state had a role in encouraging a favorable policy climate such that large business groups, such as Keiretsus in Japans and Chaebols in South Korea, or the small and medium sized firms in Taiwan, were supported.[84] In fact, Alexander Gerschenkron has argued that the state was important for late industrialization. He used the Russian example, where nineteenth-century industrialization was dominated by the interests of the state.[85] The Russian state of the 1890s assumed the role as the main agent of industrialization by financing railroads and large industrialization projects.[86]

Similarly, in Japan the Meiji government had founded state-operated industrial enterprises, since these were regarded as important for nation building. The Meiji government had been formed by members of the intelligentsia and warrior class, and management of the state enterprises was in the hands of these same people. These enterprises were large factories, requiring the organization of numerous workers. Thus, early Japanese industrialization commenced with a nucleus of government factories run according to a collective ideology.[87] In addition, from the 1880s onward, investments in infrastructure, such as roads, railways, harbors, and telegraphs, grew at the rate of 10 percent per annum.[88]

In Taiwan, initial semiconductor capabilities were acquired by a public sector research agency, the Industrial Technology Research

Institute (ITRI). One of its laboratories entered into a technology transfer agreement with the American firm, RCA, in 1976, to acquire semiconductor fabrication and design capabilities based on obsolete technology. This served as training ground for ITRI, which then diffused the skills to the private sector in 1980 by spinning off a new company, the United Microelectronics Corporation.[89] In 1986, ITRI entered into an agreement with Philips to form a new venture, giving Philips new fabrication capacity and privileged access to the Taiwanese market. In order to avoid competing directly with Philips, a new company established in 1987, the Taiwan Semiconductor Manufacturing Corporation, started producing only third-party chips. Today, Taiwan Semiconductor Manufacturing Corporation is one of the world's largest semiconductor companies. Hence, government support can create a global powerhouse in less than a generation.

There has been a revival of the big push model, whereby government can play a major role in enabling firms to industrialize rapidly, leading to late industrialization of the nation. The influential writing on Japan, by the late Chalmers Johnson,[90] and on South Korea by Alice Amsden,[91] has stressed the role that governments could play. Directly or indirectly, governments could get interventions right and propel a big push.[92] To be successful, a big push would need investment by the government in companies and subsidies and other incentives to private firms. To accelerate the volumes needed, to generate the economies of scale and learning, firms might need support. In heavy industrial sectors, such as steel and petrochemicals, the state-owned enterprises could play a central role.[93] A cohesive-capitalist state with a pro-capitalist stance could make appropriate interventions to facilitate the supply of capital, labor, and technology.[94]

In a study, the World Bank has described the policies of governments that have led to the development of the heavy and chemical industries in South Korea and Taiwan. The use of government levers has supported strategic industries' growth. The levers were tax incentives, grants for detailed engineering studies, subsidized public services, and preferential financing. The strategic industries were steel, petrochemicals, nonferrous metals, shipbuilding, electronics, and machinery. The support led to radical alterations in the industrial structure. The first three upstream sectors provided supply of inputs for further processing by downstream industries. The three downstream sectors enabled countries such as South Korea and Taiwan to crack world markets.[95]

The political psychology of late industrialization

As the Samsung case has shown, manufactured exports, it is true, accelerated the acquisition and the mastery of internationally acceptable production and marketing skills as well as the enhancement of the capabilities and cognitive skills of the labor force in firms and in industry generally. Yet, government policies alone cannot explain what the motivations were for a company like Samsung to go from no production of microwave ovens in 1979 to over 4 million units a decade later, to being a top five producer in the world today.

What were the psychological compulsions leading Yun Soo Chu, the Samsung original product designer, to work absurd hours and be called mad by his wife? Inside the black box of the firm are the functional black boxes, such as manufacturing and product development. Inside each such functional black box are further collections of black boxes that are the collective of a firm's human capital. Going deeper, within each human being is the black box of the mind where visceral desires and motives to drive human progress emerge. As a design engineer, Yun Soo Chu may have been professionally obsessive. What drives countries? What is the catharsis that generates amazing outcomes from firms in countries advancing on a late industrialization path?

The late I. G. Patel, in referring to Japan, had raised several speculative questions. He had wondered:

Why was Japan so successful? It was not easy to explain. It could not be that Japan was not colonized. Neither was Thailand. Why were Japanese savings rates high and its propensity to import low, which facilitated growth? Why was Japanese labor ready to adjust and cooperate rather than agitate? It could not be coercion or compulsion, coercive regimes were a dime a dozen then.[96]

There are several possible explanations, none of which is complete in itself. Based on its erstwhile heritage, the Japanese had assessed that industrial might equated with military might and that if they did not modernize they would be colonized.[97] The Meiji Revolution had been a revolution by the intelligentsia and a warrior class. The role of landlords and merchants, who constituted the main wealthy elite, was also an important factor for raising capital, and Japanese businessmen came from both Samurai and merchant groups.[98] Given a rich mélange of social groups in place, in which the erstwhile Samurai dominated, the Meiji government advocated a rich country and a strong army policy.[99] Since it was not possible for Japan to strengthen military capacity by relying on foreign technology alone, they had to make scientific progress themselves and develop new techniques within the country.[100]

The late Mancur Olson pointed out that economic growth could be held up by old vested interests.[101] The destruction of the old feudal social system of Tokugawa Japan in the late nineteenth century created a gateway through which members of other social groups could enter industry. Thus, it was the sheer will of the reformers of the Meiji Revolution that eliminated these interests and brought about Japanese industrialization.[102] Puritanism, associated with the Meiji revolution, was supposed to have achieved a mindset in which the effort of labor was to be performed as if it were an absolute end in itself. Entrepreneurs, too, were to view the making of profits as a divinely ordained occupation. In addition, the associated frugality meant opposition to consumption, and capital formation was carried out through frugality.[103]

All of the above explanations are necessary and important. None of the above explanations is sufficient. Another observation by Mancur Olson was that extremely rapid growth follows wars or other revolutions. Destruction permits new leadership to emerge.[104] This line of thinking can be expanded to suggest a deeper psychological explanation. Some extreme humiliation can lead to a national catharsis that then energizes the political will of the people and generates powerful economic forces to transform a nation. Disturbing events lead to powerful reactions.[105] The transformation is akin to a phase transition that Philip Ball suggests drives the physics of society. Suddenly, things happen all at once, leading to a complete break in existing social symmetry.[106] It is the occurrence of a tipping point. Things are never the same again.[107]

For Japan, the dropping of the atom bombs in August 1945 on Hiroshima and Nagasaki proved to be that point of catharsis. Driven by a national humiliation, at that time the Japanese vowed that they would get even with the United States. Militarily there was no option. But through production and exports of consumer goods, eventually it could control the levers of the American economy.[108] Thus, the maximum growth that Japan achieved in its contemporary history, as the data show, occurred between the early 1950s, after the American occupation forces had left Japan, and the early 1970s. By the 1970s, Japan was an economic might of global consequence. Centuries earlier, the fall of the Byzantine Empire, and the sacking of Constantinople in 1453, had massively influenced the renaissance in Europe.[109]

Is a similar explanation available for South Korea? South Korea had emerged in the 1950s, after decades of colonial repression by the Japanese and a brutal war that led to the division of the country. These were the cathartic events. Taiwan had experienced the 1949 Communist takeover of mainland China and the expulsion of the Kuomintang to Formosa, which renamed itself Taiwan. Perhaps the Taiwanese cathartic event was not the one that occurred in 1949, but the 1971 expulsion as a permanent member of the Security Council of the United Nations, and from the United Nations itself. The pragmatic Taiwanese then set out to become one of the world's economic powers. All three countries, Japan, South Korea, and Taiwan, were driven by a sense of urgency. Catch-up was important; but, forging ahead was even more important.

In 1905, the partition of Bengal provided an incentive for indigenous industrialization to commence, but India remained under British rule till 1947. After 1947, many lessons from Japan were adopted. Yet, Indian industry and the Indian economy did not take off. What was the cathartic event for India, propelling her into a new trajectory of economic progress?

The 1991 economic crisis, now 20 years ago, had reduced India's foreign exchange reserves to two weeks' supply of essential items. Importers had to deposit double the value of their imports in a bank before being allowed to buy items. Oil was running out. Because of the 1991 Gulf War, Indian workers' remittances had stopped. Inflation was extremely high.[110] On January 18, 1991, India's foreign exchange reserves were only ₹1,666 crores, not even enough for a day's business activity for a country of India's size. A loan of ₹3,200 crores was negotiated with the International Monetary Fund.[111] The Reserve Bank had to mortgage its gold with the Bank of England, which was the International Monetary Fund's agent, before it could acquire any further foreign exchange.[112] The Indian gold reserves had to be physically deposited as collateral in London. India was perceived as a likely defaulter of its international obligations.[113] Only then could she raise money.

Indians possess the biggest store of gold and silver in the world, in people's personal holdings.[114] Gold is important to the Indian psyche.

In Indian culture, the woman of the house treasures her gold jewelry as her soundest asset as well as the symbol of her status.[115]

The sight of armored trucks carrying India's gold to the airport, at the dead of night, to be sent out of the country, was visible to Bombay's vast nocturnal public. In spite of the best possible security precautions, word soon leaks out when an event like this takes place. The jungle drums of Bombay relayed the message all along the route, from Marine Drive, Haji Ali, Worli, Dadar, Mahim, and along the Western Express Highway, that India was in serious trouble. The route from the Reserve Bank of India headquarters, at Shahid Bhagatsingh Marg, to the international airport is 25 kilometers long. A number of people saw the armored trucks on their journey. The rest of India knew, from the newspapers the next day, that India's gold had flown abroad to a once-hated colonial master, even if the Bank of England was merely acting as an agent for the international financial community. This event was a psychological trigger that changed the context for economic activity in India and was one of the catalysts for the late, late industrial revolution to commence in real earnest.

The specter of India again becoming enslaved to foreign powers was a trauma that changed the Indian mindset to aspire to progress and wealth. Hopefully, the subsequent policy decisions and firms' strategies of the last 20 years will result in India's late, late industrialization efforts displaying the same outcomes that countries such as Japan, South Korea, and Taiwan have shown. What is vital is a sense of urgency that, first, drives the catch-up process and then propels the forging-ahead dynamic. If the visible upward trajectory in India's share of the world economic product keeps accelerating, perhaps one day India will regain its global economic stature. The next several chapters let us assess how this might happen.

6 | *Democratizing entrepreneurship*

The tale of a nationalist entrepreneur

This chapter commences with a story. The Bengalis had been inadequate in industrial capabilities, but were not short of nationalist spirit. The first technology entrepreneur in India, motivated by a spirit of national uplift, was Praphulla Chandra Ray, whose achievements we have seen in Chapter 4. On the western side of the country, a remarkable man with nationalist spirit, named Walchand Hirachand, deserves approbation as an inspirational doyen of India's manufacturing sector in the period prior to the Second World War.[1] His approach, in the first half of the twentieth century, displays the characteristics of a sense of urgency, and an unwillingness to kowtow to other countries' interests. The latter factor was a psychological component behind India's tipping-point in 1991.

Born in 1882, Walchand Hirachand belonged to a Gujarati family that had settled in Phaltan, in the Satara district of the Bombay presidency, in the nineteenth century. The family had dropped the surname of Doshi. Phaltan was an important center of cloth, oil, rice, and mango trades. Today, it is an important agriculture center in western Maharashtra. Walchand Hirachand's father, Hirachand Nemichand, had to give up school and enter business at the age of 14 because his own father had suddenly died. In a decade, he had attracted the attention of Morarjee Goculdas, a textile industry pioneer of Bombay, who had started the Sholapur Spinning and Weaving Mills. By the age of 30, Hirachand Nemichand, who was an agent of several textile mills, had entered the banking sector and accumulated a fortune in bond trading.

A sequence of family deaths also led Walchand Hirachand to give up studies and take to business, though at the later age of 21, and for some time he evaluated various possibilities. In 1904, through a serendipitous meeting with a railway contractor who had contacts but

153

no cash, he entered business as a railway contractor to build lines. One of his early construction projects, the harbor branch for the suburban services of the Central Railway in Bombay, is in existence and intensively used today. Within a decade he had established himself as a railway contractor and as a military contractor of repute in Bombay and western India.

A chance meeting in a train, in 1919, with a senior executive of a British company had alerted him to the availability of a hospital ship that India's princes, led by the Maharaja of Gwalior, Madhavrao Scindia, had donated to the Great War. Since the war was over, the ship was to be sold as surplus. Moving quickly, and articulating a nationalist vision for the enterprise, Walchand Hirachand persuaded Narottam Morarjee, of Morarjee Goculdas and Company, Kilachand Devchand and Lallubhai Samaldas to launch the Scindia Steam Navigation Company in March 1919. Since the Scindia Steam Navigation Company was a direct head-to-head competitor of Peninsular and Oriental Steam Navigation Company, then the leading shipping line between India and Britain (today a subsidiary of Maersk), the competition was brutal. The Peninsular and Oriental Steam Navigation Company was controlled by James MacKay, the founder of the Inchcape group, who had, after retirement from India, become a member of the Council of India in London.[2] The British company used the British government's good offices to enforce its retaliatory tactics. These tactics were to enforce British shipping monopoly in India's coastal shipping trade as well as in international trade.

Over the years, and several incidents later between Walchand Hirachand, an aggressive nationalist, and James MacKay, an unrepentant imperialist, the Scindia Steam Navigation Company was able to establish a position as a domestic business in India's coastal shipping trade. Meanwhile, the railway contracting firms had been bought out by the Tata group in 1920, and renamed the Tata Construction Company. The business implemented several irrigation, railway, water supply, and electricity projects in and around Bombay. Over the years, several other businesses, such as concrete pipes, were added. After the death of Dorab Tata, the Tatas, however, divested their share and the business was renamed as the Premier Construction Company. Walchand Hirachand had also started the Hindustan Construction Company, which later absorbed Premier Construction Company, and that company is still alive today. It implemented the new Bandra–Worli

Sea Link, in Bombay, and is developing the township of Lavasa, in the Poona district of Maharashtra.

Walchand Hirachand's major initiatives, as a nationalist entrepreneur in the manufacturing sector, were the Hindustan Shipyards, Hindustan Aeronautics, and Premier Automobiles. The first two are now state-owned undertakings. The third company has passed into history. Nevertheless, they were the foundations of manufacturing of items other than textiles and steel in India. The shipyards saga commenced after the passage of the Government of India Act of 1935, by which time it was clear that soon India would be self-governing. Walchand Hirachand had established a shipping concern. He explored setting up a Calcutta shipyard, but conditions were unwelcoming. Thereupon, he chose Vishakapatnam as a site in 1939 and a shipyard was established there by 1941. At that time, he realized that many opportunities lay for India's industrialization because of the Second World War, and India's role as a strategic supply platform.[3] The entry of Japan into the war in 1941, and the bombing of Vishakapatnam by the Japanese in 1942, however, forced a shift of the yard to Mazagon in Bombay. After the war ended, the yard was revived. But, in 1952 Hindustan Shipyards was taken over by government as it was in financially poor health. Also, shipbuilding had become a key industry to be placed in public sector hands.

At the outbreak of the Second World War, Walchand Hirachand had gone to the United States to investigate possible American collaborations for an automobile venture. Returning via San Francisco, he struck up an acquaintance with a fellow passenger, the head of a large American aircraft manufacturing corporation with facilities in China. Seeing air transport as a logical extension of sea travel, during the flight Walchand Hirachand used the very long journey time of those days to strike a deal with the American businessman to manufacture aircraft for the war effort in India. During the layovers, he sent off numerous telegrams. By the time he arrived in India, government had become interested in the project.

The British government in Whitehall tried to scuttle the project because Indian firms were not considered capable enough to manufacture combat aircraft.[4] The Mysore state, which had been served by exceptionally able administrators such as Albion Rajkumar Banerji ICS, M. Visvesvaraya, and Mirza Ismail, had shown interest in the project. They donated land at Bangalore, and Hindustan Aircraft was set up in 1940. Just eight months later, its first product, a trainer aircraft, was flight tested. The entry of Japan into the war, and the emergence of India as a frontline state, changed the situation. Hindustan Aircraft was taken over by government in 1942. The seed of an ambitious undertaking 70 years ago is now the core of India's potentially burgeoning aeronautics industry. Hindustan Aeronautics, as Hindustan Aircraft became, now has the capability to manufacture sophisticated Sukhoi 30 fourth-generation fighter aircraft. Hindustan Aeronautics will be the company to manufacture the advanced fifth-generation fighter aircraft, which India has contracted to develop jointly with Russia, to be based on the Sukhoi T-50 fighter plane.

One great venture of Walchand Hirachand that continued into the late twentieth century was Premier Automobiles. Negotiations on this venture had been the initial purpose of his trip to the United States in 1939, where Chrysler had been interested in providing the technology for an automobile manufacturing unit of 12,000 units per year. Again, however, the war intervened to stall this venture, and production did not commence till after 1945. The British government then stalled the venture, because they feared substantial competition from India in automobile production after the end of the Second World War. Shortage of shipping capacity to supply the efforts of the combat in the Pacific had led to an arrangement for General Motors to set up an assembly plant in India. Chevrolet cars and trucks were imported as completely knocked-down (CKD) kits and put together in India.[5]

Walchand Hirachand's automotive venture commenced making Dodge and Plymouth cars in India in the late 1940s. It continued to do so till the late 1950s. Model changes in the Bombay plant kept up with model changes made in Detroit till the 1956 model year. The production of all Dodge and Plymouth cars in India ceased in 1959. The Dodge Kingsway Custom and Deluxe models and the Plymouth Savoy model were made in India. The Premier Automobiles facility also manufactured the Chrysler and De Soto makes in the late 1940s. These makes were dropped in the early 1950s. In my childhood, one could see numerous Dodge Kingsway and Plymouth Savoy cars on Bombay roads. Bombay had a unique taxi system of "small" taxis, which were Morris Minor and Hillman Minx cars. Then there were the "big" taxis, which were the Plymouth and Dodge D24 cars of 1947 or 1948 vintage, and Chevrolet Fleetmaster cars that had been assembled in India in large numbers. In the past, Model T Fords had been assembled in India from CKD kits.[6] Many black and white movies of that era depict scenes in which such cars are to be found in the yellow and black taxi livery. The Chevrolet Fleetmaster cars were to be the mainstay of India's government car fleets till the early 1970s. Dodge, Fargo, and Chevrolet trucks were noticed all over India.

In the mid 1950s, Premier Automobiles entered into an agreement with Fiat Motors of Italy to manufacture the Fiat 1100 model in India. Manufacture of these cars continued from 1955 till 2000. Increased production commenced from the 1959 model year. Model changes in India kept pace with model changes in Italy till the 1964 model year, when the Fiat 1100D was introduced. Thereafter, the model changes stopped. Premier Automobiles' agreement with Fiat of Italy ceased in 1972, but the cars were made in Kurla, a Bombay locality, till the end of the twentieth century. Even today, about 30,000 of Bombay's taxis are Fiat 1100D descendants, all in terminally ramshackle condition. It is a good idea, before embarking on a journey in one of these ubiquitous Premier taxis, to ensure that the doors shut and ask the driver if his brakes work. During Bombay's monsoon, it is imperative to ensure that the windshield wipers operate, and the speed does not exceed 16 kilometers per hour. Journeys above that speed, in the rain, are challenging for the nervous!

Only Hindustan Construction Company, with a record of firsts in constructing iconic structures, such as the Bandra–Worli Sea Link, and the world's longest dam, is now in business, along with a food products company named Ravalgaon Industries, where farming activities were corporatized on a large scale, and Walchandnagar Industries, a heavy engineering concern. Walchand Hirachand's pioneering of large-scale organization brought modern approaches to non-traditional areas, such as shipping, shipbuilding, construction, aircraft manufacture, and automobile manufacture, in India.

Industrial policy in India from 1947 to 1991

While Walchand Hirachand's tale is inspirational, industrial policy in post-independence India might have had the opposite effect on entrepreneurs' motivations. Covering the entire pantheon of the political economy of India's industrial development in the post-independence period till 1991 is challenging. The subject deserves a separate book. I deal with the main points leading to the reforms of 1991.

The genesis of India's post-independence industrial policy lies in the work of a Reconstruction Committee that the then Governor General in Council, Field Marshal Archibald Wavell, had set up. In 1944, a separate Department of Planning and Development had been set up, with Ardeshir Dalal as member-in-charge. Ardeshir Dalal had led the production of the unofficial Bombay Plan. Officially, the Bombay Plan was translated by the Department of Planning and Development into an Industrial Policy Statement in 1945, setting out a scheme for industrial development. The two documents are virtually identical. The seeds of India's industrial policy for the next half century are contained in this statement. The statement anticipated state involvement and regulation, with 20 industries of national importance to be administered by government. The government would regulate industry by licensing new capacity, and by investments in return for management involvement. Certain industries, such as ordnance, public utilities, and railways, would be nationalized. Other industries would be state-owned if private investment capital was not forthcoming.[7]

Government regulation of private industry was justified to ensure balance of production, suitable location, equitable labor conditions, product quality, and prevention of profiteering.[8] By 1945, government was also anxious to ensure that Indians, and not British capital, benefited from a more active policy of industrial development. Government also proposed that foreign capital only hold minority interests in Indian companies in key sectors such as iron and steel, electrical and heavy engineering, machine tools, heavy chemicals, fertilizers, and pharmaceuticals. Whitehall found the proposals unacceptable and rejected them.[9] Then, of course, all issues were subordinated to succeeding political events.

Independent India's first Industrial Policy Resolution was issued in April 1948. It stated that India was to have a mixed economy in which private capital had an important place. Full state ownership was to be imposed on the railways, ordnance, and atomic energy sectors. In six sectors, coal, iron and steel, aircraft manufacture, shipbuilding, telephone and telegraphs, and minerals, the government could start new ventures if it wished.[10] Independent India had to struggle with the Herculean tasks of partition, with its associated communal carnage, refugee rehabilitation efforts, transition to a national administration, and integration of the princely states. These were completed by 1950.[11] Then, attention turned to building India. The First Five-Year Plan began in 1951. As the late I. G. Patel had put it: "the First Five-Year Plan is like the Mahabharat: there is nothing in the Indian economy which does not find a reflection in the Plan and there is nothing in the Plan which is also not found in Indian reality."[12] The industrial licensing framework was formalized, under the Industries Development and Regulation (IDR) Act of 1951, to be the principal instrument for coordinating and controlling investments in industry. It controlled entry, expansion of capacity, technology, output mix, capacity, location, and import content.[13]

India's planning approaches and economic strategy of the times were, incidentally, fully in step with prevailing fashion. The Marshall Plan's big push for European reindustrialization was contemporaneous. The idea of planning was an American export, based on the success that the techniques, particularly operations research, had achieved during the Second World War. India's planners were advised by a team from the Massachusetts Institute of Technology, some of whom were still to be found in Calcutta in the early 1970s, and by Gosplan, the Soviet Union's economic planning agency.[14] Numerous overseas economists spent time pontificating in India. Of these, the late Milton Friedman had come to India in 1955. He tried educating Indian politicians and bureaucrats about the virtues of private enterprise, but gave up when he realized his arguments fell on deaf ears.[15] Milton Friedman wrote of his experiences that India was "socialist in its orientation, its intellectual atmosphere having been shaped largely by Harold Laski of the London School of Economics, and his fellow Fabians."[16]

The plans for a state-dominated economy found approbation in Britain, where the post-war Labour government had in Stafford Cripps, a key figure in prior Indian independence negotiations, a major economic statesman. Britain had also nationalized far more of its industrial base than India.[17] A commitment to socialism, to foster growth and development, had become a central idea in government policy. The commitment was endorsed by the Lok Sabha, in 1954, and by the Congress Party in its Avadi session in 1955.[18] To meet the goals of development, heavy industrialization became the dominant strategy. This was driven by a strong modernization imperative, motivated by nationalism and a desire to achieve great power status. The modernization strategy adopted by India emulated past Japanese approaches, given Japan's track record in implementing such an approach.[19] The Second Five-Year Plan, from 1956 to 1961, was based on the idea of capital intensive and rapid heavy industrialization. This was to be led by the public sector. The state-owned firms would build the key industries to control the commanding heights of a new modern industrial economy for India, leaving the private sector to play a complementary role in the mixed economy.[20]

A new Industrial Policy Resolution was issued in 1956. This resolution referred to the socialist pattern of society as the objective of social and economic policy.[21] During the Second Plan, state-owned firms mainly invested in heavy industry as private businesses did not, or could not, become involved. The late I. G. Patel wrote:

> At the other end, I do not think Indian industry was ready then to undertake large projects like steel plants or fertilizer plants. I do not remember great enthusiasm even among the Tatas for substantial expansion of their steel production. JRD's Air India was not nationalized. He was too happy to hand it over to the Government, as he was to hand over the Tata Institute of Fundamental Research and the Tata Cancer Hospital. Sir Biren Mukherjee, despite all the support of the World Bank, was not able to manage his modest steel plant. Let us not forget that even the great and the good in Indian private industry had little access to world capital markets.[22]

From a government perspective, by the 1960s the sheer momentum of a system of administrative controls had fed on itself and created an administrative monster.[23] The late S. Bhoothalingam, a distinguished civil servant,[24] found that as the controlling authorities gained experience, the range and depth of regulation were extended well beyond the initial objective of regulating only the growth of industrial capacity. Power was centralized, with the administration becoming rigorous, rigid, and detailed.[25] The judgment of government and planners, on questions such as strategy, size, equipment, processes, and physical locations of units, prevailed over entrepreneurs' judgment.[26] The attitude adopted was that entrepreneurs were pirates and not patriots. Philip Spratt, a British Communist leader settled in India, becoming a pro-market commentator, wrote that government tended to treat the businessman "as a criminal who has dared to use his brains independently of the state to create wealth and give employment."[27]

The process of extracting a judgment or resources from government was akin to swimming in a sea of treacle. The approach of government was not constructive, as in East Asian countries,[28] but constrictive.

The regulatory and control system was based on the predilections of engineers and not economists.[29] Engineers viewed issues from a fixed-coefficients point of view, based on linear production relationships, but were unable to factor in issues of increasing returns and externalities, which the economists would have. It was as if Robert Stephenson was in charge of India's industrial economy, and not Adam Smith. The Adam Smith in question would be at least the person for whom markets and production were important, and the author of the idea of division of labor being limited by the extent of the market, if not the Adam Smith for whom moral sentiments actually mattered much more.

The creation of a protected domestic market, where entry was restricted by a complex and long-drawn-out system of licensing, import control, and capital issues control, thus materially benefited established entrepreneurs.[30] They diverted firms' resources and managerial attention towards unproductive rent-seeking activities that were stimulated by the controls.[31] Rent-seeking firms were profitable but unproductive, as expected.[32] Pre-emption of capacity by existing industrialists in the Udyog Bhavan inner circle, the building where the Ministry of Industrial Development was located, became the norm. Between the mid 1960s and mid 1970s, such capacity pre-emption was chronic. It led to the existence of huge unused manufacturing capacity. Such unutilized capacity, in turn, led to a drop in industrial growth.[33]

The late I. G. Patel wrote:

But Gandhi, Prasad and Patel died early. And Rajaji was forsaken by his business friends who initially supported the Swatantra party but soon abandoned it when they discovered that bribing politicians to get the licenses they wanted was easier than acquiring political power with a view to changing economic policy and towards greater freedom and competition. Those in business who now proclaim loudly the stupidity or cupidity of earlier political leaders should also examine the behavior of early business leaders. They wanted not competition and efficiency but to preserve and enlarge their own turf.[34]

Among the founders of the Federation of Indian Chambers of Commerce and Industry (FICCI) in the late 1930s were G. D. Birla, Purshotamdas Thakurdas, Lala Shri Ram, Kasturbhai Lalbhai, and M. C. T. Muthiah Chettiar. Among those in the group that had produced the 1944 Bombay Plan were G. D. Birla, Purshotamdas Thakurdas,

Lala Shri Ram, Kasturbhai Lalbhai, and J. R. D. Tata. Odd, that similarity of names! Of course, it could be pure and simple coincidence.

Capacity pre-emption had unforeseen effects on strategy and industrial structure. In the automotive industry, there were two principal manufacturers: Premier Automobiles, making the Fiat derivate, and Hindustan Motors, making the Morris Oxford derivative. Each firm had a manufacturing capacity of 25,000 cars. The chief executive's primary job at Hindustan Motors was to ensure that politicians received their Ambassador cars. There were no sales, marketing, or service functions, because none were needed, and no concern for quality. Employees behaved like rationing inspectors. Since very few new cars were made, a remanufacturing sub-culture started. Entire bodies were reconstructed in small workshops, and at one time Calcutta was awash with these remanufacturing units. Then, remanufactured engines and transmissions would be added. After an Ambassador car had reached the end of its useful life as a staff car in Bombay or Delhi, it would be sent to Calcutta to be used as a taxi or reconstituted if necessary. Many times, the doors of such remanufactured Ambassador taxis would not shut properly. Then drivers would tie them up with a piece of red cloth, called a *gamchha*, which they carried with them.

The administrative mechanisms for implementing the policies of the *License Raj* provided incentives to circumvent laws and regulations. Regulation was complex. It was implemented more with courage than with wisdom, covering industrial licensing, import and export regulations, price controls, capital issue controls, and the allocation of indigenously produced materials. It created large and powerful groups of vested interests. These comprised politicians, bureaucrats, and a large section of private industry.[35] Rent-extracting distributional coalitions, retardants to progress, flourished in India. As Jagdish Bhagwati stated: "I should also add that the deadly combination of industrial licensing and controls at home with import and exchange controls externally, effectively cut off the rigours of competition from all sources and made the creation of a rentier, as against an entrepreneurial, economy more likely."[36] By the middle of the 1970s, the licensing system had become more regulatory and less developmental. It led to an underground economy. The evidence shows that the licensing system was ineffective by the 1970s. Analyses in the 1960s, by Mr. Subimal Dutt, ICS, and Dr. R. K. Hazari, were landmarks.[37] Industrial growth rates,

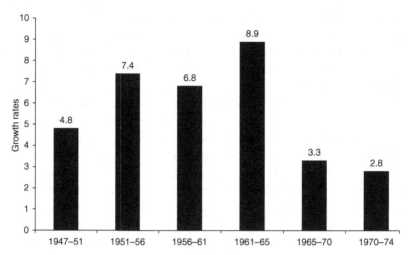

Figure 6.1. Average growth rate in industrial production over three decades.

Source: K. N. Raj, Growth and Stagnation in Industrial Development, in D. Nayyar (ed.), *Industrial Growth and Stagnation: The Debate in India*, New Delhi: Oxford University Press (1994), Table 2.

shown in figure 6.1, displayed a pattern of rise and then a fall in the mid 1960s to the mid 1970s.

The response from government in terms of adjustment, or change in direction, was minimal.[38] In the mid 1970s, an assessment of the system noted that detailed controls put strain on the administrative machinery and delayed implementation. Yet, for political compulsion, the government led by Mrs. Indira Gandhi reinforced the controls system.[39] Additional regulatory instruments, such as the Monopoly and Restrictive Trade Practices Act, and the Foreign Exchange Regulation Act, came into play in 1970 and 1973. These laws constituted major barriers to entry for new firms in Indian industry, by laying down draconian size and financing restrictions. Simultaneously, exit routes were blocked by labor legislation designed to protect employees' interests in the organized sector.[40] On Mrs. Indira Gandhi's return to power in 1980, the government considered comprehensive reforms to licensing. Mrs. Gandhi used to regularly consult J. R. D. Tata, the doyen of Indian industry, who had stated that while Indian economic performance from the mid 1950 to the mid 1960s reflected soundness of the original mixed economy idea, the opportunity in the late 1960s to open the economy to competition was lost. Otherwise, employment would have grown, production would have increased considerably, shortages would have eased, and government revenues would have materially increased.[41]

Meanwhile, in various Indian states, numerous initiatives had been taken in the 1950s and the 1960s, in the setting-up of state financial corporations (SFCs), such as the Maharashtra State Financial Corporation (MSFC), and state industrial development corporations (SIDCs), such as the Maharashtra Industrial Development Corporation (MIDC) and the West Bengal Industrial Development Corporation (WBIDC). The SFCs would provide funds, and the SIDCs would set up industrial estates in different parts of the state, to encourage entrepreneurs to set up manufacturing units. The SIDCs gave plots of land for the establishment of factories, and were explicitly established to create an environment for encouraging entrepreneurship democratization. But the entrepreneurs, while willing to invest and operate manufacturing businesses, found that they were engaged in fighting against the pathologies of the *License Raj*.

Of course, the *License Raj* and its pathologies are not a new phenomenon. One of the best examples of the phenomenon was related by John Beames over 100 years ago. John Beames was an ICS officer who had served in India from 1858 to 1893, principally in Bengal but also for a very short time in Punjab and also in Orissa, where had he had been Collector and District Magistrate of Balasore and Puri districts, and then Commissioner of Orissa. He wrote about his experiences in *Memoirs of a Bengal Civilian.* One story related to the salt trade. Salt is an important part of human diet. It was also an important source of government revenue. In the 1800s, after the British Crown took over Indian administration, the control of the manufacture, distribution, and taxation of salt in nineteenth-century Bengal and Orissa was a government activity. In fact, salt-making was a government monopoly. In the early years of British rule, salt was made by men hired by government. A large highly paid official staff supervised the work. The Salt Agent to Government, a senior ICS man, lived in a huge palace at Contai, on the Bengal coast, and received an extremely large annual salary of ₹48,000. The system was expensive and inefficient, as state-controlled systems can be. Fraud was rife. Smuggling was carried out on a large scale, since badly paid native watchmen turned a blind eye.[42]

The old salt manufacturing system was replaced, in a case of nineteenth-century privatization. Government gave up salt-making on its own account. Private individuals were invited to engage in its manufacture. Immediately, a variety of enterprising merchants, contractors, and others with a little bit of capital to spare readily embarked on this venture. These persons secured leases of tracts of land 10 or 15 square miles in area, in the salt-bearing region which was a narrow strip of low land running along the coast, and applied for contracts to make salt there.[43] Nevertheless, government could not simply let the salt contractors alone. There was a *License Raj* for the nineteenth-century salt business, which then invited an equal and opposite reaction from the entrepreneurial fraternity. Beames wrote: "Every step in the manufacture and sale of salt is surrounded with the most minute precautions on the part of Government, and there is a distinct and separate kind of fraud practiced at each stage. As each fresh precaution is evolved by the Board of Revenue, the Board of Smugglers invents a means of circumventing it."[44]

Economic regulation is necessary, its consequences are unexpected, and state intervention is often required. The issue is not whether regulation and state intervention should exist or not – there is no argument on that score – but of what kind and when.[45] Design and sequencing of regulations and state interventions are important. Otherwise, outcomes can be perverse,[46] and the opposite of original intentions, as with the *License Raj*. A key conceptual lapse in the design of the twentieth-century *License Raj* was the use of physical rather than financial controls. Also, these physical controls of manufacturing capacity continued well beyond their sell-by date. Negative oriented instruments of physical control stopped investment in specific areas and drove investments underground.[47] It also led to the creation of an administrative Frankenstein. Thus, the Directorate-General of Technical Development, popularly known as the DGTD, an agency meant for the technical upgrading of India's industrial capabilities, became the final arbiter of import, investment, and expansion decisions for India's industry.

Establishment of large-scale facilities had been ordained, since 1956, to be the province of state-owned enterprises. If private sector enterprises wanted to scale up production, they had to go through an involved process with the DGTD, which would evaluate all the technical parameters. But, since the DGTD was a technical agency, fully staffed by engineers, and not an economic agency, with economists who might understand markets, approval was rarely forthcoming.

Since it became known that approval was rarely forthcoming, and if it did come would be attached to a string of near-impossible conditions, individual firms lost motivation to expand their capabilities and size. This led to a self-displacing prophecy loop,[48] as businessmen, in general, shared this negative motivation. Since everybody expected the same behavior from DGTD, they collectively curtailed their DGTD dealings. Nobody wanted to deal with the *babus* of Udyog Bhavan.[49] By doing so, they reduced the average level of capabilities and firm and plant size in Indian industry. Thus, Indian firms lost numerous opportunities to derive economies of scale and scope, and they never had a chance to launch their own industrial revolutions.

As stated earlier, the financial and economic situation in the beginning of 1991, culminating in India's gold shipment to London, promoted a full evaluation of all aspects of Indian economic policy. Some time after taking over as the prime minister, the late Mr. P. V. Narasimha Rao realized that the opportunity to comprehensively alter policies was now or never. An institutional discontinuity could be engendered. The Principal Secretary to the Prime Minister was the late Mr. A. N. Verma, who had previously been the Industry Secretary. Between A. N. Verma and Mr. L. Mansingh, the then Joint Secretary in charge of the Secretariat of Industrial Approvals, the division of the Ministry of Industrial Development engaged actually in the task of industrial licensing, a decision was taken to delicense industrial entry. On D-Day, July 24, 1991, a notification was issued, under Mr. Mansingh's signature, opening up entry, other than in the standard strategic areas of atomic energy, defense, and railways, to any firm wanting to invest and set up business in India. India had let down institutional barriers to entry, and was again fully open for business.[50]

Dr. Nitish Sengupta, a former civil servant and politician, wrote:

In the end nothing is more important than creating an environment in which the entrepreneurs, whether in the private sector or in the public sector, can take managerial decisions, based on his own assessment, judgment and intuition within the parameters and rules of the game laid down by the government rather than under the compulsions of administrative diktats from sources far removed from the reality of the shop floor.[51]

On July 24, 1991 India's business environment was radically changed.

Institutional change and its consequences

At the heart of India's economic regulation and control processes was a post-independence necessity to exercise power for the common good. Power was derived from control over key sectors of the economy.[52] Later, the command necessity turned into a command desire, if not a command need. For several decades the exercise of economic power became a hard-to-break habit. The ownership of capital had given some industrialists a considerable hold over political processes in Indian society,[53] by creating vested interests. Similarly, control over the economy permitted exercise of direct and material power by government over the lives of people.[54]

The Nobel laureate Friedrich Hayek raised the issue not only that central direction of economic activity was possibly inefficient, but also that there was the fundamental question of how much personal and political freedom could be preserved in such a system.[55] Eventually, such a process would become pathological. It would lead to concentration of state power similar to that in Nazi Germany or the Soviet Union.[56] The historian Carlo Cipolla had noted that Europeans went into Asia with a spirit of determination to succeed that was stronger than the will of the Asian people to resist, and this accounted for European successes.[57] But even if India's businessmen were determined, possessing a strong spirit could not deliver results in the absence of resources.[58] Control over resources, and the specific parameters of their utilization, provided the mechanisms for amassing power. Because the economy was essential to human survival, command over people's autonomous economic activities yielded control over people's lives.[59] All economic questions became political questions. Control over all of the means meant that an arbitrary agency would decide which ends would be satisfied and which ones were not to be satisfied.[60]

The human factor was of paramount importance. The will to make individual progress existed among the people. But it could be dampened and needed reactivating.[61] Thus, there was little entrepreneurship in India in the period till 1991.[62] Placing limits on entrepreneurs' aspirations had important consequences. Unless the desire to increase material wealth was felt, businessmen would not have interests in new techniques or innovation. At the margin, businessmen would disdain to engage in activities yielding advantages with available opportunities, because the psychological barriers placed by institutional norms were so great.[63] Friedrich Hayek noted that "the gradual transformation of a rigidly organized hierarchic system into one where men could at least attempt to shape their own life ... is closely associated with the growth of commerce."[64] The rigidity of the *License Raj*, where businessmen could not shape their firms' destinies, was perhaps one factor leading to the decline of India's share in global commerce.

What happens when a pathological process is removed and people regain autonomy? What could the institutional discontinuity of July 24, 1991 achieve? In a sense, it was like acquiring freedom. Amartya Sen has suggested that the instrumental roles of freedom include interrelated components, such as facilitation of economic possibilities, political freedoms, social opportunities, transparency guarantees, and protective security.[65] To these items could be added the right to start and support one's own business initiatives, since these would permit individuals to fully exploit their idiosyncratic capabilities. The exploitation of one's capabilities would be achieved with the freedom to make decisions to achieve the outcomes one valued the most.[66]

Extending the range of choices and effective alternatives open to the people would be an important objective of economic development, with a measure of success being the effect on the range of entrepreneurial alternatives open to individuals.[67] In a moral sense, an open and competitive market-based economic system allowed greater expression for individual freedom, on the assumption that a multiplier effect would create further economic opportunities elsewhere.[68] A democratic society permitted the choices, initiatives, and enterprise of individual citizens to rise to the fore rather than be controlled and guided by a machine bureaucracy or organization, which aggregated preferences and mobilized the choices.[69]

Just as the Constitution of India had created a strong democratic political process, the institutional discontinuity permitted entrepreneurship democratization in India. Just as political democracy permitted moral incentives to thrive, economic democracy permitted material incentives to thrive. Indeed, Alexis de Tocqueville had found a similar phenomenon at play in early nineteenth-century America. In an environment where entrepreneurship was democratized, the burden of strategic choice would fall on the businessman. With strategic choices having been made, there arose the responsibility for their consequences. The laying at a businessman's door of the cause–effect relationship in business transactions would engender rationality. It would promote active engagement with the economic world, to minimize dissonances and maximize benefits. Entrepreneurship was the engine driving economic change.[70] The responsibility for consequences was, in other words, a link between economic self-determination and moral responsibility. Now it was no longer possible for businessmen to blame others, say the SIA or the DGTD, for non-occurrence of performance outcomes, since, as a free agent, the blame would fall squarely on entrepreneurs' shoulders. Economic freedom permitted agency. But it brought responsibilities for action. These factors would encourage entrepreneurs to develop robust business models, based on strong capabilities, so that success would follow.

The breakdown of the *License Raj* could also be compared to a reformation, which increased the drive for success and changed aspirations. The sociologist Max Weber suggested that the Protestant Reformation gave rise to an ethic that promoted efforts toward material ends, which he called the spirit of capitalism. The American psychologist David McClelland has suggested that since the Protestants had broken away from the Roman Catholics, their increased drive was to prove, via performance, that they were not one of the damned. Instead, they were the chosen. This theological schism, coupled with a chip on the shoulder, released an achievement motivation which led the Protestants to economic success.[71] A similar argument has been advanced for the Parsis, who settled in India over 1,000 years ago. As refugees from Persia, being settlers in a commercially vibrant part of India, the Parsis had a considerable amount to prove to the community accepting them that they were able to contribute out of proportion to their actual numbers. Hence, this achievement need drove the Parsis in India to aspire to significant positions in business, trade, industry, professional life, public life, and even government.[72]

When businessmen were concerned about daily survival issues during the *License Raj*, initiatives for entrepreneurial self-expression and radical outside-the-box thinking schemes were not feasible. When an assurance of prosperity was made available, businessmen could become less circumspect about husbandry and more risk-taking in their orientation and their achievement motivation levels would rise. They could be indulgent in expressing initiatives to enhance well-being.[73] Growing individualism became the result of greater freedom, and led to greater prosperity.[74] Hence, the disappearance of the *License Raj* mentality from the Indian business psyche in the last two decades has generated a flood of entrepreneurial initiatives never before witnessed in India. Indian industry has re-entered an age of autonomous thinking.[75]

Democratizing entrepreneurship

Indians have never been shy of entrepreneurship, and evidence shows that past institutional barriers retarded entrepreneurship. In the sixteenth and seventeenth centuries there were numerous political factions in India who charged traders significant customs duties for the trans-shipment of goods. These led to high prices. Harassment by customs authorities also added significant disincentives for Indian traders and businessmen.[76] Hardships still exist. India is not yet a hospitable place to start new ventures, according to many international benchmarks. Entrepreneurship was considered by many to be a negative activity, requiring unsavory characteristics. But that is no longer true. Entrepreneurship is emerging as a key determinant of economic growth,[77] just as 30 years ago it was called the fourth factor of production.[78]

After the reforms that commenced in 1991, the release of pent-up hunger has led to the emergence of numerous business initiatives across the agriculture, manufacturing, and services sectors. Tangible barriers to entry still exist but mental barriers have come down. This breakdown of barriers has led to tidal waves of entrepreneurial activity by heterogeneous individuals who might never have considered engaging in ventures. Such entrepreneurs' deeds have created opportunities for others, and generated self-created wealth. William Baumol remarked that "The entrepreneur is at once one of the most intriguing and one of the most elusive in the cast of characters that constitutes the subject of economic analysis."[79] There is an explosion of literature on entrepreneurship. Hence, the term might mean all things to all men. Yet, in the sense of Israel Kirzner, the actions of an alert individual, who recognizes opportunities arising from misallocation of resources, possesses the imagination to create options to exploit these, and the ability to mobilize resources, captures the essence of entrepreneurship.[80] This requires the ability to perceive the opening of a major opportunity in a new field, and to detect and shift to the advancing frontier rather than wrestle with crises in existing domains.[81]

An important characteristic defines new Indian entrepreneurs. They have emerged from all walks of life. Once-disenfranchised persons have turned entrepreneurs. Women like Sumangala, and men such as OM (see Chapter 1), who a decade ago would have been considered to be unlikely entrepreneurs, have emerged as India's economic value creators. To be engaged in enterprise knows no caste or class boundaries, as the phenomenon is visceral. Though much of Indian entrepreneurship activities and behavior is consistently described along caste lines in the literature, Indian entrepreneurship scholar Dwijendra Tripathi has established that caste considerations did not inhibit any group of Indians from becoming entrepreneurs.[82]

Vent for growth is universal. Its occurrence in India is not unique. It has simply happened in the world's largest political democracy today. The outcome of this process has been the world's largest ever entrepreneurship democratization. Democratization of entrepreneurship implies several things. The late Professor C. K. Prahalad, in his path-breaking development of the concept of the "bottom of the pyramid," described how democratizing commerce meant ensuring that the benefits of globalization were available to all, as micro-consumers, and as micro-producers, micro-innovators and micro-investors, thus democratizing entrepreneurship. Hence, the multitudes could exercise their democratic choice to engage in business activities, and in wealth creation.[83] Thus, while Sumangala and OM are, by nobody's stretch of the imagination, global business magnates, the process of engagement in Calcutta's IVF economy has expanded their little worlds to one that is just slightly larger. For persons like Sumangala and OM, and many others like them, engagement with the formal sector permits them access to markets. Sumangala and OM's little worlds may have been the local area of Calcutta where they reside, but they have now acquired access to the larger Calcutta hinterland. In due course of time, they may acquire access to the entire eastern India market.

Another characteristic of the process of democratization of commerce is that participants in business and enterprise become self-reliant, acquire confidence, and are capable of understanding concepts of economics and finance such as investment, returns, credit, and profit.[84] Again, in due course of time, involvement with the IVF fraternity of Calcutta will enable our two entrepreneurs to access formal sources of finance, should they have any interest in altering or expanding the scope of their activities. Such functionalities may not have immediate salience for OM. For Sumangala, as she expands the scope of her activities to supply all of the IVF centers in Calcutta with egg donors, acquiring knowledge of these functionalities could have considerable impact on the future course of her budding entrepreneurial career.

A key assumption underlying the democratization process is that the exercise of choice, as consumers, producers, suppliers, or employees, be available to all. Such choices must be volitional, autonomous, and not dictated from above. Thus, entrepreneurial individuals insist that they possess the authority to determine the contours of decisions forming part of their economic lives. The 1991 reforms were a discontinuity, bringing about a radical change in the intangible context for permitting autonomous entrepreneurial decisions. The reforms enhanced entrepreneurship democratization by permitting full entrepreneurial autonomy. They augmented the tangible environment for entrepreneurship democratization, which the formation of SFCs, SIDCs, small-scale industry development corporations (SSIDCs), and bank nationalization had tried to establish over the past few decades.

Contextual intuition and creative improvisation

A number of features define entrepreneurship democratization. Many entrepreneurial individuals have emerged from the fringes of India's urban sectors. They have had relatively little to lose other than a sense of impoverishment. This is an important enabling factor for autonomous entrepreneurial behavior to be channeled towards productive ends. Since entrepreneurial individuals have substantial wealth gains and improvements in standards of living to enjoy, the calculus of the cost–benefit trade-offs in being entrepreneurial is weighted in their favor, and the spurs to being entrepreneurial are greater.

A second key quality of entrepreneurial individuals is the possession of contextual intuition. As persons making marginal livings in urban and rural India, these individuals possess "street smarts," since this quality is a survival necessity. Economic progress has been stochastic in India. Life has been uncertain. Consequently, there has been no assurance that processes, as formally laid down via rules or systems, will work. Hence, individuals have had to possess a sixth sense to survive, get ahead, and grow.[85] The dynamics of personal evolution, whether in economic, social, or public life, motivate individuals to continuously search for opportunities to exploit asymmetries, however sudden and marginal, arising from changing contexts, differences in resource endowments, or variations among individuals, to foster a transaction, a deal, an action, or an immediate response to events. In a sense, this epitomizes evolutionary economic behavior when man is conceptualized as not just a passive agent, stimulated purely by desires for hedonistic consumption, but as continuously creating and recreating simultaneous opportunities for production and consumption.[86]

When making business plans, human beings bring in three types of knowledge: as to the laws of nature; as to extant social laws, which are contextually and temporally driven; and of specific and unique events that enable an entrepreneur to imagine the possible consequences of actions and anticipate outcomes.[87] These cumulatively act on each other. They facilitate the synchronization and coordination of activities, because an entrepreneur will have also worked out, in a flash, how others might react to her approaches, since there will exist a set of shared categories and standards among all the individuals engaged in the relevant activities.[88] An entrepreneur organizes a number of other human beings into a firm or a business. She coordinates the three types of knowledge acquired or possessed, by the imposition of a unique interpretive framework or scheme.[89] Each such interpretive framework may be different, giving each enterprise its unique character.[90] Uniquely in India, the speed of reaction by entrepreneurs, to random and stray pieces of information to which this knowledge framework has been applied, has been high. Thus, entrepreneurs' abilities to react in a split second and immediately anticipate the outcomes of an engagement or intervention have been considerable.

A polite way to describe such qualities and resultant behavior is "living by one's wits." In reality, in a stochastic environment like India, every activity is a decision point since there is never certainty that formal process outcomes will ensue. Nothing can be taken for granted. Hence, individuals have been sensitized to thinking ahead as to what alternative outcomes may be, as the likely results may deviate from officially expected results, and then rapidly reconceptualizing their next courses of action. There is continuous anticipation and reconceptualization. This reconceptualization, and the taking of resulting action, if any, will be driven by the categories of natural, social, and historical knowledge possessed by the entrepreneurs.

Let me give an example. In most cities of the world, a red light at a set of road traffic lights means that the traffic comes to a complete halt. This has not been the case in Bombay. Over the last decade, as economic growth has triggered a race for success, getting ahead has meant doing so regardless of the consequences. This disregard is applied to traffic rules and lights. Thus, a red light signifies, for Bombay's drivers, a mere suggestion that they might possibly consider slowing down. It would be considered vulgar and bad form by the drivers if the red light was an order for them to halt completely! Yet, many times at perpendicular cross-roads, traffic making legitimate progress, because their lights are green, will be moving at a fair pace. Hence, the drivers faced with the red light, not wishing to subject themselves to the complete halt required, make split-second decisions to continue at the same pace, if the cross-roads traffic seems distant, to slow down if such traffic is close by, or to halt if the traffic is upon them.

I have often been in hired cars where drivers at perpendicular cross-roads have passed each other at lights at speeds of 20 to 30 miles per hour, irrespective of which traffic lanes were subject to red and green lights. My exhortations to drivers to actually view the red light as a complete traffic halt were humored a few times as an aberration of a non-resident Indian. When my attention wandered off, the drivers resorted to their ways of driving. Yet, it is this extreme example of contextual intuition which epitomizes the Indian environment. Crashes at traffic lights, because of non-observance of rules, are so far rare, though violations of these rules have to be strictly monitored and severe sanctions applied.

Let me give another example. This was a tale recounted to me by a friend, Subrata Mukherji, now President of the ICICI Foundation. Earlier in his career he spent several years in the ICICI office in Calcutta at a time when all Calcutta taxis were the Hindustan Ambassador, which is the 1958 version of the Morris Oxford, an unlamented British brand, manufactured in India. They still are the majority of Calcutta's taxis. He used a taxi once to make a small visit somewhere. Having got to the destination, he asked the driver to wait since he would be gone for only a minute or two. The street was crowded, and Subrata enquired as to where the driver would park. The driver replied that, in spite of not an inch of parking space anywhere, there were no worries at all on that score. The taxi would be parked right outside the establishment Subrata was visiting, waiting. He stopped the car in the traffic lane outside the establishment, allowed Subrata to get out, and then immediately opened the taxi's hood and pretended that the car had broken down. It was, therefore, for a few moments, incapacitated and immobile and traffic was blocked on that lane. One can argue that had the taxi driver simply stopped the car and waited, Calcutta's excitable denizens would have brought the house down with their incessant honking of horns (many of these horns might have been the rubber bulb horns, still used in Calcutta). By the expedient of raising the hood, the taxi driver gained public sympathy and reduced noise pollution!

Of course, the use of contextual intuition can get carried too far, as the examples recounted suggest, and create substantial social costs. In fact, the term "animal spirits" might also attract opprobrium if applied to India's entrepreneurs. Yet, in conjunction with a continuous scanning of the environment, so as to pick up even the weakest of signals, this scanning activity and intuitive sixth sense have given Indian entrepreneurs an ability to develop business models tailored to the specific needs of the context. An ingenuity to make something out of nothing is a typical characteristic of businessmen in economies where resources have been very little to start with.[91] Remaining a step ahead of the next set of issues, that could impinge on the fulfillment of one's goals has meant that these entrepreneurial individuals are adaptable, ready, and willing to commence experiments into alternatives. Provided the contextual intuitions lead to important commercial insights, implemented legally, and keeping public convenience in mind, then all is well. This generation of alternatives has led to the coinage of the term *jugaad*. *Jugaad* is a generic term for describing creative improvisation as a tool for evolving business-model solutions, calling on initiative and immediate thinking, based on a resolve to quickly fulfill market demands cheaply.[92] India's former Minister for Commerce and Industry, Kamal Nath, wrote about the benefits of *jugaad* as being "innovation ... a survival tool for Indians, where every obstacle became an opportunity."[93]

The adaptability of these entrepreneurs permits flexible business organizations and fluid business models. By necessity, these business models are unique because these entrepreneurs lack precedents. As a result, no baggage attaches to these models. When conditions change, models can be rapidly altered. These business models typically start small. Because habits of personal frugality spill over into business ventures, the need for financial and physical capital resources can be small, relative to output generated, when compared with larger business enterprises. Hence, creative improvisation can lead to high capital utilization rates. Possibly, the ventures of our friend OM, whom we met in Chapter 1, suggest the high returns feasible from a fluid business model. Conversely, these entrepreneurs' leverage of intellectual and social capital enable them to piggyback on existing businesses and co-utilize other firms' resources. Finally, adaptability permits the ventures to be scalable if occasion demands.

A manufacturing entrepreneur's tale

An anecdote of Indian manufacturing entrepreneurship today reflects creative improvisation, and the leverage of intellectual and social capital. On a recent visit to Bombay, I read in the Sunday edition of a local daily newspaper, *Mumbai Mirror*,[94] about an automobile engineer. I decided to visit him. Ferdinand Rodricks, popularly known as Ferdi, is the chief executive officer of an authorized service station for Mahindra vehicles in the Parel locality of Bombay. Originally trained as an outboard marine engineer for large engines in Hong Kong, he worked as a tool and die manufacturing professional in Kandivili, a suburb of Bombay, for several years. He has an automobile engineering diploma and a mechanical engineering degree.

Parel demands description. It was once the home of the earliest governors of Bombay. It is one of Bombay's oldest and most historic localities and it looks like that in parts, broken and dirty, but it is the heart of Central Bombay. Central Bombay is the happening part of town. What used to be land full of slum tenements that housed thousands of textile mill workers has become the location for gleaming glass and aluminum skyscrapers that put contemporary real estate construction in the West to shame. Ferdi's day job also requires description. He heads the automotive service unit of a venture owned by the Roman Catholic Church. Many know that India is one of the oldest Christian countries in the world. The apostle Saint Thomas, known as Doubting Thomas, arrived in India in AD 52 and was martyred around AD 72 in Madras, now known as Chennai. He was the only apostle believed to have traveled outside the Mediterranean area.

The Roman Catholic Archdiocese of Bombay runs the St. Paul's Convent School for girls, a boy's school also called St. Paul's, an orphanage called Our Lady of Lourdes, and the Joseph Cardijn Technical School in Parel. These four establishments form four sides of a square in Parel. The Joseph Cardijn Technical School is an industrial training institute. It also runs the authorized Mahindra service station, so that

not only are customers' vehicles serviced but also the school's automotive technology students can gain hands-on practical experience. In the
grounds of the school and service center, the archdiocese has allowed
Ferdi space to set up his own small enterprise, called Ferro Equip. Its
business is to convert cars, so that people with disabilities may drive
them. As Ferdi put it, many individuals cannot walk, they may not
even have legs; their arms or hands may be withered or useless, but
they can drive. People with disabilities may be talented in many fields,
but cannot use their skills because of mobility restrictions.

Such individuals have no freedom of choice or opportunity. This
view of freedom is that of Amartya Sen, for whom freedom is both the
processes that allow freedom of actions and decisions, and the actual
opportunities that people have, given their personal and social circumstances.[95] A lack of freedom for some people arises through inadequate
opportunities for achieving what they can or would like to achieve. In
this context, Ferdi's venture provides his customers with the wherewithal to be free of the constraints of their disability, whether in their
professional or personal lives. In a sense, Ferdi is releasing them from
the dark ages of isolation and a lack of mobility that engender deep
feelings of hopelessness.[96]

In the Ferro Equip facility, Ferdi undertakes a complete modification
of cars. Anything in a car can be changed to tailor it to the needs of
a disabled person. Any make of car can be dealt with. Presently, the
costs of these modifications for a mid-range car amount to between
₹20,000 and ₹40,000 for those whose hands are disabled. While these
sums represent between 5 and 10 percent of the cost of the car, the
benefits of freedom, independence, and mobility for a person unable to
be independently mobile are priceless. Everything is customized, since
safety is paramount. Everyone has a different need. Standardized kits
may not fit correctly to the person specification. Hence, Ferdi operates a made-to-order automotive workshop where cars are redesigned,
models are built, parts are manufactured, and assembly is carried out.

The process at Ferdi's Ferro Equip workshop is not like the one at
Ford's River Rouge plant. Ferro Equip converts just two to three cars
per month, and its revenues are tiny. Many of the parts are machined
and fabricated elsewhere, based on the designs given to them by
Ferro Equip, which keeps a close watch on the quality levels. Ferro
Equip is the only company in India authorized by the Automotive
Research Association of India (ARAI), an industry body certifying the

roadworthiness of cars, to convert cars so that the public may acquire them. In awarding their certification, the ARAI had conducted extensive tests of Ferro Equip cars, and now the enterprise can sell cars for outright registration by the Regional Transport Offices, the government agency that controls vehicle certification and licensing in India. So far, Ferdi and his company, Ferro Equip, have converted over 1,000 cars, and made that many immobile persons mobile, releasing them from their darkness. While Ferdi is constrained for space in Parel, he hopes to set up a testing track and training facility outside Bombay for drivers with disabilities. This way, the driver can get used to the car, then to the process of driving on the road, and thereafter to the nightmarish traffic conditions prevalent in India. The manufacturing facility will be transferred to this unit, and Ferdi hopes to establish an integrated automotive facility for disabled people.

Ferdi's activities are a reflection of informal entrepreneurship coexisting side by side with formal sector businesses in India. As a staff member of the Roman Catholic Archdiocese of Bombay, Ferdi plays a formal role during the day as a technology and management professional. He caters to a set of customers, and also runs the service organization. As a trained technologist, via his own Ferro Equip venture, he is harnessing his engineering skills in bringing transformation to the lives of people in an unusual (so far for India, anyway) sector where entrepreneurial activities have been absent. For a group of otherwise talented customers, who have restrictions on their mobility, he has abolished their personal limitations of geography.

The late C. S. Venkatachar wrote: "In Indian history there are long and continuous periods of development and of creative energy possible because India is the terminus of recurring movements."[97] Perhaps these economic, intellectual and social movements finding their termini in India are also humanist in orientation. Like our other entrepreneurs Sumangala and OM, Ferdi does not come from an exalted and rich family background of merchants or industrialists where he might have acquired all the capital necessary to start and run his own business. Ferdi's example, as a professional and simultaneously an entrepreneur in the realm of light manufacturing, is an element of India's late, late industrial revolution.

Ferdi is not Ford! Ferdi exploits his automobile engineering expertise in an arena where the contemporary Indian society has important demands, but where response has been light. His approach is that of a job-shop, and not that of a mass-scale standardized assembly process, based on parts interchangeability. Ferdi may be a technology entrepreneur, as described by Thorstein Veblen, who was a little bit of an inventor, a little bit of a designer, and a builder of a factory, machines, and machine tools, while being a shop manager and at the same time taking care of finances.[98] While the nature of the automotive technology Ferdi is engaged in may be basic, if compared to the technologies of a BMW or a Honda, his project highlights another aspect of the process of democratization of entrepreneurship under way in India.

Emergent Indian entrepreneurship and its profile

India's first prime minister, Jawaharlal Nehru stated, in relation to the industrialized West and India, that "The old culture managed to live through many a fierce storm and tempest, but, though it kept its outer form, it lost its real content. Today it is fighting silently and desperately against a new and all-powerful opponent the *bania* civilization of the capitalist West. It will succumb to this newcomer, for the West brings science, and science brings food for the hungry millions."[99]

India missed the first and second industrial revolutions. She did not engage in late industrialization, as did her Asian sisters. In the last two decades, India has been engaged in a late, late industrial revolution. One fact is abundantly clear. India has not needed the big push by government to propel its economic activity in the last 20 years. India's entrepreneurs have not needed government to "gull them into silly schemes" of industrialization that James MacKay railed against over a century ago (see p. 124). They have engaged in innumerable silly schemes themselves! India is an inherently laissez-faire society, where a "live and let live" philosophy prevails, and this attribute expresses itself in the way her industrialization is evolving. India has moved from a cathedral style of industrial development, where top-down planning, and the commands of a dirigisme authority set the pace, to a bazaar style of functioning where bottom-up activities of million of entrepreneurs will define the industrial context.[100]

There is no scope now for a Bombay school of thought versus a Calcutta school of thought debate on industrial policy. Neither will the ghosts of Mahatma Gandhi and M. Visvesvaraya, when they view events in contemporary India, believe what the past couple of decades have wrought in the Indian industrial landscape. Between

1947 and 1991, government in India had a unique, and some would say suffocating,[101] role to play in industrialization. Contemporary entrepreneurial responses to emerging opportunities have been overwhelming, if one bases this conclusion on the aggregate data that are presented in the various chapters here. The role of government, after 1991, in promoting entrepreneurship and industrialization, has been minuscule.

With respect to the role of government, India's late, late industrial revolution is emulating the American industrial revolution, dubbed as the second industrial revolution, rather than the late industrialization of Japan, South Korea, and Taiwan. In East Asia, as recorded by the World Bank,[102] drives for growth in specific sectors, such as heavy and chemical industries, were the major policy initiatives taken by the East Asian governments. Governments in East Asia committed to move away from neutral incentives leading to industrial growth. They used tailored instruments to channel resources into targeted sectors to alter countries' industrial structures. In India, this process of industrial structure alteration is happening autonomously. Market forces have emerged to guide India's entrepreneurial decisions, and entrepreneurs have followed economic demand in being innovative. Indian firms are experimenting with strategies in unexpected ways.[103]

What are the patterns of entrepreneurial behavior to have emerged in India after the institutional change of July 24, 1991? What other examples of entrepreneurial autonomy, like Sumangala and OM, are visible? Of course, many individuals and businessmen will have behaved randomly just as Fyodor Dostoevsky suggested: "He might thus act for the shallowest of reasons; for a reason which is not worth mentioning; for the reason that, always, and everywhere, and no matter what his station, man loves to act as he likes, and not necessarily as reason and self-interest would have him do."[104] In assessing the consequences of the institutional discontinuity on emergent entrepreneurship in India, there is the question of individuals' stories. Many have done what they have liked. What did they do? The economic historian Jonathan Hughes has stated that the masses of history were represented by aggregate data. Yet, changes in the massed data as such did not lead to changes in the economy and society. The forces of history only occurred because of human action and volition. Thus, the impact of individual businessmen and entrepreneurs' actions cannot be ignored.[105]

The question of entrepreneurship and economic growth are related to the mobilization of resources. Individual entrepreneurs put together the new factor combinations, and mobilized resources to change economic flows.[106] The Nobel laureate Thomas Schelling has described the world as one where people respond to an environment that consists of other people responding to their environment. This, in turn, consists of people responding to an environment consisting of other people's responses.[107] Hence, initial acts of business creation lead to economic transactions, lead others to create businesses to supply emerging demand, and these acts of business establishment induce many other individuals to set up in business.

Friedrich von Hayek had suggested that the combined actions of individual actions could lead to unexpected outcomes. Many human achievements could have arisen without a design or mental direction. Thus, the spontaneous collaboration of free persons often created things, or led to the emergence of the big picture, which were other than what individual minds might have singly comprehended.[108] Yet, it was the random patterns of individual behavior that aggregated to the big picture of economic flow changes. While an individual's ends might be defined in advance, the engagement in action with another person, or persons, would alter those ends since collective action was based on social interaction containing a constitutive aspect which could lead to unexpected outcomes.[109] The patterns of aggregate behavior would emerge from the statistically random actions of several businessmen, all engaging in their own idiosyncratic activity but also acting collectively. The effects of these would be the inevitable aggregations. Thus, no matter how individualistic an entrepreneur might be, the resultant deeds of all entrepreneurs, each with unique motivations, would provide the details for the larger picture.[110]

What have been the motivations of entrepreneurs engaged in activities altering India's industrial structure? Data on India's entrepreneurs have emerged. In 2004, the Government of India had set up a National Knowledge Commission. That commission had sponsored research on several aspects of Indian entrepreneurship.[111] A team from the commission conducted one-on-one interviews with 155 entrepreneurs from diverse backgrounds in several cities across India. The findings of the team are presented in Table 6.1. The survey was conducted for six categories of entrepreneurship motivators: independence, family background, challenge, dream and desire, exploiting market opportunity,

Table 6.1. *Motivations for entrepreneurship in contemporary India*

Motivations

Category	Independence	Family background	Challenge	Dream and desire	Market opportunity	Idea driven	Total
Overall	21	21	11	10	19	18	100
By gender							
Female	26	8	12	12	17	25	100
Male	21	24	11	9	19	16	100
By age							
Less than 35	22	22	19	6	26	5	100
Over 35	21	22	8	11	16	22	100
By family background							
First generation	33	4	15	8	22	18	100
Second generation same	4	74	4	0	4	14	100
Second generation different	3	34	5	8	23	27	100
By period							
Pre 1991	13	31	12	15	12	17	100
1991–99	19	14	11	12	28	16	100
2000 onwards	36	12	12	2	22	16	100

Source: Government of India, *Entrepreneurship in India*, New Delhi: National Knowledge Commission (2008), Table 2.1 and Tables 2.3–2.9.

and to implement an idea. The responses across categories summed up to 100 points.

There are no unique and distinguishing features about what makes an entrepreneur become an entrepreneur.[112] Equally, India's entrepreneurs were a diversely motivated lot. For the sample of India's women entrepreneurs, the most important motivator was independence, followed by the desire to execute a potentially viable idea. The money-making opportunity, given a market, was third. Taking on a challenge or fulfilling a dream was fourth. A family background in business was the least important. For India's male entrepreneurs, a family background in business was the most important. The desire for independence was second, followed by the feasibility of exploiting a market opportunity. Executing an idea was next in importance, followed by meeting a challenge and fulfilling a dream. Clearly, gender differences in what factors have motivated men and women into entrepreneurship are significant.

Among the young entrepreneurs, those under 35, exploiting a market opportunity did matter the most, followed equally by a business family background and attaining independence. Taking on a challenge was the next motivator, while fulfilling a dream or executing an idea were relatively trivial motivators. Clearly, India's young entrepreneurs have been hungry for success, and are acquisitive. Comparatively, India's older entrepreneurs, those over 35 years old, were most motivated by an idea or had a family background, and coming next in order of importance was a desire to be independent. Exploiting a market opportunity came next, followed by fulfilling a dream. Meeting a challenge was last in engendering motivation, perhaps because some of these challenges may already have been met previously.

For first-generation entrepreneurs, being independent was the primary driver. Exploiting a market opportunity followed, succeeded by the ability to exploit an idea. Accepting a challenge was the next motivator, and then came a dream fulfillment. A family background was the least important, probably because in most cases there was none. Of course, for second-generation entrepreneurs entering the same line of business as family members, the family background was exceedingly important. Then, the next motivator was the exploitation of an idea. Almost all other motivators were trivial in importance, and having a dream to be an entrepreneur simply did not matter, because, one supposes, it was expected that the second-generation entrepreneurs would go into the same line of business as that of the family.

For second-generation entrepreneurs in a different line of business, family background mattered most, but not as much as for those entrepreneurs who had entered the same line of business. This was followed by the motivation to exploit an idea. Then was the motivation to exploit a market opportunity. Having a dream, meeting a challenge, and being independent were small motivators. In the period prior to the institutional change taking place, before 1991, entrepreneurs had been primarily influenced by family background in entering business; exploiting an idea, chasing a dream, being independent, taking on a challenge, and exploiting a market opportunity had ranked below. Between 1991 and 1999, exploiting a market opportunity was the most important. Clearly, the institutional change opened up many economic and financial possibilities to be enjoyed. Being independent was the next important motivator, while exploiting an idea followed after it. A family background, chasing a dream, and meeting a challenge followed in order.

After 2000, the beginning of a new millennium, being independent was the most important motive. Attitudes had changed. A desire to be autonomous, linked to an enhanced risk appetite, had emerged strongly. This was followed by a desire to exploit a market opportunity. This had the same proportion in this period as it had in the previous one, signaling that institutional change in India had been an important influence on entrepreneurs to engage in India's growth process. These two factors were followed by family background and meeting a challenge. Being an entrepreneur was now no longer a dream, as it was once. Instead, it was a *sui generis* activity taken for granted. Other than for a second-generation entrepreneur entering the same line of business, the desire for independence was the key motivator, given that institutional changes permitted freedom of entry into various businesses. These findings correlate well with previous findings for the United States, where 63 percent of individuals surveyed wanted to escape employment drudgery and start their own business, and 49 percent for the United Kingdom who had replied similarly.[113]

What do the results imply? In Chapter 1, I recorded growth in projected employment over the last 20 years or so in India. Yet, there has also been a marked increase in entrepreneurship. This is in spite of the fact that many small businesses may consist of just a self-employed entrepreneur and a few employees. Typically, at least in the United States, earnings of self-employed entrepreneurs are less than those of comparable employed persons.[114] An explanation as to why such a large amount of self-employment and entrepreneurship persists in the United States, in spite of a potential economic downside, is the ability to be one's own boss. This is an important non-pecuniary advantage of entrepreneurship.

The National Knowledge Commission survey shows that this particular non-pecuniary motive, as captured by the responses to the search for independence question, is very strong in India. India's viscerally driven model of entrepreneurship, and associated industrial development, may have a lot in common with that of the United States. This is a conjecture worthy of detailed examination. The next chapter deals with stories of some individuals whose actions are contributing to aggregate entrepreneurship in India. It also deals in detail with the big picture, as represented by corporate and macro industrial data. The chapter highlights salient details of India's emerging industrial scenario, to bear out the conjecture of whether India is an America-like economy. The stories provide background for the way India's industrial revolution is being conducted.

7 | Contemporary India

Contemporary Indian enterprises

The entrepreneurs' data presented in Chapter 6 suggest that a transform-ation is under way. Yet, behind the dynamics is the issue of whether this is simply a revival, as a set of reactions to past impoverishments, or genuine regenerations of an industrial spirit that also experiment with new busi-nesses and functionalities so as to make the industrial transformation a genuine revolution. Specific cases and facts address this issue. I posit that the evidence suggests not just a revival but a regeneration.

The older large business houses of India, such as Bangur, Birla, Goenka, Kilachand, Mafatlal, Modi, Sarabhai, and Shriram, are no longer dominant, if they exist at all. One of the largest Indian busi-ness groups, Martin Burn, has become extinct, falling prey to Bengalis' inabilities to be businessmen. In the place of the old names, new names have emerged. A listing of these businesses and names has been made by journalist Harish Damodaran.[1] Among these new businesses, three companies assert Indian-owned firms' emergence as serious world-stage players. These are: Arcelor-Mittal in steel, Videocon in consumer electronics and white goods, and Bharti Cellular with its Airtel brand in wireless communications.

Today a prominent global name is that of Laxmi Narain Mittal, of Arcelor-Mittal. His father, Mohan L. Mittal, bought a rolling mill in Howrah, near Calcutta, then purchased several mini steel mills and diversified operations overseas, to Indonesia, in the 1970s. The overseas operations were handled by L. N. Mittal, who then acquired several defunct steel assets in relatively obscure steel-manufacturing locations, such as Trinidad and Tobago, Ireland, and Kazakhstan, and then bought Arcelor, an extremely large European steel manu-facturer, to emerge as one of the world's largest steelmakers.

In India's domestic economy, the brand name Videocon is well estab-lished in consumer durables, white goods, and consumer electronics, and the company is the closest that India can offer to a company such as Matsushita Industries of the National or Panasonic brands fame. The origins of the group lie in a sugar mill started by Nandlal M. Dhoot, in the mid 1950s.[2] In the 1980s, the group entered into a joint venture with Toshiba Corporation of Japan to manufacture television sets. The real entrepreneurship occurred in the late 1980s. Raj Kumar Dhoot, one of N. M. Dhoot's sons, had noticed that at Bombay's Santa Cruz airport, Indian residents, mostly originating from the Indian state of Kerala, arriving from the Gulf States, would typically return with three items of luggage. One item was a stereo radio-cum-recorder, of the type called a boom box; the second item was a Dunlopillo foam mattress, and the third item was a washing machine. After clearing customs, and emerging outside the airport, these passengers would be immediately met and relieved of their Dunlopillo mattresses and the washing machines by agents. These items were purchased by the passengers for subsequent sale in India, since Dunlopillo foam mattresses had very high domestic excise taxes levied on them. A domestic agent could arbitrage on prices. Washing machines had a very large demand in Bombay, since people lived in small flats and there were no regular servants for washing clothes. Hence, the lady of the house would hand-wash all of her family's laundry herself, and wanted a washing machine for these tasks.

R. K. Dhoot concluded that a large market for washing machines and other white goods existed. He researched the regulations and found that washing machines without electronic controls, considered basic items of manufacture, were reserved for manufacture by the small-scale sector, while washing machines with electronic controls, considered complex items of manufacture, were subject to capacity controls and licensing by the Ministry of Industrial Development. Videocon would be ineligible to make the less complex washing machines reserved for the small-scale sector. Thereupon, Videocon applied for a license to make 5,000 washing machines with electronic controls, actually a very tiny number to be produced in terms of the economies of scale required to attain efficiencies in white goods production. The grant of the license led to the foundation of India's major corporation in consumer electronics and white goods.

R. K. Dhoot's noticing of a market gap, which might be explained as an Israel Kirzner type of an alert entrepreneurial act, based on spontaneous discovery,[3] may have indirectly propelled industrial sector reforms in India. Mr. L. Mansingh, as joint secretary in charge of the Secretariat of Industrial Approvals in the Ministry of Industrial Development, had to deal with the Videocon license application. On an enquiry by then Industrial Development Secretary, Mrs. Otima Bordia, as to why the Videocon license was being granted, Mr. Mansingh pointed out the absurdities of reservation and licensing, creating a dual structure for a good with economic demand and a social necessity in urban India. Thereafter, from the late 1980s, piecemeal reforms of various anomalies in the industrial licensing process started, before the Big Bang declaration of July 24, 1991.

Sunil Mittal, son of a former member of parliament, started in business at the age of 18 with ₹20,000 borrowed from his father. Initial ventures to trade bicycle parts and hosiery yarn were not remunerative. The import of portable generating sets for India's chronically energy-deficient areas was paying, but their imports were banned. While in Taiwan, he had noticed push-button phones which did not exist in India. He started marketing telephones and answering and fax machines, and in 1992 successfully bid for a mobile services license. This is how Airtel came into being.[4] The Airtel brand has since become visible in India, with the company Bharti Cellular one of the largest in terms of market share and customer coverage. It attempted twice to acquire the MTN Group, a large South Africa-based mobile services company, but this did not transpire. Since then, Bharti Cellular has acquired the African assets of Zain Telecom, to expand its market coverage to 15 African markets. In the process, it has become one of the largest emerging-market mobile services firms.

The tale of the Mittals and Dhoots still relate to scions of established businesses, albeit small businesses, engaging in manufacturing relatively standard items, within a traditional industry structure, and keenly aware of the institutional milieu of India. Steel, consumer goods, and telecommunications are erstwhile *License Raj* industries. Driving many such industries are deals, and the import–export functionalities of older days. What, however, is different today is the engaging of such entrepreneurs in large-scale operations, L. N. Mittal in steel overseas, the Dhoots in white goods and consumer electronics in India, and S. Mittal in wireless services both in India and abroad.

There is also a new breed of technology entrepreneur that has emerged in contemporary India. For them, the *License Raj* has been a theoretical concept, to be experienced via films such as my classmate

Mani Ratnam's film *Guru*. Typically, these technology entrepreneurs are engineers, often with a degree or other qualifications from the United States, and many have had work experience overseas. They have returned to India to set up businesses, often venturing into uncharted waters, where the prospects of grounding the vessel on invisible sandbanks are high. The reverse brain drain, particularly from the United States to India, may be evoking new passion in India and the United States in terms of loss of intellectual capabilities for the United States.[5] The known originator of such a reverse flow of knowledge was Gokaraju S. Raju, who had earned a master's degree from the University of California, San Francisco. In 1950, on return to India, he set up the South India Research Institute, a pharmaceutical formulations manufacturing company at Vijayawada. Since then, the SIRIS group, as it is known, has branched into the production of herbal remedies, herbal dietary products, and wine.[6]

In the pharmaceutical sector, Murali K. Divi, holder of a pharmacy doctorate who had worked in the United States, having earlier worked with Warner Hindustan, later Warner Lambert, in their Hyderabad plant, started Divi's Laboratories. The firm is engaged in research and development (R&D) based generation of new processes to produce active pharmaceutical ingredients, in other words bulk drugs, to provide inputs to the domestic Indian pharmaceutical industry. M. K. Divi had earlier set up Cheminor Drugs, in collaboration with Dr. K. Anji Reddy, which then merged into Dr. Reddy's laboratories.[7] In 1990, he set up Divi's Laboratories, now a company that generates revenues of ₹1,000 crores per year and enjoys a profit margin of almost 35 percent.[8] Similarly, Venkaiah C. Nannipeni, a pharmacist, worked in the United States for 15 years and then returned to set up Natco Pharma in 1981.[9] The company is one of India's largest contract manufacturers of pharmaceutical products, and pioneered time-release technology in India. Currently, it has four manufacturing plants and employs 1,500 persons.[10]

A relatively newer company, Bharat Biotech International, was set up in 1996 by Dr. Krishna M. Ella, an agricultural scientist who had worked with Sandoz and Bayer in India, received a doctorate from the University of Wisconsin-Madison in molecular biology, and was then on the faculty of the Medical University of South Carolina, Charleston.[11] The company introduced the world's first cesium chloride-free hepatitis B vaccine, after collaborative research with the

Indian Institute of Science,[12] and India's first new generation vaccine against typhoid. It was also the first Indian company to receive two grants from the Bill and Melinda Gates Foundation: one, to develop new vaccines against malaria, in collaboration with the United States' Centers for Disease Control, based in Atlanta, and the New Delhi-based International Center for Genetic Engineering and Biotechnology; the other against rotavirus.[13] Dr. Vijay Chandru, who had done his doctorate at the Massachusetts Institute of Technology, and then been a faculty member at Purdue University and the Indian Institute of Science, Bangalore, founded Strand Genomics in 2000. Now renamed Strand Life Sciences, the company is in the life sciences informatics area of business, engaged in data mining, predictive modeling, bioinformatics, and computational chemistry for developing drug discovery solutions. Several of the largest global pharmaceutical companies, biotechnology companies, and academic institutions are its customers.[14]

Other than reverse brain drain returnees, Indian entrepreneurs have also engaged in the biotechnology sector. A useful example is that of Shantha Biotechnics set up by Dr. K. I. Varaprasad Reddy, an electronics engineer, in 1993 to develop vaccines and therapeutics for the mass of India's population. In order to have a low cost base, the vaccine technologies were developed domestically, based on in-house R&D, in collaboration with the Osmania University and the Center for Cellular and Molecular Biology in Hyderabad. In 1997, Shantha Biotechnics developed and commercialized India's first recombinant DNA-based hepatitis B vaccine. It is now a part of the French Sanofi-Aventis group, which is one of the world leaders in the vaccine industry.[15] The research spending, at more than 25 percent of its revenues, is extremely high compared to other Indian companies where the R&D intensity is extremely slim.[16]

Somewhat related to pharmaceuticals and biotechnology are initiatives in the food sector, where an American academic turned serial entrepreneur has set an interesting precedent. Dr. Palani G. Periasamy is the holder of a doctorate in economics from the University of Pittsburgh, and had in the course of an academic career headed the business school of the University of Baltimore. After over 20 years in academia, in 1987 he started Dharani Sugars, now a quoted company, and has diversified his business activities into hotels, with a Le Meridien property, and a range of educational initiatives in his home state of Tamil Nadu.[17] In northern India, Malvinder Singh Bhinder, a marine engineer who had worked in the United States,[18] established a facility in 1992, in conjunction with the Punjab Agro Industries Corporation, to produce mushrooms. The company, since renamed Agro-Dutch Industries, is today the world's largest mushroom producer. Initially, its annual production level was 3,000 tons. Now, its annual mushroom production level is 50,000 tons.[19] It is probable that the mushrooms one buys at one's local grocery will have been supplied by Patiala's Agro-Dutch Industries.

So far, these entrepreneurship examples are of persons engaging in traditional businesses. M. S. Bhinder's mushroom farming, while an enterprising venture, is based on the solid path dependencies of a farming culture that has had its roots in the Punjab for thousands of years. Are there off-the-wall ventures developed by entrepreneurs that have trod water in an uncharted ocean, to use a cliché? The website http://yourstory.in/entrepreneurs has several stories of such emerging ventures. I will describe a few cases of emergent and home-grown entrepreneurship that caught my eye.

A venture with important social responsibility overtones is that of Sharda University. Education is very big business in India. It will remain so for the foreseeable future. In fact, if it was not for the hunger of India's youth for learning, the economies of nations such as Australia and the United Kingdom would be severely afflicted if Indian students deserted Australian and British universities. While the business model of Sharda University, in terms of products and content, is no different from any other Indian educational entrepreneurship venture, one tweak in the model sets it apart. It provides 90 percent scholarships for female students whose families cannot afford to pay their tuition fees, in the interest of reducing India's gender inequalities. One could consider it as an innovation in corporate social entrepreneurship within the framework of a traditional business model.

Similarly, novel thinking might have driven the business venture of Rouble Nagi. She is an entrepreneur in commercial art, using materials like wood, stone, and copper. Having worked in variety of media, she has executed more than 600 murals world-wide and established one of the largest mural companies in Asia. A former chemical engineer, Nalin Khanduri has set up Great Indian Outdoors, in 2000, and it has apparently become India's leading adventure tourism company. After 14 years of being a bartender, Yangdup Lama has set up a beverage consultancy. He conducts corporate and consumer workshops on beverage appreciation and experience, trains the corporate staff of the Taj Luxury Hotels chain on bar and beverage issues, and provides consulting for international spirit brands in India.[20] As a bartender, he would have made some money on tips. As a beverage consultant, he has changed the return on his human capital skills to an hourly rate probably 10 to 25 times more than he would have received via tips.

Other than India's current entrepreneurial climate, none of these individuals would have any precedents to fall back on in their choice of business activities. Their enterprises would be classified as unorganized service or trading sector businesses in the government statistics. In addition, they would all be totally flummoxed if one classified them as radically subjective entrepreneurs. Yet, a radical subjectivist label might describe India's entrepreneurs today. The destruction of a low-level centralized command and control equilibrium in India, 20 years ago, has been accompanied by the arrival of decentralized entrepreneurial disequilibrium. Indian firms have become the vehicle for her entrepreneurs to originate a stream of novel ventures, emerging from their subjective imaginations, such as a commercial mural supply company, in which a range of heterogeneous resources are combined.

These thoughts and creative actions have generated increased variety in a synthesis of dynamic creation, and are changing the order of India's industrial landscape.[21] As George Shackle had suggested, these creative acts have injected something essentially new into the world.[22] Indian entrepreneurs have, thus, created novelty by forward-looking, creative activities, whether it is in financing girls' school and college fees, leading adventure treks in India's wilderness, or making a transition from dispensing beverages to dispensing beverage knowledge. There are also some, like Ferdi, and Jagdish Khattar, whom we will meet soon, engaged in providing vehicles for people who are physically challenged, or in altering the automotive service sector in India. Their actions may eventually have repercussions on India's industrial structure. The next two sections of this chapter provide aggregate evidence of the macro landscape in India's industrial economy.

Corporate sector evolution in India

An important indicator of entrepreneurial activity in India is the growth in company registrations, and their financial patterns. The macro landscape is an aggregation of the thousands of micro views capturing the details of individual enterprises in India. The macro big picture on Indian entrepreneurship can be depicted using the details on company formation in India from the 1920s to the 2000s as data. These data, for almost nine decades, provide details of the number of companies formed annually over that period. They highlight the extent of corporate sector activity in India.

The corporate organizational form has been called an important institutional innovation in economic history, since the limited liability characteristic permits individuals to take risks without committing all of their capital. It is one way in which organized sector businesses in India can be set up. The corporate sector data were obtained from several sources. The primary source is the Ministry of Corporate Affairs (MCA) of the government of India. This is the primary agency for monitoring and regulating corporate bodies in India. Their data are at the company level. The MCA do not, however, look after the interests of businesses organized either as a proprietorship, a partnership, or a cooperative. Both organized and unorganized sector businesses in India could be set up as proprietorships, partnerships, or cooperatives. Nevertheless, firms organized as corporations account for almost 90 percent of the value of industrial output in India.[23]

The MCA data were organized as a time series for the period 1923–24 to 2009–10. Table A7 contains biennial details of the number of companies in India, and the value of the paid-up capital associated with private companies. The data coverage was for the entire population of enterprises making up the corporate sector in India. Many of these companies could be non-operational, but the numbers do indicate the growth trends. Figure 7.1 depicts the average number of companies in existence in India during each of the decades from the 1920s to the 2000s.

In 1923–24, there were 5,190 registered companies in India. In 2009–10, there were 786,774 registered companies. The number of companies in India had risen 152 times in about 90 years. In 1923–24, the total paid-up capital of the companies, in nominal terms, was ₹260 crores. In 2009–10, the total paid-up capital of the companies, in nominal terms, was over ₹1,000,000 crores. The aggregate amount invested in the corporate sector had risen 3,864 times in that period. These are data for the two-year periods at the beginning and the end of the time series. The following discussions are based on the average trends per decade reported in Table 7.1.

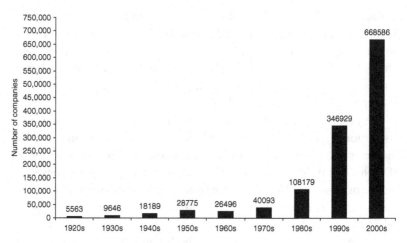

Figure 7.1. Average number of companies in existence in each decade from the 1920s to the 2000s.

Source: Table A7.

The average number of companies in each decade rose from 5,563 to 668,586 by the 2000s. The average amount of paid-up capital invested in the companies in each decade rose from ₹273 crores to ₹495,040 crores by the 2000s. The number of registered companies grew rapidly in the decade of the 1930s and 1940s, capturing the reaction of Indian businessmen to nationalist forces and the possibilities of industrialization during the Second World War. The within-decade growth in the number of companies was low in the 1950s and 1960s, but shot up to 78 percent in the 1970s. In the 1980s and 1990s, the within-decade growth was 219 percent and 153 percent respectively. By the early part of the 2000s, the absolute number of companies was high; thus, the within-decade growth in the number of companies being registered dropped to 37 percent.

The within-decade growth in the amount of overall capital invested was low in the 1920s and 1930s. It shot up to triple digits from the 1940s onwards. In the 1950s and 1960s, it was over 100 percent within the decades; it shot up to 207 percent in the 1970s. In the 1980s and 1990s, the within-decade growth in capital invested was 295 percent and 307 percent respectively. Again, by the early part of the 2000s, the absolute amount of capital invested had reached a high level, so the within-decade growth of overall capital invested

Table 7.1. *The corporate sector in India from the 1920s to the 2000s*

Decade	Average annual number of registered companies in that decade	Percentage growth in average number of companies from decade beginning to decade end	Average annual total paid-up capital in rupees crores of the companies in that decade	Percentage growth in annual average total paid-up capital from decade beginning to decade end
1920s	5,563	22	273	8
1930s	9,646	52	295	3
1940s	18,189	118	452	103
1950s	28,775	−1	1,009	109
1960s	26,496	4	2,733	145
1970s	40,093	78	8,428	207
1980s	108,179	219	31,844	295
1990s	346,929	153	140,359	307
2000s	668,586	37	495,040	104

Source: See Table A7.

dropped to 104 percent between the beginning and the end of the 2000s. The amount of capital invested per company is an excellent indicator of businessmen's motives. Since it is easy to start a company but funding it requires considerable and consistent commitment, the growth in the average amount of paid-up capital per company over time reflects continuing support for the cause of one's corporate activity.

Figure 7.2 depicts the average amount of paid-up capital per company for the biennial years between 1971–72 and 2009–10. Table A8 lists the amount of paid-up capital, per year, and the growth for all of the biennial years between 1923–24 and 2009–10. Figure 7.2 shows that the average amount of paid-up capital per company increased from ₹15 lakhs in 1970–71 to ₹33 lakhs in 1990–91. Hence, there was a doubling of amount invested per company. Between 1990–91 and 2009–10, the amount invested per company rose from ₹33 lakhs to ₹1.28 crores. In other words, there was a quadrupling of amount invested per company in the period of twenty years.

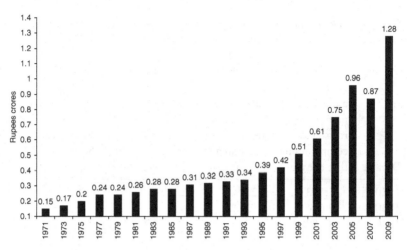

Figure 7.2. Average paid-up capital per company in rupees crores from 1971–72 to 2009–10.

Source: Table A7.

Over the 40 years evaluated, the average amount of paid-up capital per company rose almost ten times. A caveat is necessary. These are nominal values. A computation in real values will show that this rise is six times. Nevertheless, as a prima facie indicator of commitment by company promoters to the cause of their businesses, these data are compelling. Another important indicator is the between-decade growth in the amount of paid-up capital per company, and that is depicted in figure 7.3. Figure 7.3 shows that the growth within the decade in the average paid-up capital per company was negative in the 1920s, 1930s, and the 1940s. More companies were being started than money was being put into them. From the 1950s, the growth was positive and substantial. In the 1960s, the growth was over 20 percent. The growth was in double digits in the 1970s and 1990s, but somewhat lower in the 1980s. By the 2000s, the growth was over 20 percent again. Two conclusions follow: the growth in company formations reflects the basic process of economic growth under way in India, an unsurprising finding; the growth in the paid-up capital per company reflects that businessmen and entrepreneurs have been willing to put more of their resources into potentially risky ventures, with this facet of corporate behavior depicting the enhanced risk propensity of Indian entrepreneurs.

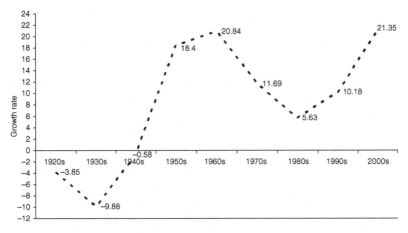

Figure 7.3. Decadal growth rates in average paid-up capital per company. *Source:* Table A7.

From policy and intellectual standpoints, the aggregate data can be further analyzed. The corporate demography approach, feasible with aggregate company formation and capital information data, reveals important trends. Using company formation data for the years 1957–58 to 2001–02, which gave information for the number of both private sector and public sector government companies for those years, I investigated issues of crowding out.[24] Crowding out is an important economic construct capturing how the business environment has evolved,[25] and how the investment activity of firms has unfolded. The industrial structure of an economy is materially affected, as one group of firms displaces another in the environment. Consistent with the industrial policy of government, in the 1950s and 1960s there was growth of the public sector. The growth in the share of government companies effectively crowded out private enterprises in India's corporate sector from access to funds, from the mid to late 1950s to the early 1990s. That trend was reversed with the resurgence in private enterprise growth after the introduction of reforms in 1991. There was crowding in by private enterprises, displacing government companies from their position as holders of a large portion of equity capital, and private companies increased their financial scale by substantially augmenting the level of equity invested per company.[26] Such analyses complement the data in this chapter.

The industrial initiatives landscape

The next analyses, highlighting entrepreneurial and industrial activity in India, relate to growth in India's organized manufacturing sector. In the years after the institutional discontinuity, between 1990–91 and 2008–09, the big picture on manufacturing initiatives in India depicts a trend similar to that depicted by the corporate sector. The data on organized sector manufacturing enterprises are collected via the Annual Survey of Industries, popularly known as the ASI. These have been widely used. Data at plant or manufacturing unit level are collected annually and released in the aggregate. These aggregate data depict an important aspect of India's manufacturing reality.

A clarification is required. Many, if not all, of these units will also have been incorporated as companies. Nevertheless, a large chunk of the organized manufacturing enterprises in India is also organized as proprietorships and partnerships. Jean-Baptiste Say[27] articulated, over 300 years ago, that an entrepreneur unified different elements such as workers and financial resources with the goal of creating a product or service. How these elements are then to be organized, for such unity of elements to be attained, is a second-order question as to the precise organizational form used. There are no data overlaps between the ASI data, and the corporate sector data also released in the aggregate by the Ministry of Corporate Affairs. What both datasets show is whether the broad trends are similar. Let me use the analogy of a view of Bombay. The first big view is a depiction of Bombay from the harbor, looking westwards towards the Gateway of India; the second big view looks eastwards, and depicts Bombay from the sea, highlighting the buildings of Nariman Point. Both views are of the same broad area of Bombay, but each is from a different perspective. Similarly, the ASI and companies' data reflect different realities of India's economy.

The ASI data show that in the roughly 20 years between 1990–91 and 2008–09, the number of manufacturing factories had grown at a rate of 2 percent per year. Employment in these factories had risen by 2 percent per year. Real investment in these units had grown by 6 percent, while the real output growth from these factories was 15 percent per annum. Clearly, the organized manufacturing sector was growing and contributing to India's overall growth.[28] The specific annual growth in each of these parameters, number of factories, employment, real investment and real output, are depicted in figures 7.4 to 7.7.

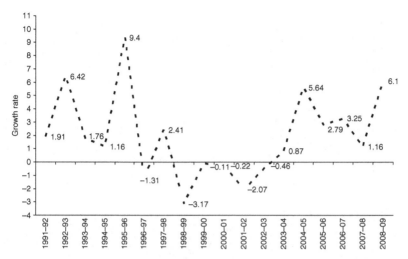

Figure 7.4. Growth in the total number of factories in the organized manufacturing sector from 1991–92 to 2008–09.

Source: Annual Survey of Industries, various years.

Figure 7.4 shows that after 1991 and till 1996, the number of factories being established grew rapidly. These are net growth data, as the data on actual exits and entries are not provided. Hence, the actual number of new factories to be established could be quite a bit larger than the numbers depicted. There was net decline in factory establishments till 2002–03. Then, the trend is again positive. Figure 7.5 depicts employment growth in these factories.

Figure 7.5 again depicts the same time series trends, with the same dip in the late 1990s and early 2000s, though the actual magnitude of the growth rates is considerably larger than those for factory establishment. It has been suggested that a specter of jobless growth hangs over the Indian economy. One would suggest that such a specter could be exorcised, at least for the manufacturing sector. Relatively healthy organized manufacturing sector employment growth of 7.41 percent in 2004–05, 7.78 percent in 2005–06, 13.35 percent in 2006–07, 1.20 percent in 2007–08, and 8.37 percent in 2008–09 occurred. Of course, organized sector manufacturing employment of 11 million is trivial, at 1 percent, relative to India's total population of 1.1 or 1.2 billion. Yet, Indian entrepreneurs have responded to incentives by enhancing manufacturing employment over time.

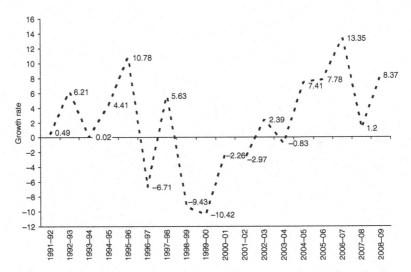

Figure 7.5. Growth in total employment in the organized manufacturing sector from 1991–92 to 2008–09.

Source: Annual Survey of Industries, various years.

Table 7.2 lists some manufacturing industries in which entrepreneurs have created jobs. These data relate to the period between 1993–94 and 2003–04, a decade in which the influence of institutional change will have been felt by firms, with the employment results becoming verifiable. I discuss five of the industries. In the automotive and motor vehicles sector, annual employment has risen at over 14 percent; in the accounting and computing machinery sector annual employment has risen at over 7 percent; in the leather sector, annual employment has risen at almost 5 percent; in the fabricated metals sector, annual employment has risen at well over 4 percent; and in the apparels sector annual employment has risen at over 4 percent. These sectors are important for economic development and India's exports.

Figures 7.6 and 7.7 depict the growth in real levels of investment and output, in aggregate, over time. Other than dips in 1998–99 and 2000–01, levels of real investment rose in all of the years. In the last four years evaluated, the growth rates were 15.19 percent in 2005–06, 13.80 percent in 2006–07, 13.75 percent in 2007–08 and 11.01 percent in 2008–09. Similarly, other than in 1998–99, when there was a relative decline, real output growth rates were robust. After 2000–01, real output growth rates were very robust. They were 22.26 percent

Table 7.2. *Average annual percentage employment growth for a sample of segments of Indian industry in the manufacturing sector between 1993–94 and 2003–04*

Annual employment growth

Industry	Growth	Industry	Growth	Industry	Growth
Food and beverages	0.85	Paper	4.00	Basic metals	−0.11
Tobacco	1.51	Printing and publishing	5.07	Fabricated metals	4.47
Textiles	0.96	Petroleum products	−1.92	Machinery and equipment	−1.38
Apparels	4.20	Chemicals	2.04	Accounting and computing machinery	7.44
Leather	4.84	Rubber and plastics	2.03	Electrical machinery	3.94
Wood products	4.27	Other minerals	3.04	Radios and television sets	−3.51
Furniture	3.18	Motor vehicles	14.56	Medical instruments	8.80
		Transport equipment	−0.79		

Source: Ministry of Statistics and Programme Implementation, Annual Survey of Industries, various years.

for 2004–05, 10.70 percent for 2005–06, 20.85 percent for 2006–07, 9.73 percent for 2007–08, and 9.14 percent for 2008–09.

Two indicators of manufacturing sector progress are whether there is capital–labor substitution taking place, and if manufacturing scale is being attained. These issues are evaluated, at an aggregate level, for the organized manufacturing sector. As stressed, capital–labor substitution and attainment of scale reflect industrialization at work. The enhancements of the ratios are important indicators of an economy going through an industrial revolution.[29] Figure 7.8 depicts the levels of real capital investment made per employee in India's organized manufacturing sector. In the near 20 years between 1990–91 and 2008–09, the levels of real capital investment made per employee have doubled. The amount was approximately ₹2.4 lakhs per employee. By 2008–09,

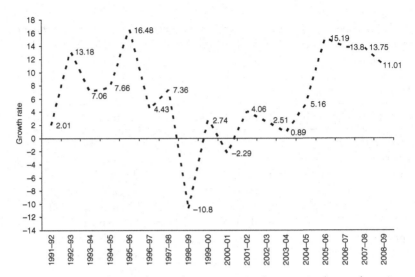

Figure 7.6. Growth in real capital investment in the organized manufacturing sector from 1991–92 to 2008–09.

Source: Annual Survey of Industries, various years.

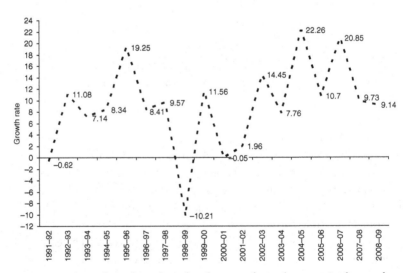

Figure 7.7. Growth in the value of real output from the organized manufacturing sector from 1991–92 to 2008–09.

Source: Annual Survey of Industries, various years.

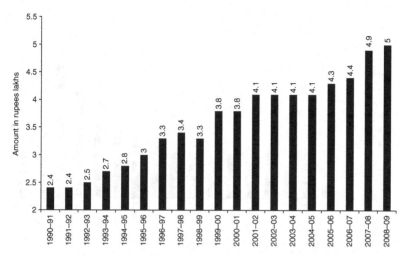

Figure 7.8. Levels of real capital investment per employee from 1990–91 to 2008–09.

Source: Annual Survey of Industries, various years.

it had touched ₹5 lakhs per employee. The amount has been rising steadily since the early 1990s. It jumped by over 10 percent between 2006–07 and 2007–08. Since changes in the capital–labor substitution ratio are a prima facie indicator of technology diffusion within the manufacturing sector, the aggregate indicators for India suggest improvements in manufacturing functionalities.

A second issue relates to manufacturing scale. Figure 7.9 depicts the level of real output per factory over the almost 20 years between 1990–91 and 2008–09. An indication that manufacturing scale is being achieved is depicted by increases in the amount produced per factory. This may also imply achievement of efficiencies. Since efficiencies are also driven by scale effects, the improvements in the ratio can suggest scale effects being finally triggered in Indian industry. Figure 7.9 displays the levels of real output per factory over time. The levels of real output per factory have increased from ₹2.46 crores in 1990–91 to ₹7.80 crores in 2008–09. Again, the growth has been steady. The amounts of real output per factory have trebled in a period of less than 20 years. While the increase of real output per factory was less than double between 1990–91 and 1999–2000, between 2000–01 and 2008–09 the amounts have doubled. I reiterate a point made some years ago that India is finally engaged in a supply side revolution.[30]

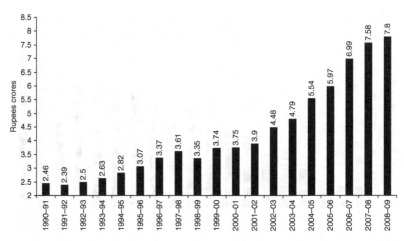

Figure 7.9. Levels of real output per factory from 1990–91 to 2008–09.

Source: Annual Survey of Industries, various years.

A second set of facts relating to scale is presented in Table 7.3. The table documents the size distribution of factories for the year 2008–09, by size of employment. There are eight categories of size. These are units employing between zero and 49, between 50 and 99, between 100 and 199, between 200 and 499, between 500 and 999, between 1,000 and 1,999, between 2,000 and 4,999 and over 5,000 persons.

The smallest size factories, which employ between zero and 49 persons, account for over 72 percent of factories in India, but for less than 10 percent of capital invested and just over 11 percent of output by value. At the other end of the scale, factories employing more than 5,000 persons, the mega-factories, account for 0.18 of all factories in India. If the factories employing 2,000 to 4,999 persons are taken into account, these factories in total account for just 0.64 percent of all Indian factories. The large units employing more than 5,000 persons account for over 12 percent of capital investment, about 8 percent of employment, and just over 10 percent of organized manufacturing sector output. The large units employing more than 2,000 persons, which is a sum of the two last size categories, account for 0.64 percent of factories, for over 25 percent of capital investment, over 16 percent of employment, and 23 percent of organized manufacturing sector output by value.

Hence, the size distribution of organized manufacturing sector factories is skewed. Yet, the existence of these factory units, producing considerable output, is a precedent for other Indian manufacturing

Table 7.3. *Size distribution of organized sector manufacturing*
establishments in India for 2008–09 – size range by employment

Panel (A)	Factories	Capital invested	Employment	Output
0 to 49	72.04	9.41	17.23	11.63
50 to 99	12.33	6.25	11.55	8.94
100 to 199	7.25	8.89	13.23	9.83
200 to 499	5.00	18.67	18.42	17.13
500 to 999	1.82	16.41	13.05	15.69
1,000 to 1,999	0.93	14.48	9.88	13.53
2,000 to 4,999	0.46	13.82	8.72	12.80
5,000 and above	0.18	12.06	7.92	10.45

Panel (B)	Cumulative percentage	Cumulative percentage	Cumulative percentage	Cumulative percentage
0 to 49	72.04	9.41	11.63	17.23
50 to 99	84.37	15.66	20.57	28.78
100 to 199	91.62	24.55	30.40	42.01
200 to 499	96.62	43.22	47.53	60.43
500 to 999	98.44	59.63	63.22	73.48
1,000 to 1,999	99.37	74.11	76.75	83.36
2,000 to 4,999	99.83	87.93	89.55	92.08
5,000 and above	100.00	100.00	100.00	100.00

Source: Ministry of Statistics and Programme Implementation, Annual Survey of Industries, 2008–09.

units to scale up their operations, which is a necessary condition for successful industrialization. When the key features of industrial progress, a substitution of capital for labor and an enhancement of manufacturing scale, are evaluated for the Indian organized manufacturing sector, the data indicate the progression of very late large-scale industrialization in India.

The small-scale sector in India

There are many aspects to India's industrialization. India is a heterogeneous economy. The largest part of India's private sector consists of small entrepreneurs, craftsmen, traders, and petty professionals. The process of India's entrepreneurship democratization is driven by elements in the small-scale sector. Many such businesses are engaged in manufacturing. While writing about Indian industry is based around the role of the organized manufacturing sector, that sector forms a small part of the economy.[31] Small-scale industries hold an iconic status among industrial policy issues in India. At one time, many consumer products could only be made by small-scale firms. India's lack of manufacturing prowess might have resulted from the reservation policies made for small-scale firms, and Indian industry was unable to reap the benefits of scale economies.[32]

Small-scale enterprises belong to organized and unorganized sectors. The distinction of scale is based on size characteristics. In the manufacturing sector, a micro enterprise is one with investment in plant and machinery not exceeding ₹25 lakhs. A small enterprise is one with investment in plant and machinery over ₹25 lakhs but not exceeding ₹5 crores. A medium enterprise is one with investment in plant and machinery over ₹5 crores but not exceeding ₹10 crores. In the services sector, a micro enterprise is one with investment in equipment not exceeding ₹10 lakhs. A small enterprise is one with investment in equipment over ₹10 lakhs but not exceeding ₹2 crores. A medium enterprise is one with investment in equipment over ₹2 crores but not exceeding ₹5 crores.[33]

The small-scale industries grew rapidly in India during the Second World War in response to emerging defense supply needs. There was no distinction between cottage and small-scale industries. With the fall in demand after the Second World War ended, a large number of units disappeared.[34] The First Five-Year Plan recognized the importance of the small-scale sector for providing employment for educated persons and for women in their homes. Thus, a concern with employment, and an anxiety about shortage of funds, led to initial reservations for small-scale and cottage industries.[35]

The Second Five-Year Plan identified features of these units as urban or semi-urban locations and use of power, machines, and modern techniques. They were generally run by small entrepreneurs. Their link with large-scale units was more as suppliers against orders rather than as well-established subcontractors. The Third Plan found that that the growth of a vigorous class of small entrepreneurs had been a significant development in the 1950s.[36] The first formal definition of small-scale and ancillary units was given in 1955. In 1967, reservation of production of 47 items by the small-scale sector was introduced. By March 1987, the reservations had been extended to 850 items. In 1977, a category of tiny, now called the micro category, industries was introduced.[37]

In many states, such as Maharashtra, small-scale industries corporations had been set up. The Maharashtra Small Scale Industries Development Corporation (MSSIDC) was established in 1962, to create an atmosphere for entrepreneurship democratization by permitting businessmen to develop industrial capabilities. Several economic development initiatives in the public sphere were given to bodies such as MSSIDC to implement. In the case of public health programs, the central government might place a contract with a state government, such as that of Maharashtra, to provide medicines for mass distribution. The implementing agency would be MSSIDC, which would then farm out the production of tablets to several small-scale units that were looking for business opportunities. While such an approach sacrificed economies of scale in the manufacture of medicines, it led to skills acquisition by many firms and the development of a vibrant pharmaceutical manufacturing sector in the region.[38]

Lupin Laboratories is one such pharmaceutical sector small-scale enterprise story. In the late 1960s, Desh Bandu Gupta, an associate professor of chemistry at the Birla Institute of Technology and Science, Pilani, had come to to Bombay to become an entrepreneur. He had sold his wife's jewelry to start the business, and commenced operations in a Bombay suburb with a single tablet-making machine. With no financial and production track record to display to bankers, he found securing funds difficult, and only the personal interventions of senior government officials, standing personal surety, enabled him to obtain loan financing. Today, Lupin Laboratories has annual sales of approximately $1 billion, and obtains almost 70 percent of its revenues from export markets. It is also one of the world's largest producers of anti-tuberculosis (TB) drugs and cephalosporins, an important class of antibiotics.[39]

While the industrial policy changes of July 24, 1991 did not deal with the question of reservation, a later committee, chaired by Abid Husain, recommended the abolition of reservations. The Abid Husain Committee had found that more than half the number of small-scale units manufactured only non-reserved items. The committee had also found that 68 items out of the total 850 items, being manufactured by 83 percent of the units, accounted for 81 percent of the total sales value.[40] Reservations were no longer required. They were, in fact, counter-productive. The natural drive and professionalism of numerous entrepreneurs had made reservations unnecessary.

The case of Bharat Forge further illustrates the fact that giants were once small too. Bharat Forge in Poona, now India's and one of the world's largest forgings and stampings company specially for automotive components, started life as a small-scale unit in the late 1960s. Started by Dr. Neelkanth Kalyani, and now managed by his son Baba Kalyani, a graduate of the Massachusetts Institute of Technology, Bharat Forge started as a captive plant for Tata Engineering and Locomotive Company (TELCO), as Tata Motors used to be called. It was specifically set up as a small-scale sector ancillary unit to supply TELCO with parts. By the late 1980s and early 1990s, TELCO had over-reached and Bharat Forge was in despair. Business was drying up for a collapsing automobile ancillary belt around Poona, because of TELCO Poona's performance crisis. Subsequently, a very badly misguided dear-money policy of the Reserve Bank of India in the 1990s, with extremely high domestic interest rates, made Bharat Forge's financial situation somewhat precarious because general domestic demand had dried up.

At this juncture, Baba Kalyani went on a 20-day trip around the world to see what other business could be done, and came back with the idea that the global market could be supplied if quality standards were met. To meet global quality standards would need considerable technology investments on the shop-floor and personnel retraining. Bharat Forge bit the bullet to make the necessary business model changes. The number of blue-collar shop-floor workers was minimized, and all production work was handled by engineering graduates.[41] Full automation was implemented, and Bharat Forge relaunched itself, initially in a small way, to supply products for the global automotive market. Some years later, Germany's largest forgings company went bankrupt. Bharat Forge stepped in as a purchaser. Under German law, companies interested in acquiring another had to make presentations to workers, and the German company's workers chose Bharat Forge over other purchasers. The acquisition enabled Bharat Forge to obtain world-class technology, and German engineers and technicians came to India to facilitate technology transfer. Now, Tata Motors accounts for a tiny percentage of Bharat Forge sales, Bharat Forge has diversified

Table 7.4. *Details of the number of units, combined production, and combined employment in the organized and unorganized micro-scale, small-scale, and medium-scale manufacturing sector in India*

Year	Number of units in millions	Percentage growth	Output value in rupees crores	Percentage growth	Employment in millions	Percentage growth
2006–07	26.10	—	709,398	—	59.46	—
2007–08	27.28	4.52	790,759	11.47	62.63	5.33
2008–09	28.52	4.55	880,805	11.39	65.94	5.29

Source: Government of India, *Handbook of Indian Statistics* (New Delhi: Ministry of Statistics and Programme Implementation, 2011).

into equipment for the nuclear power and oil-drilling sectors, and via acquisitions of other companies has emerged as one of Germany's largest manufacturers of forged items.[42]

What has been the contribution of the small-scale sector, or rather the micro, small- and medium-scale sector as it is now classified as, in the aggregate? Table 7.4 provides some details about the contributions of the sector to Indian industry. The data relate to manufacturing activities carried out in the organized as well as unorganized manufacturing sectors by micro, small- and medium-scale firms. There are over 25 million units in the micro, small- and medium-scale sector firms, and over the course of the period evaluated the number of units has grown at over 4 percent per year. These units employed, in 2008–09, almost 66 million persons. The levels of employment have grown at over 5 percent per year in 2007–08 and 2008–09. Figure 7.10 depicts the employment levels in just the micro and small-scale sector over a 35-year period between 1973–74 and 2007–08. These data now relate to employment in both manufacturing and service sector activities. Figure 7.10 shows that there has been a consistent increase in employment levels in the micro and small-scale sector over the period. In 1973–74, the employment levels were just under 4 million. By 2007–08, the employment levels had reached over 32 million persons. In 1990–91, employment levels were around 11 million persons. The 2007–08 employment levels are almost treble that amount.

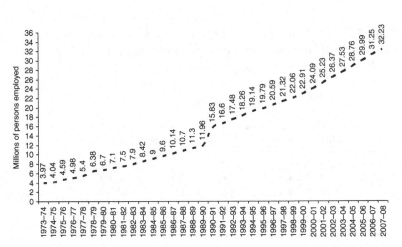

Figure 7.10. Employment in small-scale industries in millions from 1973–74 to 2007–08.

Source: Reserve Bank of India Database on the Indian Economy, Table 35.

The sharp employment increase in the period after the institutional change was put through reflects a substantial response by India's micro and small-scale entrepreneurs towards opportunities to do business in India. Hence, these data highlight the democratization of entrepreneurship in India, since the micro and small entrepreneurs have responded strongly by increasing the number of persons engaged in business activities by an order of magnitude.

Beneficial dualism or bipolar disorder

So far the preceding discussions have been based mainly on the industrial sector. The unorganized trading, services, and manufacturing sectors account for a bulk of India's employment. As shown, organized sector manufacturing employs just 1 percent of India's total population. The micro, small, and medium sector is an important component of industrial growth and employment. The real India, sustaining the common man, is in the numerous shops, workshops, and automotive remanufacturing units of Calcutta and in the streets of Bombay, and numerous towns and villages of India.

On a recent trip to Bombay, I took a drive from the tip of Colaba, all along the north–south spine of eastern Bombay on what is now called P. D'Mello Road and then Rafi Ahmed Kidwai Marg, all the way to

Sion, turned around, stopped, had a very decent cup of South Indian coffee at Sion Circle and came back home, near Mantralaya, along the road which is the major north–south spine of central Bombay called variously Dr. B. R. Ambedkar Marg, Jamsetjee Jeejeebhoy Marg and Mohammedali Road. I was intrigued by what I would find as manufacturing establishments, on this 20-mile stretch. I was not disappointed. I discovered an entire thriving manufacturing ecosystem. There were hundreds of small manufacturing units, all approximately 250 or 300 square feet in size, since their frontages were between 12 and 15 feet and the establishments had a depth of about 20 feet. They were located in what is now very expensive real estate.

The factories started at Bhau Laxman Ajinkya Chowk, near the Yellowgate entrance to Bombay's docks. These were small automotive reconstruction shops. Along P. D'Mello Road, at the spot known as Darukhana, a retail stores cluster supplied hardware for automotive engineering. Then, between Darukhana and the Reay Road station, I found a number of light engineering works catering to the automotive sector, and to the varied requirements of Bombay port's businesses, such as haulage contractors and suppliers of containers. These light engineering works had names such as Startek Engineering Works, K. G. Engineering Works, Salim Engineering Works, New Hindustan Engineering Works, Regal Engineering Works, Best Bharat Engineering Works, Premdev Engineering Works and New Laxmi Engineering Works. Eventually, the cluster of small manufacturing units petered out at Cotton Green. This was once the trading heart of Bombay. Now, there is neither cotton nor green. Instead, situated at Cotton Green is a large grease factory owned by Balmer Lawrie, once a British managing agency house and now a state-owned enterprise.

These workshops, light engineering works, retail outlets, many wholesale outlets, and service businesses reflect the vast unorganized sector of the Indian economy engaged in manufacturing, trading, and service activities. It is conceivable that, like Bharat Forge, once a small-scale unit, any one of these businesses could evolve into a global giant. But we must first understand them, and what they comprise in the aggregate, since they are a neglected segment of Indian business in analysis. What does the unorganized sector of the Indian economy look like in the aggregate? What have been trends in their performance? What have been the salient features of progress for the unorganized sector manufacturing in India? These are important questions,

Table 7.5. *Details of the number of units and combined employment in the unorganized manufacturing, services, and trading sectors of India for various years*

Year	Unorganized manufacturing sector Number of units in millions	Employment in millions	Unorganized services sector Number of units in millions	Employment in millions	Unorganized trading sector Number of units in millions	Employment in millions
1989–90	16.29	—	—	—	—	—
1994–95	14.49	33.23	—	—	—	—
1997	—	—	—	—	14.50	22.15
2000–01	17.03	37.08	14.48	26.56	—	—
2005–06	17.07	36.44	—	—	–	–

Source: See Tables A9 and A10.

as one evaluates contemporary Indian industrialization. In addressing these questions, there are data constraints. The unorganized sector is unorganized as to records. The facts are scattered. Nor are they contemporary. By foraging, I put together facts indicating the scale of operations of the unorganized sector.

The Central Statistical Organization, now in the Ministry of Statistics and Programme Implementation, conducts a National Sample Survey every five years. One is currently under way. Data on many aspects of Indian life are collected, to estimate the contours of the landscape. Ad hoc surveys are carried out from time to time. The National Sample Surveys, popularly called the NSS Rounds, have attempted to estimate the size of India's manufacturing sector. I list the data, in summary form, in Table 7.5. Unorganized manufacturing units are classified as own account manufacturing enterprises (OAME), where there is simply an entrepreneur, non-directory manufacturing enterprises (NDME) where there are up to five employees and directory manufacturing enterprises (DME) where there are more than five employees.

In Table A9, I detail the number of units that belonged to each category, and whether these were located in urban or rural areas, for the survey year 1989–90. No other data were available for that period. The table also details the number of units and employment, and whether these were located in urban or rural areas, by category such as OAME, NDME, and DME, for the survey year 1994–95. Table A9 also details the number of units and employment, by category such as OAME, NDME, and DME, and whether these were located in urban or rural areas, for the survey years 2000–01 and 2005–06. The 2000–11 survey is under way. Take Ferdi Rodrick's enterprise, Ferro Equip, which we came across in Chapter 6. It will be classified as an OAME in the unorganized manufacturing sector. Like it, there are millions of small manufacturing businesses and entrepreneurs creating and delivering value, via the products that they make, to India's markets.

Data on unorganized service and trading enterprises are sparse. In Table A10, I list the number of units and employment, by category such as own account enterprise, and enterprises with employees, for service sector enterprises, and whether these were located in urban or rural areas, for the survey year 2000–01. For example, Sumangala and OM would be classified as urban-based, own account entrepreneurs in the service sector. For trading enterprises, the data are older. In Table A10, I additionally detail the number of units and employment, by category such as own account enterprise and enterprise with employees for service sector enterprises for the survey year of 1997, whether these were retail or wholesale enterprises, and whether these were located in urban or rural areas. I summarize these details in Table 7.5, and base my discussion on that summary. There are over 17 million manufacturing units in India's unorganized sector. Since these would be classified as small units, they would also contribute to the total for small-scale units as shown in Table 7.4. These unorganized sector manufacturing units employed over 33 million persons in 1994–95, the first year for which employment data were available, and this had increased by 10 percent in 2005–06.

Older data, for 2001–02, show that there are 15 million unorganized sector service businesses in India. They employ over 26 million persons. Even older data, for 1997, show that there are about 15 million unorganized sector trading businesses in India, employing over 22 million persons. Let me make an attempt at forecasting. If by 2010–11 the number of businesses in the unorganized manufacturing, services and trading sectors are, say, 18 million, 16 million, and 16 million respectively, these sum up to 50 million businesses in India's unorganized sector. Attempting a forecast of employment, if by 2010–11 the number of persons engaged in the unorganized manufacturing, services, and trading sectors are, say, 38 million, 28 million, and 24 million respectively, these items sum up to 90 million persons engaged in India's unorganized sector.

These 50 million unorganized sector businesses are an important entrepreneurial asset in India. The 90 million persons engaged in the unorganized sector businesses are a vital human capital component. Relative to the organized manufacturing sector, which employs 1 percent of India's population, the unorganized sector as a whole employs almost 10 times the number of persons. The level of such employment comes close to 10 percent of India's population. As a proportion of India's working-age population, the number will be larger, and five industry groups have engaged 71 percent of persons who work in unorganized manufacturing enterprises. These groups are: manufacture of food products and beverages, 17 percent; manufacture of textiles, 17 percent; manufacture of apparel, 14 percent; manufacture of tobacco products, 12 percent; and manufacture of wood products, 11 percent. The other sectors together have engaged 29 percent of the persons employed.

Yet, a discordant note arises. Based on data for 2000–01, collating the NSS and ASI manufacturing sector facts together, labor economist Dipak Mazumdar suggested that there was a dualism in India's industrial structure. The unorganized manufacturing sector, while accounting for 83 percent of all manufacturing sector employment, accounted for a small portion of manufacturing value-added in India. The OAME entrepreneurial units accounted for 56 percent of persons employed in manufacturing, but could generate a small amount of manufacturing value-added per person engaged. Similarly, the units with employees, the NDME and DME units, could generate small amounts of value-added relative to the organized sector. According to a basic productivity index, productivity of entrepreneur-owned units was 4 percent that of manufacturing units in the organized sector.[43]

Just as the organized manufacturing sector has responded to the institutional discontinuity engendered in India, the unorganized sector, in trading, services, and manufacturing, will have responded with equal alacrity, if not with the same level of professionalism or resources. Nevertheless, the relative discordance between the performance of the unorganized and organized sectors reflects the opportunity to engender yet another industrial transformation. The skewness in output and productivity distribution, between the organized sector and unorganized sector activities, particularly in manufacturing, suggests that a bipolar disorder may afflict India's economy. Such an industrial structure could, instead, be an important asset. The decentralized industrial order of Germany, consisting of thousands of small and medium firms, is an important economic resource.[44] India's decentralized industrial sector firms, which unorganized sector firms are, can be flexible specialists. Tackling the bipolar disorder, and converting it into a beneficent dualism, is a challenge in translating entrepreneurship democratization into a flourishing industrial revolution.

Hence, the recognition by government agencies and international organizations of the possible bipolar disorder has led to some steps, albeit small ones, to translate it into a beneficial dualism. Let us take an example. For historical reasons, the region around Jaipur, a city of marble and pink palaces and one of India's premier tourist destinations, has emerged as the ball-bearing capital of India. The origins may lie simply in serendipity, as a major manufacturer located here and attracted other firms to the area. India rolls, rotates, and revolves due to the industriousness of Jaipur's bearing-cluster firms. Ball-bearings are machine elements used in the rotating parts of virtually every machine. Since every piece of machinery rotates, and industrial success is based on machinery, the role of bearings in India's industrialization is paramount.[45]

The Ministry of Small and Medium Sized Enterprises (MSME) of India's central government has collaborated with the United Nations Industrial Development Organization (UNIDO) in a series of cluster development initiatives. A cluster is a sector-specific and geographic concentration of small and medium-sized firms. There exist 350 small and medium-sized firms' clusters, and 2,000 rural and artisan firms' clusters, across different industries, in India. These clusters contribute 60 percent of India's manufactured exports. They have a high share in employment generation.[46] Implicit in this cluster development approach is a recognition of path dependencies, since spatial and agglomeration economies had been conceptualized, and clustering policies implemented, 4,500 years ago during the Indus Valley Civilization.

In Jaipur, the bearing cluster has its origins in a manufacturing unit set up by the Birla Group in 1946, called National Bearing Company. Over time, a number of other firms co-located to Jaipur. Now, the bearings cluster consists of over 100 small and medium-sized manufacturing units and 2,000 tiny units run by artisans that carry out work for the rest. There is a large-scale bearing manufacturing unit at

Jaipur called National Engineering Industries (NEI). The Jaipur bearing cluster units supply components to all large-scale bearing manufacturers in India. A non-trivial aspect of cluster management has been the development of a website for the Jaipur bearing cluster. There, I discovered a number of firms who might be willing suppliers of bearing components, if I was a medium-scale machine-tool manufacturer from Fort Worth, Texas, and I wanted to set up an Indian unit because I was impressed by India's growth story. In that website, I discovered, among the many companies listed, a 20-year-old company named Manu Yantralaya, manufacturing ball-bearing cages, dust shields, and turned races. Manu Yantralaya was a supplier to FAG India and NEI. Manu Yantralaya also had a technical collaboration with Toho Industrial Company of Japan, and had received the ISO 9001 certification for its manufacturing quality.

Most of all, I was deeply impressed by the company's vaulting ambitions, aspirations, and desire to change the world. To cite them directly: "Manu Yantralaya has been setting higher and higher targets each year and all of us here at Manu have been working hard to achieve them. Our future plan is to seek exponential growth in every endeavor, developing global relations and try removing all the possible friction from this world with our components."[47] The future plan statement of Manu Yantralaya is evocative of the deep transformation under way in contemporary industrial India. Hopefully, one could issue a similar statement about the forthcoming impact of India's industrial transformation on world peace!

8 | *The services sector debate*

The services sector role in India

The previous chapters have dealt with contemporary Indian entrepreneurship and industrial development. A macroeconomic approach helps in understanding the structure of India's economy. I ask two questions. Which sectors produce India's output and income, and in what proportions? And from which sectors has India's gross domestic product growth come from? There are three main sectors of the economy: agriculture, industry, and services. Their activities comprise the national income statistics. The discussion revolves around the relative performance of these three sectors. When we talk about manufacturing industries and service industries, the term "industry," in national accounts statistics, refers to the actual manufacturing, mining, electricity, gas, and water sectors. The term "services" refers to construction, trade, hotel, transport, communications, finance, insurance, real estate, professional business services, community services, social services, and personal services.

Is India's growth story a service sector growth story? The manufacturing sector in India has performed well and, relatively, brilliantly in relation to its past performance. Yet India's growth has been unleashed by her service sector businessmen. This phenomenon is considered consequential.[1] In the last six decades, agriculture, which was the sector providing the key economic sustenance to India's millions, has shrunk. Its share of national income was almost 54 percent in the 1950s, during the decade as a whole. It had shrunk to 20 percent by the first decade of the new millennium.[2] Which other sectors have absorbed the slack generated?

Comparatively, the service sector accounted for about 35 percent of India's gross domestic product in the 1950s. By the 2000s, the share of services in national income had increased to just over 60 percent. The share of the industrial sector, as defined, was just under 12 percent in

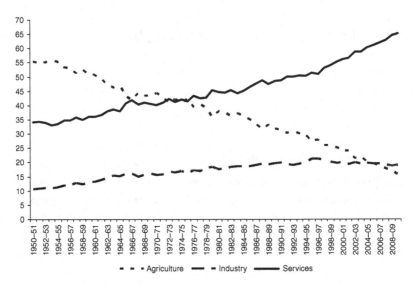

Figure 8.1. Share of agriculture, industry, and services in India's national income, 1950–51 to 2008–09.

Source: Derived from the Reserve Bank of India Database on the Indian Economy, Table 3.

the 1950s. By the 2000s, the share was just below 20 percent. These trends are brought out by figure 8.1. For the six decades as a whole, agriculture's share of India's gross domestic product was 37 percent, industry's share was 17 percent and the share of services was 46 percent. Thus, India was an agricultural country, and now she is a services producing country. She is not a manufacturing country yet, though the share of industry in India's gross domestic product has risen. These details are supported by the data in table A11.

How have different sectors' contributions changed? The analysis of the changes in the shares of each sector in gross domestic product portrays an economic transformation in progress. Between the 1950s and 1960s, the share of agriculture in gross domestic product declined 15 percent. Between the 1960s and 1970s, its decline was 10 percent. Between the 1970s and 1980s, the decline was 14 percent. Between the 1980s and 1990s, the decline was 19 percent, and between the 1990s and 2000s the decline was 30 percent. The story for industry is different. Between the 1950s and 1960s, the share of industry in gross

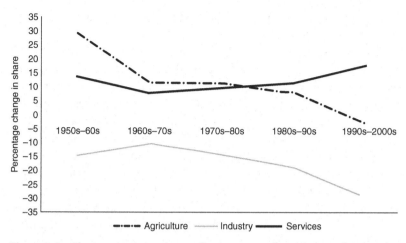

Figure 8.2. Changes in sectoral contributions to national income by decades from the 1950s to the 2000s.

Source: Derived from the Reserve Bank of India Database on the Indian Economy, table 3.

domestic product rose at 29 percent. Between the 1960s and 1970s, the rise was 11 percent. Between the 1970s and 1980s, the rise was also 11 percent. Between the 1980s and 1990s, the rise was 7 percent, but between the 1990s and 2000s the share of industry fell by 3 percent. This is the decade in which the industrial revival should have kicked in.

Between the 1950s and 1960s, the share of services in gross domestic product rose at 13 percent. Between the 1960s and 1970s, its rise was 8 percent. Between the 1970s and 1980s, its rise was 9 percent. Between the 1980s and 1990s, its rise was 11 percent, and between the 1990s and 2000s it rose by 17 percent. From the 1980s onwards, the decline in the share of agriculture in the national income was taken up by growth in the share of the services sector. These trends come into view in figure 8.2. The details of changes in each sector's share per decade are provided in Table A11. The decline in agriculture's share in national income being taken up by growth in the services sector is a unique characteristic of India's overall growth. There is no case like it recorded in history. The share of industry in national income has remained the same, unlike in other countries which experienced mass industrialization. Such a trend is noted in developed countries and not developing countries.

Because the service sector is structurally different from the agricultural or industrial sectors, the growth of services in India reorders the sequence of economic development that a country goes through. Economic development is a three-stage sequential process, with the primary agriculture, secondary industrial manufacturing, and the tertiary services sector following on from each other in the development process.[3] In India, the share of the services sector has risen before the manufacturing sector has had a chance to catch up. India, whether by accident or design, is following the development path of countries such as Ireland and Israel, rather than the development path of China and Japan.[4] No theory suggests this to be an appropriate development model. Manufacturing should be the master, and services the servant. Yet, in India the services servant is the main boss in the economic household. The current economic travails of Portugal, Ireland, Greece, and Spain (PIGS) suggest this to be a short-sighted and short-lived strategy. What happens in contemporary Britain will show whether a fully services-driven economy has any survival hope. The question is should Ireland and Spain be the contemporary countries emulated by India? Or should the countries to be emulated by India be South Korea, China, and Taiwan?[5]

What is India's service sector made up of? This is an important question. It is a peculiar mixture of high-performance categories, such as finance and telecommunications, which cannot employ too many people, and low-performance petty services, where the poor are driven to work because of lack of prospects in low-performance agriculture. Of the specific services making up the sector as a whole, the construction category accounts for 13 percent, the trade, hotels, transport, and communications category accounts for 38 percent, the finance, insurance, and banking services segment accounts for 20 percent and the community, business, and personal services category accounts for 28 percent of the total.

The details of different items' shares making up the services sector are provided in Table 8.1. The statistics reflect patterns for six decades. Over the course of this period, the construction sector' share in the services category has shrunk, while there has been growth in the shares of trade, hotels, transport, and communications categories. This is due to the growth of telecommunications services, with

Table 8.1. *Contributions of different items to total services sector income in India*

	Construction	Trade, hotels, transport, and communications	Finance, insurance, and banking	Community, business, and personal services
1950s	14	34	22	30
1960s	16	37	18	29
1970s	15	38	17	30
1980s	13	39	19	29
1990s	11	39	23	27
2000s	11	43	23	23

Proportion of contributions of the different items to total service sector income

Source: Reserve Bank of India Database on the Indian Economy, Table 3, and author's calculations.

the rapid diffusion of mobile telephones and an increase in telephone density. Yet, the decline in construction sector share causes concern. Infrastructure-building consumes considerable construction services. In a rapidly industrializing economy, construction services' consumption, and the share of construction services in the gross domestic product, ought to be rising. The share of the finance, insurance, and banking services segment has stayed the same, while the share of the community, business, and personal services category has shrunk.

So far the discussion has related to an assessment of the static shares of each category in the overall gross domestic product or national income. What about the growth in income for each broad category of activity? How have the three specific sectors, agriculture, industry, and services, grown in income? Which sectors in India have contributed to overall income growth? A computation of the growth in gross domestic product for 60 years reveals interesting trends. The assessment is based on data for each decade. Over the 60 years, India's overall gross domestic product growth was just under 5 percent, with agriculture income growth at just under 3 percent, industrial income growth at 6 percent, and service sector income growth also at 6 percent. The

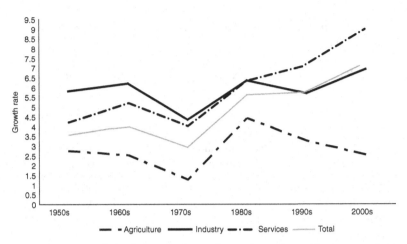

Figure 8.3. Growth in the gross domestic product of specific sectors of the Indian economy from the 1950s to the 2000s.

Source: Derived from the Reserve Bank of India Database on the Indian Economy, Table 3.

time series trends reveal volatility and then stagnation in agricultural income growth. Industrial incomes have risen, but slowly. Conversely, service sector incomes have grown substantially. In the 1950s, service incomes grew by just over 4 percent. In the 2000s, service sector incomes have grown by almost 9 percent, or at more than double its growth performance two generations ago. The trends are presented in figure 8.3, based on data in Table A12.

Do these trends raise a warning flag? Is the situation sustainable in the long run? There are three issues arising: (1) in spite of the rising share of services in income and trade, there has not been a corresponding rise in the share of services in employment; this has led to an observed jobless growth phenomenon;[6] (2) the growth in the service sector has not been uniform across all service categories; some services have grown fast in terms of their share in income, and in terms of their share in trade and foreign direct investment; (3) and income from the service sector can be growing in excess of the demand generated for services by the agriculture and industry sectors. Since disposable incomes often grow faster than efficiency growth in the services sector, in the absence of endogenous productivity gains, service-led growth can seriously perpetrate inflation, create income distribution inequalities, and exacerbate negative balance of payments, due to Baumol's Cost Disease.[7]

Diffusion of services may make an economy efficient. The use of information technology and communications services by firms, to coordinate the production of manufactured goods and services, can enhance efficiencies. In fact, the diffusion of information technology and communications hardware is associated with efficiency growth, as the evidence for developed economies shows.[8] Yet, such efficiency growth is secondary. The order-of-magnitude capacity expansion that genuinely generates productivity growth and wealth for a nation comes via manufacturing sector scale effects. Countries such as the United States which outsource manufacturing to concentrate on services production based on symbolic analysis, such as the work of accountants, lawyers, financial analysts, journalists, and media specialists, eventually also outsource design, development, and innovation. Thereby, they break their chain of experiences. Countries engaging in contract manufacturing, such as the East Asian countries and particularly China, have gained from learning-by-manufacturing and design-by-adaptation. For these countries, the step to being the world's primary innovators is small.[9]

A substantial amount of attention that India's service sector gets is due to the performance of information technology and software firms in the global outsourcing of business back-office services. This model is predicated on an East–West wage arbitrage model. This wage arbitrage is a short-term financial opportunity. It has led to the mass digital shipping of the efforts of India's human bodies. It has not led to the utilization of high-quality human capital, but to the production of commodities by means of commodities.[10] The primary items delivered are customer care, call center, and medical transcription services. While numerous information technology-enabled services, such as managing physical hardware operations, maintaining business software, undertaking routine legal paperwork, preparing tax returns, and conducting financial analysis, are now provided,[11] the intellectual architecture has been developed overseas. Indians simply complete the low-end execution work. Knowledge embodiment has taken place overseas. Indian firms have been unable to exploit the high gains accruing from intellectual property development.

The business back-office services do not embody knowledge, because Indian information technology and software sector firms do not create any knowledge. They do not conduct material research and development (R&D) activities.[12] In recent analysis, I had found that the R&D intensity of Indian information technology and software firms was trivial. These development efforts will not lead to creating knowledge-embodying value-added products to be supplied to domestic and overseas clients digitally. No country has gotten rich by wage arbitrage, or by exporting slaves, in embodied or disembodied form. In the nineteenth century, Indians went overseas as indentured sugarcane plantation labor. In the twenty-first century, white-collar workers provide basic and low-technology back-office services, on-line, to customers overseas. India has simply progressed from exporting sugar-coolies to exporting cyber-coolies.

The seeds of national human development are not sown by this coolie-progression approach. To suggest that the information technology and software services sector is going to drive long-run growth in India, such that a Kaldor–Verdoorn law starts operating, is wishful thinking. Once real wages in the East catch up with real wages in the West, as Western living standards decline or as the East converges in income, India's advantage disappears. Globalization will lead to wage convergence.[13] Wage arbitrage will be unfeasible. Ignoring manufacturing means de-industrialization. Foreign firms have adopted a "make or buy" strategy by outsourcing to India. This will cease. The outsourcing business will disappear. Then, Indian firms will have to "make or die!"

For India to grow rich, manufacturing matters. After all, making products and selling them to a demanding world is entrepreneurship's essence. Manufactured products add sustainable value to be enjoyed by consumers. Manufacturing of a product means creating something to be inventoried, and later acquired by customers. A product is not instantly perishable, though a few may be unless immediately consumed. When acquired by a customer, a manufactured product can be repeatedly used till the end of its useful life. In some cases, the useful product life is infinite: a piece of software can be used any number of times as long as one possesses it. In other cases, its life may be a day, like that of a newspaper. A manufactured good embodies intellectual property in the product design and in the manufacturing process. Once a product has been designed, it can be reproduced infinitely, assuming that the tools and dies for making the reproductions have not worn out. In India, the tools and dies for the 1958 Morris Oxford car, shipped from Cowley, in Oxfordshire, to Uttarpara, in West Bengal, are still available. Their upgrades produce the Ambassador car in 2011. While some body changes have been made, the factory can change the tooling back to the original dies so as to reproduce a twenty-first-century version of the car as made in 1958!

Conversely, any service has spatial, temporal, and person specificity. It is an item to be consumed, at a particular time and place, by a particular person or organization to which it has been directed. By definition, a service is a low value-added unit of sale because the intellectual property component in the actual service, and in the process of delivery, is low if not non-existent.[14] There may be certain services embodying substantial intellectual property. But these are highly specialized and customized services which are not infinitely reproducible. There are no scale economies in providing such services. The critical limitation is the unique human skill of the service provider. In contrast, a manufactured product transfers a stream of continuous value to a consumer, since the skill embodied in the product has a long life.

Productivity of the Indian services sector

How productive is India's service sector? If India's service sector is what it is made out to be, and the service sector is an important engine of India's growth, then it should be highly productive. These will be reflected in statistics. Unfortunately, no work has evaluated India's service sector productivity. This has proved challenging. Conclusions and judgments should be based on evidence. Hence, I carried out some analysis, using the data available in the Reserve Bank of India Database on the Indian Economy, to assess service sector performance over the course of the last six decades. To do so, I used data on the composition of India's gross domestic product by category. These data were the output variables. The data covered the period 1950–51 and 2008–09. The three outputs used were: the gross domestic product generated by the agricultural sector, the gross domestic product generated by the industrial (in other words, manufacturing) sector, and the gross domestic product generated by the services sector.

The key constraint in the analysis of service sector productivity has been the availability of inputs data. While some recent analysis, using just data on services sector employment, has emerged, a long time series of data on what the services sector has used as inputs to generate the outputs is simply not available from any source. Hence,

I used an alternative approach to assess service sector productivity. Data envelopment analysis (DEA) is an innovative operations research technique for efficiency measurement. It can handle multiple outputs and multiple inputs in assessing economic performance.[15] The DEA technique generates an efficiency score for each observation, comparing that observation relative to all others in the data set assessed.[16] DEA is a flexible technique useful in estimating productive efficiencies. Inefficiency represents the manifestation of an inability to extract maximal output from the given inputs. In a DEA sense, those observations defining the frontier, attaining a score of 100, on a scale of 0 to 100, are efficient. These are the observations which have utilized their full potential. Therefore, observations which score less than 100 are inefficient, and the efficiency rating for each observation denotes a precise estimate of the empirically assessed inefficiencies that may be present.[17]

For the analysis of service sector productive efficiency, the inputs to be used by the Indian economy every year, in generating the various types of its gross domestic product, were the varieties of investments made in the economy in the formation of capital to engage in business and economic activities. These variables were the aggregate household sector gross domestic capital formation, private sector gross domestic capital formation, and public sector gross domestic capital formation.[18] These three inputs would generate the three categories of outputs for the Indian economy – the gross domestic product generated by the agricultural sector, the gross domestic product generated by the industrial (manufacturing) sector, and the gross domestic product generated by the services sector. The analysis would reveal how efficient the Indian economy had been over time, each year considered in relation to others. More importantly, the analysis would reveal where exactly the sources of inefficiencies lay in a particular inefficient, or below optimal, year which was the particular unit of analysis.[19] Could India have generated more agriculture output, more industrial output or more services output, if the economy was operating optimally?

In a particular year, when the economic performance of the Indian economy was below optimal levels, to become efficient the economy could have generated additional agricultural, additional industrial, and additional services output. If the ratio of, say, additional agricultural output to be generated relative to the agricultural output actually generated was greater than the ratio of additional industrial output to

Table 8.2. *Total output augmentation possibilities in rupees crores for each sector by decade if optimal economic performance had been achieved*

	Amount of actual output augmentation possible		
	Sector		
	Agriculture	Industry	Services
Decade	Amount of possible agricultural output augmentation	Amount of possible industrial output augmentation	Amount of possible services output augmentation
1950s	1,533	181	138
1960s	1,977	212	0
1970s	5,188	493	2,377
1980s	10,815	1,150	2,845
1990s	13,071	25,286	90,349
2000s	82,361	0	380,277

Source: Author's calculations.

be generated relative to the industrial output actually generated, then one could conclude that the agriculture sector was relatively inefficient compared to the industrial sector. Similar assessment of the agriculture sector relative to the services sector, and of the industrial sector relative to the services sector, could be performed. The objective of the assessment was to derive conclusions on the relative performance of India's service sector relative to the agriculture and industry sectors. In Table 8.2 I summarize the additional output generation that would have been possible, by each output category, had the inefficient years of observation been as optimally efficient as the other years. The detailed data of year-by-year output enhancements feasible at maximum efficiency, so as to compute the overall average additional outputs amounts by decade, are given in Table A13. Table 8.2 highlights these additional output amounts per decade that might have been generated.

In the 1950s and the 1960s, the agriculture and industry sectors were relatively inefficient as they could have generated considerably more outputs if optimal economic performance were attained in all of the years. The additional incremental output values would have been ₹1,533 crores as agriculture output, ₹181 crores as additional industrial output, and ₹138 crores as additional services output in the 1950s. In the 1960s, the additional incremental output values would have been ₹1,977 crores as agriculture output and ₹212 crores as additional industrial output. The services sector was relatively efficient in the 1960s. In the 1970s, the services sector additional output possible became greater than that of the industrial sector, at ₹2,377 crores versus ₹493 crores. The agriculture sector was still the most inefficient, with lost output due to inefficiencies of ₹5,188 crores. In the 1980s, the same trend continued. The agriculture sector was more inefficient than industry or agriculture, but the industry sector was more efficient than the services sector. The additional incremental output values would have been ₹10,815 crores as agriculture output, ₹1,150 crores as additional industrial output, and ₹2,845 crores as additional services output in the 1980s.

The liberalized era in India dates from the 1990s, with the services sector being touted as the economic savior. This is simply untrue. In fact, in the 1990s, and continuing into the 2000s, the services sector has been very inefficient compared to both the agriculture and industry sectors. If optimal performance were attained, the additional incremental output values would have been ₹13,071 crores as agriculture output, ₹25,286 crores as additional industrial output, and ₹90,349 crores as additional services output in the decade of the 1990s. In the 2000s, the additional incremental output generated would have been ₹82,361 crores as agriculture output, implying that agriculture had taken a beating, but no additional industrial output would accrue as the industrial sector was relatively efficient and did not incur any output losses. Comparatively, an amount of ₹380,277 crores as additional output could have been generated by the services sector in the 2000s, given optimal performance. The analysis shows that since the 1970s the services sector has been more inefficient relative to the industrial sector, and in the 1990s and 2000s even relative to the agriculture sector.

The preceding discussion has dealt with absolute values. Figure 8.4 displays the ratios of additional outputs possible but lost due to inefficiency, relative to actual outputs for each of the sectors for each of the decades. The relative performance of the services sector versus the agriculture or the industry sectors is weak. The services sector, as a whole, is a mish-mash of high-performance and low-performance business categories. The latter predominate and drive down average

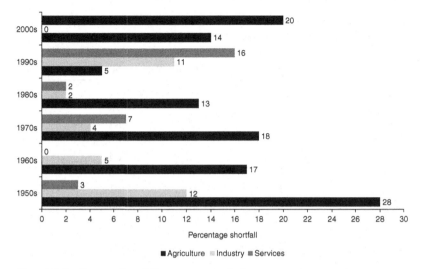

Figure 8.4. Output shortfall percentage relative to actual output due to sector inefficiency.

Source: Author's calculations.

sector productivity. In the 1990s and 2000s, when the touted services revolution occurred in India, the services sector slipped badly in relative performance. Over the years, the agriculture and industry sectors have become relatively more efficient, as the decline in the ratios displayed in figure 8.4 indicates. Also, over the years the services sector has become much more inefficient as the increase in the ratios show. If productivity of the services sector versus the manufacturing sector is a concern guiding investment in the services sector, then the services sector has simply failed to deliver, relative to the manufacturing sector. For several reasons, India's economic performance has to be driven by the manufacturing sector. Manufacturing has to be the growth engine. Based on the actual efficiency parameters revealed, the services sector cannot be India's growth engine. To suggest otherwise is mischievous and misleading.

Comparison with other countries

What do other countries' data show? I compared the sector-by-sector shares of national income for the income pecking order of nine

Table 8.3. *Share of agriculture, industry, and services sectors in the national income of nine countries for 2007*

	Agriculture	Industry	Services
United States	1	22	77
United Kingdom	1	23	76
Germany	1	31	68
New Zealand	6	25	69
Finland	3	33	64
South Korea	3	37	60
Mexico	3	36	61
Turkey	9	28	63
India	18	20	62

Source: US Census Bureau 2012 Statistical Abstract, Table 1350, sectoral contributions to gross value-added: 1997 and 2007, accessed January 11, 2011 and author's computations.

countries. These were the United States, the United Kingdom, Germany, New Zealand, Finland, South Korea, Mexico, Turkey, and India. These data are from the United States Census Bureau, which has collated global financial statistics. The data relate to 2007. The first three countries are the super-rich developed nations. The next three are developed medium-rich nations. In fact, by 2007, the year for which data are used, the real per capita gross domestic product of South Korea was $25,021. The latter three are emerging nations. While the service sector accounts for more than 75 percent of the national income in the United States and the United Kingdom, in other countries the percentage share of services is in the 60s. In Germany, it is 68 percent, while Mexico and South Korea have smaller service sectors than India at 61 and 60 percent respectively. Details of these sector shares are given in Table 8.3.

Relative to India's income share from manufacturing at 20 percent, four of the selected countries, ranked in descending order, South Korea, Mexico, Finland, and Germany, have an income share from manufacturing of over 30 percent.[20] The evidence of a services-intensive economy is supported by employment composition data for India, and compared to data for China. In India, for the 1950–60 decade the shares of employment in agriculture, industry and services were 72,

10, and 18 percent. By the 1990–2000 decade, these shares were 67, 13, and 20 percent.[21] Comparatively, in China the share of services in employment was 16 percent in the 1950–60 decade and 13 percent in the 1990–2000 decade.[22] In aggregate, India is displaying the statistical and structural characteristics of a developed country without actually being one in terms of income or development indicators. She is skipping a stage of growth, bypassing the manufacturing phase. There is no historical precedence for this contingency. Theory does not support this process. Is this a brilliant development strategy?[23] Or, will it end in tears? I am a Cassandra on this issue.

There is a large and significant correlation between industrial growth and income growth, as measured by the growth in real gross domestic product. Using data from the Census Bureau and the Bureau of Labor Statistics of the United States, I collected details of real per capita gross domestic product for 15 countries.[24] These were Australia, Austria, Belgium, Canada, Denmark, France, Germany, Italy, Japan, Netherlands, Norway, Spain, Sweden, the United Kingdom, and the United States. I collected data on the index of industrial production for these countries. I collected data on real per capita gross domestic product and on the index of industrial production for 23 years between 1986 and 2008. This is a substantial time-series data set for the world's developed countries, all of which ascended to the top of the league tables on manufacturing strength. Each has a substantial service sector as well.

I analyzed the relationship between changes in the real per capita gross domestic product and changes in the index of industrial production for these countries. Since this is a first-differencing approach, it is a very stringent method of statistical analysis that considerably removes the stochastic variations present in the data. I found that for these countries, with economies highly geared towards the service sector, the correlation coefficient between changes in the real per capita gross domestic product and changes in the index of industrial production was positive and large at 0.69.[25] Hence, even for developed countries, with a large services sector, industrial and economic growth are highly correlated. This finding does not impute causation. More sophisticated analysis is required. But the strength of the correlation supports the idea that a strong manufacturing sector drives a country's long-run real income growth. If there is a strong service sector, that is the icing on the cake. It is not the cake itself. The cake has to be first manufactured at the bakery.

The tale of South Korea

The story of South Korea has been called a development miracle of the twentieth century. It has been retold several times by specialists in this genre of work.[26] I suggest that recent South Korean data are reviewed, and appropriate conclusions drawn to be extrapolated for Indian conditions. In 1960, the Korean economy was an agriculture and mining economy. The manufacturing sector supplied very simple consumer products. Exports were 3 percent of gross domestic product. They consisted almost entirely of primary products such as seaweed, ginseng, and various minerals. Now, 50 years later, the economy is dominated by the manufacturing sector, exports exceed 40 percent of gross domestic product, and manufactured products constitute more than 90 percent of exports.[27]

In 1960, South Korea's per capita gross domestic product was US$1,877. By 2007, that sum was $25,021. In 2008, it was $25,498. Comparatively, Germany's per capita gross domestic product was $11,702 in 1960 and $33,363 in 2008. How rapid has the rise in South Korea's income levels over the past half-century been? What has been the magnitude of catch-up? The disparity ratio between South Korea and Germany narrowed to 1.32 in 2008, from 6.23 in 1960, in the course of about 50 years. Similarly, the per capita gross domestic product of the United States was $15,644 in 1960 and $43,250 in 2008. The disparity ratio between South Korea and the United States narrowed to 1.69 in 2008 from 8.33 in 1960, in the course of 50 years.

I computed similar numbers in respect of South Korean income and the income of the United Kingdom. The per capita gross domestic product of the United Kingdom was $12,382 in 1960 and $34,356 in 2008. The disparity ratio between South Korea and the United Kingdom has narrowed to 1.35 from 6.60 in the course of the last 50 years. The catch-up process can be expressed another way. In 1960, South Korea's income was 16 percent of Germany's, 15 percent of the United Kingdom's, and 12 percent of that of the United States. In 2008, her income was 75 percent of that of Germany, 74 percent of that of the United Kingdom, and 59 percent of that of the United

States. The process of catching up in wealth highlights the importance of a large manufacturing sector in South Korea. Among the nine
countries listed in Table 8.3, South Korea has the smallest service sector proportion, and the largest manufacturing sector share in its gross
domestic product.

Two analyses provide further support for the manufacturing sector
impact story. The Census Bureau and the Bureau of Labor Statistics
data show that even in 1990 South Korea was a manufacturing laggard, relative to countries such as Germany, Japan, and the United
States. The indices of industrial production for these countries have
been computed on a comparable basis. They are used to evaluate
trends between countries. Given an index base for the year 2005 as
100, in 1990 the relative industrial production index value for South
Korea was 31.7. By 2008, it had become 199.9. Even though South
Korea had been a laggard, the speed of catch-up was substantial.
Comparatively, the industrial production index values for Germany,
Japan, and the United States were 85.7, 96.9, and 65.0 in 1990. By
2008, the equivalent industrial production index values were 113.8,
103.8, and 101.5. Putting things together, the proposition that South
Korea's massive manufacturing catch-up and growth have led to its
massive income catch-up and growth is supported.

A final set of analyses for South Korea is instructive. Based on data
relating to the industrial production index and real per capita gross
domestic product, I analyzed the relationship between changes in
the real per capita gross domestic product and changes in the industrial production index for South Korea between 1991 and 2008. The
results indicate a one-to-one mapping of growth in per capita real
gross domestic product with the growth in industrial output. The
results are a broad indicator. No causality can be imputed. There are
leads, lags, and feedbacks inherent in the relationship. More analysis is warranted. Yet, the data and results are too strong to ignore,
to pay short shrift to manufacturing sector contributions, and to
suggest that national income growth occurs via the services sector.
Manufacturing, unsurprisingly, has been all-important for generating
income in South Korea.

How did South Korea do it? By now, there are masses of material on the topic. To sum up, South Korea became extremely competitive in world markets on the basis of manufacturing. It invested
its money where its competitive advantage lay. South Korean firms

were oriented toward production, and not towards sales or finance.[28] Firms that became major players did so by making key investments in facilities and personnel, so as to acquire the technologies of production, enabling them to become large enough to achieve economies of scale and scope cost advantages.[29] An advantage that South Korea had in the late twentieth century, versus firms in the United States and Western Europe a century earlier, was the amount of available knowledge applicable to production. The knowledge stock applicable to production had increased dramatically over the last century on account of new discoveries and innovations. Once South Korea commenced knowledge adoption, it experienced a development miracle as it used the knowledge stock available to her.[30] There are enough lessons, from such precedents, for India to absorb in acquiring and utilizing globally available stocks of knowledge for engendering production.

India's China manufacturing syndrome

India has many China syndromes. China, too, perhaps has many India syndromes. If there is one China syndrome India needs to acquire, it is the manufacturing syndrome. India is in a long-term race with China in which it is badly lagging behind. China has a smaller service sector than that of India. Much of China's growth has come from the manufacturing sector. China's service sector activity, as a proportion of gross domestic product, went from 34 percent in 1990 to 40 percent in 2004.[31] Yet, China is a manufacturing country. India is a services producing country. Does this matter? It matters for a country's presence in world trade. A recent news item highlights that China's foreign exchange reserves have topped $3 trillion.[32] These trends have had a major impact on the nature of Chinese engagement with the world. Chinese manufactured exports grew at the rate of 14 percent, in the 15 years between 1981 and 1996. Till 2000, these exports grew at over 20 percent. China has captured attention as the world's workshop, in comparison to every other developing nation, because of its manufacturing focus.

Comparatively, Indian manufactured exports grew at 11 percent between 1981 and 1996, but this growth dropped to 6 percent in the period till 2000.[33] Clearly, India has lagged behind.[34] Analysis of Chinese and Indian income yields important insights. The World Bank has collated real gross national income data, expressed in US dollars,

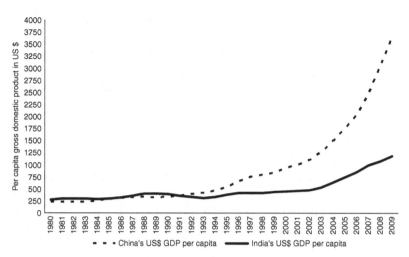

Figure 8.5. Comparative gross domestic product per capita in US$ for China and India from 1980 to 2009.

Source: World Bank.

for India and China. I use these data for almost a 30-year period, between 1980 and 2009.[35] In 1980, China's real per capita income was $220. At that time, India's per capita income was $270. By 2009, the tables had turned. For that year, China's real per capita income was $3,650, and India's per capita income was $1,180. Figure 8.5 charts the growth in Chinese and Indian incomes, expressed in US dollar values, for the 30-year period.

In the space of just a generation, China managed to increase its real per capita income levels 16.6 times, from $220 to $3,650. India had managed to raise hers, comparatively, only 4.4 times. China's average income increased at an annual rate of about 10.5 percent, while India's income increased at an average rate of 5.5 percent. By 2009, the Chinese, who were poorer than Indians in 1980, had become three times richer. The Chinese were poorer than Indians till 1990. In 1991, Chinese and Indian incomes were the same. Within less than two decades, between 1992 and 2008, Chinese incomes leapt massively ahead. By 2000, the Chinese were two times richer than the Indians. By the end of the first decade of the new millennium, they were three times richer. Details of Chinese and Indian incomes are provided in Table A14. If China's income keeps growing at the rate of 10.5 percent for the next 20 years, as it has been doing for the past several years, by 2030 the Chinese will be earning $29,709 annually. If the Indians' incomes grow at 5.5 percent, which was the average rate between 1980 and 2009, then by 2030 the average annual Indian income will be $3,632. In 30 years, Chinese incomes will be eight times greater than those of Indians.

Why will this have happened? The evidence is clear. Manufacturing goods efficiently generates national wealth. There can be no industrial revolution, which will comprise fundamental transformations in service as well as manufacturing industries, without a critical role for the manufacturing sector. Manufacturing is the master. A service sector fetish, for that is what India possesses at the moment, cannot make Indians relatively richer in the world. If India wants to reach the level of expected Chinese incomes by 2030, the per capita income growth rate has to be between 16 and 17 percent. Indian industry has to engage in emulative behavior with respect to the South Korean, Taiwanese, and Chinese examples. The data indicate that a paean for manufacturing is necessary. A high income growth rate can be consistently achieved only if there is a manufacturing breakthrough in India. Whether these goods are consumed domestically or exported is a second-order issue. As the South Koreans and Chinese examples have shown in the last 20 years, chronic income laggards can rapidly catch up via manufacturing.

There may be a potential silver lining in India's China cloud. India may hope to catch up in manufacturing, since Chinese labor shortages have driven wages up and eroded China's cost advantages. Chinese manufacturing wages have increased by 20 percent recently. These increases will have reduced her low costs advantages. Both labor and raw material shortages may end the era of cheap Chinese goods, such as clothing and furniture, in Western markets.[36] Manufacturing by Chinese firms, in many spheres, has already moved to other Asian locations with relatively lower wages, such as Bangladesh and Vietnam. Yet, these are small countries unable to supply in large volumes. Being relatively backward in manufacturing, India could conduct a manufacturing labor wage arbitrage vis-à-vis China. Thereby, she can start capturing market share for items that China sells in the West. Within Indian industry, there is an indication that firms are considering manufactured exports seriously. In 2010–11, India's exports surged by 37 percent, driven by an 85 percent increase in engineering exports, to

$60 billion.[37] While the absolute sum is low, given global consumption of manufactured items, the relatively large increase, albeit from a low base, signals important transition.

In encouraging this transition further, however, a cautionary tale of firms' manufacturing experiences in China and India is useful, so that Indian firms can take cognizance of their performance divergences with Chinese firms. An American technology manager, Alan Keizer, is the chief technology officer for a medium-sized telecommunications equipment manufacturer named FibreFab, based in the United Kingdom. That company has its principal manufacturing plant in China's Shenzen region, located on the mainland opposite Hong Kong. The market supplied is in the European Union. Alan previously occupied a similar role in a company called Opterna, also based in the United Kingdom, and with its principal manufacturing plant in Cochin, India. Both companies manufacture very similar fiber-optic connectors. These are products to lay broadband and data lines seamlessly in communications and data networks. These precision products ensure network connectivity. Otherwise, the passages of light, voice, and digital data flows are compromised.

In the Shenzen region, there is an active cluster of over 2,000 electronics manufacturing firms of all sizes. The presence of such a cluster has enabled FibreFab to obtain components, materials, manufacturing equipment, and testing equipment within two hours if necessary, but certainly within the day, to modify production processes, modify products, or manufacture products. The availability of a large number of electronics firms in the Shenzen ecosystem enables FibreFab to put together components and fiber-optic cabling as modular products to meet special market needs. In the process, FibreFab can offer higher value-added products. As Alan recounted, the lack of a commercial or manufacturing cluster, supplying anything other than basic office and generic factory consumables, in the Cochin region meant that when he was coordinating manufacturing operations at Opterna, the minimum wait for any item was at least five days, if supplied by air, and longer otherwise. The network externalities and spillovers present in a cluster, that FibreFab now enjoys at Shenzen, were completely absent at Cochin.

In Alan's judgment, the Chinese cost levels are 50 percent of Indian costs levels. FibreFab's Shenzen plant enjoys an over two-to-one value-added advantage over the Opterna Cochin plant, for identical products. The Chinese manufactured products enjoy an over two-to-one quality advantage over Indian manufactured items. In a global market, such an advantage is lethal. Writing a century ago, historian Jadunath Sarkar stated:

Speaking generally, the greatest weakness of Indian manufacturers is their inability to keep to the same standard of excellence in production. Increased out-turn is almost always followed by deterioration of quality. This result is sometimes due to dishonesty but more often to inability to increase the trained labour supply. Its effect is most irritating to the purchaser and fatal to the good name of Indian manufactures.[38]

Alan Keizer's experiences, highlighting the divergences between Chinese and Indian manufacturing performance, is a wake-up call for Indian industry. Facts indicate not much has changed by the twenty-first century. Given draconian global quality standards, the India brand may not command value in competition with China. While such grass-roots tales seem trivial, they highlight the advantages that serious attention to manufacturing gives nations. They also highlight the nature of the multiple challenges India faces in engendering a manufacturing transformation. Since manufacturing is an important activity, the next chapter deals with conceptual issues associated with manufacturing, and its role in a nation. Thereafter, key issues required to be dealt with, to propel this manufacturing transition and support India's industrial journey, are discussed in the final chapter.

9 | A paean for manufacturing

Why manufacturing matters

The term industry is used interchangeably between manufacturing and services sectors, though in government documents it refers to manufacturing industries alone. Many lessons are to be learnt from the first and second industrial revolutions. At the heart of the first and second industrial revolutions were innovations in manufacturing that changed the economic equations. One lesson from the industrialization revolution experiences is that the transformation of raw items into valuable manufactured items changed human functionalities for the teeming mass of people making up society. These changed human functionalities generated the economic outcomes leading to wealth creation. The chapter specifically evaluates manufacturing functionalities, and their vital importance, in the context of national economic development.

India's economy has fundamentally shifted towards the services sector. This has been documented in Chapter 8. In this chapter, I make a paean for manufacturing. Only a deeper focus on the manufacturing sector will make India rich and developed.[1] I ground my arguments in the philosopher David Hume's belief that the determinants of a nation's prosperity, and the subsequent resources available to the state, are based upon real, as opposed to monetary, factors. This view was conditioned by his observations of the Indian eighteenth-century economic phenomenon. The acquisition of bullion could be generated by trade, but such a bullion hoard was impermanent.

It was the attraction of manufactured items that provided incentives for undertaking economic activity to businessmen and farmers alike. In turn, manufacturers were attracted by trade, so as to showcase their talents via the diffusion of goods in various markets. Indeed, Indian manufacturing talent had produced goods which were being showcased globally in the seventeenth century. Walt Rostow had written that "Like all men and, especially, women of his time, Hume was conscious of the quite extraordinary and, ultimately, revolutionary impact on Europe of the expansion, despite inhibitions, of Indian textile imports, starting around 1670."[2] Much earlier than David Hume, in 1581, a British author, John Hale, had observed the role of a manufacturing multiplier in generating national pride and wealth, and stated that: "What groseness of wits be we of ... that will suffer or owne commodities to go and set straungers at worke, and then buy them againe at theyr hands."[3]

The two important late nineteenth- and early twentieth-century examples of manufacturing-led growth are those of Germany and the United States. While in most of the nineteenth century, the economic and technological leader was the United Kingdom, during the second half of the nineteenth century United States and Germany both started to catch up and substantially reduced the British lead. They did so by developing new ways of organizing production. In other words, by a single-minded focus of comprehensively altering the manufacturing function, and the associated function of distribution, they became rich countries. In the case of the United States, this manufacturing focus led to the development of a new system, based on mass production and exploitation of scale and scope economies.[4] Germany introduced new ways of manufacturing in the chemical and engineering industries. Subsequently, Japan caught up rapidly with the West by altering its manufacturing paradigm completely. In the late twentieth century, this manufacturing paradigm ruled the ideas world.

The industrial leadership of the United States only emerged worldwide at the very end of the nineteenth century. In per capita levels of industrial output, the United States had actually been a weak fourth in the world in 1880.[5] It surpassed Britain only after 1900. By 1900, after key scientific, technical, and organizational breakthroughs, the United States led the world in industry.[6] In those two decades, the composition of manufacturing exports changed consistently, away from products of animal or vegetable origin toward those of mineral origin.[7] In these products, capital and natural resources were complementary factors of production.[8] Continuous process methods of mass production, associated with modern forms of organization,[9] led to high throughput and efficiency of the moving assembly line and other quasi-flow processes.

Why does manufacturing matter? First, economic development is a qualitatively distinctive phenomenon from economic growth.[10]

Development is growth plus change. The qualitative dimensions of the development processes deepen the economy. Growth occurs in an economy through a quantitative widening process.[11] Economic development activities involve experiments, changes, and mimetic behavior that leads to the adoption of others' changes and experiments. Since national wealth generation is a function of the adoption of new techniques for achieving productivity gains,[12] India has to initiate change in the structure of its economy by becoming a manufacturing nation based on new methods and techniques.

An early illustration of the role of manufacturing was given by Charles Babbage, the nineteenth-century inventor of the computer, or the calculating engine as he called it. He had shown that 1.6 million pounds of raw cotton, imported from, say, India or the United States, at a cost of £120,000, when spun would yield 1 million pounds of yarn valued at £500,000. When the yarn was woven into cloth, it would produce 6.75 million square yards of powerloom cloth valued at £421,875, 15.75 million square yards of handloom cloth valued at £1,378,125, and 150,000 square yards of fancy cloth valued at £26,250. There was a 14-times value addition to the raw cotton, of £1,706,250, by the process of manufacturing, for an initial cost of £120,000. The value addition in the process of weaving cloth from spun yarn alone was £1,206,250.[13]

Not being a manufacturing nation impoverished a country, and could lead to de-industrialization, as happened in India. Well before de-industrialization, however, Charles Babbage wrote:

The cotton of India is conveyed by British ships round half our planet, to be woven by British skill in the factories of Lancashire: it is again set in motion by British capital; and, transported to the very plains whereon it grew, is repurchased by the lords of the soil which gave it birth, at a cheaper price than that at which their coarser machinery enables them to manufacture it themselves.[14]

Of course, India might have got cheaper cloth, but what was foregone in terms of lost manufacturing value added was immense.

A nation that wishes to be rich must become skilled in the use of machinery.[15] Economic historians have shown that there was a direct relationship between the scientific revolution and the industrial revolution. Hence, machinery and manufacturing processes have always incorporated the most recent and relevant scientific principles in their

design throughout human history.[16] The changes wrought by manufacturing-driven industrialization have been transformational.[17] A historian of the industrial revolution, Thomas Ashton noted the changes
were not merely scientific and industrial, but also social and intellectual. These changes had commercial, financial, agricultural, and political ramifications. The word revolution also implied a suddenness of
change that was, in fact, unexpected. These changes were revolutionary because they brought about intellectual changes which enabled
other changes to occur.

Thorstein Veblen defined manufacturing entrepreneurship as a process
of incorporating many of the numerous intellectual elements, writing:

> The beginnings of the captain of industry are to be seen at their best among
> those enterprising Englishmen who made it their work to carry the industrial
> promise of the Revolution out into tangible performance, during the closing
> decades of the eighteenth and the early decades of the nineteenth century.
> These captains of the early time are likely to be rated as inventors, at least in
> a loose sense of the word. But it is more to the point that they were design-
> ers and builders of factory, mill, and mine equipment, of engines, processes,
> machines, and machine tools, as well as shop managers, at the same time that
> they took care, more or less effectually, of the financial end … Something
> to much the same effect is due to be said for the pioneering work of the
> Americans along the same general lines of mechanical design and perform-
> ance at a slightly later period. To men of this class the new industrial order
> owes much of its early success as well as of its later growth. These men were
> captains of industry, entrepreneurs, in some such simple and comprehensive
> sense of the word as that which the economists appear to have had in mind
> for a hundred years after, when they have spoken of the wages of manage-
> ment that are due the entrepreneur for productive work done. They were a
> cross between a business man and an industrial expert, and the industrial
> expert appears to have been the more valuable half in their composition.[18]

Manufacturing, particularly modern manufacturing, involves
machinery usage. The usage of machinery is the primary approach
towards engendering productivity for the same human effort. In fact,
one of India's most distinguished post-independence civil servants, the
late H. M. Patel wrote: "I will only make one rather obvious point. A
country with limited resources of men, money and material that wishes
to improve its standard of living quickly must ensure that there is no
wastage in the utilization of its resources."[19] Manufacturing matters
in engendering productivity and rapid growth.[20] When an individual

works with a machine, they engage in a transformative act. Often, some chemical and metallurgical processes change the raw material into something more valuable. There is a rearrangement, initially, of the key natural elements. Thereafter, the resulting product is combined with other rearranged items to create a final product completely different from the basic raw materials that the process began with.[21] Hence, a transformative process alters the constitutive components into an item or a product, providing functionalities that the constitutive components separately could not.

In engendering the transformative process, machinery within the manufacturing sector incorporates embodied as well as disembodied technologies. These technologies are based on and have incorporated scientific principles. By definition, machinery makes work smart and reduces overall costs. That outcome is a function of the knowledge applied to the design of the machine, as well as of the intelligence embodied within the machine itself.[22] Capital equipment, of which machinery is a key component, is valued not for the visible physical metal but for the ideas embodied in the functionalities of the machine, and the activities then made feasible.[23]

This logic can be taken further. The item or product, as generated by the use of machinery, *ipso facto* will incorporate some or all of the knowledge originally embodied in the machine itself, though by an indirect process. Machinery in the manufacturing sector incorporates a considerable amount of intellectual capital, a priori, and the work of each individual is influenced by this incorporated knowledge. As each individual works with machinery, not only is output enhanced by the contribution of such capital, but the quality of the human capital pool improves since it has now to work with physical capital that embodies knowledge. As such, the presence of a large manufacturing sector dramatically improves the human capital pool in an economy as a whole.

The capital goods that are employed in other sectors are produced in the manufacturing sector. The output of the manufacturing sector *ipso facto* incorporates such knowledge. The manufacturing sector helps diffuse knowledge to other economic sectors, such as the service sector. These are the linkage and spillover effects. Linkage effects are the direct backward and forward linkages between different sectors. These linkage effects lead to the utilization of abilities and resources that are scattered, hidden elsewhere, or badly organized.[24] Spillover effects are the disembodied knowledge flows between sectors, and externalities of investment in knowledge and technology. When the efforts of labor, in conjunction with other resources, are used in the production activity, they yield external economies since the knowledge embodied in machines leads to the acquisition of on-the-job knowledge by workers. The acquisition of on-the-job knowledge not only increases individual skills, but also increases the average level of skills in the firm and the economy as a whole. This has a spillover effect on performance elsewhere, and leads to knowledge-based endogenous growth.[25]

The existence of linkage and spillover effects has been recognized in India. As recounted by the late Sharad Marathe,[26] the then government of India's Industry Secretary, the statement of industrial policy laid before parliament in December 1977 by George Fernandes, then Minister for Industry, made several important points. A point of departure in the 1977 statement was an effort to relate industry and industrial policy to the needs of the economy as whole, and to define the role of the large-scale industrial sector in the social and economic context of the country. Industry was important neither in itself, nor as a contributor to the growth of national income. It was an instrument for rapid development of agriculture and activation of rural manpower, and the technical and managerial skills developed over the last several decades.

Not only was a substantial part of the industrial production based on domestic agricultural production, but also the level of agricultural production and productivity growth was dependent upon the availability of inputs like power, fertilizers, and pesticides, which had to be produced by industry. The lack of adequate power or cement or steel was as important for levels of agricultural output as it was for industrial output. The recognition of the interaction between agricultural and industrial sector reflected experiences in India and other countries. The policy statement also recognized for the first time an important facet of India's economic reality, that prosperity and distribution of income arising from the broad growth of agricultural and related activities in the countryside provided the demand for a wide range of industries producing articles of consumption.

The economic consequences of manufacturing

Contemporary thinking on a theory, and the economic consequences, of manufacturing can be grounded in the ideas of Thorstein Veblen.[27] For

Veblen, the modern age, as experienced at the height of the American manufacturing boom, was the machine age. Machine processes set the pace for the rest of the economy. It was more comprehensive than aggregating appliances for the mediation of human labor, and something fundamentally transformative. Chemical properties of minerals, the extraction of metallurgical processes, and the sequence of processes involved interacted in such a way that the materials reshaped themselves with the help of mechanical apparatus.

In this process, there was interdependence of all processes. Each followed some and preceded others in an endless sequence. Thus, the set of processes was interlocked. This required adaptation and permitted accuracy, which in turn led to the enforcement of uniformity and standardization. Consequently, coordination of the process passed out of the category of craftwork into the realm of professional management. Because of this professionalization, major productive efficiency gains ensued. From a market dimension, the elimination of irregularities and departures from standard measurements led to ready usability of products. Hence, for standardized consumable goods the demand became certain and led to business growth.

In the next set of steps, business transactions permitted the organization of industrial process, involving relationships with other firms in the economy. This was a decisive factor leading to pecuniary gains. The motive of business was gain, and modern manufacturing enterprises generated substantial pecuniary gains. Before the advent of modern manufacturing industry, business enterprises would invest in the goods as they passed from producer and consumer. Now, entrepreneurs invested in the production processes themselves. Instead of relying on the uncertainties associated with market trading, the entrepreneurs tried to control the conjunctures arising from the interplay of the industrial processes within firms.

Similarly, instead of relying on the vagaries of global trade in information technology services that is driving India's service sector incomes, a sharpened focus on manufacturing can reduce the conjectures and uncertainties that Indian firms face in global trade, and enable them to engage in mass production of standardized goods which face ready demand, both domestically and globally. Rather than Indian firms, specifically those in the information technology and software sector, operating as investors in commoditized human capital whose services are then sold to foreign buyers, it makes much more sense for Indian firms to invest in actual process capabilities that add value, and which can be coordinated by professional managers.

The other important effect of manufacturing is to enhance national wealth via a process of market expansion. The domestic market can be catered for through substitution of imports. Then, the manufacturing for export markets approach, successfully adopted first by Japan, then by South Korea, and now by China, opens up global markets substantially and helps override the limitations of a narrow domestic market.[28] These increases in market size facilitate the realization of scale economies, bring about reductions in costs and prices, and trigger demand expansion. The late P. C. Mahalanobis had similar views. His biographer wrote:

To quote his own words: independently of any theory, on the basis of empirical evidence, I believed the industrialization growth which has started in India is likely to gain momentum even if slowly and help in the modernization of Indian society. Changes of outlook are occurring which are of significance for the future. Businessmen, particularly big industrialists, are becoming increasingly dependent for purpose of production on goods manufactured in different parts of India and also on country wide market for selling their own manufactures. The mutual self interest of industrialists is likely to become increasingly a strong cohesive force to hold India together. Organized labor is perhaps beginning to understand the risks and danger of a narrow provincial isolation.[29]

The importance of manufacturing for India had, however, been formally recognized much earlier. M. Visvesvaraya postulated that the industries of a country reflected the productive capacities and the executive abilities of its inhabitants. These capacities and abilities formed key components of a nation's productive efficiency. A purely agricultural country, that maintained itself by producing raw materials, would always remain poor. Conversely, items manufactured within a country would reflect exactly the nation's needs, and the funds to procure the items would remain within the country, hence adding to the national wealth.[30]

Historically, too, the cult of manufacturing led to increases in economic growth in the time of Tudor England, Renaissance Italy, and elsewhere in Europe. A manufacturing multiplier led producers to obtain anywhere between 2 and 100 times the cost of the embodied raw materials as the final price for the product sold in the market.[31] As

John Hicks had articulated, the capacity to save increases as growth leads to rises in real incomes. The stimulus to investment is strengthened by realizing increasing returns in the wider markets that trade provides. By allowing economies of scale in production to be enjoined, market access makes it profitable to adopt better and advanced techniques of production requiring more capital. Hence, the opportunities for productive investment of capital are greater than they would be if the market is limited to the small domestic sphere.[32] The exploitation of these opportunities stimulates increasing returns, which fuel progress.[33]

The consequence of the Kaldor–Verdoorn law of cumulative complex causation is that higher productivity generates higher growth. In fact, it is common sense to note that manufacturing output leads to the sale of goods to other sectors in the economy. The manufacturing sector, in turn, buys products and services from these sectors. Manufacturing spurs demand for raw materials, intermediate components, software, financial, legal, health, accounting, transportation, and other services. Higher growth also generates higher productivity by means of learning-by-doing,[34] economies of scale, and investments embodying knowledge, perhaps from foreign designs. The productivity and growth dynamic becomes a closed loop involving the cumulative causality of productivity and output.[35]

A large manufacturing sector provides the big push for a nation's growth trajectory to take off.[36] The contemporary income growth of China and South Korea in the 1990s and 2000s proves the point well. In a sense, manufacturing becomes the mechanism for mass-scale economic development.[37] In the modern literature, these ideas have been salient since the 1940s when Paul Rosenstein-Rodan diagnosed the problem of poverty as a failure of capital investment.[38] His context was the lesser developed European countries of central and eastern Europe, which were badly affected by the Second World War. Hence, subsequent investment in heavy manufacturing capacities would translate into an accelerated growth outcome for these nations.[39] The most famous case of the major post-war big push in Europe was the $15 billion Marshall Plan of 1948, which provided Germany with the wherewithal to reindustrialize.

The consequences of a big push, when applied to the manufacturing sector, can be staggering. From Chapter 2, we have seen that the manufacturing-based industrial revolution in Britain led to sustained increases in productivity. The expansion of national wealth, and purchasing power of the people, constantly outstripped population growth. Britain's population rose by 1.25 percent annually in the nineteenth century. Its national income product rose as much as 14 times in the same period. The primary reason for this transformation lay in the productivity increases originating from manufacturing processes engendered during the industrial revolution. The mechanization of spinning in Britain led to productivity in that sector rising by a factor of over 300. Hence, Britain's share of total world manufacturing rose dramatically.[40]

Other European countries and the United States imitated Britain's manufacturing approach. Hence, their per capita levels of industrialization and national wealth rose steadily. In Germany and the United States, an industrial revolution was under way in new fields such as electricity, the internal combustion engine, and organic chemistry.[41] Income distribution conditions, and tastes in the United States, had favored the manufacture of standardized goods for a mass market. Entrepreneurs designed machinery to permit low-cost and high-volume production.[42] The Ford Model T, by virtue of its product design and manufacturing process, redefined human transportation and the nature of economic activity and human society for all time to come.[43]

General purpose technology investments

What were the consequences of the manufacturing-based industrial revolutions on employees and employment? After all, one of the most important objectives of economic policy is to expand both the quantity and quality of employment so that real wages can rise. An economic consequence of the industrial revolutions was the democratization of markets. What happened within firms? The adoption of new practices and technology substituted physical capital for unskilled labor but not skilled labor. To cite Charles Babbage, who foresaw it all over a century and a half ago: "At each increase of knowledge, as well as on the contrivance of every new tool, human labour becomes abridged."[44] The demand for skilled labor rose, as did the level of wages for such skilled individuals. In other words, physical capital and human skills complemented each other.[45] Shifts in technology, rather than changes in relative factor prices, were more important across history in altering the ratios of capital to output and of capital to labor.

As particular technologies, such as batch and continuous process methods of production, spread widely capital, technology, and skill complementarities emerged. This trend was reinforced by another technological change, the switch to electricity from steam and water power. Thus, the shift to continuous process or batch methods produced manufacturing skills development. Electrification reinforced the change through the automation of materials handling, and finished goods hauling.[46] The shift in manufacturing practices reinforced an increased demand for educated labor, for selling, installing, and servicing technologically advanced products. Ample and cheap electricity made the production of various materials, such as aluminum and other electricity-based chemicals, feasible. Cheap electricity permitted reorganization of the workshop floor, encouraged intensive machine use, and increased demand for skilled maintenance personnel. Electricity production moved from small-scale primitive processes to giant power stations.[47]

The technologies that made it possible for capital and skills to complement each other were general purpose in nature. General purpose technologies are technologies[48] that reshape production so that the returns to human capital increase in both technology-producing and technology-purchasing firms.[49] General purpose technologies open up new opportunities. They are pervasive in use. They create innovation complementarities and require reorganization of production and different factor mixes. These processes occur for the customers utilizing the technologies, as inputs in their work, as well for firms producing these technologies as outputs. Consequently, in industries deploying general purpose technologies, there is a shift in demand for higher skilled and better paid human capital.[50] Such a phenomenon has implications for changing the national capital-to-labor ratio within industries, and for the speed of an industrial revolution.

New work practices have transformed many jobs. For example, production and clerical jobs have evolved from specialized tasks with little by way of powers to make decisions to more broadly defined jobs with higher levels of accountability. These new work practices have created a demand for a set of new skills for workers. The new skills comprise soft skills such as communication and interactive skills and hard skills such as numerical and analytical skills.[51] Interactive skills are necessary for workers to work within a team environment, to send and receive data between departments within an organization, and to communicate with external entities including customers and suppliers. Numerical and analytical skills are important to operate equipment. These are skills commanding wage premiums in firms and on the shop-floor. Thus, rapid industrialization via manufacturing, by facilitating the rapid diffusion of general purpose technologies and changing the relationships between people and technology, has had important consequences for wages and employment. Such considerations are extremely important in India's development.

The political dimensions of manufacturing

The political dimensions of engaging in a manufacturing-driven domestic and world trade are equally if not more significant. In the absence of a manufacturing-driven global trading base, a country's ability to project economic power abroad is diminished as it depends more and more on major foreign nations for financing its consumption. The implication of not making things is importing them, and then borrowing large sums to finance the imports. This is the twenty-first-century trade and fiscal deficit phenomenon faced by the United States and the United Kingdom.

In medieval times, and during the period of the Renaissance, small countries like the Netherlands and city-states like Venice did not possess much arable land. Yet, they were rich because they had specialized in manufacturing. Florence, a city not on the Italian coast, had acquired wealth through the efforts of craftsmen and manufacturers. Manufacturing represented 30 percent of employment in the Netherlands, and the shipyards of Venice employed over 40,000 persons.[52] Henry VII, a future ruler of England, had lived as a child and youth in Burgundy. There, he had observed great wealth in an area devoted to woolen production, based on English wool. Having observed industrial wealth, acquired because of manufacturing prowess, when Henry VII became king he formalized reasons, based on what we call political economy, to implement policies so that England would not remain a raw materials exporter but become a textile producing nation.[53] Thereafter, till the early part of the twentieth century, British policy had been based on the premise that manufactured goods exports and raw materials imports would give it wealth. With the associated wealth came political power. This idea was recognized in the nineteenth century by Friedrich List, the German political economist.[54]

Similarly, in the mid nineteenth century, the rulers of Japan were forced to accept instant industrialization to stave off potential economic subjection, after the visit of Commodore Matthew Perry and his fleet of ships, belching black smoke, to the Japanese port of Kyoto, in 1853–54.[55] The Japanese response to the arrival of the ships of an industrial power, the United States, on their shores was similar to that of the United States a century earlier. Then, the Americans, too, had realized that the alternative to developing indigenous industry was to remain a low-level raw material supplier of items that would be turned into high-value goods by British or European machines.[56] The alternative was enslavement, potential in the Japanese case, and actual, as had already once occurred, in the case of the early Americans.

Since war created empires as tribute-collecting machines,[57] the ability of nations to engage in war, helped by arms production, could expand the revenue base of states that possessed a manufacturing base. War permitted the discovery that men as well as animals could be domesticated. Instead of killing a defeated enemy, he could be enslaved. In return for his life, he could be made to work. Thus, by early historic times, slavery was a foundation of ancient industry and a potent instrument for the accumulation of capital.[58] The Japanese, having come face to face with the West, and its navy, had acknowledged the East–West technology gap that existed. The alternative to defeat was the immediate creation of a manufacturing base. Immediately after the Meiji Revolution of 1868, Japan assimilated and absorbed Western European science at high speed. Between 1878 and 1900, the Meiji government successfully achieved take-off for the Japanese economy.[59]

Such nationalist and political considerations had also influenced the early investments in manufacturing made by Indian entrepreneurs in the earlier part of the twentieth century. Because of British colonial rule, there had been shrinkage in the range of occupations that Indians could pursue. This had led to mounting pressure on cultivable lands. The productivity of Indian agriculture grew slowly, while population growth was fast-paced in the first half of the twentieth century. In this milieu, India began manufacturing so as to add value to resources on its own, instead of merely exporting raw materials as it had done during the British colonial rule.[60] The results were unpromising.

Are there theoretical precedents for industrialization to be undertaken for national political and security considerations? The ideas of

Friedrich List, the founder of the national system of political economy, are fundamental.[61] In his work, *The National System of Political
Economy*, List stated that the source of national power was productive prowess. While a nation could be wealthy, it was important to ask
why it was wealthy. Hence, List drew a distinction between the causes
of wealth and wealth itself. Wealth was not simply created by material
capital, but by the interactions between material capital and human
skills, ingenuity, and initiative. In other words, technology, innovations, and entrepreneurship mattered for wealth creation. Productivity
mattered at a national political level. A country that possessed the
power of producing a larger amount of articles of value than it could
consume could become rich. A country could have natural capital or
natural resources, and the capital of matter or what we now refer to as
physical capital. To List, it was the conversion of these, by the manufacturing process, and the application of the capital of mind or mental
capital, that generated wealth.[62]

In a sense, List was the first of thinkers to argue that strong national
industrial capabilities were a "tonic for the national spirit."[63] They
led to a strong global political footprint. Economic security led to
national security. Butter led to guns. Around the time that List was
writing, by the early nineteenth century, it was evident that industrialization gave rise not only to wealth but also to military prowess.
Nations which remained economically backward were vulnerable, as
they were liable to be defeated on the battlefield and become subservient to a foreign power.[64] This was an important motivation behind
Japan's industrialization.[65] Indian economists, too, thought similarly.
In the late nineteenth century, the political economist Justice Mahadev
Govind Ranade had believed that, to be strong, India needed to
develop all productive powers of society. Given India's initial conditions, an increase in industrial employment was vital.[66] Justice Ranade
stated that: "This Dependency has come to be regarded as a plantation, growing raw produce to be shipped by British agents in British
ships, to be worked into fabrics by British skill and capital, and to
be re-exported to the Dependency by British merchants to their corresponding British firms in India and elsewhere."[67] Justice Ranade
had visualized manufacturing industry as allowing more scope than
other sectors for "art manipulation," or applying modern technology
to production processes.[68]

The penultimate word on how industrial changes could make obsolete even formidable political powers without an industrial base belongs to the historian Geoffrey Hudson. As he put it:

the collapse of the power of the nomads with so slight a resistance, after they had again and again turned the course of history with their military powers, is to be attributed not to the degeneracy of the nomads themselves but to the evolution of the art of war beyond their capacity of adaptation. The Tartars in the seventeenth and eighteenth centuries had lost none of the qualities which had made so terrible the armies of Attila and Baian, of Jenghiz Khan and Tamerlane. But the increasing use in war of artillery and musketry was fatal to a power which depended on cavalry and had not the economic resources for the new equipment.

Once artillery began to be manufactured elsewhere, the Mongols were consigned to the trash bin of history as losers.[69]

The ultimate word in support of a political economy dimension for manufacturing comes from an analysis of the Second World War. The two principal theaters were the battles between Germany and the Soviet Union on the Eastern Front, and the battles in Burma between the Allies and the Japanese, in which the Indian army contributed almost 80 percent of manpower and equipment. Let me deal with the German and Soviet Eastern Front battles which took place between 1941 and 1945, because these were indeed a "clash of Titans,"[70] as the facts show. At the peak of the clashes, in 1943, Germany had put forth 2.7 million men, 1,336 tanks, and 6,360 guns to face the might of the Soviets who had 5.8 million men, with over 6,000 tanks and 20,000 guns assembled to face the enemy.[71]

The eventual Soviet victory over Adolf Hitler and Nazism could only be achieved because Josef Stalin, as well as being a major war leader, had also emerged as one of the greatest manufacturing strategists of the twentieth century. In some areas, notably trucks and jeeps, the Soviets were deficient in material items, and were supplied over 400,000 trucks and almost 50,000 jeeps by the Allies.[72] In other areas, Soviet manufacturing production was immense. In the overall period of the conflict, between 1941 and 1945, the Soviets had produced almost 20 million rifles, almost 100,000 tanks and self-propelled guns, over 500,000 artillery guns and mortars, over 120,000 combat aircraft and 70 ships.[73] The scale of Soviet production was staggering. It was the production of these material items which led to the eventual destruction of fascism in Europe.

Among the Axis powers, Japan, too, had substantially harnessed its manufacturing capabilities in this conflict. During the period of its engagement in the Second World War, between December 1941 and August 1945, Japan's shipyards completed 15 aircraft carriers, 6 cruisers, 126 submarines, 63 destroyers, 70 transport ships, 168 coastal defense ships, and a few other vessels for a total of 682 naval vessels. In the civil sector, 720 cargo ships and 271 oil tankers were also built. About 60,000 military aircraft was also produced in the period.[74] Clearly, manufacturing might mattered for the assertion and projection of one's global political power.

In fact, both Professor Mahalanobis and Pandit Jawaharlal Nehru had strategized similarly, not from a logical assessment of the political economy of India, the resources, social structure, and the needs of her people, but by analyzing a model of what a modern industrial society, also a big military power, might look like in the twentieth century. Thus, past methods used by the big industrial and military powers to achieve their status were important to emulate. For both Professor Mahalanobis and Pandit Nehru, heavy industry and manufacturing played a key role for India's development. These would lead India to become a military and an industrial power. Their mental models were based on the Soviet Union's achievements, overlaid with political considerations.[75]

Guns and butter

Does a political economy dimension to manufacturing suggest that there be a trade-off between guns and butter? An emotive topic of debate has been the relationship between defense expenditures, including on production, and economic development. The issue of how defense sector activities can play a role in India's manufacturing-led reindustrialization is dealt with in this section.

About 40 years ago, Emile Benoit postulated a positive relationship between defense spending and economic growth, thereby activating controversy.[76] The debate has been inconclusive, as the facts have been equivocal. Emile Benoit suggested that defense activities and organizations might help feed, clothe, and house individuals who would otherwise have to be alternatively fed, clothed, and housed; the defense sector could provide education and medical facilities; it could engage personnel in works projects; and it could engage scientific and technical talent in research facilities for military use but also of civilian consequence.[77]

As stated, the emerging evidence has been equivocal,[78] but the key issues are managerial and industrial, and not political, in nature.[79] The important issue, from an industrialization perspective, is the nature of spillovers that may occur between defense industrial activities and civilian industrial activities.[80] The late Vernon Ruttan noted that "Knowledge acquired in making weapons was an important source of the industrial revolution."[81] To bore the condenser cylinders for his steam engines James Watt had utilized the skills of John Wilkinson, a cannon-borer, who had invented the one machine in all England that could drill through a block of cast iron with accuracy.[82]

Howard Rheingold has put the concern appropriately: "If necessity is the mother of invention, it must be added that the Defense Department is the father of Technology; from the army's first electronic digital computer in the 1940s to the Air Force research into head-mounted displays in the 1980s, the US military has always been the prime contractor for the most significant innovations in computer technology."[83] At least in the United States, the Department of Defense was the final customer for a large number of production facilities. A study found that almost 49 percent of all manufacturing plants in the United States had defense contracts, and probably 40,000 manufacturing plants throughout the United States were engaged in defense contracting at that time.[84] There was a vast and hidden defense subcontracting base, consisting of firms with no direct dealings with the Department of Defense. There was a substantial pass-through of defense spending from prime contractors to lower-tier suppliers.[85]

Chapter 2 discussed the rise of the American manufacturing system. This system led to the dramatic growth of the United States manufacturing sector. In 1800, the sector had accounted for 10 percent of national income. A century later, it accounted for 50 percent of that income.[86] The American system of manufacturing, involving goods produced by specialized machines, based on highly standardized and interchangeable parts, came to notice in firearms production.[87] After that, mass production of items started in the clocks, watches, bicycles, sewing machines, and wood and metalworking industries.[88] In its most developed form, the mass manufacturing system emerged as Henry Ford's assembly process for automobiles manufacture.

In armaments, prior manufacturing efforts had been based on handicraft techniques used in Britain, where the filing was done by hand and the individual components put together for guns by individual craftsmen. Because of the need for precision, this required skill and patience. It was slow and painstaking work. Interchangeability required little skill. It vastly simplified gun production, and cut down on the number of specialists required to fit a new part or repair a damaged gun.[89] The armaments industry in the United States, called the New England Armory System, created organizational innovations. An inside contract system, or the putting-out of work, was the forerunner of modern subcontracting.[90] For example, the Springfield Armory, in Massachusetts, allowed a machine tool developer named Thomas Blanchard to co-locate his lathe manufacturing workshop within the armory, so that the armory could obtain his machines to make gunstocks.[91] This development of the machine tool sector led to the development of the machine-building and capital goods sector in the United States as a spillover from the armaments manufacturing sector.

In Japan, there had been defense spillovers which led to the development of civilian industries. Early Dutch and Portuguese merchants had introduced firearms to an already militarist society in the sixteenth century. Japanese sword and armor, regarded as the world's finest, had been exported throughout East Asia. During the decline of the Tokugawa Shogunate, in power between 1603 and 1868, by the early nineteenth century there was resurgence of arms manufacture.[92] The Meiji Revolution, in power between 1868 and 1912, had adopted a "rich nation and strong military" approach, with the causality running from butter to guns. When Japanese industrialization took off, the past mastery of the production of guns and the production of gunpowder established a strong base for the manufacturing of other mechanical and chemical goods.[93]

In the late twentieth century, military procurement has had a decisive effect on modern technologies, and modern goods and services. There is considerable symbiosis and deep interdependencies between military and civilian production activities. The requirements of a sophisticated military sector can lead to the development of scientific and technological capabilities of supplier firms.[94] The political scientist

Richard Samuels has discussed the relationships between military and civil production activities as spin-off, spin-away, and spin-on. Spin-off describes the development and production of mass-market civilian products which had initially been developed for military applications. Spin-away describes phenomena where there are no military and civil relationships, and spin-on describes items developed for civilian use finding military applications.[95]

The examples of military to civilian spin-offs are numerous. They notably include jet engines and airframes. After all, the Boeing 747 jumbo jet is the descendant of the Boeing B-52 bomber, whose own ancestor was the Boeing B-29 bomber of Second World War origins. The Boeing B-29 had also spawned the Boeing 377 Stratocruiser, the first aircraft to be conceived for mass air travel. The Boeing 707 airliner was developed from the Boeing KC-135 air-refueling tanker. The civilian aircraft sector has experienced the most defense-related spin-offs. Other defense-related spin-offs include insecticides, microwave ovens, developed as a spin-off by Raytheon from its radar activities, commercial satellites, lasers, medical diagnostic equipment, digital displays, integrated circuits, and nuclear power.[96] Probably every important material aspect of our contemporary lives has been influenced by military research of one type or another.

The important contemporary example is the Internet. The Internet is a basic element of life. The development of the Internet involved the transformation of a computer network, initially established in the 1960s by the Defense Department's Advanced Research Projects Agency (DARPA). The project involved interconnecting computers at a number of academic, industrial, and government computer centers supported by DARPA. In early 1972, DARPA contracted with a small Massachusetts firm to develop an interface computer for the network. At an October 1972 conference, in Washington, DC, the project team displayed a prototype called ARPANET, in which computers made by different manufacturers could communicate with each other at different sites across the country. It took a number of years to work out the protocols for connecting different kinds of computers and for sending messages across network interfaces. In 1983, the Defense Department established a separate MILNET, dedicated to military applications, while continuing to support ARPANET as a defense-related research network with operational responsibility transferred to the Defense Communication Agency (DCA). It was not until ARPANET was decommissioned in 1990, however, that military responsibility for the Internet was finally terminated.[97] In the last 20 years, the diffusion of the Internet has radically changed modern society and civilization.

The economic consequences of defense procurement, production, and research on civilian life are enormous, and nobody has really measured the full impact. The issue for India is whether her industrial sector can harness the benefits of procurement, production, and research activities conducted in her defense sector. India's defense sector is actually extremely large, as befits a nation with one of the world's largest standing armies. India's overall defense spending, in absolute terms, is large. It is also now one of the world's largest arms purchasers. The number of persons employed in defense-related procurement, production, and research activities, additionally, runs into several hundred thousand, though exact numbers are secret. The monetary value of these activities is very large, though the amounts are also secret.

The procurement, production, and research activities are primarily organized departmentally via the Indian Ordnance Factories Board (IOFB), the Defence Research and Development Organization (DRDO), and several production units in the corporate sector that are owned by the government of India. Within the main Indian Ministry of Defence are departmental units such as the Directorate-General of Quality Assurance (DGQA) that play an important quality maintenance role. In Table A15, I list the ordnance factories in India, and their capabilities. There are now 40 ordnance factories in India, with a diverse range of capabilities in chemistry, metallurgy, electrical engineering, mechanical engineering, optics, and textiles technology.

India has a long history, as long as those of the arsenals at Harper's Ferry, Virginia, and Springfield, Massachusetts, in the United States, in the manufacture of modern ordnance and arms. In 1775, a board of ordnance was established in Fort William, Calcutta. Subsequently, a gunpowder factory was established at Ishapore in 1787. At the same location, a rifle factory was established in 1904. In 1801, a gun carriage factory was established at Cossipore, in Calcutta, which has since become the Gun and Shell Factory, Cossipore. This was the first industrial ordnance factory establishment in India. The Ishapore and Cossipore factories are still in existence. In 1917, an Indian munitions board was set up to coordinate India's role as a military supplier.[98]

In Chapter 4, I have noted how iron used to be wrought in India, and Damascene swords were forged from the steel made in the furnaces at Konasamundram and Dimdurti. Tipu Sultan's ammunition factories produced muskets at Bednur, and rockets. It transferred rocket technology to the Woolwich arsenal in Britain for development of rockets in Britain. Similarly, the Mughals had a substantial arsenal at Agra where field guns of substantial magnitude were manufactured. The Sikh arsenals and foundries, in locations such as Amritsar and Lahore, employed at times between 50,000 and 75,000 persons and turned out numerous heavy guns.[99] The Zamzama gun, or Kim's gun as immortalized by Rudyard Kipling in his novel *Kim,* was cast in a Lahore foundry in 1757. It is still visible in Lahore as a showpiece. Thus the armies of Indian rulers that fought the British had considerable firepower, but the problem was one of standardization of guns. The number of designs of guns created field training and logistics problems. Comparatively, the British standardized on three types of guns, and the field commanders paid close personal attention to ordnance and logistics issues.[100] Hence, they won later victories in battle. It is with respect to this fundamental dimension of ordnance manufacture, the standardization aspect, that the American experience becomes important.

There is considerable manufacturing history, of over 300 years, with all of its associated path dependencies, in manufacturing world-class ordnance items in India. Thus, the scope for engendering spillovers to manufacturing establishments in the civilian sector is actually very considerable. Table A16 lists in full the research and development establishments that have been organized under the aegis of the DRDO. Again, these are an extremely diverse lot of establishments that conduct research and development in numerous areas which are also of potential benefit to the civilian population, as well as to civil sector firms. The spillovers from these can be very substantial.

To take just a few examples, the learning and capabilities in airframes and engines design for fourth advanced generation fighters, being developed at the Aeronautical Development Agency at Bangalore, could be utilized for the development of small high-speed regional jet aircraft for civilian travel. Similarly, the competencies and capabilities of the Vehicle Research and Development Establishment (VRDE), at Ahmednagar, can spill over into the design of heavy transport vehicles for India's relatively difficult-to-use road system where there is still a premium for robust vehicles. The research on fuel cells, for Indian Navy submarines, carried out at the Naval Materials Research

Laboratory (NMRL), at Ambernath, can find numerous applications in fuel-hungry India, at a time when environmental pollution and energy efficiency issues are fundamental concerns. One can go down the list of laboratories and draw on several examples for civil–military strategic partnerships.

Finally, there are 11 medium- to large-scale production firms, organized as corporate sector firms, owned by the government of India. A list of these firms is given in Table A17. Some of these firms, such as Bharat Dynamics, Brahmos Aerospace, and Mishra Dhatu Nigam, are specialized entities, catering to a narrow market for missiles of different types, and their components, where there could be export market possibilities in the global arms trade. The other eight firms might possess potential for engendering civilian sector spillovers.

Of the other firms in the corporate sector, at least five of these, Hindustan Shipyards, Cochin Shipyards, Garden Reach Shipbuilders and Engineers, Goa Shipyard, and Mazagon Docks, are shipyards. Clearly, the process of manufacture of ships for naval and civil purposes is extremely similar, if not identical. While the manufacture of giant cruise ships may be a specialist art, to be found in the shipyards of Hamburg or the Norwegian fjords, the correlations between processes to make an aircraft carrier of 75,000 deadweight tons and an oil tanker of 100,000 deadweights tons are very high. Hence, there is considerable scope for defense shipbuilding skills to regenerate the civilian shipbuilding sector that India possessed thousands of years ago, during the time of the Indus Valley Civilization.

It is worth taking a little detour back into the history of Indian shipbuilding. In the late seventeenth century, the East India Company, which had recently obtained Bombay as a marriage dowry, set up a shipyard in Bombay where small vessels were built. In 1736, facing a shortage of British carpenters, some Parsis were taken on and trained as carpenters and shipwrights, and of these Parsi carpenters the Wadia family became the most prominent shipwrights of the Bombay dockyard for a century. By the late eighteenth century, the Bombay dockyard produced ships in the range of 500 to 1,000 tons, for civilian use. During the Napoleonic Wars, the British Royal Navy, facing timber and space shortage at home, ordered ships from the dockyard. By the first quarter of the nineteenth century, over 22 Royal Navy ships had been built at Bombay.[101] One of these Royal Navy ships built in Bombay, HMS *Trincomalee*, a Leander-class frigate of its day, is still afloat. It is the oldest Royal Navy ship afloat, anchored as a floating museum at Hartlepool, in Cleveland, UK.

The funds that the Parsis generated through their shipbuilding ventures in Bombay, in the eighteenth and nineteenth centuries, were fed back into modern industries of the day, such as textiles.[102] The Wadias, who own Bombay Dyeing Textiles, are descendants of the shipbuilders. Thus, diffusion of skills occurred in the late nineteenth century from the defense sector to the civil sector in areas where the Indian businessmen had participated as industrialists. There is considerable past history of defense–civil spillovers in India taking place not that long ago. Thus, one may not have to appeal to the Lothal shipbuilding experiences acquired during the Indus Valley Civilization. The fact that HMS *Trincomalee* is still around suggests that high-quality workmanship defined the Bombay dockyard's activities. Clearly, the defense-civil sector spillover phenomenon can recur in the contemporary dockyards of Bombay, Calcutta, Cochin, Goa, and Vishakhapatnam, where the modern Indian defense dockyards are located.

How are guns turned into butter? How does the spillover from defense operations to the civilian sector actually occur? The standard corporate strategy prescriptions apply for the engendering of spillovers. These are via the use of the subcontracting mechanisms, through licensing of technologies, through alliances, and by the diversification of firms.[103] A number of the factories run by the IOFB use subcontractors from the private sector. This usage can intensify so that smaller private sector firms can gain scale economies, and perhaps learn about the use of interchangeable parts and standardization practices that may be followed at IOFB factories. Many of the laboratories and establishments run by the DRDO can license technologies for further development and commercialization to a wider public. Hence, this is one pathway for technologies developed by defense laboratories to be made available to a wider public. It is also possible that many DRDO laboratories can engage in alliances with private manufacturing companies to have the products that they have developed manufactured for a commercial market. DGQA, as an independent agency, can monitor compliance with standards and verify quality. Hence, pathways exist to engender extensive and beneficial civil–military tie-ups. Finally, defense sector firms owned by government can diversify their activities. This is relevant in the case of the five shipyards, as well as for Hindustan Aeronautics.

Hindustan Aeronautics was a private venture, established by Walchand Hirachand, taken over by government in 1942, during the Second World War, and used for maintaining and repairing the aircraft that the Americans had begun to station in India in large numbers. After the end of the hostilities, it continued life as a remanufacturer of damaged DC-3 Dakota and the B-24 Liberator aircraft that had been brought to India during the Second World War and left behind.[104] There were a large number of pilots, aircraft engineers, and aircraftsmen available after 1945 in India. Their skills were harnessed in the salvage and remanufacture of the numerous planes left behind. The remanufacture operations were carried out at Bangalore and Kanpur. These Dakota and Liberator aircrafts were refurbished for civilian use and Indian Air Force use, respectively.

The B-24 Liberators had a further life of 20 years. They served in India's heavy bomber and maritime reconnaissance squadrons till 1968, operating out of the Lohegaon Air Force Base at Poona. One of the only two B-24 Liberators in flying condition left in the world, operated by the Collings Foundation, is an aircraft that was remanufactured by Hindustan Aircraft in the late 1940s. It had originally been manufactured at the Fort Worth plant of Consolidated Aircraft. Earlier in its life, it had been tasked for operations in the Burma theater. After independence, it served in the Indian air force till 1968, and then as a test and training aircraft in Bangalore till 1981. Its continued existence suggests that it was high-quality remanufacture. The domestic national airline established in 1953, Indian Airlines, was started with a fleet of remanufactured Dakotas.[105]

J. M. Shrinagesh, an ICS officer who had successively been general manager, managing director, and chairman of Hindustan Aircraft, later renamed Hindustan Aeronautics, recounted that an important challenge had been to convert the company into a genuine manufacturing unit, to include the manufacture of aircraft engines. Because Hindustan Aircraft had been manned by American technicians during the Second World War, the company had the advantage of imbibing American management systems in its workshop processes. Earlier, in typical British craftsmen tradition, Hindustan Aircraft technicians had been used to making parts and fitting them onto sub-assemblies and aircraft assemblies by "a little tap here and a little grinding there."[106] After conversion to the American system, they had to make parts so accurately that they fitted each sub-assembly and assembly accurately across all aircraft.[107]

Hindustan Aeronautics subsequently manufactured the Avro HS-748 aircraft for the Indian air force and Indian Airlines. Hence, considerable civil aircraft manufacturing capabilities were, at one time, embodied within Hindustan Aeronautics. Further diverse aircraft engine manufacturing skills would have been available earlier, as Rolls-Royce had offered to license the manufacture of all the car engines, aircraft piston engines, aircraft jet engines, and rocket engines that it designed and manufactured, to Hindustan Aircraft. This manufacturing possibility was negotiated by a high-level delegation consisting of the Air India chairman, J. R. D. Tata, the Chief of Air Staff, Air Marshal Subroto Mukherji, and the chairman of Hindustan Aircraft, J. M. Shrinagesh, who had visited London for detailed discussion with Rolls-Royce. The Indian Ministry of Finance, considering itself the final authority on India's aircraft engine manufacturing program, issued an opinion that Hindustan Aircraft and the Indian Air Force did not need any aircraft engines other than the Rolls-Royce Orpheus that had been contracted for. The Orpheus engines were considered adequate.[108]

Hindustan Aeronautics, which has had practical exposure to concepts associated with large-scale manufacturing, such as standardization and interchangeability, can resume, albeit after a break, the mass production of aircraft for civilian needs. The market for civil aircraft is large in India. A major impact by the defense sector on civilian quality of life can be made rapidly by Hindustan Aeronautics' adoption of product and market diversification strategies. Based on this example, there are other possibilities for India's industrial sector to harness the benefits of procurement, production, and research activities conducted in her defense sector. India's defense sector manufacturing capabilities are not insubstantial. The contemporary survival of the Zamzama gun, the frigate HMS *Trincomalee*, and one of the two still-flying B-24 Liberator bomber aircraft testify to the competencies. Effectively harnessing these defense sector manufacturing capabilities is important for India's industrial progress.

A political economy rationale for enhancing the manufacturing functionality implicitly factors in national interests. The cornerstones of such interests are not only an enhancement of wealth, but also projection and protection of that wealth, as well as the projection of capabilities for wealth protection. Hence, in almost every major industrial power, the defense sector has played an important role, as it has to now in India. There is a substantially long way to go, yet, for Indian industry in terms of issues such as standardization and interchangeability, concepts that have been developed from defense manufacturing practices. Civilian–defense spillovers, via close interactions, can help diffuse the concepts throughout Indian industry. In addition, relevant concepts for Indian industry to go forward are modularity and manufacturing flexibility, based on the adoption of modern information and communications technology systems. These concepts, along with some steps to facilitate the industrialization journey, are discussed in the next and final chapter of the book.

10 | *Reindustrializing India*

Heat and light

India's late, late industrial revolution demands many transformations, some of which are under way. The numerous institutional transitions that have occurred are just the first step. Many more are required. One's own predilections lead to the discussion of just a few structural transitions considered critical. This chapter deals with some of the issues and discusses how a few necessary, but by no means sufficient, transformations ought to be wrought as India proceeds to reindustrialize herself. Each item demands a separate book-length treatment. Each topic is massive. Thus, what is discussed in the section, on that topic, only scratches the surface of an important issue in a shallow way.

This first section deals with the energy imperative, since that is vital in industrialization, for mass manufacturing and in enhancing general welfare. Thereafter, other important contingencies are discussed. There is no particular order among them. All are equally important and necessary contingencies. Yet, no item is sufficient in itself. The second section highlights possible changes in industrial structure occurring because of entrepreneurial actions. The third section deals with how fragmented industry segments may consolidate. The fourth section deals with the information technology sector, while the fifth section sums up the major issues of the book by discussing new age manufacturing. Finally, there is a summary of the various themes in the book.

A vital and necessary condition for a successful late, late industrial revolution outcome for Indian firms will be energy usage. The energy imperative was critical in the first and second industrial revolutions, both of which involved a change from animate to inanimate energy usage. This inanimate energy was based on coal-driven steam power. It was coal-based thermal energy that generated electricity and electrical power. Though windmills and watermills had been invented in

265

the twelfth century, their power was low, just in the range of five horsepower or so. From the twelfth to the eighteenth centuries, a lack of adequate energy resources condemned industrial life, such as it was, to semi-immobility and a low productivity trap.[1] Steam power changed that.

The use of electric power, in place of water power or steam power, was a major source of growth, development, and change in the first half of the twentieth century.[2] The loss of mechanical energy, when it had to be transmitted by belts, pulleys, gears, and take turns, led to an absolute limit on plant size.[3] This limited the enjoyment of scale efficiencies. Electric power removed the constraints on the enjoying of scale efficiencies in manufacturing processes. Electricity made possible the redesign of entire systems of manufacturing technology.[4] Because of electricity usage, which was made possible by Thomas Edison's efforts at creating an electricity supply system, per capita energy consumption in the United States doubled between 1880 and 1910. This is the period when the second industrial revolution made its mark. The late Vernon Ruttan had documented the ratio of energy consumption to gross national product (GNP), based on GNP amounts deflated to 1992 US$ amounts. He found the largest growth in the ratio occurred between 1895 and 1900, and 1900 and 1905.[5] After that, the growth in the ratio tapered off. By then, the American GNP as well as energy consumption amounts had become very substantial. To propel her industrialization, the United States consumed energy at an ever-rising rate. See Table A18 for the details of numbers.

Since China and India are the economies of contemporary interest, figure 10.1 plots the per capita energy consumption in these countries between the years 1990 and 2007. The per capita energy consumption is expressed in British thermal units (BTUs). China has historically been a bigger energy consumer than India. It has become even bigger, relative to India, over time. Whatever India's consumption growth rate, China's consumption growth rate has been double that. The great leap forward, in China's energy consumption, occurred in the twenty-first century. The dragon has acquired more and more fire. Comparatively, India's energy consumption growth has been more sedate, at the pace of an elephant.

India's position is also usefully compared relative to a few developed countries, such as Germany, Japan, and the United States, and to the other late industrializing countries, such as Brazil, China and

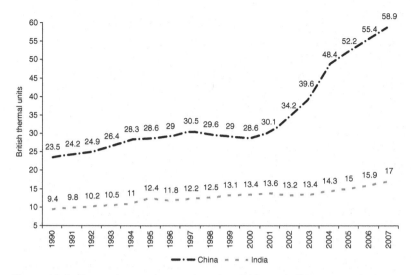

Figure 10.1. Per capita energy consumption: India and China.

Source: Derived from Energy Consumption by Country, United States Bureau of the Census, 2011 Statistical Abstracts, International Statistics, Table 1383.

South Korea. Table 10.1 highlights the per capita energy consumption, in BTUs, which is an average for the entire period of time between 1990 and 2007. First of all, India's large population skews meaningful statistic. Yet, India's consumption has been just 12.7 BTUs during the period, compared to 340.8 BTUs for the United States and 34.5 BTUs for China. Of course, the United States is the world's largest consumer of resources, and that is a polemic issue. Nevertheless, China consumes three times the energy that India does. South Korea's consumption is 154.6 BTUs, and it is now a developed nation. South Korea's energy consumption is 12 times that for India. Brazil, too, is no laggard at a consumption of 45.4 BTUs, which is three times that of India's, but it does have own energy sources.

The growth in energy consumption has been the highest for South Korea and China, followed by India. In analyses of contemporary industrialization, South Korea and China lead the global pack. Rising energy consumption has played a role. India's consumption has risen too, while the energy consumption of the developed countries has stagnated, primarily because these are countries that have reached a consumption plateau. Figure 10.2 plots the growth in per capita energy

Table 10.1. *Per capita energy consumption in British thermal units for a selection of countries for the period 1990 to 2007*

	Average per capita energy consumption for the entire period	Percentage growth in average per capita energy consumption for the period
Brazil	45.4	1.90
China	34.5	5.73
Germany	175.2	–0.14
India	12.7	3.61
Japan	169.7	0.91
South Korea	154.6	4.92
USA	340.8	–0.02

Source: Calculated from Table 1383, Energy Consumption by Country, United States Bureau of the Census, 2011 Statistical Abstracts, International Statistics.

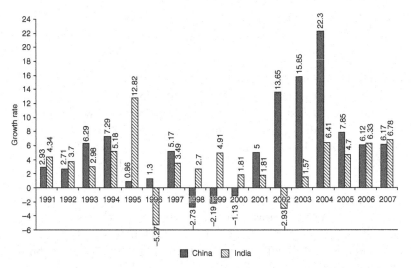

Figure 10.2. Growth in per capita energy consumption for India and China.

Source: Derived from Energy Consumption by Country, United States Bureau of the Census, 2011 Statistical Abstracts, International Statistics, Table 1383.

consumption expressed in BTUs in China and India between the years 1990 and 2007. The twenty-first century is of interest in this figure. Chinese energy consumption growth, in the twenty-first century, has been almost equal to that of India for the years 2006 and 2007, or greater than India's between 2001 and 2005.

Table 10.2. *India's per capita energy consumption in percentages relative to a group of countries*

	India's consumption as a percentage of each country's consumption					
	Relative to Brazil	Relative to China	Relative to Germany	Relative to Japan	Relative to South Korea	Relative to USA
1990	24.71	39.98	5.32	6.20	10.49	2.78
1991	25.13	40.53	5.48	6.27	9.79	2.94
1992	26.10	40.92	5.84	6.51	9.23	3.04
1993	26.26	39.65	6.03	6.66	8.61	3.11
1994	26.81	38.87	6.39	6.75	8.44	3.25
1995	28.97	43.48	7.08	7.42	8.81	3.63
1996	26.26	40.66	6.70	6.92	7.94	3.37
1997	26.18	40.01	6.96	7.01	7.62	3.51
1998	26.43	42.25	7.16	7.34	8.37	3.63
1999	27.64	45.31	7.63	7.56	8.17	3.79
2000	27.66	46.69	7.71	7.56	7.99	3.81
2001	28.89	45.27	7.67	7.78	7.93	4.03
2002	28.06	38.67	7.60	7.59	7.47	3.89
2003	28.53	33.90	7.58	7.72	7.40	3.97
2004	29.63	29.49	8.01	7.99	7.67	4.17
2005	30.25	28.64	8.56	8.37	7.78	4.40
2006	31.46	28.69	8.95	8.81	8.20	4.75
2007	32.51	28.86	9.88	9.63	8.50	5.04

Source: Calculated from Table 1383, Energy Consumption by Country, United States Bureau of the Census, 2011 Statistical Abstracts, International Statistics.

Table 10.2 highlights India's per capita energy consumption in percentages relative to the group of countries discussed for each of the years between 1990 and 2007. Let us deal with the countries of contemporary interest. Relative to China's energy consumption, India's energy consumption was 40 percent for the first half of the 1990s. By the last half of the 2000s, for which data are available, India's consumption has been 30 percent of that of China. Similarly, with respect to South Korea, India's energy consumption was about 9 percent for the first half of the 1990s. By the second half of the 2000s, for which data are available, India's energy consumption has been between 7 and 8 percent of that of South Korea. The literature on whether energy consumption is related to economic growth and national development is unequivocal. Like all literatures, it is large.[6] The consistent finding is of a significant and positive relationship. What is the outcome, in economic terms, of India's low energy availability? It is estimated that firms lose over 8 percent in value of their sales because of a lack of power. At a macroeconomic level, production losses due to the lack of power facing firms amount to over 1 percent of the gross domestic product.[7]

There is a salutary lesson from Britain's economic history. At the turn of the twentieth century, Britain was an important shipbuilding nation. Yet, the inability, or unwillingness, of British yards to provide workers with electrical powered tools in the first part of the twentieth century led British ships to be uncompetitive, as they were hand-riveted and not electric-welded.[8] By the twentieth century, electric welding had become standard in shipbuilding. As mentioned in Chapter 5, these welding innovations allowed Japanese shipbuilders to eventually produce ships of 500,000 tons deadweight capacity. Conversely, to acquire electric power sources, British shipbuilders were forced to invest in their own electrical power sources, adding to production costs and making their products globally uncompetitive.[9] Today, there is no British shipbuilding industry left.

Energy production and consumption issues remain crucial. Energy will be the most critical constraint for India's late, late industrial revolution. What is India's track record in the energy production dimension? India has a long history of electricity use. The first firms to use electricity did so in the 1880s, using their own generating sets. The first town lit by electricity was Darjeeling, in 1896, and Kolar Gold Fields was electrified in 1903. The Tatas set up the Tata Hydro Electric Power Supply Company in 1910.[10] Today, India's electric power is mainly generated by thermal energy, as coal-fired power stations provide over 53 percent of the generating capacity. Hydroelectric power is the next major source, accounting for almost 25 percent of generating capacity. Nuclear power accounts for less than 3 percent of India's generating capacity. The total generating capacity in India is 170,229 megawatts. Panel (A) of Table A19 details the categories of installed production capacity for electricity in India.

In the decade of the 2000s, for which data have been released, production has increased between 3 and 8 percent. The average, for all of the years and by all of the categories, is just over 5 percent in the entire

Table 10.3. *Growth in power generation in India in the 2000s*

	Growth by categories					
	Thermal	Hydro	Nuclear	Total utility sector	Private generation	Grand total
2001–02	3.52	−1.05	15.22	3.24	3.43	3.26
2002–03	5.87	−13.00	−0.44	2.95	3.52	3.01
2003–04	5.07	17.54	−8.30	6.08	6.77	6.16
2004–05	4.40	12.45	−4.33	5.19	4.76	5.15
2005–06	2.47	19.96	1.84	4.94	3.11	4.74
2006–07	6.60	11.83	8.53	7.51	11.08	7.89
2007–08	8.72	6.07	−9.81	7.75	10.61	8.06
2008–09	5.56	−5.24	−13.23	3.32	6.00	3.62

Source: Computations based on data in Ministry of Power, Table 16.9, http://powermin.nic.in, accessed March 9, 2011.

decade. The data for specific years, and by electricity generation source, are given in Table 10.3. Comparatively, there has been greater growth in consumption. In the 2000s, consumption has increased by between 1.85 percent in 2001–02 to over 10 percent by 2006–07 and 2007–08. The average, for all years and by all categories, is over 7 percent in the decade. The data for the specific years, and by source of electricity generation, are given in Table 10.4. What accounts for the discrepancy between production and consumption growth? India's electricity sector has suffered from transmission losses. This is a euphemism for theft, as individuals, at risk to their lives, download electricity from passing wires. These transmission losses were over 30 percent of net electricity available for supply, but they have reduced considerably over the decade. Yet, because supply from public utility sources may often be unreliable, many firms install their own captive power stations. This leads to a waste of resources, as these small plants are inefficient and uneconomic.

Consumption is rising, albeit influenced by lower transmission losses, but production growth is less dynamic. What is the growth pattern in the primary sources of raw materials for electricity generation? Table 10.5 details the production and growth in production of the primary raw materials for generating power. There has been considerable growth in the production of subterranean raw materials sources such

Table 10.4. *Growth in power consumption in India in the 2000s*

Year	Growth by categories						Total consumption	Transmission losses
	Industry	Agriculture	Domestic	Commercial	Railways	Others		
2001–02	-0.30	-3.61	5.37	7.07	-1.30	20.65	1.85	3.41
2002–03	7.14	3.44	4.59	5.38	8.52	4.70	5.32	-4.65
2003–04	8.36	3.08	7.66	10.87	4.69	-1.93	6.28	0.38
2004–05	10.45	1.68	6.60	11.28	3.09	5.99	6.98	-3.93
2005–06	10.15	1.96	4.63	14.61	4.73	2.49	6.67	-2.68
2006–07	13.02	9.67	10.90	11.83	8.61	-2.61	10.65	-5.81
2007–08	10.58	5.21	8.93	16.07	2.85	26.69	10.14	-5.10
2008–09	10.58	5.21	8.93	16.07	2.85	26.69	10.36	-0.83

Source: Computations based on data in Ministry of Power, Tables 16.10 and 16.11, http://powermin.nic.in, accessed March 9, 2011.

Table 10.5. *Production and growth in production of primary raw materials as sources of power*

	Panel (A): Annual production volumes by category				
	Coal	Lignite	Coal and lignite	Crude petroleum	Natural gas
	In million tons				In billion cubic meters
2000–01	313.70	22.95	336.65	32.43	29.48
2001–02	327.79	24.81	352.60	32.03	29.71
2002–03	341.27	26.02	367.29	33.04	31.39
2003–04	361.25	27.96	389.21	33.37	31.96
2004–05	382.62	30.34	412.96	33.98	31.76
2005–06	407.01	30.07	437.08	32.19	32.20
2006–07	430.83	31.29	462.12	33.99	31.75
2007–08	457.08	33.98	491.06	34.12	32.40
2008–09	492.76	32.42	525.18	33.51	32.85

	Panel (B): Production growth by category				
	Coal	Lignite	Coal and lignite	Crude petroleum	Natural gas
2001–02	4.49	8.10	4.74	−1.22	0.79
2002–03	4.11	4.88	4.17	3.15	5.65
2003–04	5.85	7.46	5.97	1.00	1.82
2004–05	5.92	8.51	6.10	1.83	−0.63
2005–06	6.38	−0.89	5.84	−5.27	1.39
2006–07	5.85	4.06	5.73	5.59	−1.41
2007–08	6.09	8.60	6.26	0.38	2.06
2008–09	7.80	−4.59	6.95	−1.79	1.37

Source: Computations based on data in Ministry of Power, Table 16.2, http://powermin.nic.in, accessed March 9, 2011.

as coal, and oscillating growth in surface sources such as lignite. Since India relies on coal and lignite based power, and has the world's largest coal reserves, the growth rates are unusually low. The growth of coal and lignite production has been 6 percent in the decade. Because of industrial demand, there is a flourishing world trade in coal, and Indian firms are buying up coal mines abroad, in Africa, Indonesia, and elsewhere. Cement companies belong to one major group of firms buying coal mines abroad. India is also highly deficient in petroleum and natural gas reserves, and the production growth figures for these categories of materials reflect that deficit.[11]

India's per capita energy consumption is low, and she needs to treble or quadruple this consumption level to power the industrialization under way. A critical sector for investments is energy. The proposed capacity additions amount to 78,700 megawatts over the next five years. The specific details, by category of energy source of the proposed additions to power capacity in India, are given in panel (B) of Table A19. Is this program of additions enough? Let us take the case of India versus other countries in per capita energy consumption. Table 10.2 indicates that India's per capita consumption is about one third of that of China or Brazil, one tenth that of South Korea, and one twentieth that of the United States. China, South Korea, and the United States are India's industrialization benchmarks. To have even a relatively remote chance of catching up with these countries, let alone leapfrogging and charging ahead, the proposed 78,700 megawatts of capacity addition is trivial. The additions to the power capacity should be at least 787,000 megawatts.

The sobering point is hammered home if one reviews the installed capacity in the United States. The details are shown in Table A20. There is over 1 million megawatts of installed power capacity in the United States, where there is a much smaller population, about one third that of India's, and where transmission losses are trivial. Hence, the per capita energy consumption level of the United States is over 20 times that of India. If India wants to emulate the United States in economic development, then planned Indian energy investments should be in the range of 1 to 2 million megawatts. What is the key message to emerge? If there is one sector in which investment has to be supplied urgently for industrialization to succeed, it is energy. India's power supply discrepancy can stall her industrialization. Conversely, it can be viewed as an economic opportunity in India of magnificent proportions.

Entrepreneurial sector transformation

An anecdote relates entrepreneurship in the organized automotive sector to potentially far-reaching changes in industrial structure, but it also involves an unlikely entrepreneur figure. It is possible that other examples of such entrepreneurship can have far-reaching and unexpected changes in other parts of India's industrial structure. Such entrepreneur-driven alteration of segment structures is an important contingency that can reindustrialize India. Hence, India may witness processes of transitions in its industrial structure because of entrepreneurial activities and actions. This is, of course, precisely the disequilibrium outcomes that the radical subjectivist school of thought on entrepreneurship would welcome.[12]

The entrepreneur we meet is Jagdish Khattar, who, at publication date, is 70 years old. In 2007, he retired at the age of 65 as the managing director of Maruti Udyog, India's largest manufacturer of cars. Jagdish Khattar should not have held the managing director position of Maruti Udyog in the first place. He ought to have retired in 2002, as perhaps a secretary to the government of India, perhaps even the Cabinet Secretary, a position that might have been theoretically attainable since he belonged to the Indian Administrative Service (IAS) cadre with a career apparently on the right trajectory.

Maruti Udyog was a once state-owned enterprise, set up in 1981 to implement a small car project that had been the brainchild of Sanjay Gandhi, the late Indira Gandhi's son. Sanjay Gandhi had been unable to complete the project. It was taken over for implementation by the state after his death. It eventually established a relationship with Suzuki Motors of Japan, to make the Suzuki range of small cars in India. Today, it is a subsidiary of Suzuki. It has the distinction of being the only company in India to make the transition from being a state-owned (SOE) enterprise to being a multinational company (MNC) subsidiary. Maruti now manufactures cars in India for the global market. It is aimed to make Maruti Udyog the global supply platform for all of Suzuki's small car range. That transition is a story to be told later. As a state-owned enterprise, Maruti might deploy IAS officers, on deputation as the term was technically called, from time to time. These officers could retain a lien on their parent service, and return to it any time they, or their cadre controlling authority, wanted. Jagdish Khattar joined Maruti after quitting the IAS.

Jagdish Khattar did not foresee returning to government, since he thought himself to be a non-political person and wanted the freedom of initiative. Hence, he carried on as the chief executive of Maruti till attaining retirement age. In fact, he even turned down the offer of continuing as Maruti's managing director for some more time since he wanted to do something different from being a bureaucrat, whether in a corporate or government setting. On retiring from Maruti, on December 18, 2007, Jagdish Khattar found the prospect of a retired bureaucrat's life underwhelming.[13] As he mentioned, he did belong to four golf clubs, but did not know how to play golf! He did, however, by then know the automotive sector extremely well. He visualized India's potential emergence as a world-class global player in the automotive sector and, most of all, he knew the anomalies within the automotive sector. On January 3, 2008, Carnation Auto was incorporated and Jagdish Khattar was in business. In October 2008, Azim Premji, one of India's information technology billionaires, came on board, via his venture capital fund, to provide venture financing.

Carnation Auto, according to Jagdish Khattar, provides one-stop shopping for all of India's car servicing needs. Under a single umbrella of the Carnation brand, the company will provide parts, servicing facilities, insurance products, second-hand car sales, and eventually any services required by customers after they have purchased a car. In a sense, the Carnation Auto brand rolls the businesses of O'Reilly Parts, Carmax, Firestone, and Geico products and services (to those familiar with these United States brands) under one umbrella. According to the advertising copy, Carnation Auto will be a cradle-to-grave service provider for all post-purchase requirements that enhance Indian customers' automotive experiences. Standardization, quality, reliability, and predictability of service are performance facets to be enhanced in the post-purchase automotive service market. The Carnation Auto business will mainly supply the post-warranty requirements, when the demand for automotive services becomes higher. The number of car fleets in India is rising. Car-fleet owners will find it easier to deal with a Carnation Auto outlet than a local service provider. Currently, there are 24 Carnation sites throughout India, and the company has an annual turnover of over ₹100 crores. Within three more years, a total of 200 Carnation outlets, including franchises, are expected to be *in situ* throughout India.

India's automotive service sector is extremely fragmented, personalized, and localized. While firms in the sector epitomize the activities of *jugaad* to the utmost, carrying creative improvisation to the extremes, the technology profile of the firms is primitive. Such technological backwardness in post-sales facilities and services is incompatible with the internal content of modern cars on India's roads today. Almost all of India's automotive service enterprises belong to the unorganized sector. The used Ambassador cars, shipped from Bombay, Delhi, and elsewhere to be remanufactured in Calcutta for subsequent use as taxis, are processed in small workshops once found on almost every corner of Calcutta's residential localities. In a typical middle-class residential area of Calcutta, called Bhawanipur, there are numerous small automotive workshops. On Romesh Mitter Road, a leafy residential road, there are rows of car repair and manufacturing units, close to a park for children, which itself is close to houses and apartments.[14] In these workshops, cars are stripped to the chassis and put together again from the ground up. Many of the body panels will be new, but not manufactured using giant presses. Rather, the metal shapes will have been formed by hand. Similarly, the engine components will have been made using small machine tools at these workshops. Surprisingly, these remanufactured cars do run, after a fashion.

The Carnation Auto business model is designed to change, in a small and limited way, what is a primitive, localized, and possibly inefficient but burgeoning automotive services sector. It is a sector that also has to grow more rapidly than the growth of the number of cars in India. There are now more cars in India than there is road capacity to handle the traffic, or competent service stations to deal with service requirements. A structural challenge is to transition the automotive services sector into the organized business segment category from the unorganized category. It is simple to suggest that Jagdish Khattar is someone utilizing his native contextual intuition, that he is an Israel Kirzner type of entrepreneur who has been alert to entrepreneurial opportunities, is a radical subjectivist who has imagined a different future in India's automotive sector, and has mobilized the necessary resources to create the visualized economic image. Some features of the story are important. A person who might have become a top Indian civil servant is now, past retirement date, an entrepreneur interested in transforming India's business landscape. In contemporary India, bureaucrats are turning businessmen. Age is not an entrepreneurship barrier. This exemplifies across-the-board democratization. Next, a notoriously unorganized sector of Indian business may become organized. The bipolar disorder in India's industrial structure, which is one of the most pressing industrial problems that characterizes many industries, is curable by entrepreneurs' innovative business models.

Fragmentation and consolidation

Democratization of entrepreneurship is having important effects on the late, late industrial revolution in India. Entrepreneurs such as Jagdish Khattar can develop unique business models that organize a sector with bipolar tendencies by bringing in scale economies and the use of modern practices and professionalism into transactions and activities that may have been extremely informal in their orientation. Of course, the consolidation of a fragmented and informal sector leads to the destruction of thousands of entrepreneurial livelihoods. The spread of fast-food chains, where food preparation and service has been industrialized, via the standard McDonald's model, has led to the disappearance of many small food outlets, cafés and restaurants. The McDonald's model promises quality and consistency, at a cheap price, but at the loss of ambience.

By definition, the scaling, consolidation, and corporatization of small, local, informal, or unorganized sector enterprises leads to the disappearance of entrepreneurship. Hence, there is a growth and survival trade-off between a Carnation Auto outlet and the local auto remanufacturing workshop on Romesh Mitter Road in Calcutta, just like the trade-off between a McDonald's outlet on Preston Road in Dallas versus the local Ostrogorski da Schnitzel Dhaba nearby on Dilbeck Lane. The presence of a Carnation Auto outlet or a McDonald's can crowd alternative suppliers out of the market. This has been a dilemma in the organization of economic activity. The very qualities that make entrepreneurial firms successful, such as task orientation, single-mindedness, and working in isolation, inhibit scaling-up processes.[15] Yet, there are economic necessities of efficiency that a large firm engenders, versus the psychological demands of autonomy that a small firm allows its owners to enjoy. The flip side of the trade-off between autonomy and control is the conflict between creativity and coercion.

Smaller companies, led by dynamic individuals, often create new markets. Yet, while making a product that is innovative, these companies may not be able to conquer the new markets because they do not have the resources to engender the scale economies that create mass markets. These small firms may have colonized a new niche, but can never consolidate the empire because they lack resources or abilities. Such mass-market creation can be done by consolidators that are large firms, with structures, bureaucracies, and discipline that can actually grow a market or utilize an item designed and manufactured by a small, specialized firm efficiently. These large firms may not be innovative, but they are effective in scaling up for mass-production and mass-marketing activities.[16]

An important issue in dealing with industrial structure is engendering relationships between the small firms from the fragmented segment and the large firms which can consolidate markets. The evidence, across a range of European countries, shows that small and creative firms are unable to compete with larger firms. Numerous experiments to engender flexible specialization have been tried in various countries, with clusters, industrial districts, and other organizational models implemented to bring together small and creative firms, in a focused and organized way, with the larger consolidator firms. These processes generate the scale economies. Hence, based on experiences, focus on the subcontracting process becomes important.[17]

The use of subcontracting has been an important approach towards handling the potentially debilitating dimension of emerging industrial structure in India. Yet, we do not know, at the aggregate level, how quantitatively important subcontracting relationships are for small and large firms alike. The subcontracting model has driven one aspect of the growth of India's information technology and software sector. Does it work elsewhere? The topic of subcontracting is vast, deserving a separate chapter, or even a book. There are many issues, such as those dealing with the boundary of the firm, make versus buy decisions relating to bought-out parts and components, vertical integration strategies and the minimization of transaction costs, and the role of outsourcing in international trade, that arise with the topic. These issues are skipped. This section deals with one rather small aspect of the issue.

In the manufacturing field in India, a subcontracting approach has salience towards resolving the bipolar disorder highlighted by the presence of numerous small firms and a couple of giant suppliers or manufacturers. The literature on subcontracting in India is slim.[18] There is a suggestion, however, that at least in the automotive sector, MNCs have shifted production to India to take advantage not just of a potentially large market, but also of the services of numerous small and medium-sized suppliers, and have created relationships with these.[19] Because India's strict labor laws sometimes make it difficult to terminate employment, in the textiles sector companies outsource considerable amounts of their weaving requirements to small handloom and powerloom units in the unorganized sector. Also, excise arbitrage makes it useful for firms to outsource cloth manufacture to small weavers, who operate a few looms, rather than to large weaving establishments.[20]

An example is Gokaldas Exports. It turns out 2 million garments per month for prominent global brand labels.[21] The workforce of Gokaldas Exports can produce items in 900 different styles, switching production techniques to suit fashion trends. Unlike Chinese garment production units, which might employ 300,000 persons each, Gokaldas Exports employs 33,000 people.[22] Contemporary hiring and employment practices at Gokaldas Exports have skewed the capital-to-labor ratio higher, as many staff members are highly qualified graduates using fashion software to design clothes on computers. Contracts for the actual production of clothes are given to several small units across Bangalore, where Gokaldas Exports is located. The labor-intensive work is carried out by these numerous small firms, and the high value-added work is done by the principal contractor. This has not only taken Gokaldas Exports higher up the economic value-added chain,[23] but also provided employment to many small units in the Bangalore region.

Similar subcontracting relationships can bring the numerous small, but possibly quite creative, firms in India's unorganized services and manufacturing sectors into deep relationships with large firms in the organized sector, and in the process enable the transfer of best practices to these small units. The smaller units will then become a part of the organized sector. The activities of the larger firm, in consolidating the numerous manufacturing and marketing activities, can bring mutual benefits for the small as well as large firms. The bipolar disorder can become a beneficial dualism. From a conceptual angle, associated with an analysis of industrial structure, subcontracting relationships can solve the trade-off riddle between autonomy and control. The need for efficiency which large firms engender is paramount in India. The autonomy feature in the unorganized sector, however, permits small firms to engage in *jugaad*. This attribute is badly needed. It captures indigenous grassroots innovation. Subcontracting relationships can dissipate the tensions between autonomy and interdependence in the context of managing complex industrial operations. The trade-off between craft production, based on craftsmen's creativity, and mass production, based on machinery, can be dealt with via subcontracting relationships, permitting millions of India's small firms to engage in specialized activities for which they have the flexibility.

These millions of firms may be extremely tiny in some cases, with low productivity, because they have not had access to finance, and have not built up marketing and infrastructure assets. They also do not possess business capabilities to make their enterprises successful because of basic skills and education deficits.[24] The subcontracting relationship is one way to engage the small and medium firms in India with large firms in the Indian corporate ecosystem. Of course, as Karl Marx suggested, such relationships, by bringing together the individualized and scattered means of production into a socially concentrated mechanism, transform a dwarf-like property of many into the giant-like property of the few. It could lead to the expropriation of the means of subsistence from the instruments of labor, and transfer these to those controlling large capital stocks.[25] This resource-extraction process may destroy the spirit of autonomy for the sake of economic efficiency. Yet, there is a conflict between efficiency and equality, necessitating the design of appropriate mechanisms and social organizations to mitigate the trade-offs.[26] Thus, an appropriate social organization can foster an effective subcontracting process.

How can one drive a subcontracting agenda? I have discussed how cluster recognition, and the development of websites, could help small and medium firms in Jaipur's ball-bearing cluster engage with the world. The Government of India has implemented other support programs for industrial development, and no longer behaves like Dr. No! An initiative by the Ministry of Small and Medium Sized Enterprises (MSME) of India's central government, with the United Nations Industrial Development Organization (UNIDO), has been the development of a series of subcontracting and partnership exchanges (SPX).[27] The website www.shaadi.com has changed the way marriages are made in contemporary India, and the website called www.match. com has changed the way relationships are struck up in the United States. Similarly, the SPX website enables matchmaking between firms for contractual relationships, specifically subcontracting relationships. The SPX focuses on three sectors: the auto component sectors in the national capital region around Delhi, Poona, and Madras, these being the main automobile production hubs in India; the leather sector in Tamil Nadu, since that state contributes 60 percent of the total leather production in India; and on footwear in Tamil Nadu, since there has been an important transition of the leather manufacturers from shoe component subcontractors to complete shoe exporters.[28]

Clearly, the implications of such an initiative are to reduce information asymmetries and lower the transaction costs for firms of doing business in India. As economies industrialize, there is a necessity for formal and informal structures that minimize uncertainty for buyers and sellers. By creating markets, that clear, for small and medium firms' products and services, the SPX initiative reduces moral hazard and adverse selection issues for buyers and sellers in the market for subcontracted products and services.[29] The SPX initiative improves the flows of information and knowledge between potential contractual service providers and those needing services. This information flow between parties help entrepreneurs balance demand, supply, and cost relationships.[30] It makes business systems predictable and business models profitable for all parties.

In addition, the initiative establishes monitoring and contracting services because all firms, whether large, medium, or small, must be vetted to join the exchange and to receive recommendations or connections from the exchange. In a sense, Sumangala provides identical intermediation and market-making services for a group of disenfranchised women, vetted by her, by weaving them into the business firmament of the formal medical profession in Calcutta, and making them suppliers of important raw materials. For the IVF clinics, Sumangala's services help them balance demand and supply factors in a sector where formal structures of business relationships have not existed. The IVF clinics are more accurately able to predict their costs, since there is now a standard tariff plan. This aspect of the relationship helps them reduce the uncertainties inherent in the cost of providing services to potential customers.

The long-term structural implications of SPX, this time of a joint entrepreneurial initiative by a government department and an international organization, is to engage the numerous small and medium-scale enterprises in subcontracting relationships with larger manufacturing units, and alter the bipolar disorder into a beneficial dualism. The SPX initiative has created an alliance structure midway between the total fragmentation of an industry segment such as automobile services, in which Jagdish Khattar is developing his consolidated business model, and a completely concentrated structure that may exist in many sectors where scale economies are extremely high, such as the oil and gas sector. Finally, for specialist entrepreneurs, such as Ferdinand Rodricks, the SPX initiative offers a means for making connections with another entrepreneur, such as Jagdish Khattar, to market his specialist services under the Carnation umbrella at a few select locations.

The SPX intermediation initiative starts imposing the semblance of a formal structure on the numerous diverse and heterogeneous segments of Indian industry that comprises the unorganized sector, as well as the small and medium-scale sector, by engaging firms in potentially ever-deepening ties with large-scale manufacturing firms. By intermediating exchange, the SPX initiative enables the existence of markets where none existed. This intermediation initiative brings small entrepreneurs into the organized sector without a sacrifice of the freedom and autonomy that is their hallmark. Those with a belief in grassroots entrepreneurship are adequately provided for, since the intermediation initiative can engender efficiency by bringing these smaller firms into the large-firms' transaction sets, where scale and scope economies can spill over from the larger to the smaller firms, and enhance the value-addition process by small firms. As contemporary facts show, interesting structural transformations are occurring in India's industrial landscape.

Information technology industrialization

This section contains a discussion of the changing role of India's information technology and software sector. The next section contains a discussion on what may emerge as a potential world-class manufacturing sector via the possible diffusion of new age manufacturing practices in India. Ideas in these sections are linked. Information technology industrialization and new age manufacturing can become India's unique and perhaps only way of defining the contours of her own late, late industrial revolution that the world can emulate.

Prognostication on Indian industrialization ought to be grounded in sobering evidence. The Indian information technology and software sector is an important driver for her growth.[31] If the much-touted Indian information technology sector is, indeed, one of the world's greatest, and is the standard-bearer for India's overall economic growth, then why does not a single Indian company figure in the list of the world's top 100 software revenue earners?[32] Is it because of a major focus on information technology services, and not on digital goods or software products? The research that my colleagues, Ashok Nag and Kenneth Simons, and I have carried out shows that low value-added services, often pejoratively called body-shopping and off-shoring, in the popular press and literature, account for the vast bulk, perhaps as much as 95 percent, of Indian information technology and software firms' revenues.[33] These services involve labor-intensive and repetitive coding of software that has already been designed, and the debugging of problems. Body-shopping activities involve the Indian companies' sending their staff abroad. Off-shoring involves the conduct of work in India, and the transmittal of completed tasks to clients via data links.[34] This is the consequence of unbundling activities where feasible, because communications facilities make the performance of cheaper and low value-added tasks in lower wage nations possible.[35]

Labor of reasonable quality is, generally, a scarce resource in many economies. In such cases, firms adopt a strategy of substituting labor by capital. In India, labor is an abundant resource. The strategy of Indian firms is to substitute capital by labor. This is counter-factual to a strategy of climbing the ladder of comparative advantage by moving into more capital-intensive areas of economic activity. In the case of information technology and software services, this capital intensity arises from the application of knowledge resources. Such an approach, in the twenty-first century, trading the benefits of capital by utilizing abundant and cheap labor, may be fraught with considerable risk. Fernand Braudel recognized that a perversion of incentives in India, in the late eighteenth and early nineteenth centuries, may have been a reason, among several, that led to her textiles industry becoming backward, and then almost extinct. Because labor was plentiful and cheap, even if Indian businessmen had investible capital, there were no motivations to mechanize textile production.[36] This might, perhaps, have contributed to India's de-industrialization.

India is a service-based economy. It is an economy celebrating the role of its information technology services and software sector.[37] It is worth keeping the labor-for-capital substitution phenomenon in mind when assessing the nature of modern capital in general, and the type of capital to be found in the information technology services and software sector. The generic features of service operations are relevant to an understanding of information technology and software services. Services are imitable; service innovations are easily imitable. Services are perishable, since they are not produced in advance; demand and supply balancing is difficult to achieve, affecting the attaining of operational scale; and services are heterogeneous, with every value-added service offering becoming unique, as customer needs vary, affecting standardization.[38] A service has spatial, temporal, and person specificity. A service is an item to be consumed at a particular time and place by a particular person or organization. By definition, a service is a low value-added unit because the intellectual property component in the service and delivery process is low or non-existent.[39] A service is labor intensive. It has lower profitability.[40]

Let me provide an example. There may be certain services, such as cancer surgery, which embody a very high intellectual property component in the surgeon's skills. Over and above the surgeon's skills, the instruments and processes used today, for example in laparoscopic or robotic surgery, embody substantial knowledge elements and intellectual property. Only a surgeon, highly trained in both general surgery and the various automated surgical processes, can utilize these new technologies. Each operation is an extremely high value-added transaction, in commercial and quality-of-life dimensions. It is a service with unique temporal, spatial, and person specificities, involving considerable intellectual property utilization.

But these highly specialized and customized services are not infinitely reproducible on a large scale. There are no economies of scale in providing value-added services. It is only the no-value-added or low-value-added services, delivered in a routine manner, that generate economies of scale. Thus, economies of scale are found in call center services, or in services involving routine maintenance issues. Provisions of these services are not going to develop a country, or enrich it in the long run, though the company owners may benefit in the short term. A few individuals will become immensely wealthy, because they have leveraged the efforts of a large pool of people for a period of time to generate cash flows. Exploiting economies of scale in wage arbitrage, which is what Indian information technology and software firms are currently engaged in,[41] is a short-term phenomenon.

What does making an information technology or software product imply? The lines of code necessary for a software algorithm to work are transcribed on to a CD. Then that disk is packaged in a colorful box, with an attractive brand logo, shrink-wrapped, and sold in retail outlets. The product disk embodies a considerable amount of knowledge and human effort encapsulated within it. The value addition to society comes from making these knowledge efforts available to a wider public. Yet, in creating value, basic coding is necessary. Information technology has yielded a digital or information good.[42] The Microsoft Office disk has been manufactured in the billions and sold to customers who may use it forever. This product alone generates a substantial portion of Microsoft's market capitalization of several billion dollars.

Of course, not all products developed will succeed. Writing a successful software product is like producing a hit film or writing a bestseller. There are attendant failure risks. But these risks apply to all product development efforts, and to all business initiatives. As is well known, only a small number of business initiative attempted ever hit the jackpot. Nevertheless, software companies that have greater product revenues have greater growth and profit potential, since it is easier to sell numerous copies of a standardized product than it is to sell tailored services in bulk.[43] The business models of products versus services are contradictory with respect to scale economies. Software is a capital good, in the same way that a piece of equipment is a capital good. Just as a piece of machinery embodies ideas and knowledge in its design, functionalities, and operations, leading to the production of other goods and services when it is used, so does software incorporate ideas and knowledge in design and functionalities.[44] What is true for capital goods is true for digital goods with respect to knowledge embodiment. Software enables the production of other goods and services. While capital goods may be visible on the shop-floor, a digital good resides inside a machine and is invisible; *ipso facto*, it is an intangible item. Machinery too, however, contains large amounts of embedded intangible intellectual property.

The harnessing of old-fashioned manufacturing principles and values to the production of digital or information goods has led to the industrialization of information technology in the United States and elsewhere. The reproduction of a digital good or product is almost costless. Because of the Internet, distribution is almost costless if not free. The act of transformation of code into a digital product, embodying ideas and knowledge, deliverable as a CD by mail, or via the Internet, has led to an explosion in the digital goods industry. Books, music, and software are digital goods produced because of the industrialization of the information technology and software sector. There are millions of applications for mobile web-based products created and distributed in the last few years. Indian firms' participation in these activities is trivial.

Let us take an example. Accounting routines that companies and individuals use are now over 500 years old. These accounting routines were coded as software commands, packaged, and sold as the Quicken brand of accounting software.[45] We can all buy Quicken products. Similarly, SAP sells products for enterprise resource planning and supply chain management tasks. The purchasers of these are individual businesses. A company called SAS sells statistical software packages. Companies like Quicken, SAP, and SAS have industrialized themselves in the information technology and software sector. They create digital products, produced and sold via mass manufacturing and marketing techniques reminiscent of the second industrial revolution in the United States a century ago.

India's software firms engage thousands of individuals to write code. The output of code is used to provide a service, at low cost, to specific companies, perhaps in India or anywhere in the world. Employees working in Infosys, Wipro, or Tata Consultancy Services write accounting and enterprise resource planning codes all day. The labor of these individuals is sold as a cheap commodity. It is not embodied in differentiated digital products adding value to the activities of daily living of a multitude of consumers all over the world. Yet, it is precisely because firms such as Quicken, Microsoft, and SAP have added value to the activities of a mass market, whether individuals or businesses, that they have become big and rich. They have been able to develop products requiring manufacturing, even if the manufacturing process does not take place in a facility where there are pools of grease and metal shavings lying on the floor.

Production and manufacturing activities have been reorganized. But they still exist. They need to be undertaken, even for information technology and software products. If India is an information technology powerhouse, then several Indian companies ought to be selling vast amounts of digital goods and information technology and software products to the world's mass markets. Nevertheless, in the list of the top 100 global software revenue earners there are two Chinese, seven Japanese, and two South Korean companies listed, but not a single Indian company appears.[46] We understand that China, Japan, and South Korea are primarily manufacturing nations, and India is a nation growing rich primarily on information technology. Is that the case? The crude optimism that software and information technology services will be India's savior can lead to exacerbation of income inequalities and inflation. It is worth considering that information technology and software sector growth is not a panacea for future development.[47]

So where do the world's information technology and digital products come from? If they do not come from India, pointed out as the world's most successful information technology sector growth example, and if Indian firms cannot manufacture software and digital products, then can the Indian information technology and software sector be held up as a role model? According to Sudipto Deb, a senior software industry executive based in northern India, such product-oriented companies account for just 5 percent of information technology sector activities in India.[48] The remaining 95 of percent of information technology sector companies is purely service oriented.

The present work carried out by India's information technology sector companies is conceptually similar to being an OEM contractor for goods. Companies from several Asian countries, such as China, South Korea, and Taiwan, began life as OEM contractors.[49] Later, these Asian contract manufacturers developed their own brands. They became own label manufacturers (OLM). Only then could Asian companies such as Canon and Mitsubishi become global giants. In the software sector, Indian companies are OEM oriented. To have a branded product, or suite of products, means being OLM oriented. Indian information technology and software companies that are OLM oriented are small in number. Without products and manufacturing, even of items that owe their origins to the information technology and software sector, such as digital products, India's national income cannot keep rising to higher levels.

In this analysis, there is some hope. A recent analysis of India's information technology and software sector lists a few small firms engaged in product development.[50] A company originally named Peutronics, now called Tally Solutions, created an accounting software product named Tally, while Punjab Communications created and sold a product named Wisdom Workhorse to large Indian companies. Thus, there yet might be market space for Indian companies to develop software products in specific niches. Indian companies can, however, hardly take on the likes of Microsoft in standard office applications, or SAP,

SAS, or PeopleSoft in enterprise resource planning (ERP) products. In focused areas, such as computer-based training for airline crews, image compression, and pattern recognition, Indian firms can create digital products. Sankhya Infotech developed integrated resource management products for airline operators, and Geometric Solutions, a feature recognition algorithm company, developed algorithms extensively used in machine tool manufacturing and the design of computer-aided manufacturing products.[51] The issue in these information technology industrialization initiatives is achieving economies of scale.

In respect of scale-driven information technology industrialization, the case of Financial Technologies (FT) deserves mention. Founded by Jignesh Shah, a former design engineer with the Bombay Stock Exchange (BSE), FT has developed trading products extensively used by India's broking and trading communities. The origins of FT, founded jointly with Dewang Narella, lie in the design of the BSE on-line terminal (BOLT), which Jignesh Shah and Dewang Narella had a development role in, during the mid 1990s. At that time, a critical constraint for all on-line applications in India was bandwidth. There was not enough bandwidth to go around. The delays, called latencies in technical parlance, in computer-to-computer connections and communications severely limited on-line activities since speed was essential in trading.[52] This was a constraint in the diffusion of information and communications technologies in India's businesses.

Using functionalities developed overseas, FT developed a trading platform, along the lines of a Bloomberg platform, which was oriented towards Indian infrastructure constraints. The platform was developed in a Microsoft environment, making development costs cheaper. In the mid 1990s, an alternate stock exchange, the National Stock Exchange (NSE), had also been set up and this was to be a fully on-line exchange only. There was to be no physical trading floor. By 2000–01, an Indian stock market boom had occurred, with NSE capturing the largest share of market transactions, and there was considerable demand for trading terminals that incorporated the FT product. Within a few years, FT's own stock market valuation had touched $1 billion.[53]

Scale matters, and in some segments of the software sector the benefits of scale can be achieved. The spillovers from trading terminal product development led FT into creating a commodity exchange, based on its exchange algorithms, named Multi Commodity Exchange (MCX). A commodity exchange named the National Commodity and Derivatives Exchange (NCDEX) had been set up by India's state-owned financial institutions so that farmers could trade agricultural commodities. Yet, NCDEX did not do well because it did not have the pulse of India's trading community. MCX concentrated on the trading of items such as gold, silver, energy, and oil, as these were items with prices that did not fluctuate wildly across different sub-markets. Gold as a standardized item, with quality certifiable by assay, also attracted a large clientele given India's predilections for bullion as well as for trading, two behavioral characteristics discussed in earlier chapters. This feature gave MCX considerable scale and volume, leading to an extensive daily trading turnover that has made it a very large firm in India's financial sector.

The FT and MCX examples suggest that industrialization of the information technology sector is feasible in India, with branding and volumes based on scale economies being attainable. Also, India's information technology and software sector firms, through the industry association, the National Association of Software and Service Companies (NASSCOM), have excellent relationships with government.[54] Hence, concerted cooperative market development, in India and overseas, is possible. Developments by other Indian information technology and software firms, in the manufacturing and sale of digital products, could one day lead Indian companies to appear in the list of the top 100 companies of the world, as ranked by software revenues. A transition from the sale of commoditized people-based services to branded value-added products, including digital products, can enhance the financial and real wealth of India's information technology sector.

New age manufacturing

To connect the dots, I return to manufacturing as a vital contingency for India's reindustrialization. Michael Cusumano has stated that "Software has the power to change the world, especially when treated as a business by managers, programmers, and entrepreneurs who also want to change the world."[55] Actually, software might have the power to change the world of Indian manufacturing, since embedded software can give rise to a new manufacturing age for Indian firms. A focus on embedded software can lift the Indian information technology and software sector from the low value-added services trough it presently is in. Especially in the automotive sector, where India has considerable potential to be a global manufacturing power, new age manufacturing, with embedded software functionalities, can alter the balance in India's favor and transition her information technology and software sector towards a products orientation.

What is new age manufacturing? Over four decades ago, Wickham Skinner argued that manufacturing ought to be the centerpiece of a firm's competitive strategy, as well as being of consequence for a nation's fortunes. As the decades of the last century passed, manufacturing came to be looked at as a technical process, to be managed from the bottom upwards. The received world-view of the manufacturing function in firms was to perceive it as a set of daily low-grade routines, full of details and minutiae, and even the content of its academic courses consisted of quantitative analysis and industrial engineering materials. Hence, within firms, particularly in the United States, manufacturing had been relegated in both its corporate role and its national role.[56] It was not considered a value-enhancing functionality. There was also an economic issue. The American manufacturing system epitomized mass production, with high-volume output of standard products made with interchangeable parts, using dedicated machinery, operated by semi-skilled labor, and based on predetermined tasks. In this system, large-scale manufacturing volumes implied rigidity since production fixed costs were high. Thus, product changes or volume reductions were not cheap.

Some decades ago, at least in the United States, manufacturing still had a mass production distinction, characterized by rigidity, associated with it. Nevertheless, in the interim a variety of advanced manufacturing techniques had been developed so as to obtain productivity from the processes.[57] While these advanced manufacturing techniques yielded short-term advantages in cost savings, they were palliatives. They did not address the long-term structural transformation in progress.[58] This structural transformation occurred because of an industrial transformation leading to the diffusion of information and communications technologies through all aspects of a firm's operations. Many, if not all, of a firm's processes became digital processes.[59] Manufacturing had changed radically since the days of Henry Ford.

The diffusion of information and communications technologies as a general purpose technology has changed the role of manufacturing, and redistributed value among various production activities. Many products are assembled in one location, but the various components are sourced from all over the world. Hence, global sourcing and manufacturing networks are the norm. There has been a considerable reorganization of production, with the emergence of production supply chains, or global value chains, as a substitute for own manufacturing facilities. The technologies of computers and electronics communications have dispersed power and knowledge. Therefore, traditional industrial formations have dispersed and altered the nature of industrial activity.[60]

An important aspect of modern manufacturing is miniaturization. In many products, the conceptual heart of the product may be a tiny component in which the intellectual property associated with the value inherent in a particular product resides. This is true of the computer. A desktop computer is physically large. Yet, the motherboard is a small, even tiny, device in which the analytical and computational horsepower of the computer resides. The chip, even smaller in size relative to the rest of the machine, is the core value-enhancing functionality providing the engine for the computation operations. Another aspect is modularization. Putting together a computer, or for that matter a car, today involves the use of modules. By this process, many ready-made modules are assembled together to prepare the final assembled product that the customer buys. Hence, component and module manufacturing operations need not be within a single firm. In the final assembly process, the use of software-driven robots has changed manufacturing functionalities. Thus, the diffusion of general purpose technologies has changed the nature of manufacturing. Substantial value addition still takes place via manufacturing, but in entirely different ways.[61]

Since manufacturing implies manipulating things and materials, and of putting something together from components and parts, the way these manipulations and assembly occur has changed radically. Manufacturing, as a specific case of physical production, still exists, but the processes have changed. The key aspects of this process change have been driven by developments in information technology and communications. Just like old-fashioned mass-production technologies, modular systems embody standardization. Older systems of mass production standardized the products or processes. Modular components standardize functionality rules.[62] Take the modular manufacture of cars. It does not matter to the automobile assembler, say Volkswagen, what the detailed internal processes and manufacturing techniques related to an electronic engine management system are, if the engine management system module can be bolted on to the engine, and the module then integrates its activities seamlessly with the rest of an engine's and a car's functionalities. Standardized engine management system modules can be made in India, in bulk, and shipped to Augsburg in Germany to be incorporated into Volkswagen cars.

Similarly, take the manufacture of personal computers. They can be assembled like the Meccano toys children play with. Each of the modules will have substantial knowledge and critical intellectual properties embedded within them. The manufacturer of each module can undertake its own development and manufacturing activities, as long as all of the modules eventually integrate together to form a viable product generating customer value. An example of extreme engineering, based on principles of modularization, is the annual manufacture by a South Korean shipyard of 40 super-sized container ships and tankers, in a cost-efficient way. Modularization leads to assembly-line type scale economies even in job-shop type industries. Manufacturing modularization leads to the dispersal of many activities across regions or countries. A car or computer manufacturer may not make all the modules. If it does not, it simply needs to coordinate the processes involved in final manufacturing. General purpose information and communications technologies assist in coordination. What a car manufacturer like Volkswagen achieves is manufacturing flexibility.

Information and communications technologies are contemporary general purpose technologies with a major influence on manufacturing flexibility and overall performance.[63] The impact of information and communications technologies at the firm level is profound. This impact occurs not because of the usage of equipment, but because of changes in the organization of production within the firm and the industry and across industries. This arises because of complementarities between the diffusion of information and communications technologies and in the use of higher skilled employees.[64] For instance, higher bandwidth communications technology can transmit complex process, product, and service information very cheaply. The telegraph and the telephone changed coordination processes in the late nineteenth century, leading to manufacturing specialization by firms, market integration, the engendering of scale and scope economies, and the birth of professional management. Similarly, contemporary technologies of coordination make flexible manufacturing an efficient form for value addition. Information can be shared instantly, and inexpensively, among many people in many locations and the value of centralized decision making decreases.[65] These organizational efficiencies lead to the enhancement of economic value-added.

Based on the preceding discussion, one can state that a very important innovation possibility for India's manufacturing firms is in the use of modular manufacturing approaches in domestic operations, and in the manufacturing of modules for assembly in other parts of the world. These will involve the very heavy use of embedded software permitting automation of the manufacturing function. The corresponding opportunity for information technology and software sector firms, then, is to become the major designers and suppliers of this embedded software. These pieces of embedded software translate functionality rules into digital code for subsequent standardization and mass production. An embedded system consists of computer processes, performing one or more dedicated functions, incorporated in another device.

Embedded software converts human or mechanical processes into digital processes. A wireless phone instrument contains many processes involving embedded software. Modern cars contain numerous pieces of embedded software, for their directional, navigation, engine management, braking, air conditioning, entertainment systems, and safety systems. Modern aircraft and flight control systems are virtually run by these pieces of embedded software. In theory, from the start of its take-off roll to eventual landing after a flight, a fully loaded Boeing 777 can fly itself via its embedded software. The pilots are there to take over if things go wrong, but need not intervene if things are going according to plan. Embedded software products, therefore, find potential mass markets. They can be mass-produced, thus benefiting from economies of scale.

I have consistently used the automotive sector for examples throughout the book. In Chapter 1, I described the three criteria necessary for an economy to take off. One criterion was the existence of at least one sector, if not several, possessing world-class scale, quality, and product demand characteristics. India's automotive sector has consistently met Walt Rostow's criterion of being a unique sector displaying world-class scale and growth[66] so that it can drive her economic take-off. To illustrate the role of embedded software, I use an example from this sector. The example deals with whether the automotive sector can be a possible world-leader and growth-driver, based on industrialization of information technology and new age manufacturing. The design, development, and use of embedded software products can help transform the information technology and software sector as well as Indian manufacturing practices generally. The illustration of what embedded software might do is based on an example that I observed in Munich some time ago.

While visiting a Bavarian Motor Works (BMW) plant, which was situated next to BMW's world headquarters and the research and development center in Munich, I had occasion to observe the manufacturing of the 3-series BMW cars in the plant. The plant is one of the oldest in the BMW family, and small by BMW standards. It is located in what has become the congested northern part of the Munich city, near the Olympic stadium, and is 400,000 square meters in size. The plant employs 9,000 persons. It operates three shifts in the press shop, where car bodies are made, and two assembly shifts. On average, 900 BMW 3-series cars are assembled daily and the annual production of the plant is over 200,000 cars. The annual production value is over $7 billion from a small plant.

Because of space constraints, the assembly line, in aggregate almost four kilometers long, is constructed on many levels. The plant consumes 600 tons of steel per day, made up of approximately 20 coils. A coil of steel goes in to the plant at one end, and it is cut and shaped into several bodies, with 66 bodies being cut and shaped by the giant presses per hour. According to the production plan, the required body parts, which have been stored in the interim, are spot-welded together to a one-tenth millimeter precision, other components are added, the body is married to the power train consisting of the engine and transmission, and a week later emerges a finished BMW 3-series car for sale anywhere in the world. The coil-to-car time is less than a week. The plant makes every variant of the 3-series BMW car.

All cars are made per customers' orders. A customer can change an order up to six days before production commences. Each of the over 200,000 cars produced annually in that plant is unique. There is an infinite number of variations possible, based on body style, steering wheel location, pollution requirements, number of doors, light placement requirements, and many other features. Yet, the rejection rate is nil. In fact, an American visitor asked a guide what the rejection rate was, and the guide did not understand the question as he did not know what rejection meant! How does this happen? One explanation is that it is through the extensive use of information and communications technology and embedded software. The shaped body parts, cut from the steel, are generic; they are based on the current product and model designs. These cut body parts are stored in the body shop awaiting assembly. Once an order is placed, a vehicle identification number (VIN) is given. After that, everything is specific. Each car becomes unique. Based on a detailed production specification sheet, the production plan for a number of days is spelt out in detail in advance. The detailed specifications are then placed in a digital transponder box for each car.[67] The processor in every digital box has the same computational power contained in each Apollo space vehicle used on erstwhile lunar missions. The box is attached to the largest body part kept in the body shop that will eventually become part of the finished car.

Production is fully automated, though there are 3,000 employees per shift. These employees change tools and dies, and keep a check on quality. The plant uses 650 robots, in mobile production cells, with eight robots per cell on average. These robots can conduct operations on six planes or axes. There are some robots that can also operate along seven axes, the seventh axis being the lateral one. The robots are pre-programmed with specific instructions as to what to do when faced with a specific car variant. When a car of a particular variant, say a four-door saloon car for the right-hand drive British market, comes to a robot station for a specific bodywork task, the robot has explicit instructions embedded in its software as to what operation to conduct for such a car and body style.

The production plan and every order variation is pre-programmed in the robots' software, and the digital transponder box associated with a particular VIN communicates with the robot so that exactly the correct operation is carried out. Thus, the exact activity required is matched to model specifications. As the next VIN to be processed by a robot may be for a completely different order, say for a left-hand drive two-door convertible for the American market, the robot has to change certain tools, and these tool changes are carried out in five seconds. Eventually, a completed 3-series BMW car will contain 22 pounds of fiber optic cabling. It will, additionally, contain 40 different electronic controllers, coordinating and controlling every aspect of the automobile's operations. The production processes for the cars, and the subsequent operations in day-to-day ownership, are based on embedded software. The embedded software has made the processes of manufacture and operational handling extremely efficient. Thus, the BMW cars are justly prized for their build quality, handling, and operations. The high retail prices that they command are a function of the knowledge embodied in these cars.

Embedded software items are products which may not be visible when in use for general purpose commercial or entertainment activities consumed en masse. They are, nevertheless, digital goods used for the production of almost all other goods and services in our contemporary society. These embedded software items are ubiquitous in today's world. They are continuously being updated and redeveloped. The use of embedded software products is found in consumer items, manufacturing processes, and service delivery processes. India's domestic market, which is burgeoning in all sectors, is potentially extremely large for embedded software items that alter the functionalities of other goods and services consumed by the public at large. Embedded software will find a major market in modular new age manufacturing processes, in all types of manufacturing plants across India. India's companies have to emulate the likes of manufacturing companies such as BMW, so that India may become one of the key manufacturing nations of the world. The fact that BMW has recently located some of its manufacturing facilities to India, at Chennai, albeit for small volumes of production initially, is useful for engendering possible capability spillovers to other automotive plants in the region.

While it could be too late for Indian information technology and software firms to become a Microsoft or an SAP, there are other opportunities for these firms to become global market leaders in specific embedded software domains. The intellectual energies of India's vast army of information technology and software professionals can be channeled into embedded software development. Because India is reputed to be now a global information technology power, India can leapfrog many emerging economies into the new generation of flexible manufacturing functionalities. Based on embedded software product development, she can enter a manufacturing new age. India can become a global player in the production of embedded software products to create digital machines, because this is what machinery with embedded software is. This manufacturing new age will be based on modularization, driven by embedded software functionalities, and arising because of the industrialization of information technology.

Resetting the clock

The political psychologist Ashish Nandy has speculated that it is human nature to create a future unencumbered by the past, and yet be informed by it.[68] Lessons from the complexities of the past help reorganize the perplexities of the present. In contemporary India, a moral economy of prosperity has taken root. A will to make progress, once dampened, has been released. While India is heterogeneous, such an attribute has transcended ideologies and united Indians in a common homogenous purpose. John Strachey wrote: "This is the first and most essential thing to learn about India – that there is not, and never was an India, or even any country of India, possessing, according to European ideas, any sort of unity, physical, political, social, or religious; no Indian nation, no 'people of India,' of which we hear so much."[69] Such a comment was an excuse for colonization. Today, such a sentiment is utterly repugnant. The contemporary unifying theme of improving one's material lot transcends all ethnic divisions in India.

The Indian state, once a command and control regime, has taken a back seat in giving directions. It is an infrastructure creator, deal facilitator, and partner. Supporting these tasks are financial institutions, and decentralized bodies like SFCs, SIDCs, SSIDCs, SPXs, and SEZs. The markets versus socialism debates wasted time and energy in the twentieth century. The government-led industrialization epoch is in India's past. Contemporary India has not needed state-led big push industrialization. India possesses a rich industrial history. Harnessing path dependencies, along with emulating others' experiences, can lead to comprehensive entrepreneur-led reindustrialization. On this note, I return to Walt Rostow's recommendation that for take-off there has to be at least one, if not more, world-class industrial sector. The production of cars has increased 30 times in 30 years. Today, every make of car is available, there are 15 million cars in India and by 2015 that number may be 25 million. The automotive sector has started displaying world-class characteristics. A world-class automotive sector can work wonders for India's global economic standing. India can become the world's supply platform, in the small and medium-sized category of cars.

Automotive production is recognized as a sunrise sector.[70] Expansion of automotive production will have considerable welfare consequences, in terms of domestic mobility for Indians,[71] in impacting world trade,

and for the direction of India's trade balances, as India becomes a global automotive manufacturing hub. Hence, a determination to turn
India into the word's pre-eminent global automotive hub finds expression in the worthy sentiment: "To emerge as the destination of choice
in the world for design and manufacture of automobiles and auto
components with output reaching a level of $145 billion accounting
for more than 10% of the GDP and providing additional employment to 25 million people by 2016."[72] But, how will such an eventu-
ality occur? For translating these extremely ambitious sentiments into
doable reality, the example that I have described, of BMW's Munich
manufacturing plant, and its use of embedded software and information and communications technologies for enhancing manufacturing
quality and output, should find many takers among Indian automotive sector firms. The internalization of these lessons by the automotive industry, and other industries too, in the development of digital
machines can be of considerable impact in India.

The late Leonard Setright stated that: "Revolution, you see, is like
any other turnaround, like a clock-hand, like a spinning wheel: when
it has turned full circle, it is back where it started."[73] In 1500, India's
share of the world's gross domestic product was almost 25 percent,
as we have seen from Chapter 5. By the mid 1970s, it had dropped
to 3 percent. It then started rising, so that by the end of the twentieth
century it was over 5 percent. Clearly, the clock hand, keeping track
of India's position in world income tables, is on its upward trajectory
now. To be back to where it started, so that India's share of the global
gross domestic product is substantial, if no longer at 25 percent, is a
challenge. But, such a challenge is a visceral goal. Given the entrepreneurship democratization taking place, and the flood of firms emerging from this process, the harnessing of business talent can ensure
that the current late, late industrial revolution in progress is taken
seriously and the goal attained.

The Indian economy has a significant amount of catching up to do.
Yet, oddly enough, that is an extremely important advantage. The relative backwardness of a country as it is taking off, relative to other
comparable but not backward countries, provides conditions for subsequent industrialization success. A series of eruptive spurts, driven by
intergenerational technology leapfrogging, can transform a disadvantage into a sustainable competitive advantage. Intergenerational technology leapfrogging can occur in the manufacturing sector. Income

distribution conditions and tastes in India support standardized goods manufacture for a mass market. The Bombay Plan postulated ambitious targets. To achieve a doubling of per capita income, the planners proposed to raise the net output of industry by five times from then current levels.[74] Such ambitions have to be rearticulated. Entrepreneurs who use machinery, permitting low-cost and high-volume production, will realize their goals and expectations. Conversely, India cannot be taken seriously as an industrial nation if she does not enter the mass-manufacturing age.

One thing is absolutely clear. India cannot compete globally on the basis of low wages. She has to compete globally based on manufacturing capabilities. Some of these capabilities will be developed via equipment use; some will arise via the organizational discipline that needs to be inculcated; and other capabilities will develop via the use of state-of-the-art processes. India's firms have to focus on large-scale manufacturing, turning out high-quality standardized products by the millions, as the American, Japanese, South Korean, Taiwanese, and Chinese companies have done, to advance her late, late industrial revolution. There is no escaping that approach. This strategy paid off handsomely for the United States, Japan, South Korea, and Taiwan. It is now doing the same for China. This process will generate the mass incomes and fiscal resources required for poverty amelioration. It will make cheap goods widely available. It will influence income distribution and employment generation. Additionally, the paradox of a rapidly growing manufacturing base, but a stagnant share of manufacturing in national income, will correct itself.

India's mass manufacturing approach has to be modern. The economic development of the world in the last three centuries occurred because of simultaneous multiple scientific, technological, institutional, and organizational innovations. These innovations made possible the growth of firms and economies. Experiences and knowledge accumulated, as a corpus of learning opportunities, for others to utilize in creating national mass-manufacturing platforms.[75] These lessons are applicable to countries commencing industrialization. The lessons for industrialists and policy makers in India, and elsewhere, from the first industrial revolution are: the application of science and technology for producing goods and services that enhance material wellbeing; the substantial use of energy in operations; and a substitution by capital of labor effort. The use of science and technology by firms is possible if governments have created the appropriate educational infrastructures. Firms collectively alter the capital to labor utilization ratio in an economy. In energy use by firms, governments need to provide incentives for consumption and production, and are often energy suppliers.

The lessons from the second industrial revolution are: the standardization and interchangeability of processes; the adoption of general purpose technologies; the substantial use of electric power; the engendering of scale and scope economies; and the democratization of invention and markets. Firms standardize manufacturing and operational processes. While the adoption of general purpose technologies is also achieved by firms, they cannot do so in the absence of appropriate incentives provided by governments. Similarly, the role of government in creating the institutional environment for electricity use is important. Firms will engender scale and scope economies, but government actions matter greatly for the democratization of inventions and markets. Finally, lessons from Asian countries' experiences with late industrialization are: a strong focus on operations; the engendering of scale economies; organizational learning; enhancing human capital quality; and alteration of management practices.

There are numerous contemporary examples of India's entrepreneurs' interests in applying science and technology to achieve profitable ends and improve human progress. An ideology of commercial gains has become linked in Indian entrepreneurial minds with technological applications. Now, there are numerous examples of science-based biotechnology entrepreneurs. Firms such as the wireless telecommunications services operators, some of which have become global firms, are using the latest technology in their services networks. The data in Chapters 1 and 7 show that a capital-for-labor substitution is in progress. This indicates shifts in Indian entrepreneurs' attitudes to technology. Indian entrepreneurial character may no longer correspond to historian Damodar Kosambi's conjecture that "The Indian bourgeoisie was a specific kind of bourgeoisie, characterized by ravening greed and a mania for speculation rather than initiative or efficiency in developing production."[76] Times might have changed.

Many key lessons of the first and second industrial revolutions and late industrialization relate to management and organizational practices, to be emulated by firms. The American industrialization experiences, driven by the American system of manufactures, were studied in the Soviet Union and Germany.[77] Indian firms can do the same. As to whether there has been democratization of Indian markets, with consumer goods prices falling in real terms, because firms use resources frugally, demands further analysis. The issue also requires analyses of concerns such as inflation, income growth, and distribution. The record of patenting by Indian entrepreneurs and firms is patchy. Endogenous innovation is important for self-sustaining growth. Patenting is an outcome of such innovation. Whether the packages of institutional changes have led to the democratization of invention, and consequent patenting growth, therefore, requires analysis.

In general, India's information technology and software sector now utilizes commodities, the cheap human capital employed, to create other commodities. These are the daily accounting services digitally transmitted to foreign clients. It can, instead, develop high-value digital machines to manufacture other machines. These machines, based on the incorporation of embedded software, can in turn be used to manufacture yet other machines and durable and non-durable tangible goods, and to provide services. In a sense, we come back to the strands of the Bombay ideology, oriented towards consumer goods production, versus the Calcutta school of thought, based on building machines to build other machines. Machine-produced machines lead to the development of mass-produced automatic machine tools. Knowledge embodiment, via digital means, in automatic machine tools enables the mass production of consumer goods. We do not change our minds about consumer goods being more important than capital goods, and vice versa. Both are equally important for growth. They will remain so. Indian industry will not only manufacture consumer goods, but also build machines that manufacture consumer goods, and build machines that build other machines. Now, the fundamental change is that the process of machine building, or consumer goods production, will be driven by new age manufacturing principles and practices, and mediated by the functionalities emerging from the industrialization of information technology.

Having missed out on participation in the earlier industrial revolutions, and not having participated in Asia's late industrialization, Indian industry has to actively utilize all the functionalities of modern information and communications technologies for catching up and resetting the clock. Her industrialization example can be emulated by other emerging nations engaged in the industrialization process. She can be an important driver of the global economy, based on extensive industrialization of the information technology sector and the adoption of new age manufacturing functionalities. These can be some of India's unique ways of defining the contours of her late, late industrial revolution. India's experiences of a modern industrial transformation can be a force to reorient global economic development along a new trajectory, with the model altering the contents of business and economic discourse in the 2010s, and beyond.

Appendix

Table A1. *Percentage growth in the index of industrial production over the years (1980 = 100)*

1980s		1990s		2000s	
Year	Growth	Year	Growth	Year	Growth
1980–81	—	1990–91	8.95	2000–01	5.35
1981–82	7.93	1991–92	–0.76	2001–02	2.85
1982–83	1.34	1992–93	2.16	2002–03	6.01
1983–84	5.68	1993–94	6.09	2003–04	7.38
1984–85	8.00	1994–95	9.81	2004–05	9.13
1985–86	9.66	1995–96	13.60	2005–06	9.15
1986–87	9.39	1996–97	8.61	2006–07	12.52
1987–88	7.87	1997–98	3.59	2007–08	8.98
1988–89	8.72	1998–99	4.40	2008–09	2.75
1989–90	8.59	1999–2000	7.16	2009–10	10.92

Average growth for the decade

1980s	1990s	2000s
7.46	6.36	7.50

Source: Reserve Bank of India Database on the Indian Economy, Table 28, and author's calculations; computations expressed in percentages based on data at factor cost and in constant rupees.

Table A2. *Trends in the growth of gross domestic product of India over six decades*

1950s		1960s		1970s		1980s		1990s		2000s	
—	—	1960–61	7.1	1970–71	5.0	1980–81	7.2	1990–91	5.3	2000–01	4.4
1951–52	2.3	1961–62	3.1	1971–72	1.0	1981–82	5.6	1991–92	1.4	2001–02	5.8
1952–53	2.8	1962–63	2.1	1972–73	–0.3	1982–83	2.9	1992–93	5.4	2002–03	3.8
1953–54	6.1	1963–64	5.1	1973–74	4.6	1983–84	7.9	1993–94	5.7	2003–04	8.5
1954–55	4.2	1964–65	7.6	1974–75	1.2	1984–85	4.0	1994–95	6.4	2004–05	7.5
1955–56	2.6	1965–66	–3.7	1975–76	9.0	1985–86	4.2	1995–96	7.3	2005–06	9.5
1956–57	5.7	1966–67	1.0	1976–77	1.2	1986–87	4.3	1996–97	8.0	2006–07	9.7
1957–58	–1.2	1967–68	8.1	1977–78	7.5	1987–88	3.5	1997–98	4.3	2007–08	9.2
1958–59	7.6	1968–69	2.6	1978–79	5.5	1988–89	10.2	1998–99	6.7	2008–09	6.7
1959–60	2.2	1969–70	6.5	1979–80	–5.2	1989–90	6.1	1999–2000	6.4	2009–10	7.4

Decade average

1950s	1960s	1970s	1980s	1990s	2000s
3.6	4.0	2.9	5.6	5.7	7.3

Each decade relative to the 2000s

1950s	1960s	1970s	1980s	1990s	2000s
0.49	0.55	0.41	0.77	0.78	1.00

Source: Reserve Bank of India Database on the Indian Economy, Table 224, and author's calculations; computations expressed in percentages based on data at factor cost and in constant rupees.

Table A3. *Indian companies ranked in the global top 2,000 for 2009*

Company	Industry	Revenue $ billion
Indian Oil Corporation (state owned)	oil and gas	51.66
Reliance Industries	oil and gas	46.00
Tata Steel	steel	32.77
Bharat Petroleum (state owned)	oil and gas	27.71
Hindustan Petroleum (state owned)	oil and gas	25.43
Oil and Natural Gas Corporation (state owned)	oil and gas	24.04
State Bank of India (state owned)	banking	22.63
ICICI Bank	banking	15.06
Hindalco Industries	metal	14.87
Steel Authority of India Limited (state owned)	steel	9.82
National Thermal Power Corporation (state owned)	power	9.63
Tata Motors	capital goods	8.54
Larsen & Toubro	capital goods	7.30
Bharti	telecommunications	6.73
Mahindra & Mahindra	automotive	5.92
Tata Consultancy Services	software and services	5.70
Wipro	software and services	4.98
Bharat Heavy Electricals (state owned)	capital goods	4.81
Gas Authority of India Limited (state owned)	oil and gas	4.69
Reliance Communications	telecommunications	4.26
Grasim Industries	textiles	4.23
Canara Bank (state owned)	banking	4.19
Infosys Technologies	software and services	4.16

Company	Sector	Value
Punjab National Bank (state owned)	banking	4.15
ITC Limited	tobacco and food	3.65
Bank of India (state owned)	banking	3.62
Bank of Baroda (state owned)	banking	3.56
DLF Universal Limited	property	3.50
HDFC Bank	banking	3.09
Union Bank of India (state owned)	banking	2.66
Hero Honda Motors	automotive	2.57
IDBI Bank (state owned)	banking	2.51
Indian Overseas Bank (state owned)	banking	2.25
Central Bank of India (state owned)	banking	2.22
HDFC	banking	2.21
Axis Bank	banking	2.20
Syndicate Bank (state owned)	banking	2.20
Oriental Bank of Commerce (state owned)	banking	1.86
Allahabad Bank (state owned)	banking	1.81
UCO Bank (state owned)	banking	1.81
Indian Bank (state owned)	banking	1.56
National Mineral Development Corporation (state owned)	materials	1.42
Jindal Steel and Power	materials	1.36
Power Finance Corporation (state owned)	finance	1.26
National Aluminum Company	metal	1.24
Power Grid Corporation of India (state owned)	power	1.15
Sun Pharmaceuticals	pharmaceuticals	0.82

Source: List of Companies of India, Wikipedia.

Table A4. *The 75 largest Indian business groups, by revenues in rupees lakhs, in the mid 1960s*

Number	Company	Revenue	Number	Company	Revenue
1	Tata	32,498	39	Turner Morrison	1,925
2	Birla	29,024	40	Jai Dayal Dalmia	1,907
3	Martin Burn	10,872	41	Parry	1,891
4	Thapar	7,061	42	Nowrosjee Wadia	1,809
5	Bangur	6,529	43	Thyagaraja	1,796
6	Sahu Jain	6,106	44	Jaipuria	1,778
7	Shri Ram	5,985	45	Ruia	1,720
8	Bird Heilgers	5,829	46	Bhagirath Kanoria	1,678
9	J. K. Singhania	5,443	47	G. V. Naidu	1,605
10	Sarabhai	5,429	48	Thakersey	1,500
11	Walchand	5,402	49	Khatau	1,423
12	Soorajmull Nagarmull	4,483	50	Mangal Das Parekh	1,390
13	Associated Cement Companies	4,413	51	Amin	1,331
14	Goenka	4,356	52	Seshasayee	1,322
15	Mafatlal	4,311	53	R. K. Kanoria	1,316
16	Imperial Chemical Industries	3,816	54	Finlay	1,316
17	Andrew Yule	3,430	55	Chinai	1,306
18	Amalgamations	3,343	56	Shapoorji Pallonji	1,264
19	Jardine Henderson	3,142	57	Kamani	1,255
20	Bajaj	2,925	58	Tube Investments	1,134

21	British India Corporation	2,905	59	Podar	1,103
22	Macneill and Barry	2,698	60	V. Ramakrishna	1,052
23	Kasturbhai Lalbhai	2,620	61	Talukdar Law	1,028
24	Binny	2,540	62	J. P. Srivastava	1,013
25	Killick Nixon	2,445	63	Gillanders Arthbutnot	802
26	Rallis	2,445	64	Indra Singh	777
27	Kilachand	2,430	65	Shriyas Prasad Jain	764
28	Swedish Match	2,392	66	Wallace and Company	763
29	T. V. Sundaram Aiyangar	2,333	67	Mangaldas Jaisinghbhai	707
30	Balmer Lawrie	2,168	68	V. Rangaswamy Naidu	618
31	G. D. Kothari	2,155	69	Kothari Madras	579
32	Kirloskar	2,146	70	Ram Kumar Agarwal	502
33	A & F Harvey	2,114	71	R. K. Dalmia	412
34	Mahindra and Mahindra	2,111	72	Muthia	405
35	Modi	2,082	73	Pierce Leslie	360
36	Scindia Steamships	2,062	74	Shaw Wallace	333
37	Vissanji	2,062	75	Jatia	65
38	B. N. Elias	2,044			

Source: Government of India, *Report of the Monopolies Inquiry Commission*, Chairman Justice K. C. Dasgupta, ICS (New Delhi: Ministry of Finance, 1965). Originally the groups were ranked by asset values. They are ranked in this list by sales amounts. Hence many groups with large asset values could have low sales.

Table A5. *Percentage shares of world manufacturing output by various countries from 1750 to 1980*

Year	West	China	Japan	India	Russia	Others
1750	18.2	32.8	3.8	24.5	5.0	15.7
1800	23.3	33.3	3.5	19.7	5.6	14.6
1830	31.1	29.8	2.8	17.6	5.6	13.1
1860	53.7	19.7	2.6	8.6	7.0	8.4
1880	68.8	12.5	2.4	2.8	7.6	5.9
1900	77.4	6.2	2.4	1.7	8.8	3.5
1913	81.6	3.6	2.7	1.4	8.2	2.5
1928	84.2	3.4	3.3	1.9	5.3	1.9
1938	78.6	3.1	5.2	2.4	9.0	1.7
1953	74.6	2.3	2.9	1.7	16.0	2.5
1963	65.4	3.5	5.1	1.8	20.9	3.3
1973	61.2	3.9	8.8	2.1	20.1	3.9
1980	57.8	5.0	9.1	2.3	21.1	4.7

Source: Calculated from Paul Bairoch, International Industrialization Levels from 1750 to 1980, *Journal of European Economic History*, 2 (1982), 268–333, various tables.

Table A6. *Gross domestic product for a selection of countries from* AD *0 to 1998, expressed in 1990 US$ thousands*

Panel (A): India's aggregate GDP and that of other countries

Year	GDP of India	GDP of China	GDP of Japan	GDP of Western Europe	GDP of United States	World GDP
0	33,750	26,820	1,200	11,115	0	102,356
1000	33,750	26,550	3,188	10,165	0	116,790
1500	60,500	61,800	7,700	44,345	800	247,116
1600	74,250	96,000	9,620	65,955	600	329,417
1700	90,750	82,800	15,390	83,395	527	371,369
1820	111,417	228,600	20,739	163,722	12,548	694,442
1870	134,882	189,740	25,393	370,223	98,374	1,101,369
1913	204,241	241,344	71,653	906,374	517,383	2,704,782
1950	222,222	239,093	160,966	1,401,551	1,455,916	5,336,101
1973	494,832	740,048	1,242,932	4,133,780	3,536,622	16,059,180
1998	1,702,712	3,873,352	2,581,576	6,960,616	7,394,598	33,725,635

Table A6. (*cont.*)

Panel (B): Ratio of India's aggregate GDP to that of other countries

Year	Ratio of India's GDP to itself	Ratio of India's GDP to China's GDP	Ratio of India's GDP to Japan's GDP	Ratio of India's GDP to GDP of Western Europe	Ratio of India's GDP to GDP of the United States	Percentage of India's GDP to world GDP
0	1.00	1.26	28.13	3.04	N/A	33.00
1000	1.00	1.27	10.59	3.32	N/A	29.00
1500	1.00	0.98	7.86	1.36	75.63	24.00
1600	1.00	0.77	7.72	1.13	123.75	23.00
1700	1.00	1.10	5.90	1.09	172.20	24.00
1820	1.00	0.49	5.37	0.68	8.88	16.00
1870	1.00	0.71	5.31	0.36	1.37	12.00
1913	1.00	0.85	2.85	0.23	0.39	8.00
1950	1.00	0.93	1.38	0.16	0.15	4.00
1973	1.00	0.67	0.40	0.12	0.14	3.00
1998	1.00	0.44	0.66	0.24	0.23	5.00

Source: Worldeconomy.org.

Table A7. *Number of registered companies in India and aggregate paid-up capital in rupees crores over the last nine decades*

Year	Number of companies	Paid-up capital	Year	Number of companies	Paid-up capital	Year	Number of companies	Paid-up capital
	—	—	1951–52	28,532	775.4	1981–82	62,714	16,357
1923–24	5,190	259.8	1953–54	29,312	897.6	1983–84	82,903	23,056
1925–26	5,204	275.5	1955–56	29,779	983.1	1985–86	109,309	30,597
1927–28	5,526	276.9	1957–58	29,357	1,078	1987–88	140,670	43,968
1929–30	6,330	279.3	1959–60	27,403	1,516	1989–90	180,328	57,704
1931–32	7,328	282.7	1961–62	26,149	1,819	1991–92	224,452	74,798
1933–34	8,715	286.5	1963–64	25,622	2,256	1993–94	276,854	94,055
1935–36	9,842	304	1965–66	26,221	2,843	1995–96	353,292	136,019
1937–38	11,229	311.5	1967–68	27,027	3,402	1997–98	450,950	190,519
1939–40	11,114	290.4	1969–70	28,024	3,974	1999–2000	511,990	263,359
1941–42	11,638	309.6	1971–72	30,322	4,503	2001–02	589,100	357,247
1943–44	12,770	336.1	1973–74	34,356	5,749	2003–04	612,155	457,059
1945–46	14,859	389	1975–76	40,580	8,201	2005–06	679,649	654,021
1947–48	21,853	478.7	1977–78	45,866	10,880	2007–08	743,678	649,490
1949–50	25,340	628.3	1979–80	51,518	12,575	2009–10	786,774	1,003,888

Source: Calculations based on data in Nabagopal Das, *Industrial Enterprise in India* (2nd edn., Calcutta: Orient Longmans, 1956), appendix 1, 179; S. K. Majumdar, Crowding Out: The Displacement of Private Enterprise in India and Its Consequences for Competitiveness, *Industrial and Corporate Change*, 18, 1 (2009), 165–207; and Ministry of Statistics and Programme Implementation, *Handbook of Indian Statistics* 2011.

Table A8. *Average paid-up capital per registered company in India in rupees crores and growth in average paid-up capital over the last nine decades*

Year	Average paid-up capital per company	Growth	Year	Average paid-up capital per company	Growth	Year	Average paid-up capital per company	Growth
—	—	—	1951–52	0.027	9.61	1981–82	0.261	6.85
1923–24	0.050	—	1953–54	0.031	12.68	1983–84	0.278	6.63
1925–26	0.053	5.76	1955–56	0.033	7.81	1985–86	0.280	0.65
1927–28	0.050	−5.35	1957–58	0.037	11.23	1987–88	0.313	11.66
1929–30	0.044	−11.94	1959–60	0.055	50.66	1989–90	0.320	2.38
1931–32	0.039	−12.57	1961–62	0.070	25.74	1991–92	0.333	4.14
1933–34	0.033	−14.78	1963–64	0.088	26.58	1993–94	0.340	1.94
1935–36	0.031	−6.04	1965–66	0.108	23.14	1995–96	0.385	13.33
1937–38	0.028	−10.19	1967–68	0.126	16.09	1997–98	0.422	9.73
1939–40	0.026	−5.81	1969–70	0.142	12.66	1999–2000	0.514	21.75
1941–42	0.027	1.81	1971–72	0.149	4.72	2001–02	0.606	17.89
1943–44	0.026	−1.06	1973–74	0.167	12.68	2003–04	0.747	23.12
1945–46	0.026	−0.53	1975–76	0.202	20.77	2005–06	0.962	28.88
1947–48	0.022	−16.33	1977–78	0.237	17.38	2007–08	0.873	−9.24
1949–50	0.025	13.19	1979–80	0.244	2.90	2009–10	1.276	46.10

Source: Calculations based on data in Nabagopal Das, *Industrial Enterprise in India* (2nd edn., Calcutta: Orient Longmans, 1956), appendix 1, 179; S. K. Majumdar, Crowding Out: The Displacement of Private Enterprise in India and Its Consequences for Competitiveness, *Industrial and Corporate Change*, 18, 1 (2009), 165–207; and Ministry of Statistics and Programme Implementation, *Handbook of Indian Statistics 2011*.

Table A9. *Details of number of units in the unorganized manufacturing sector of India in 1989–90 and number of units and employment in 1994–95, 2000–01, and 2005–06*

	Own account manufacturing enterprises	Non-directory manufacturing enterprises with employees	Directory manufacturing enterprises with employees	Total
1989–90	Number of units in millions			
Rural	11.28	0.74	0.22	12.24
Urban	2.82	0.89	0.34	4.05
Total	14.10	1.63	0.56	16.29
1994–95	Number of units in millions			
Rural	9.53	0.67	0.29	10.49
Urban	2.71	0.93	0.36	4.00
Total	12.24	1.60	0.65	14.49
1994–95	Employment in millions			
Rural	17.86	1.84	2.46	22.15
Urban	4.82	3.06	3.20	11.08
Total	22.68	4.90	5.66	33.23
2000–01	Number of units in millions			
Rural	11.06	0.63	0.25	11.94
Urban	3.61	1.08	0.40	5.09
Total	14.67	1.71	0.65	17.03
2000–01	Employment in millions			
Rural	19.15	1.93	2.91	23.99
Urban	5.91	3.63	3.55	13.09
Total	25.06	5.56	6.46	37.08
2005–06	Number of units in millions			
Rural	11.11	0.74	0.27	12.12
Urban	3.50	1.03	0.42	4.95
Total	14.61	1.77	0.69	17.07
2005–06	Employment in millions			
Rural	18.02	2.38	3.06	23.46
Urban	5.67	3.40	3.91	12.98
Total	23.69	5.78	6.97	36.44

Source: Ministry of Statistics and Programme Implementation, *Unorganized Manufacturing Enterprises in India: Salient Features*, vols. 1 and 2, NSS 51st Round, July 1994–June 1995; *Unorganized Manufacturing Sector in India, 2000–01, Key Results*, NSS 56th Round, July 2000–June 2001, and NSS 62nd Round, July 2005–June 2006.

Table A10. *Details of number of units, combined production, and combined employment in the unorganized services sector of India for the year 2000–01 and details of number of units and employment in the unorganized trading sector of India in 1997*

Panel (A): Number of units, combined production and combined employment in the unorganized services sector of India for the year 2000–01

	Number of units in millions		
	Own account enterprises	Enterprises with employees	Total
Rural	7.53	1.06	8.59
Urban	4.56	1.33	5.89
Total	12.09	2.39	14.48

	Number employed in millions		
	Own account enterprises	Enterprises with employees	Total
Rural	9.92	4.16	14.08
Urban	5.92	6.56	12.48
Total	15.84	10.72	26.56

Panel (B): Details of number of units and employment in the unorganized trading sector of India in 1997

	Number of units in millions		
	Own account enterprises	Enterprises with employees	Total
Rural	8.10	0.31	8.41
Urban	5.18	0.91	6.09
Total	13.28	1.22	14.50

	Number of units in millions		
	Own account enterprises	Enterprises with employees	Total
Wholesale	0.59	0.22	0.81
Retail	10.98	0.96	11.94
Others	1.71	0.04	1.7
Total	13.28	1.22	14.50

Table A10. (*cont.*)

	Persons engaged in millions		
	Men	Women and children	Total
Wholesale	1.44	0.07	1.51
Retail	15.23	2.42	17.65
Others	1.84	1.15	2.99
Total	18.51	3.64	22.15

Source: Ministry of Statistics and Programme Implementation, *Unorganized Services Sector of India, Characteristics of Enterprises 2001–02, NSS 57th Round, July 2001–June 2002; Small Trading Units in India and their Basic Characteristics of Enterprises*, vol. 2, 1997, NSS 53rd Round, January–December 1997.

Table A11. *Share of agriculture, industry, and services sectors in India's national income*

Sector shares	Agriculture	Industry	Services
Overall average	37.31	16.94	45.75
For the 1950s	53.80	11.66	34.54
For the 1960s	45.71	15.06	39.23
For the 1970s	40.93	16.78	42.29
For the 1980s	35.04	18.66	46.30
For the 1990s	28.40	20.09	51.51
For the 2000s	19.99	19.39	60.62
Percentage changes in each sector's share	Agriculture	Industry	Services
From the 1950s to the 1960s	−15.04	29.14	13.60
From the 1960s to the 1970s	−10.46	11.44	7.79
From the 1970s to the 1980s	−14.39	11.20	9.49
From the 1980s to the 1990s	−18.96	7.66	11.26
From the 1990s to the 2000s	−29.62	−3.47	17.68

Source: Reserve Bank of India Database on the Indian Economy, Table 3, and author's calculations.

Table A12. *Gross domestic product growth in specific sectors of the*
Indian economy

	Specific sectors			
	Agriculture	Industry	Services	Overall
1950s	2.72	5.82	4.20	3.57
1960s	2.51	6.20	5.19	4.00
1970s	1.26	4.35	4.03	2.91
1980s	4.41	6.36	6.30	5.62
1990s	3.24	5.68	7.09	5.68
2000s	2.52	6.92	8.97	7.23
Average for overall period	2.78	5.89	5.99	4.86

Source: Reserve Bank of India Database on the Indian Economy, Table 3, and
author's calculations.

Table A13. *Additional output augmentation values for each of the inefficient years for the Indian economy in rupees crores*

1950s

	Agriculture	Industry	Services
1951	–	–	–
1952	146.97	0	138.07
1953	–	–	–
1954	–	–	–
1955	–	–	–
1956	798.69	105.98	0
1957	0	26.98	0
1958	0	36.14	0
1959	–	–	–
1960	587.48	12.09	0
Sum	1,553.14	181.19	138.07

1960s

	Agriculture	Industry	Services
1961	441.1	78.05	0
1962	–	–	–
1963	898.58	0	0
1964	–	–	–
1965	–	–	–
1966	0	133.53	0
1967	637.43	0	0
1968	–	–	–
1969	–	–	–
1970	–	–	–
Sum	1977.11	211.58	0

1970s

	Agriculture	Industry	Services
1971	0	0	150
1972	658.8	0	0
1973	–	–	–
1974	–	–	–
1975	–	–	–
1976	0	492.91	0

1980s

	Agriculture	Industry	Services
1981	–	–	–
1982	0	0	2,845.23
1983	–	–	–
1984	–	–	–
1985	1,303.13	0	0.02
1986	3,362.08	343.95	0

Table A13. (*cont.*)

1970s

	Agriculture	Industry	Services
1977	–	–	–
1978	–	–	–
1979	–	–	–
1980	4,529.37	0	2,227.43
Sum	5,188.17	492.91	2,377.43

1980s

	Agriculture	Industry	Services
1987	6,150.2	806.41	0
1988	–	–	–
1989	–	–	–
1990	–	–	–
Sum	10,815.45	1,150.36	2,845.25

1990s

	Agriculture	Industry	Services
1991	–	–	–
1992	0	3,764.96	2,502.64
1993	0	2,037.98	10,865.82
1994	–	–	–
1995	2,715.74	0	21,162.22
1996	10,355.47	0	41,584.04
1997	–	–	–
1998	–	–	–
1999	–	–	–
2000	0	19,483.16	14,233.92
Sum	13,071.21	25,286.10	90,348.64

2000s

	Agriculture	Industry	Services
2001	–	–	–
2002	–	–	–
2003	–	–	–
2004	–	–	–
2005	20,773.26	0.34	51,295.21
2006	10,352.88	0	61,343.33
2007	35,600.01	0	122,430.90
2008	15,635.33	0	145,207.20
2009	–	–	–
Sum	82,361.48	0.34	380,276.60

Source: Author's calculations.

Table A14. *Gross domestic product values for China and India expressed in US$ for the period 1980 to 2009*

Year	China's US$ GDP per capita	India's US$ GDP per capita	Growth of Chinese income	Growth of Indian income	Difference between China and India in US$	Ratio of Chinese to Indian income
1980	220	270	—	—	−50	0.81
1981	220	300	0.00	11.11	−80	0.73
1982	220	290	0.00	−3.33	−70	0.76
1983	220	290	0.00	0.00	−70	0.76
1984	250	280	13.64	−3.45	−30	0.89
1985	280	300	12.00	7.14	−20	0.93
1986	310	320	10.71	6.67	−10	0.97
1987	320	360	3.23	12.50	−40	0.89
1988	330	400	3.13	11.11	−70	0.83
1989	320	400	−3.03	0.00	−80	0.80
1990	330	390	3.13	−2.50	−60	0.85
1991	350	350	6.06	−10.26	0	1.00
1992	390	330	11.43	−5.71	60	1.18
1993	410	310	5.13	−6.06	100	1.32
1994	460	330	12.20	6.45	130	1.39
1995	530	380	15.22	15.15	150	1.39
1996	650	410	22.64	7.89	240	1.59
1997	750	420	15.38	2.44	330	1.79
1998	790	420	5.33	0.00	370	1.88
1999	840	440	6.33	4.76	400	1.91
2000	930	450	10.71	2.27	480	2.07
2001	1,000	460	7.53	2.22	540	2.17
2002	1,100	470	10.00	2.17	630	2.34
2003	1,270	530	15.45	12.77	740	2.40
2004	1,500	640	18.11	20.75	860	2.34
2005	1,760	750	17.33	17.19	1,010	2.35
2006	2,050	850	16.48	13.33	1,200	2.41
2007	2,490	990	21.46	16.47	1,500	2.52
2008	3,050	1,080	22.49	9.09	1,970	2.82
2009	3,650	1,180	19.67	9.26	2,470	3.09

Source: The World Bank and author's computations.

Table A15. *Indian ordnance factories: locations and capabilities*

Name	Location	Capabilities
Ammunition Factory	Khadki	Chemistry
Cordite Factory	Aruvankadu	Chemistry
Engine Factory	Avadi	Mechanical engineering
Field Gun Factory	Kanpur	Mechanical engineering
Gun Carriage Factory	Jabalpur	Mechanical engineering
Grey Iron Foundry	Jabalpur	Metallurgy
Gun and Shell Factory	Cossipore	Metallurgy; Mechanical engineering
Heavy Alloy Penetrator Project	Tiruchirappalli	Chemistry
High Explosive Factory	Khadki	Chemistry
Heavy Vehicle Factory	Avadi	Mechanical engineering
Machine Tool Prototype Factory	Ambernath	Mechanical engineering
Metal and Steel Factory	Ishapore	Metallurgy
Ordnance Clothing Factory	Avadi; Shahjahanpur	Textiles
Ordnance Cable Factory	Chandigarh	Electrical engineering
Ordnance Equipment Factory	Kanpur; Hazratpur	Mechanical engineering
Ordnance Factories	Ambernath; Bhandara; Bhusawal; Bolangir; Kanpur; Chandrapur; Dumdum; Dehu Road; Dehra Dun; Itarsi; Khamaria; Katni; Muradnagar; Tiruchirapalli; Varangaon	Chemistry; metallurgy
Ordnance Factory Projects	Nalanda; Medak	Chemistry; metallurgy
Opto Electronics Factory	Dehradun	Optics; electronics
Ordnance Parachute Factory	Kanpur	Textiles
Rifle Factory	Ishapore	Mechanical engineering
Small Arms Factory	Kanpur	Mechanical engineering
Vehicle Factory	Jabalpur	Mechanical engineering

Source: Indian Ordnance Factories Board.

Table A16. *Indian defense research and development establishments and locations*

Name	Location	Name	Location	Name	Location
Aeronautical Development Agency	Bangalore	Defence Research Laboratory	Tejpur	Institute of Technology Management	Mussorie
Advanced Numerical Research and Analysis Group	Hyderabad	Defence Institute of High Altitude Research	Leh	Instruments Research and Development Establishment	Dehradun
Aerial Delivery Research and Development Establishment	Agra	Defence Institute of Physiology and Allied Sciences	Delhi	Integrated Test Range	Balasore
Armament Research and Development Establishment	Pune	Defence Institute of Psychological Research	Delhi	Laser Science and Technology Centre	Delhi
Centre for Artificial Intelligence and Robotics	Bangalore	Defence Laboratory	Jodhpur	Microwave Tube Research and Development Centre	Bangalore
Centre for Fire, Explosive and Environment Safety	Delhi	Defence materials and Stores Research and Development Establishment	Kanpur	Naval materials Research Laboratory	Ambernath
Centre for Military Airworthiness and Certification	Bangalore	Defence Metallurgical Research Laboratory	Hyderabad	Naval Physical and Oceanographic Laboratory	Cochin
Centre for Air Borne Systems	Bangalore	Defence Research and Development Laboratory	Hyderabad	Naval Science and Technological Laboratory	Vishakapatnam

Table A16. (*cont.*)

Name	Location	Name	Location	Name	Location
Combat Vehicles Research and Development Establishment.	Chennai	Defence Research and Development Establishment	Gwalior	Proof and Experimental Establishment	Balasore
Defence Agricultural Research Laboratory	Pithoragarh	Defence Scientific Information and Documentation Centre	Delhi	Research and Development Establishment	Pune
Defence Avionics Research Establishment	Bangalore	Defence Terrain Research Laboratory	Delhi	Research Centre Imarat	Hyderabad
Defence Bioengineering and Electro Medical Laboratory	Bangalore	Electronics and Radar Development Establishment	Bangalore	Scientific Analysis Group	Delhi
Defence Electronics Application Laboratory	Dehradun	Gas Turbine Research Establishment	Bangalore	Snow and Avalanche Study Establishment	Chandigarh
Defence Electronics Research Laboratory	Hyderabad	High Energy materials Research Laboratory	Pune	Solid State Physics Laboratory	Delhi
Defence Food Research Laboratory	Mysore	Institute of Nuclear Medicine and Allied Sciences	Delhi	Terminal Ballistics Research Laboratory	Chandigarh
Defence Institute of Advanced Technology	Pune	Institute of Systems Studies and Analyses	Delhi	Vehicle Research and Development Establishment	Ahmednagar

Source: Defence Research and Development Organization.

Table A17. *Indian defense production undertakings in the corporate sector owned by the state*

Name	Location	Activities
Bharat Dynamics Limited	Hyderabad	Missiles
Bharat Earth Movers Limited	Bangalore	Heavy equipment
Bharat Electronics Limited	Bangalore	Electronics
Brahmos Aerospace Limited	Thiruvananthapuram	Cruise missiles
Cochin Shipyard Limited	Cochin	Shipyard
Garden Reach Shipbuilders and Engineers Limited	Calcutta	Shipyard
Goa Shipyard Limited	Vasco Da Gama	Shipyard
Hindustan Aeronautics Limited	Bangalore	Aircraft
Hindustan Shipyard Limited	Vishakhapatnam	Shipyard
Mazagon Dock Limited	Bombay	Shipyard
Mishra Dhatu Nigam Limited	Hyderabad	Special metals

Source: www.sarkaritel.com.

Table A18. *Energy consumption to gross national product ratio for the United States in thousands of British thermal units per 1992 US$*

Year	Energy consumption to GNP ratio	Percentage change in the ratio in each 5-year period
1890	18.84	—
1895	18.89	0.27
1900	21.75	15.14
1905	26.08	19.91
1910	26.71	2.42
1915	27.77	3.97
1920	30.85	11.09
1925	25.30	−17.99
1930	26.06	3.00
1935	24.51	−5.95
1940	23.20	−5.34
1945	18.76	−19.14
1950	20.68	10.23
1955	19.74	−4.55
1960	19.25	−2.48
1965	18.16	−5.66
1970	19.44	7.05
1975	18.07	−7.05
1980	16.26	−10.02
1985	13.84	−14.88
1990	13.20	−4.62
1995	12.86	−2.58
2000	11.71	−8.94

Source: V. W. Ruttan, *Technology, Growth, and Development: An Induced Innovation Perspective*, New York: Oxford University Press (2001), Table 7.1, 254.

Table A19. *Installed production capacity for various categories of power sources in India and plans for augmenting generating capacity*

Panel (A): Installed capacity

Fuel type	Megawatts	Percentage
Thermal capacity		
Coal-fired capacity	92,638	53.3
Gas-fired capacity	17,456	10.5
Oil-fired capacity	1,200	0.9
Total thermal capacity	111,294	64.6
Hydro capacity	37,368	24.7
Nuclear capacity	4,780	2.9
Renewable energy sources capacity	16,787	7.7
Total installed capacity	170,229	100.0

Panel (B): Generating capacity augmentation plans

Fuel type	Central government sector	State government sector	Private sector	Total for all sectors
	Megawatts			
Hydro capacity	8,654	3,482	3,491	15,627
Coal-fired capacity	22,600	19,535	8,435	50,570
Lignite-fired capacity	750	450	1,080	2,280
Gas-fired capacity	1,490	3,316	2,037	6,843
Total thermal capacity	24,840	23,301	11,552	59,693
Nuclear capacity	3,380	0	0	3,380
Total capacity	36,874	26,783	15,043	78,700

Source: Ministry of Power.

Appendix

Table A20. *Installed production capacity for various*
categories of power sources in the United States

Fuel Type	Megawatts	Percentage
Coal	337,300	30.54
Petroleum	63,655	5.76
Natural gas	454,611	41.16
Other gases	2,262	0.20
Nuclear	106,147	9.61
Hydroelectric	77,731	7.04
Wind	24,980	2.26
Solar	539	0.05
Wood	7,730	0.70
Geothermal	3,280	0.30
Other biomass	4,854	0.44
Pumped storage	20,355	1.84
Other	1,042	0.09
Total	1,104,486	100

Source: United States Energy Information Administration, Form
EIA 860 Annual Electric Generator Report.

Notes

Preface

1 Seymour Martin Lipset, The Social Requisites of Democracy Revisited, *American Sociological Review*, 59 (1994), 1–22, and Robert Barro, *The Determinants of Economic Growth: A Cross-Country Empirical Study* (Cambridge, MA: MIT Press, 1997), 52–61.

2 Alexis de Tocqueville, *Democracy in America*, edited, translated and with an introduction by Harvey C. Mansfield and Delba Winthrop (University of Chicago Press, 2000 [first published 1835]), 515.

3 Mira Kamdar, *Planet India: The Turbulent Rise of the World's Largest Democracy* (New York: Pocket Books, 2007), 22.

4 India's first Prime Minister, Pandit Jawaharlal Nehru, had presided over the simultaneous establishment of infrastructures for democracy and industrialization. According to the late Rajeshwar Dayal, ICS, once India's Foreign Secretary, Pandit Nehru "raised a weak and fractured nation to the heights of world eminence. He enabled it to regain its pride and self-respect after two and a half centuries of foreign domination." See Rajeshwar Dayal, *A Life of Our Times* (London: Sangam Books, 1998), 548.

5 In political matters, India has established yet another record. The latest elections to state assemblies in India have given the states of West Bengal and Tamil Nadu women as Chief Ministers. These are Ms. Mamta Banerjee and Ms. Jayalalitha. Taking the state of Uttar Pradesh, with its Chief Minister Ms. Mayawati into consideration, this suggests that over 400 million people in India reside in states that have women as heads of government. When one notes that the current Chief Minister of Delhi, Smt. Sheila Dikshit, and the present President of India, Smt. Pratibha Patil, are women, then India sets the standard for involving women in governance.

6 Jagdish Bhagwati, Poverty and Public Policy, *World Development*, 14, 5 (1988), 538–555.

7 Eric Hobsbawm, *Industry and Empire: From 1750 to the Present Day* (London: Pelican Books, 1969), 323.

8 Jonathan Hughes, *The Vital Few: The Entrepreneur and American Economic Progress* (New York: Oxford University Press, 1986), xiii.

9 Partha Chatterjee, *A Princely Impostor: The Strange and Universal History of the Kumar of Bhawal* (Princeton University Press, 2002), xi.

10 Phyllis Deane, *The First Industrial Revolution* (2nd edn., Cambridge University Press, 1979), 1.

11 The government targeted six strategic industries for support in South Korea: steel, petrochemicals, nonferrous metals, shipbuilding, electronics, and machinery. It pushed the large business groups to aggressively pursue advanced technology and scale. To attain efficiency, an automobile plant had to produce 300,000 vehicles a year, well beyond South Korea's market to absorb then. Export market development was vital, as was creating domestic demand. See Daniel Yergin and Joseph Stanislaw, *Commanding Heights* (New York,

Touchstone, 1998), 171. The issue of whether East Asian and Japanese industrialization was government-led or entrepreneur-led is controversial, with Edward Chen stating that it was entrepreneur-led, and that: "state intervention is largely absent. What the state provided is simply a suitable environment for the entrepreneurs to perform their functions." See Edward Chen, *Hyper-growth in Asian Economies: A Comparative Study of Hong Kong, Japan, Korea, Singapore and Taiwan* (London: Macmillan, 1979), 41. Received wisdom suggests otherwise, though there is a view suggesting that there could be an initial amount of intervention and government-led industrialization. After a particular stage, when firms have matured, the ladder of support is kicked away leaving entrepreneur-led industrialization to progress. See Ha-Joon Chang, *Kicking Away the Ladder: Development Strategy in Historical Perspective* (London: Anthem Press, 2002), though he argues that Western countries, having used a government-led approach in their own past, would want to deny it to newly emerging countries, urging them to adopt a full entrepreneur-led development model *a priori*, and thus kicking away the ladder enabling a rise in the world.

12 Such a statement may be untrue with respect to sectors such as telecommunications, where the role of India's contemporary government and firms has become mired in an on-going controversy. In this book, I do not deal with telecommunications issues but leave that for subsequent examination.

13 In this respect, the shrill and intemperate India-bashing that many Western publications routinely engage in, about the inabilities of entrepreneurs to effectively engage in business in India, seems prejudiced, uninformed, and unfortunate.

14 To cite Brooks Adams, an American historian: "Very soon after Plassey, the Bengal plunder began to arrive in London, and the effect appears to have been instantaneous, for all authorities agree that the 'industrial revolution,' the event which has divided the nineteenth century from all antecedent time, began with the year 1760. Prior to 1760, according to Baines, the machinery used for spinning cotton in Lancashire was almost as simple as in India; while about 1750 the English iron industry was in full decline because of the destruction of the forests for fuel. At that time four-fifths of the iron used in the kingdom came from Sweden ... Plassey was fought in 1757, and probably nothing has ever equalled the rapidity of the change which followed. In 1760 the flying-shuttle appeared, and coal began to replace wood in smelting. In 1764 Hargreaves invented the spinning-jenny, in 1779 Crompton contrived the mule, in 1785 Cartwright patented the power-loom, and, chief of all, in 1768 Watt matured the steam-engine, the most perfect of all vents of centralising energy. But, though these machines served as outlets for the accelerating movement of the time, they did not cause that acceleration. In themselves inventions are passive, many of the most important having lain dormant for centuries, waiting for a sufficient store of force to have accumulated to set them working. That store must always take the shape of money, and money not hoarded, but in motion." See Brooks Adams, *The Law of Civilization and Decay* (London: S. Sonnenschein and Company, 1895), 259–260.

15 Nayan Chanda, *Bound Together: How Traders, Preachers, Adventurers and Warriors Shaped Civilization* (New Delhi: Penguin, 2007), 75.

16 Keith Thomas, History and Anthropology, *Past and Present* (1963), 3–24 at p. 24.

17 Lloyd Reynolds, *Economic Growth in the Third World: 1850–1980: An Introduction* (New Haven, CT: Yale University Press, 1985), 30.

18 Jagdish Bhagwati, *India in Transition: Freeing the Economy* (New York: Oxford University Press, 1993), 97.

19 Thomas S. Ashton, *The Industrial Revolution, 1760–1830* (Oxford University Press, 1948), 161.

20 Ashton, *The Industrial Revolution*, 161.
21 Deane, *The First Industrial Revolution*, 1.
22 Eric Hobsbawm, *The Age of Revolution: 1789–1848* (London: Abacus, 1962), 46.
23 On this topic, I digress to comment on the stark contrasts depicted by films made in Calcutta versus films made in Bombay. Calcutta films, made in the studios of Tollywood, typically depicted rural poverty, emaciated people, misery, and bleak, dank, and dark backgrounds, all produced in black and white cinematography. Most film characters were intensely depressed individuals. After watching such a film, one could feel miserable for hours. Conversely, films made in Bombay's Bollywood studios depicted even poor people as cheerful, eager to get ahead, hustling, engaged in various schemes, creating ventures and conning others into joining these. Even if the films were made in black and white, the accent was on wealth creation even among the humblest. It is unsurprising that Indian academics examining poverty reduction are from Bengal, an extremely fertile land so there really should be no excuse for poverty, while Indian scholars examining wealth creation are from the other parts of India.
24 Chidambaram Subramanian, *Hand of Destiny: Memoirs*, vol. II, *The Green Revolution* (Bombay: Bharatiya Vidya Bhavan, 1995), 23.
25 Dhananjaya R. Gadgil, *The Industrial Evolution of India in Recent Times* (4th edn., Oxford University Press, 1944).
26 Morris D. Morris, The Growth of Large Scale Industry, in D. Kumar and M. Desai (eds.), *The Cambridge Economic History of India, Volume 2, c.1757–c.1970* (Cambridge University Press, 1983), 553–669.

1   Vent for growth

1 Bruno Amable, *The Diversity of Capitalism* (New York: Oxford University Press, 2003), 3.
2 In India, as elsewhere, the urge to raise a family is primordial. India's large young population means that, even with a stable birth rate, a very large number of children are born every year.
3 It is likely that the tensions of life accompanying the economic boom may have hindered natural family acquisition processes. Thus, IVF treatment has opened a way for many couples to enrich their lives with a little bit of assistance.
4 On entrepreneurial experiments see Mark Casson, *Enterprise and Competitiveness* (Oxford: Clarendon Press, 1990), 46, and Reuven Brenner, *Betting on Ideas: Wars, Invention, Inflation* (University of Chicago Press, 1985), 75. There are not yet that many IVF centers in India but these numbers are growing every day. The city of Bombay (now called Mumbai) may have 30 such centers. Delhi, along with Gurgaon and NOIDA, may have 20 centers while Calcutta has 10. There are, possibly, 170 other IVF centers spread across India. Interestingly, the state of Gujarat, and particularly Ahmedabad, has a number of IVF centers. Perhaps because the Indian diaspora overseas consists of a large number of individuals whose origins lie in Gujarat, the cities of Gujarat have emerged as major hubs of the medical tourism industry. In total, the sector generates about ₹2 billion in revenues. This is growing rapidly.
5 As with all emerging sectors, the IVF sector displays diversities in its ecology and organization. Mikku's center is organized as a private corporation in the formal and organized sector of India's economy. There are a number of highly professionally qualified young doctors like her who provide the backbone for India's emerging IVF sector. This sector model is typical of the corporate model of health care, common in the West, and particularly in the United States.

Given its growth, and future prospects, the Indian IVF sector has attracted considerable interest among private equity investors interested in cashing in on India's health care opportunities.

6 The technology of reproduction via the IVF route is standard. The processes are well understood and documented. When a couple cannot conceive naturally, an egg from the woman may be fertilized outside the body with sperm from the man and the fertilized egg then re-implanted in the woman's womb so that gestation of the embryo may commence and proceed to its eventual conclusion. There are, however, many instances when the woman's eggs cannot be fertilized or when the man's sperm does not excite the egg. The egg is not turned on! In such instances, eggs from another woman are fertilized with the man's sperm and then implanted. If the man's sperm cannot be used, the woman's eggs may be fertilized with a donor's sperm. In numerous cases, though, it is necessary to use both donor egg and donor sperm so that a fertilized egg may be implanted and the woman can eventually give birth.

7 Because of confidentiality issues in the IVF sector in India, her name is disguised.

8 Confidentiality issues lead me to disguise his name.

9 www.financialexpress.com/news/panasonic-jhajjar-plant-to-start-production-by-may/752023/, retrieved February 19, 2011.

10 www.financialexpress.com/news/panipat-naphtha-cracker-inaugurated/750518/, retrieved February 19, 2011.

11 www.financialexpress.com/news/shell-to-sell-british-refinery-to-essar/752230/, retrieved February 19, 2011.

12 www.financialexpress.com/news/venus-to-enter-super-specialty-oncology-segment/750550/, retrieved February 19, 2011.

13 Jan de Vries, *The Industrious Revolution: Consumer Behavior and the Household Economy, 1650 to the Present* (Cambridge University Press, 2008), 177.

14 The capital goods segment has been given a weight of 16.43 percent; the consumer durables segment has been weighted at 2.55 percent; the basic goods segment has been given a weight of 39.42 percent; the intermediates goods segment has been given a weight of 20.51 percent; and the basic consumer non-durables segment has been given a weight of 21.10 percent as its contribution to overall industry output, as its contribution to overall industry output. In the three decades, of the 1980s, 1990s, and 2000s, the index of industrial production for the basic goods segment has grown at 8 percent, 6.17 percent, and 5.58 percent respectively. For the capital goods segment, the index has grown at 11 percent, 6.74 percent, and 11.50 percent respectively in the 1980s, 1990s, and 2000s. For the intermediate goods segment, the index has grown at 6.05 percent, 6.68 percent, and 5.7 percent respectively in the 1980s, 1990s, and 2000s. Similarly, for the consumer durables segment the growth of the index has been at 14.23 percent, 9.65 percent, and 10 percent respectively in the 1980s, 1990s, and 2000s, and for the consumer non-durables segment the growth of the index has been at the rate of 5.43 percent, 4.18 percent, and 7.46 percent in the 1980s, 1990s, and 2000s respectively. In the latest year for which data are to hand, 2009–10, the index has risen at 7.18, 19.34, 13.64, 26.23, and 1.32 percent, for each of the basic goods, capital goods, intermediate goods, consumer durables, and consumer non-durables segments, over the preceding year.

15 Leela Fernandes, *India's New Middle Classes: Democratic Politics in an Era of Economic Reform* (Minneapolis: University of Minnesota Press, 2006), 206.

16 Neil McKendrick, The Consumer Revolution of Eighteenth-Century England, in N. McKendrick, J. Brewer, and J. H. Plumb (eds.), *The Birth of a Consumer Society: The*

Commercialization of Eighteenth Century England (Bloomington: Indiana University Press, 1982), 9–33.

17 For similar ideas, see Kamdar, *Planet India*, 19.

18 Naushad Forbes, Doing Business in India: What Has Liberalization Changed?, in A. O. Krueger (ed.), *Economic Policy Reforms and the Indian Economy* (New Delhi: Oxford University Press, 2002), 129–167.

19 Gurcharan Das, *India Unbound: The Social and Economic Revolution from Independence to the Global Information Age* (London: Profile Books, 2002), 56.

20 Paul Kennedy, *The Rise and Fall of the Great Powers: Economic Change and Military Conflict from 1500 to 2000* (New York: Random House, 1987), 149.

21 On de-industrialization, see Amiya K. Bagchi, *The Political Economy of Underdevelopment* (Cambridge University Press, 1982), 31–35.

22 Kennedy, *The Rise and Fall of the Great Powers*, 148.

23 Tirthankar Roy, *The Economic History of India: 1857–1947* (Oxford University Press, 2006), 223.

24 Angus Maddison, *Class Structure and Economic Growth: India and Pakistan since the Moghuls* (New York: Norton, 1971), 76.

25 In the mid 1970s, commentators pointed out that the two striking features of the industrial growth experience between the mid 1960s and the mid 1970s were a sharp decline in the rate of growth of industrial output since the mid 1960s, and the existence of large unutilized manufacturing capacities. See K. N. Raj, Growth and Stagnation in Industrial Development, in Deepak Nayyar (ed.), *Industrial Growth and Stagnation: The Debate in India* (New Delhi: Oxford University Press, 1994), 53.

26 The information on industrial growth rates was extracted from C. Rangarajan, Industrial Growth: Another Look, Table 2, in Deepak Nayyar (ed.), *Industrial Growth and Stagnation: The Debate in India* (New Delhi: Oxford University Press, 1994), 292. In India, by the 1950–60 decade, the shares of employment in agriculture, industry and services were 72, 10, and 18 percent. By the decade of 1990–2000, these shares had become 67, 13, and 20 percent. Agriculture was still dominant and industry still a relatively small source of employment.

27 Fernand Braudel, *A History of Civilizations* (London: Penguin Books, 1993 [first published 1963]), 250.

28 Deepak Lal, *Unfinished Business: India in the World Economy* (New Delhi: Oxford University Press, 1999), 39.

29 Maurice Zinkin, *Development for a Free Asia* (London: Chatto and Windus, 1963), 34

30 Lloyd Rudolph and Susanne H. Rudolph, *The Pursuit of Lakshmi: The Political Economy of the Indian State* (University of Chicago Press, 1987), 26.

31 Mukesh Eswaran and Ashok Kotwal, *Why Poverty Persists in India: An Analytical Framework for Understanding the Indian Economy* (New Delhi: Oxford University Press, 1994), 103.

32 Zinkin, *Development for a Free Asia*, 34.

33 Robyn Meredith, *The Elephant and the Dragon: The Rise of India and China and What It Means for All of Us* (New York: W. W. Norton and Company, 2007), 13.

34 Michael Spence, *The Next Convergence: The Future of Economic Growth in a Multiconnected World* (New York: Farrar, Straus and Giroux, 2011), 191–193.

35 Haridas Mukherjee, The Swadeshi Movement of 1905: A Turning-Point in India's Struggle for National Liberation, lecture delivered June 30, 2006, Ramakrishna Mission Institute of Culture, Calcutta, 1.

36 Gerald Meier, *Biography of a Subject: An Evolution of Development Economics* (New York: Oxford University Press, 2005), 70.

37 I am grateful for extensive conversations with Mr. Labanyendu Mansingh, former chairman of India's Petroleum and Natural Gas Regulatory Board. As a joint secretary, he handled the Secretariat of Industrial Approvals in the Ministry of Industrial Development in 1991 when these changes were put through, and, on behalf of the President of India, in whose name all government business is transacted, he issued the delicensing notification of July 24, 1991. He was involved with all aspects of delicensing. He subsequently was the Director General of Foreign Trade, an office earlier called the Chief Controller of Imports and Exports, and thereafter Secretary in the Department of Consumer Affairs, the government department which coordinated all internal trade within India.

38 See George Akerlof and Robert Shiller, *Animal Spirits* (Princeton University Press, 2009), 14.

39 If 1937 is taken as the base year and accorded an index value of 100, the overall index of industrial production value was 120 in 1945. The index of production for steel had risen to 142.9, the index of production for chemicals to 134.1, and the index of production for cement to 196.5. See Pestonji A. Wadia and Kanchanlal T. Merchant, *Our Economic Problem* (6th edn., Bombay: Vora and Company, 1959), 360.

40 Production commenced in the late 1940s with the pre-war Morris 10 being made and sold as the Hindustan 14. The Morris Oxford MO model, of the early 1950s, was also made in India and sold as the Hindustan. The Morris Minor was made in India and sold as the Baby Hindustan, and the Morris Oxford Series II was made and sold in India as the Landmaster. The Morris Oxford Series III was introduced in India, and the production of the model continues to this day as the Ambassador. In the late 1950s, new designs introduced either in Britain or the United States stopped being introduced in India simultaneously. The Indian automotive industry went through a time warp for a generation.

41 Brian Tomlinson, *The Economy of Modern India: 1860–1970* (Cambridge University Press, 1993), 144.

42 Cadambi Sesachar Venkatachar, *Witness to the Century: Writings of C. S. Venkatachar, ICS*, ed. S. Sapru and Commodore K. M. Acharya (Bangalore: published privately, 1999), 140. Since the late Mr. Venkatachar was one of the few Indians accepted into the Indian Political Service, both before and after independence his reputation being high, his views, now unknown, should carry weight.

43 See Patrick French, *Liberty or Death: India's Journey to Independence and Division* (London: HarperCollins, 1997) for a sympathetic account of the political role played by Field Marshal Wavell in India during the time he was the Viceroy of India (1943–46).

44 The memorandum was published as Purshotamdas Thakurdas, J. R. D. Tata, G. D. Birla, Ardeshir Dalal, Shri Ram, Kasturbhai Lalbhai, A. D. Shroff and John Mathai, *A Plan of Economic Development for India: Parts I and II* (Harmondsworth: Penguin, 1945). An example of the symbiosis is seen in the career of Ardeshir Dalal, who moved from the ICS to the Tatas, and then back to public life when he became the member of the Governor General's Executive Council responsible for the Department of Planning and Development, in the Government of India. After independence, he returned to the Tatas as a director of Tata Sons Limited.

45 I. G. Patel, *Glimpses of Indian Economic Policy: An Insider's View* (New Delhi: Oxford University Press, 2002), 190.

46 Sharad S. Marathe, *Regulation and Development: India's Policy Experience of Controls over Industry* (2nd edn., New Delhi: Sage Publications, 1989), 34–35.

47 Their sales ranks were the Tata group first, the Birla group second, the Martin Burn group third, the Bangur group fifth, the Associated Cement Companies (ACC) group thirteenth, the Thapar group fourth, the Sahu Jain group sixth, the Bird Heilgers group ninth, the J. K. Singhania group tenth and the Soorajmull Nagarmull group twelfth respectively.

48 These items are infrastructure goods and inputs such as electricity, steel, fertilizers, cement, forgings, sulphuric acid, caustic soda, and heavy structures; capital goods such as automobile ancillaries, shipbuilding and ship repairs and boilers; intermediate goods such as petroleum products; and consumer goods such as beer, phones, and watches.

49 Only in one instance, boilers, has the production growth in the 1980s been greater than the production growth of the 1990s or 2000s. In the case of all other items, production growth in the 1990s or the 2000s has been greater than production growth in the 1980s.

50 Hobsbawm, *Industry and Empire*, 68.

51 See Angus Maddison, Explaining the Economic Performance of Nations, 1820–1989, in William Baumol, Richard Nelson, and Edward Wolff (eds.), *Convergence of Productivity: Cross-National Studies and Historical Evidence* (New York: Oxford University Press, 1994), Table 2–1, 22–23.

52 The figure displayed is based on industrial licensing data issued by the Department of Industrial Policy and Promotion of the Ministry of Commerce and Industry.

53 Alice Amsden, *Asia's Next Giant: South Korea and Late Industrialization* (New York: Oxford University Press, 1989), 19.

54 Lal, *Unfinished Business*, 131–132.

55 Morris, The Growth of Large Scale Industry.

56 Das, *India Unbound*, 42.

57 Gunnar Myrdal, *Asian Drama: An Inquiry into the Poverty of Nations* (New York: Vintage, 1971), 193.

58 Amsden, *Asia's Next Giant*, 3.

59 Braj Kumar Nehru, *Nice Guys Finish Second* (New Delhi: Viking, 1997), 270.

60 John P. Lewis, *Quiet Crisis in India* (Garden City, NY: Anchor Books, 1964), 5.

61 Corelli Barnett, *The Lost Victory: British Dreams, British Realities, 1945–1950* (London: Pan Books, 1995), 213.

62 They were the academic standard-bearers of the Bombay School in which a tradition of team research had been initiated by Professor K. T. Shah. The late Professor Shah's academic successor was Professor C. N. Vakil, who continued the trend and built up the influential Bombay way of thinking in industrial economics. Others associated with this school were Messrs. P. A. Wadia, A. D. Shroff, K. T. Merchant and P. R. Brahmananda. See Bhabatosh Datta, The Teaching of Economics in India, in C. T. Kurien, E. R. Prabhakar and S. Gopal (eds.), *Economy, Society and Development* (New Delhi: Sage Publications, 1991), 298.

63 Patel, *Glimpses of Indian Economic Policy*, 40.

64 A standard-bearer for the Bombay School was M. R. Pai of the Forum of Free Enterprise in Bombay, a non-governmental body founded by A. D. Shroff. Important associations existed with the Swatantra Party, a pro-market party in dirigiste India, whose leader in Bombay was Mr. Narayan Dandekar, a retired ICS officer, and later a Member of Parliament. Mr. Dandekar had the distinction of having qualified as a chartered accountant in London while he also sat for the ICS examination. A member of the Finance and Commerce Pool, he prematurely quit the ICS, while a member of the Central Board of Revenue in New Delhi, to join industry. He was chairman of many Indian companies, and had served a term as President of the Bombay Chamber of Commerce and Industry.

65 Professor Mahalanobis did not think that planning or statistical models had any permanent value of their own but were to be used as scaffolding to be dismantled as soon as their
purpose had been served. See Ashok Rudra, *Prasanta Chandra Mahalanobis: A Biography*
(New Delhi: Oxford University Press, 1999), 225.

66 Sonti Venkata Ramamurti was a distinguished ICS officer who had been the first Indian
Chief Secretary of Madras, and then the Prime Minister of Jodhpur prior to independence.

67 For this fact, I thank Professor Tapan Raychaudhuri. E. P. Moon, a British ICS officer, quit
the ICS in 1944, after a run-in with the government, and left India. He returned to India,
before independence. He initially served in Bahawalpur, a princely state, as its Revenue
Minister. After 1947, initially he was the Deputy Chief Commissioner of Himachal Pradesh
and then the Chief Commissioner of Manipur. After its formation in the early 1950s, till
1961, when he left India, E. P. Moon was an adviser in the Planning Commission. I thank
Professor Amiya Bagchi for pointing out that E. P. Moon and Professor Mahalanobis did
not get along well. Tarlok Singh, a member of the Finance and Commerce Pool, had earlier
been Private Secretary to the Prime Minister, Pandit Jawaharlal Nehru, and in that capacity
had moved to the Planning Commission at its inception since the Prime Minister was also
ex-officio Chairman of the Planning Commission. Tarlok Singh's career progressed rapidly,
and by 1964 he was himself a member of the Planning Commission.

68 Nehru, *Nice Guys Finish Second*, 270.

69 Isher Judge Ahluwalia, *Industrial Growth in India: Stagnation since the Mid-Sixties* (New
Delhi: Oxford University Press, 1985), 147.

70 Myrdal, *Asian Drama*, 164.

71 The late Professor B. R. Shenoy, whom I used to meet as a schoolboy in Delhi, was influential enough that he had to be completely marginalized by restriction of his access to all government appointments. Such appointments, whether full-time, or part-time, to membership
of boards, commissions, or committees, allow participants a platform, access to data, and
the ear of the policy maker. In India, as elsewhere, these appointments have been important
sources of patronage. Also, someone of substance can be very influential via these avenues
of participation. The Cassandra-like statements of Professor Shenoy kept him out of the
loop for the rest of his life.

72 Patel, *Glimpses of Indian Economic Policy*, 41. The late I. G. Patel has written that the
frontal objection to the consensus came only from B. R. Shenoy, for whom bold industrialization meant large budget deficits and inflation which he would not have. Professor Shenoy
was a crusader for fiscal virginity.

73 Lewis, *Quiet Crisis in India*, 21–22.

74 Cited in Braudel, *A History of Civilizations*, 253.

75 Cited in Braudel, *A History of Civilizations*, 253–254.

76 George Rosen, *Contrasting Styles of Industrial Reform: China and India in the 1980s*
(University of Chicago Press, 1992), 98–99; Sumit K. Majumdar, Government Policies
and Industrial Performance: An Institutional Analysis of the Indian Experience, *Journal of
Institutional and Theoretical Economics*, 152, 2 (1996), 380–411.

77 http://new.visionuvce.in/sirmvpdf, retrieved on September 29, 2010.

78 http://new.visionuvce.in/sirmvpdf, retrieved on September 29, 2010.

2   *Industrial revolutions*

1 Simon Kuznets, *Modern Economic Growth* (New Haven, CT: Yale University Press, 1966),
9.

2 Maddison, *Explaining the Economic Performance of Nations*, 31.

3 An unfortunate "Heart of Darkness" view is one that David Landes advances (*The Wealth and Poverty of Nations: Why Some Are So Rich and Some So Poor* (New York: W. W. Norton, 1998), 516–517). Landes concludes that the history of economic development suggests it is culture that makes all the difference. If this were the case, then all generic human qualities, prevalent since the dawn of evolution, would dissolve into an irreducible dermatological variable which would explain all variations across countries.

4 Carlo Cipolla, *Guns, Sails and Empires: Technological Innovation and the Early Phases of European Expansion, 1400–1700* (Manhattan, KS: Sunflower University Press, 1965), 19.

5 Cipolla, *Guns, Sails and Empires*, 81.

6 Cipolla, *Guns, Sails and Empires*, 146.

7 Geoffrey Owen, *From Empire to Europe: The Decline and Revival of British Industry since the Second World War* (London: HarperCollins, 1999), 10.

8 Kennedy, *The Rise and Fall of the Great Powers*, 145.

9 Hughes, *The Vital Few*, 126.

10 Owen, *From Empire to Europe*, 10.

11 Margaret Jacob, *Scientific Culture and the Making of the Industrial West* (New York: Oxford University Press, 1997), 6.

12 Kennedy, *The Rise and Fall of the Great Powers*, 145.

13 Kennedy, *The Rise and Fall of the Great Powers*, 145.

14 Leonard Setright, *Drive On: A Social History of the Motor Car* (London: Granta Books, 2002), 7–8.

15 Paul Kennedy had found that while the population of the United Kingdom rose from 10.5 million in 1801 to 41.8 million in 1911, at an annual increase of 1.26 percent, its national product rose by as much as 14 times over the course of the nineteenth century; see Kennedy, *The Rise and Fall of the Great Powers*, 146.

16 Kennedy, *The Rise and Fall of the Great Powers*, 147.

17 Kennedy, *The Rise and Fall of the Great Powers*, 148.

18 Jane Jacobs, *The Nature of Economies* (New York: The Modern Library, 2000), 47.

19 Patrick O'Brien, Modern Conceptions of the Industrial Revolution, in Patrick O'Brien and Roland Quinault (eds.), *The Industrial Revolution and British Society* (Cambridge University Press, 1997), 13–14.

20 Rondo Cameron, *A Concise Economic History of the World: From Paleolithic Times to the Present* (3rd edn., New York: Oxford University Press, 1997), 164.

21 Cameron, *A Concise Economic History of the World*, 165–166.

22 Cameron, *A Concise Economic History of the World*, 167.

23 Cipolla, *Guns, Sails and Empires*, 146.

24 Ashton, *The Industrial Revolution*, 2.

25 Jacob, *Scientific Culture*, 4.

26 Jacob, *Scientific Culture*, 4.

27 Cameron, *A Concise Economic History of the World*, 167.

28 Gerald Holton, *The Scientific Imagination* (Cambridge, MA: Harvard University Press, 1998), xi.

29 Holton, *The Scientific Imagination*, xxix.

30 Holton, *The Scientific Imagination*, xxxvi.

31 Jacob, *Scientific Culture*, 4.

32 Holton, *The Scientific Imagination*, 256.

33 Jacob, *Scientific Culture*, 4.

34 Cameron, *A Concise Economic History of the World*, 167.

35 Cipolla, *Guns, Sails and Empires*, 130.

36 Hobsbawm, *Industry and Empire*, 56.

37 Hobsbawm, *Industry and Empire*, 56.

38 Braudel, *A History of Civilizations*, 378.

39 Braudel, *A History of Civilizations*, 381.

40 Someone operating several looms driven by power could produce 20 times the output of a hand worker. A mule driven by power had 200 times the capacity of a spinning wheel. See Kennedy, *The Rise and Fall of the Great Powers*, 148.

41 Hobsbawm, *Industry and Empire*, 58–59.

42 Hobsbawm, *Industry and Empire*, 60.

43 Hobsbawm, *Industry and Empire*, 69.

44 Hobsbawm, *Industry and Empire*, 114.

45 Hobsbawm, *Industry and Empire*, 109.

46 Hobsbawm, *Industry and Empire*, 35.

47 Both before and after the formal conquest of Bengal, the British had used its re-export trade with India, import substitution in textiles, and the tributes extracted from India after conquering it, to acquire the enormous resources to advance the British industrial revolution; these resources also helped the British in winning in the Anglo–French war from 1789 to 1815. See Amiya K. Bagchi, *Colonialism and Indian Economy* (New Delhi: Oxford University Press, 2010), xv–lii.

48 Vernon Ruttan, *Technology Growth and Development: An Induced Innovation Perspective* (New York: Oxford University Press, 2001), 100–108.

49 Kenneth Pomeranz and Stephen Topik, *The World that Trade Created: Culture, Society and the World Economy, 1400 to the Present* (Armonk, NY: M. E. Sharpe, 1997), 17.

50 Landes, *The Wealth and Poverty of Nations*, 154.

51 Chanda, *Bound Together*, 77.

52 In fact, the words calico, chintz, and gingham are Indian in origin. See Braudel, *A History of Civilizations*, 381.

53 Arnold Pacey, *Technology in World Civilization: A Thousand-Year History* (Cambridge, MA: MIT Press, 1990), 120.

54 Hobsbawm, *Industry and Empire*, 57.

55 Chanda, *Bound Together*, 77.

56 Pacey, *Technology in World Civilization*, 117.

57 Hobsbawm, *Industry and Empire*, 63.

58 Walt W. Rostow, Jr., *Theorists of Economic Growth from David Hume to the Present* (New York: Oxford University Press, 1990), 22.

59 Fernand Braudel, *The Wheels of Commerce* (New York: Harper and Row, 1979), 178.

60 Ephraim Lipson, *The Economic History of England*, vol. 3 (London: A. & C. Black, 1931), 39.

61 As Britain slumps irretrievably, a tangled web of myths is emerging to prop up a story of past greatness. In recent analysis, Joel Mokyr writes that two mutually reinforcing motivating factors, practical utility and moral improvement, were behind the origination of the useful knowledge central to the industrial revolution; these created a so-called British enlightenment. The primary driver of textile mechanization was a cost-saving and profit-boosting motive, which had a deleterious effect on the Indian textiles sector. When the amounts extracted from India by the East India Company, in the period that Mokyr deals in, are also taken into consideration it is improper and unfeasible to suggest that a moral improvement

motive was at play. See Joel Mokyr, *The Enlightenment Economy: An Economic History of Britain, 1700–1850* (New Haven, CT: Yale University Press, 2010), 35. Gregory Clark, *A Farewell to Alms: A Brief Economic History of the World* (Princeton University Press, 2007), 10–11, correctly attributes motives for the British industrial revolution to an English culture of ravening bourgeois greed; but, though well-versed in details of the Indian textiles sector, he ignores the role that the substitution of Indian textiles played in promoting British industrialization.

62 Pacey, *Technology in World Civilization*, 117.
63 Robert Allen, in a recent re-analysis of the British industrial revolution, acknowledges the role of cotton textiles as the wonder sector that drove the industrial revolution. He takes an excessively narrow view in attributing all innovations to a cost-saving motivation, because relative British wages were high, and ignores the role of other market, political economy, and fiscal factors that initially triggered the industrial revolution in the textiles sector. See Robert C. Allen, Why the Industrial Revolution Was British: Commerce, Induced Invention, and the Scientific Revolution, *Economic History Review*, 64, 2 (2011), 357–384.
64 Chanda, *Bound Together*, 77.
65 Maddison, *Class Structure and Economic Growth*, 55.
66 Lal, *Unfinished Business*, 18.
67 Tomlinson, *The Economy of Modern India*, 105.
68 Tomlinson, *The Economy of Modern India*, 106.
69 Tomlinson, *The Economy of Modern India*, 109.
70 Sumit Sarkar, *Modern India: 1885–1947* (New Delhi: Macmillan, 1983), 24.
71 Adam Smith, rather than Napoleon, had disparagingly called England a nation of shop-keepers because it regarded its colonial subjects simply as captive customers for its manu-factured goods; see Gavin Weightman, *The Industrial Revolutionaries: The Creation of the Modern World, 1776–1914* (London: Atlantic Books, 2007), 388.
72 Sarkar, *Modern India*, 24.
73 Pacey, *Technology in World Civilization*, 129.
74 Kennedy, *The Rise and Fall of the Great Powers*, 148. The de-industrialization literature of India is large. The influential statement remains that by Bagchi, *The Political Economy of Underdevelopment*, 31–35. The classics of the genre are the works by Dadabhai Naoroji, *Poverty and Un-British Rule in India* (London: Sonnenschein, 1901) and Romesh Chandra Dutt, *The Economic History of India*, vol. 1, *Under Early British Rule* (New Delhi: Publications Division, 1960 [originally published, 1901]) and Romesh Chandra Dutt, *The Economic History of India*, vol. 2, *In the Victorian Age, 1837–1900* (New Delhi: Publications Division, 1960 [originally published, 1903]).
75 Jacob, *Scientific Culture*, 4. In fact, the Royal Society of London as early as the 1680s dis-cussed the labor-saving value of machines; see Jacob, *Scientific Culture*, 113.
76 Albert E. Musson and Eric Robinson, *Science and Technology in the Industrial Revolution* (Reading: Gordon and Breach, 1969), 3.
77 Jacob, *Scientific Culture*, 113.
78 Jacob, *Scientific Culture*, 9–10.
79 Jacob, *Scientific Culture*, 113.
80 Margaret Jacob, The Cultural Foundations of Early Industrialization, in Maxine Berg and Kristine Bruland (eds.), *Technological Revolutions in Europe: Historical Perspectives* (Cheltenham: Edward Elgar, 1998), 67–85.
81 Jacob, *Scientific Culture*, 6–7.
82 Jacob, *Scientific Culture*, 2.

83 Hobsbawm, *Industry and Empire*, 60.
84 Jacob, *Scientific Culture*, 112.
85 Stanley Chapman, *Merchant Enterprise in Britain: From the Industrial Revolution to World War I* (Cambridge University Press, 1992), 58–68.
86 Jacob, *Scientific Culture*, 114.
87 Jacob, *Scientific Culture*, 115.
88 Braudel, *The Wheels of Commerce*, 181.
89 Hobsbawm, *Industry and Empire*, 68.
90 Eric Hobsbawm, *The Age of Capital: 1848–1875* (London, Abacus, 1975), 60.
91 Hughes, *The Vital Few*, 122.
92 Hughes, *The Vital Few*, 123.
93 Piers Brendon, *The Decline and Fall of the British Empire, 1781–1997* (London: Vintage Books, 2007), 11.
94 Hughes, *The Vital Few*, 125.
95 Hughes, *The Vital Few*, 133.
96 Hughes, *The Vital Few*, 134.
97 Hughes, *The Vital Few*, 137.
98 Owen, *From Empire to Europe*, 17.
99 Hobsbawm, *Industry and Empire*, 68.
100 Nathan Rosenberg, *Exploring the Black Box: Technology, Economics and History* (New York: Cambridge University Press, 1994), 111.
101 Rosenberg, *Exploring the Black Box*, 116.
102 Owen, *From Empire to Europe*, 15; the literature on this topic is large. The topic owes its popularity to the work on wages by John Hicks, *The Theory of Wages* (London Macmillan, 1932). See the work by Yujiro Hayami and Vernon Ruttan, *Agricultural Development: An International Perspective* (2nd edn., Baltimore: Johns Hopkins University Press, 1985) on capital and labor substitution issues.
103 A survey of the resource allocation literature is found in Ruttan, *Technology Growth and Development*, 100–108.
104 Hughes, *The Vital Few*, 138; Owen, *From Empire to Europe*, 15.
105 Rosenberg, *Exploring the Black Box*, 110.
106 David Hounshell, *From the American System to Mass Production, 1800–1932* (Baltimore: Johns Hopkins University Press, 1984), 32–33.
107 Owen, *From Empire to Europe*, 92.
108 Rosenberg, *Exploring the Black Box*, 117.
109 Hughes, *The Vital Few*, 183.
110 Hughes, *The Vital Few*, 179–180.
111 Hughes, *The Vital Few*, 186.
112 Owen, *From Empire to Europe*, 17.
113 Alfred D. Chandler, Jr., *Scale and Scope: The Dynamics of Industrial Capitalism* (Cambridge, MA: The Belknap Press of Harvard University Press, 1990), 65.
114 Hughes, *The Vital Few*, 197.
115 Owen, *From Empire to Europe*, 17.
116 Hughes, *The Vital Few*, 283.
117 Setright, *Drive On*, 8.
118 Hughes, *The Vital Few*, 291.
119 Hughes, *The Vital Few*, 325.
120 Hughes, *The Vital Few*, 303.

121 Hughes, *The Vital Few*, 294.

122 Hughes, *The Vital Few*, 325.

123 In industries such as apparel, textiles made from natural fibers, lumber, furniture, printing, and publishing, improvements in equipment and plant design did bring economies of scale but these were not extensive. A sharp reduction of unit costs did not accompany an increase in the volume of materials processed by the plant. See Chandler, *Scale and Scope*, 21–23.

124 Nathan Rosenberg and Luther Birdzell have observed that the change from the coherent, fully integrated feudal society of the late Middle Ages to the plural society of Europe in the eighteenth century implied a relaxation of political and ecclesiastical control of all spheres of life; see Nathan Rosenberg and Luther Birdzell, *How the West Grew Rich: The Economic Transformation of the Industrial World* (New York: Basic Books, 1986), 24.

125 Rosenberg and Birdzell, *How the West Grew Rich*, vi.

126 Rosenberg and Birdzell, *How the West Grew Rich*, 22.

127 Rosenberg and Birdzell, *How the West Grew Rich*, 24.

128 Rosenberg and Birdzell, *How the West Grew Rich*, 22; see Joel Mokyr, Intellectual Property Rights, the Industrial Revolution, and the Beginnings of Modern Economic Growth, *American Economic Review*, 99, 2 (2009), 349–355.

129 Nathan Rosenberg, *Inside the Black Box: Technology and Economics* (New York: Cambridge University Press, 1982), 11.

130 Douglas North and Robert Thomas, *The Rise of the Western World: A New Economic History* (Cambridge University Press, 1973), 155–156.

131 Harry I. Dutton, *The Patent System and Inventive Activity during the Industrial Revolution, 1750–1852* (Manchester University Press, 1984), 3.

132 B. Zorina Khan and Kenneth L. Sokoloff, The Early Development of Intellectual Property Institutions in the United States, *Journal of Economic Perspectives*, 15, 3 (2001), 233–246.

133 Khan and Sokoloff, *The Early Development of Intellectual Property Institutions*.

134 B. Zorina Khan and Kenneth L. Sokoloff, Institutions and Democratic Invention in Nineteenth-Century America, *American Economic Review*, 94, May (2004), 395–401.

135 Kenneth L. Sokoloff and B. Zorina Khan, The Democratization of Invention during Early Industrialization: Evidence from the United States, 1790–1846, *Journal of Economic History*, 50, 2 (1990), 363–378.

136 Khan and Sokoloff, *The Early Development of Intellectual Property Institutions*.

137 Chandler, *Scale and Scope*, 21–23.

138 These included production processes for the refining, processing and distilling of sugar, petroleum, animal and vegetable oil, whiskey, and other liquids. They were used for the refining and smelting of iron, steel, copper, and aluminum and for the mechanical processing and packaging of grain, tobacco, and other agricultural products.

139 Chandler, *Scale and Scope*, 24.

140 The rationalization could make it possible to concentrate a quarter of the world production of kerosene in three refineries, each with an average daily charging capacity of 6,500 barrels. The reorganization of refining facilities brought a sharp reduction in average cost of producing a gallon of kerosene. In 1880, the average cost at plants with a daily capacity of 1,500 to 2,000 barrels was approximately 2.5 cents per gallon. By 1885, the average cost had been reduced to 1.5 cents. To maintain this cost advantage, the refineries had to have a continuing daily throughput of 5,000 to 6,500 barrels.

141 Owen, *From Empire to Europe*, 16.
142 Chandler, *Scale and Scope*, 26.
143 Chandler, *Scale and Scope*, 63.
144 Chandler, *Scale and Scope*, 66.
145 David J. Teece, The Dynamics of Industrial Capitalism: Perspective on Alfred Chandler's *Scale and Scope*, *Journal of Economic Literature*, 31, 1 (1993), 199–225.
146 The McCormick Agriculture Machinery Company and the Singer Sewing Machine Company are examples often used in the literature. In the early 1880s, these firms adopted mass production methods of fabricating and assembling fully interchangeable parts. Perfected techniques permitted McCormick to double output in its Chicago works from 30,000 machines in 1881 to 60,000 annually by the mid 1880s. In the late 1870s, the Singer Sewing Machine Company built a plant in New Jersey; by 1883, full interchangeability of fabricated parts had been perfected. Within a few years, the plant was producing more than 500,000 machines a year. In 1886, the company built a factory of comparable size and capacity in Scotland to produce machines for markets in Europe and the eastern hemisphere. By the late 1880s, these two plants made an estimated 75 percent of the world's sewing machines. Hounshell, *From the American System to Mass Production*, 4
147 In the decade between 1840 and 1850, there were 7,000 miles of railway in the United States, 6,000 miles in Britain and 13,000 in the rest of Europe. Between 1850 and 1860, there were 24,000 miles in the United States, 4,000 in Britain and 17,000 in the rest of Europe. By 1880, the mileage had reached 51,000 in the United States, 5,000 in Britain and 31,000 in the rest of Europe. See Hobsbawm, *Industry and Empire*, 115.
148 Railways transformed the United States retailing sector by allowing nationwide catalog sales. See Alfred D. Chandler, Jr., *The Visible Hand: The Managerial Revolution in American Business* (Cambridge, MA: Harvard University Press, 1977), 230–233.
149 Chandler, *Scale and Scope*, 29.
150 Chandler, *Scale and Scope*, 29.
151 Eric Hobsbawm, *The Age of Extremes: A History of the World, 1914–1991* (New York: Vintage Books, 1994), 97.
152 Rostow, *Theorists of Economic Growth*, 78.
153 de Vries, *The Industrious Revolution*, 37–39.
154 Hobsbawm, *Industry and Empire*, 261.
155 Hobsbawm, *Industry and Empire*, 264.
156 Hobsbawm, *The Age of Extremes*, 266.
157 Hobsbawm, *Industry and Empire*, 268.
158 Kennedy, *The Rise and Fall of the Great Powers* 149.
159 Octavio Paz, *In Light of India* (New York: Harcourt Brace, 1995), 90.
160 Venkatachar, *Witness to the Century*, 328.
161 Paul Bairoch, International Industrialization Levels from 1750 to 1980, *Journal of European Economic History*, 2 (1982), 268–333.
162 Kennedy, *The Rise and Fall of the Great Powers*, 149.
163 Maddison, *Explaining the Economic Performance of Nations*, Table 2-1, 22–23.
164 The exigencies of the First World War led to the unsurprising discovery that India was not in a position to manufacture enough for her own industrial needs and for military defense. This led to the commencement of policies of government direct participation in India's industrial development. See Hobsbawm, *The Age of Extremes*, 206.

3 Aspects of Indian enterprise history

1 Charles Allen, *In Search of the Buddha: The Men Who Discovered India's Lost Religion* (New York: Carroll and Graf, 2002), 219.
2 Abraham Eraly, *The Gem in the Lotus: The Seeding of Indian Civilization* (London: Phoenix, 2000), 16.
3 Eraly, *The Gem in the Lotus*, 18.
4 Eraly, *The Gem in the Lotus*, 18.
5 Eraly, *The Gem in the Lotus*, 31.
6 Eraly, *The Gem in the Lotus*, 31.
7 Eraly, *The Gem in the Lotus*, 32.
8 Cotton was a major item of manufacture and trade in the Indus Valley, and numerous spindle whorls have been found in Indus Valley Civilization houses. In Mohenjo Daro, a silver vase with bits of red-dyed cotton cloth sticking to its side was found, and elephant tusks were found among the skeletons of a group of people, suggesting that ivory work was an established craft. Other craft products found were metal wares in copper, bronze, lead, gold, electrum, and silver, bowls and blades in stone, beads of semi-precious stones, metals, shell, paste, and ivory, stone sculptures, pottery, faience products like beads, inlays and seals, stoneware ornaments and terracotta figurines. See Eraly, *The Gem in the Lotus*, 33.
9 Shereen Ratnagar, Harappan Trade in Its World Context, in Ranabir Samaddar (ed.), *Trade in Early India* (New Delhi: Oxford University Press, 2001), 102–127.
10 Himanshu P. Ray, *The Winds of Change: Buddhism and the Maritime Links of Early South Asia* (New Delhi: Oxford University Press, 1994), 12.
11 Chanda, *Bound Together*, 74.
12 Eraly, *The Gem in the Lotus*, 33.
13 Eraly, *The Gem in the Lotus*, 33.
14 Ratnagar, *Harappan Trade in Its World Context*.
15 Vere Gordon Childe, Archaeological Ages as Technological Stages, *Journal of the Royal Anthropological Institute*, 74 (1944), 7–24.
16 Ratnagar, *Harappan Trade in Its World Context*.
17 Amaury de Riencourt, *The Soul of India* (London: Honeyglen Publishing, 1986 [first published, 1960]), 18.
18 De Riencourt, *The Soul of India*, 29.
19 Lal, *Unfinished Business*, 36.
20 Eraly, *The Gem in the Lotus*, 422.
21 Eraly, *The Gem in the Lotus*, 382.
22 Eraly, *The Gem in the Lotus*, 431.
23 Ray, *The Winds of Change*, 6–7.
24 Eraly, *The Gem in the Lotus*, 431.
25 Ray, *The Winds of Change*, 48.
26 Ray, *The Winds of Change*, 49.
27 Paz, *In Light of India*, 91.
28 Eraly, *The Gem in the Lotus*, 382.
29 Eraly, *The Gem in the Lotus*, 382.
30 Eraly, *The Gem in the Lotus*, 382.
31 Eraly, *The Gem in the Lotus*, 382.
32 Christopher Bayly, *Indian Society and the Making of the British Empire* (Cambridge University Press, 1988), 36.

344

33 Bayly, *Indian Society and the Making of the British Empire*, 36.
34 Kirti Narain Chaudhuri, Markets and Traders in India during the Seventeenth and Eighteenth Centuries, in Kirti Narain Chaudhuri and Clive Dewey (eds.), *Economy and Society: Essay in Indian Economic and Social History* (New York: Oxford University Press, 1979), 143–162.
35 Thomas R. Metcalf, *Ideologies of the Raj* (New Delhi: Foundation Books, 1998), 66.
36 Cited in Metcalf, *Ideologies of the Raj*, 70.
37 Sanjay Subrahmanyam and Christopher Bayly, Portfolio Capitalists and the Political Economy of Early Modern India, in Sanjay Subrahmanyam (ed.), *Merchants, Markets and the State in Early Modern India* (New Delhi: Oxford University Press, 1990), 242–265.
38 Between the eleventh and the sixteenth centuries, a feature of mercantile activity in southern India was the presence of merchant guilds which negotiated trader relationships with the temple or a state authority. These guilds were a mechanism for taxes to be paid and donations to be made. See Subrahmanyam and Bayly, Portfolio Capitalists.
39 Subrahmanyam and Bayly, Portfolio Capitalists.
40 Subrahmanyam and Bayly, Portfolio Capitalists.
41 Kirti Narain Chaudhuri, *Asia before Europe* (Cambridge University Press, 1990), 297.
42 Lisa Jardine, *Worldly Goods: A New History of the Renaissance* (London: Macmillan, 1996), 288–289.
43 Chaudhuri, Markets and Traders in India.
44 Chaudhuri, Markets and Traders in India.
45 Subrahmanyam and Bayly, Portfolio Capitalists.
46 Subrahmanyam and Bayly, Portfolio Capitalists.
47 Vladimir I. Pavlov, *Historical Premises for India's Transition to Capitalism: Late Eighteenth to Mid Nineteenth Century* (Moscow: Nauka Publishing House Central Department of Oriental Literature, 1978), 222.
48 Tomlinson, *The Economy of Modern India*, 97.
49 Tomlinson, *The Economy of Modern India*, 97.
50 Subrahmanyam and Bayly, Portfolio Capitalists.
51 Subrahmanyam and Bayly, Portfolio Capitalists.
52 Bayly, *Indian Society and the Making of the British Empire*, 36.
53 Bayly, *Indian Society and the Making of the British Empire*, 37–38.
54 Geoffrey Moorhouse, *India Britannica* (Chicago: Academy Chicago Publishers, 1983), 117.
55 Pavlov, *Historical Premises for India's Transition to Capitalism*, 155.
56 John Keay, *India: A History* (New York: Grove Press, 2000), 397.
57 Keay, *India: A History*, 398.
58 Keay, *India: A History*, 398.
59 Keay, *India: A History*, 399.
60 Pacey, *Technology in World Civilization*, 133.
61 Bayly, *Indian Society and the Making of the British Empire*, 4.
62 Bayly, *Indian Society and the Making of the British Empire*, 47.
63 Bayly, *Indian Society and the Making of the British Empire*, 4.
64 Bayly, *Indian Society and the Making of the British Empire*, 34.
65 Bayly, *Indian Society and the Making of the British Empire*, 4.
66 Edward Said, *Culture and Imperialism* (London: Vintage Books, 1993), 10.
67 Bayly, *Indian Society and the Making of the British Empire*, 5.

68 Claude Markovitz, *The Global World of Indian Merchants: Traders of Sind from Bukhara to Panama* (Cambridge University Press, 2000), 14.
69 Sarkar, *Modern India*, 24.
70 Benita Parry, *Delusions and Discoveries: India in the British Imagination, 1880–1930* (London: Verso Press, 1998), xi.
71 Said, *Culture and Imperialism*, 10.
72 Parry, *Delusions and Discoveries*, 11.
73 Mark Tully, *The Heart of India* (London: Penguin Books, 1995), vii.
74 Shankar Nath Maitra, *A Collector's Piece* (Calcutta: Writer's Workshop, 1997), 107. Shankar Nath Maitra had headed the Cachar district as Deputy Commissioner, a Burma war frontline location, at the time of the 1944 Kohima battle, had then been the Chief Commissioner of the Andaman and Nicobar Islands after independence, had become a diplomat, as India's High Commissioner in Pakistan, being present when the military seized power in 1958, and Indian Ambassador to the Philippines. He quit the ICS to become a tea planter in southern India for a decade. His grassroots knowledge and experiences were very diverse, and more important in reaching conclusions than academic pronouncements.
75 Professor Samuel Martin Burke was the longest-lived Indian ICS officer, being over 104 at his death in 2010. His achievements included four careers: as a district and sessions judge prior to 1947; a second post-independence career as Ambassador and High Commissioner for Pakistan; a third post-diplomatic career as a professor at the University of Minnesota; and a fourth post-academic retirement career as a South Asian historian and biographer in London.
76 Samuel Martin Burke and Salim Al-Din Quraishi, *The British Raj in India: An Historical Review* (Karachi: Oxford University Press, 1995), 7.
77 Moorhouse, *India Britannica*, 59.
78 Keay, *India: A History*, 376.
79 Bayly, *Indian Society and the Making of the British Empire*, 5.
80 Moorhouse, *India Britannica*, 117.
81 Said, *Culture and Imperialism*, 10.
82 Mir Jafar was an Arab adventurer and parvenu of Iraqi extraction at the court of Siraj-ud-Daula, then Nawab of Bengal.
83 Governor Drake, who fled Calcutta and missed the black hole episode, got £31,500. A Mr. Watts, who had run risks and played a vital part in the Plassey battle as the chief of the British factory at Kasimbazar, received £117,000. Major Kilpatrick got £60,750, Mr. Walsh £56,250, Mr. Manningham £27,000, Mr. Scrafton £22,500, Messrs. Boddam, Frankland, Mackett and Collett £11,367 apiece, Messrs. Amyatt and Pearce £11,366 each, Major Grant £11,250 and a Mr. Lushington just £5,625. See Moorhouse, *India Britannica*, 39.
84 Moorhouse, *India Britannica*, 39.
85 Tapan Raychaudhuri, *Perceptions, Emotions, Sensibilities: Essays on India's Colonial and Post-Colonial Experiences* (New Delhi: Oxford University Press, 1999), x–xi
86 Bayly, *Indian Society and the Making of the British Empire*, 51.
87 Clive had boasted to the British House of Commons in 1769 that the East India Company had taken possession of a rich, well-populated, and fruitful country, which was larger than France and Spain combined, and control over the resources, labor, industry, and manufactures belonging to 20 million persons. See Huw Bowen, *The Business of Empire: The East India Company and Imperial Britain* (Cambridge University Press, 2006), 5.

88 Pradip Sinha, Calcutta and the Currents of History, 1690–1912, in Sukanta Chaudhuri (ed.), *Calcutta, The Living City*, vol. 1, *The Past* (New Delhi, Oxford University Press, 1990), 31–45.

89 Bayly, *Indian Society and the Making of the British Empire*, 49.

90 Bayly, *Indian Society and the Making of the British Empire*, 49.

91 Bayly, *Indian Society and the Making of the British Empire*, 35.

92 Percival Griffiths, *The British Impact on India* (London: Macdonald, 1952), 374.

93 Griffiths, *The British Impact on India*, 375.

94 Cited in Griffiths, *The British Impact on India*, 375.

95 Sanjay Subrahmanyam, Introduction, in Sanjay Subrahmanyam (ed.), *Merchants, Markets and the State in Early Modern India* (New Delhi: Oxford University Press, 1990), 13.

96 Madhav Gadgil and Ramachandra Guha write that at a stroke a number of activities pursued by a substantial population of pre-colonial India became obsolete. These included the occupations of river ferrymen, itinerant traders, and nomadic entertainers. Also suppressed were activities such as shifting cultivation. See Madhav Gadgil and Ramachandra Guha, *Ecology and Equity: The Use and Abuse of Nature in Contemporary India* (New Delhi: Penguin Books, 1995), 29.

97 For a contemporary treatment of these early East India Company civil servants, see Nicholas Dirks, *The Scandal of Empire: India and the Creation of Imperial Britain* (Cambridge, MA: Harvard University Press, 2006).

98 Nick Robins, *The Corporation that Changed the World: How the East India Company Shaped the Modern Multinational* (Hyderabad: Orient Longman, 2006), 76.

99 Dirks, *The Scandal of Empire*, 151.

100 Dirks, *The Scandal of Empire*, 145–146.

101 Sarkar, *Modern India*, 25–26.

102 This is a theme also echoed by professional historians. According to Brian Tomlinson, *The Economy of Modern India*, 101, the political and economic changes accompanying the British rise to power in India during the nineteenth century seriously affected domestic manufacturing, led to de-industrialization, destroyed handicraft industries, ruined their workforce by commercializing agriculture, promoted imports of manufactured consumer goods, and inhibited India's established exports of cloth.

103 William Digby, *"Prosperous" British India: A Revelation from Official Records* (London: Unwin, 1901), 634.

104 Percival Griffiths has estimated the home charges for 1849–50. In that year the charges amounted to £2,435,337 and were made up as follows: dividends to proprietors of East India Company stock £629 435, interest on bond debt £173,723, furlough and retired pay for civil and military officers £742,959, payment on account of troops serving in India £250,999, expenditure connected with the British administration of Indian affairs £505,678, expenditure connected with the establishment of steam communications with India £120,543, and the diplomatic mission to the Court of Persia £12,000. See Griffiths, *The British Impact on India*, 401.

105 Dadabhai Naoroji was the acknowledged high priest of the drain theory, and from May 1867 till almost the second decade of the twentieth century he launched a staunch campaign against the wealth drain. On his role, see Bipan Chandra, Mridula Mukherjee, Aditya Mukherjee, K. N. Panikkar, and Sucheta Mahajan, *India's Struggle for Independence* (New Delhi: Penguin, 1987), 97.

106 Sarkar, *Modern India*, 27.

107 Sarvepalli Gopal, *Modern India* (London: Historical Association, 1967), 36.

108 Bayly, *Indian Society and the Making of the British Empire*, 104.
109 Bronwyn H. Hall, The Financing of Research and Development, *Oxford Review of Economic Policy*, 18, 1 (2002), 35–51, and Sumit K. Majumdar, Retentions, Relationships and Innovations: The Financing of R&D in India, *Economics of Innovation and New Technology*, 20, 3 (2011), 233–257, deal with the issues of financing of innovative activities.
110 Adams, *The Law of Civilization and Decay*, 259–260.
111 Digby, *"Prosperous" British India*, 30–31.
112 Robins, *The Corporation that Changed the World*, 179.
113 Gadgil and Guha, *Ecology and Equity*, 29.
114 Mahadev Govind Ranade, *Essays on Indian Economics* (2nd edn., Madras: G. A. Natesan and Company, 1906), 112–113.
115 Moorhouse, *India Britannica*, 118.
116 Dirks, *The Scandal of Empire*, 142.
117 Dirks, *The Scandal of Empire*, 143.
118 Moorhouse, *India Britannica*, 118.
119 Sunil K. Sen, Economic Transition in Bengal, in *Renascent Bengal (1817–1857): Proceedings of Seminar Organized by the Asiatic Society* (Calcutta: The Asiatic Society, 1972), 21–26.
120 Dirks, *The Scandal of Empire*, 144.
121 Maitra, *A Collector's Piece*, 114.
122 Maitra, *A Collector's Piece*, 115.
123 The issue of business and government relationships is important and deserves full treatment in another book.
124 Maitra, *A Collector's Piece*, 116.
125 In my days as a young professional in Calcutta, I had heard stories about the tea estate managers' bungalows and their lavish lifestyles. In particular, the bungalows of managers of the Jorehaut and Bishnauth companies' estates were reputed to be the grandest. The residences of superintendents, who were senior to the managers and oversaw a group of tea estates and gardens, were even more luxurious and equaled the splendor of the Government Houses, later Raj Bhavans, established by the British in locations such as Bombay or Nagpur.
126 Maitra, *A Collector's Piece*, 117.
127 Maitra, *A Collector's Piece*, 118.
128 Griffiths, *The British Impact on India*, 441.
129 Moorhouse, *India Britannica*, 118.
130 Griffiths, *The British Impact on India*, 441.
131 Griffiths, *The British Impact on India*, 441.
132 Griffiths, *The British Impact on India*, 441.
133 Griffiths, *The British Impact on India*, 442.
134 Moorhouse, *India Britannica*, 120.
135 Moorhouse, *India Britannica*, 120.
136 Moorhouse, *India Britannica*, 120.
137 Griffiths, *The British Impact on India*, 442.
138 E. R. Gee, The History of Coal Mining in India, *Mining Engineer*, 6, 3 (1940), 313–318.
139 See the Coal India site: http://coal.nic.in/abtcoal.htm, accessed February 1, 2011.
140 Percival Griffiths was a historian of British India whose work is important for anyone wishing to understand the role of the British in India. Percival Griffiths belonged to the

ICS, having joined it in 1921. He was the District Magistrate of Midnapore, a district affected by terrorism in the 1930s, and then was the Deputy Commissioner of Darjeeling, an important tea production district. He quit the ICS in 1937 to join industry and was a member of India's Central Legislative Assembly till 1947, where he represented commercial interests, especially those of the tea industry. His work on the history of the Indian tea industry remains a classic. His administrative, field, and political experiences gained in India shed more revealing insights than those of historians who may have read others' works, or shuffled paper, and then reached their opinions and conclusions.

141 Griffiths, *The British Impact on India*, 443.
142 Chaudhuri, *Asia before Europe*, 330.
143 Tomlinson, *The Economy of Modern India*, 127.
144 Tomlinson, *The Economy of Modern India*, 127.
145 Two cases are that of N. Dandekar, who quit after service of over two decades, and N. M. Wagle, who quit in 1947 to become an industrialist and later was the Chairman of Greaves, Cotton and Company Limited in Bombay. Later, he was also the President of the Bombay Chamber of Commerce and industry for a term, as had been N. Dandekar.
146 Griffiths, *The British Impact on India*, 444.
147 Tomlinson, *The Economy of Modern India*, 127.
148 Tomlinson, *The Economy of Modern India*, 128.
149 Tomlinson, *The Economy of Modern India*, 128.
150 Dennis H. Buchanan, *The Development of Capitalist Enterprise in India* (New York: Macmillan, 1934), 450.

4   The emergence of modern industry

1 Siddharta Ghosh, Calcutta's Industrial Archaeology, in Sukanta Chaudhuri (ed.), *Calcutta, The Living City*, vol. 1, *The Past* (New Delhi, Oxford University Press, 1990), 246–255.
2 Radhey Shyam Rungta, *The Rise of Business Corporations in India: 1851–1900* (Cambridge University Press, 1970).
3 Ghosh, *Calcutta's Industrial Archaeology*.
4 Ghosh, *Calcutta's Industrial Archaeology*.
5 Ghosh, *Calcutta's Industrial Archaeology*.
6 Ghosh, *Calcutta's Industrial Archaeology*.
7 Rungta, *Rise of Business Corporations in India*, 45.
8 Sen, Economic Transition in Bengal.
9 See Rungta, *Rise of Business Corporations in India*, 46. There were seven banking companies, five insurance companies, ten tea companies, five cotton mill companies, one jute mill company, one jute baling and pressing company, eight navigation companies, eight coal companies, four printing companies, three companies reclaiming waste lands, one bazaar company, eight manufacturing companies, and five trading companies.
10 Marika Vicziany, Bombay Merchants and Structural Change in the Export Community: 1850 to 1880, in Kirti Narain Chaudhuri and Clive Dewey (eds.), *Economy and Society: Essays in Indian Economic and Social History* (New York: Oxford University Press, 1979), 163–196.
11 Sarkar, *Modern India*, 40.
12 Vicziany, Bombay Merchants and Structural Change in the Export Community.
13 There is some question as to whether it was in 1855.

14 Dinsha E. Wacha, *The Life and Life Work of J. N. Tata* (2nd edn., Madras: Ganesh and Company, 1915), 5.

15 Tomlinson, *The Economy of Modern India*, 106.

16 Roy, *The Economic History of India*, 232.

17 Tomlinson, *The Economy of Modern India*, 109.

18 Tomlinson, *The Economy of Modern India*, 111.

19 Rajnarayan Chandavarkar, Industrialization in India before 1947: Conventional Approaches and Alternative Perspectives, *Modern Asian Studies*, 19, 3 (1985), 623–668.

20 Tomlinson, *The Economy of Modern India*, 112.

21 Roy, *The Economic History of India*, 245.

22 Rajnarayan Chandavarkar, *The Origins of Industrial Capitalism: Business Strategies and the Working Classes in Bombay, 1900–1940* (Cambridge University Press, 1994), 407.

23 Tomlinson, *The Economy of Modern India*, 113.

24 Vicziany, Bombay Merchants and Structural Change in the Export Community.

25 Vicziany, Bombay Merchants and Structural Change in the Export Community.

26 Vicziany, Bombay Merchants and Structural Change in the Export Community.

27 Vicziany, Bombay Merchants and Structural Change in the Export Community.

28 Vicziany, Bombay Merchants and Structural Change in the Export Community.

29 Vicziany, Bombay Merchants and Structural Change in the Export Community.

30 Vicziany, Bombay Merchants and Structural Change in the Export Community.

31 Several European trading firms operated inland ginning and pressing companies. Nicol and Company managed the Moffusil Press and Ginning Company, Volkart Brothers ran the United Press Company, and Gaddum and Company controlled the Berar Company. The Berar Company owned ginning factories at Budnaira and Khamgaon, and pressing factories at Jalgaon, Khamgaon, Akot and Amravati. See Vicziany, Bombay Merchants and Structural Change in the Export Community.

32 Gadgil and Guha, *Ecology and Equity*, 29.

33 Rungta, *Rise of Business Corporations in India*, 17.

34 Tomlinson, *The Economy of Modern India*, 127.

35 The benefits of railway construction in terms of encouraging the steel and machinery sector benefited British industry as suppliers. Nationalist economists, such as G. V. Joshi, saw the expenditure on railways as an Indian subsidy to British industries. See Chandra *et al.*, *India's Struggle for Independence*, 96.

36 Sarkar, *Modern India*, 38.

37 Tomlinson, *The Economy of Modern India*, 127.

38 Sarkar, *Modern India*, 38.

39 The myth spread about the Bengalis was their risk-aversion, effeteness, and pusillanimity. On this topic, see Moorhouse, *India Britannica*, 132. Hence, beliefs do not reconcile with reality in accounting for the fact that several acknowledged Indian Air Force heroes were Bengalis. A Bengali officer, Indra Lal Roy, was the first Indian to win a Distinguished Flying Cross during the First World War. During the Second World War, the first Distinguished Flying Cross to an Indian, for Burma operations in providing air cover protection during Alexander's rout by the Japanese, was awarded to a Bengali officer, Wing Commander Karun Krishna "Jumbo" Majumdar, who went on to win another Distinguished Flying Cross for Normandy operations in 1944. His cousin, Joyonto Nath Choudhuri, was a cavalry officer and the only Indian to command a tank regiment during the Second World War. Later, as a general, he headed India's army. After independence, the first pilot to be

awarded the Ashok Chakra, India's highest non-battlefield valor award, was Bengali Flight Lieutenant Suhas Biswas.

40 The Lieutenant Governor of East Bengal and Assam, with its capital at Dacca, was Joseph Bampfylde Fuller. He had achieved notoriety as a heavy-handed administrator. He eventually had to resign as the Lieutenant Governor, since his actions in suppressing popular sentiment were not considered appropriate. He too was from the Central Provinces and had spent the bulk of his career in the area of agriculture. There is a story, perhaps apocryphal, relating to him. In the late 1880s, J. B. Fuller was Director of Agriculture and Settlements in the Central Provinces. He affected a monocle. He had gone on an inspection visit into the interior, where a group of young tribal women with scythes would demonstrate crop cutting and yields in a typical farm. The women were assembled, waiting in orderly rows, when the young civil servant accompanying and assisting in the process, who was a practical joker, told the women in the vernacular that a great wizard was soon coming, and as soon as he put a glass in his eye and looked at them they would immediately turn barren. Fuller arrived, duly reached into his pocket for his monocle, and as soon as he started putting it to his eye the young women abandoned their scythes and ran in all directions, shrieking and screaming as they fled the field.

41 Sarkar, *Modern India*, 107.

42 Andrew Fraser, *Among Indian Rajahs and Ryots* (Philadelphia: J. B. Lippincott Company, 1911), 312–326.

43 Sarkar, *Modern India*, 107.

44 Sarkar, *Modern India*, 108.

45 Sarkar, *Modern India*, 109.

46 Amiya Bagchi, *Private Investment in India: 1900–1939* (Cambridge University Press, 1972), 10.

47 Sarkar, *Modern India*, 117.

48 Nabagopal Das, *Industrial Enterprise in India* (2nd edn., Calcutta: Orient Longman, 1956), 2.

49 Sarkar, *Modern India*, 117.

50 Subrata Dasgupta, *The Bengal Renaissance: Identity and Creativity from Rammohun Roy to Rabindranath Tagore* (New Delhi: Permanent Black, 2007), 131.

51 Dasgupta, *The Bengal Renaissance*, 133.

52 Dasgupta, *The Bengal Renaissance*, 132.

53 Dasgupta, *The Bengal Renaissance*, 138–139.

54 Dasgupta, *The Bengal Renaissance*, 142.

55 Acharya Praphulla Chandra Ray demolished the Bengali indolence myth that the British regularly spread and established the Bengalis' status as British equals in industrial capabilities; on the indolence myth, see Sudipta Sen, *Distant Sovereignty: Nationalist Imperialism and the Origins of British India* (New York: Routledge, 2002), 102.

56 Sinha, Calcutta and the Currents of History.

57 Omkar Goswami, Sahibs, Babus and Banias: Changes in Industrial Control in Eastern India, 1918–1950, *Journal of Asian Studies*, 48, 2 (1989), 289–309.

58 Roy, *The Economic History of India*, 272–275.

59 Sinha, Calcutta and the Currents of History.

60 Sinha, Calcutta and the Currents of History.

61 Sinha, Calcutta and the Currents of History.

62 Sinha, Calcutta and the Currents of History.

63 Sinha, Calcutta and the Currents of History.
64 See the website of Girdhari Lal and Company, who have been solicitors to the works for several decades; www.glvirendra.com/partners.html, retrieved March 6, 2011.
65 Rajat K. Ray, *Industrialization in India: Growth and Conflict in the Private Corporate Sector, 1914–1947* (New Delhi: Oxford University Press, 1979), 149.
66 Sinha, Calcutta and the Currents of History.
67 I owe the Amul and Gujarat State Fertilizer Company stories to Mr. L. Mansingh.
68 I am grateful to Professor Amiya Bagchi for this point.
69 Pavlov, *Historical Premises for India's Transition to Capitalism*, 226.
70 See Amalendu Guha, The Comprador Role of Parsi Seths, 1750–1850, *Economic and Political Weekly*, November 28 (1970), 1933–1936. An extensive literature documents the role of the Parsis in the opium trade between China and India, the role of the Baghdadi Jews, such as those belonging to the Sassoon family, and the role of the Marwari traders settled in Calcutta in the opium trade. The Birlas had gained access to this trade in the nineteenth century; on this topic, see Gita Piramal and Margaret Hedreck, *India's Industrialists*, vol. 1 (Boulder, CO: Lynne Rienner Publishers, 1985), 63. In Calcutta and Bombay, Baghdadi Jews were very active in the China opium trade; on this topic, see Joan G. Roland, Baghdadi Jews in India and China in the Nineteenth Century: A Comparison of Economic Roles, in Jonathan Goldstein (ed.), *The Jews of China, Volume 1, Historical and Cultural Perspectives* (New York: M. E. Sharpe, 1999), 141–156; see also Chiara Betta, From Orientals to Imagined Britons: Baghdadi Jews in Shanghai, *Modern Asian Studies*, 37, 4 (2003), 999–1023.
71 Roy, *The Economic History of India*, 248.
72 Prakash Tandon, *Beyond Punjab* (New Delhi: Thompson Press, 1971), 106.
73 Tandon, *Beyond Punjab*, 47.
74 Roy, *The Economic History of India*, 249.
75 Wacha, *The Life and Life Work of J. N. Tata*, 3.
76 Wacha, *The Life and Life Work of J. N. Tata*, 4.
77 Russi M. Lala, *The Creation of Wealth* (New Delhi: Penguin Portfolio, 2004), 4.
78 Lala, *The Creation of Wealth*, 13.
79 Ritter von Schwartz had managed the Raniganj coal area for the government. See Griffiths, *The British Impact on India*, 445.
80 Lala, *The Creation of Wealth*, 20.
81 Griffiths, *The British Impact on India*, 445.
82 Griffiths, *The British Impact on India*, 446.
83 Lala, *The Creation of Wealth*, 22.
84 A news item dated March 20, 2011 reported that a person who had ventured out late at night and gone into fields a kilometer away from his home was attacked by a lurking tiger. The tiger later dragged the body some distance to devour it before going back into the jungle. Later, villagers found the mutilated remains lying near a stream. The tiger had eaten some part of the body. See http://timesofindia.indiatimes.com/city/nagpur/Tiger-kills-man-in-Nagbhid-tehsil/articleshow/7745652.cms, retrieved March 23, 2011.
85 Lala, *The Creation of Wealth*, 23.
86 Griffiths, *The British Impact on India*, 446.
87 Lala, *The Creation of Wealth*, 23.
88 Pramatha Nath Bose, the son-in-law of Romesh Chunder Dutt, was the first Indian appointed to the Geological Survey of India. P. N. Bose discovered the Assam oilfields. See

Meenakshi Mukherjee, *An Indian for All Seasons: The Many Lives of R. C. Dutt* (New Delhi: Penguin Books, 2009), 80.
89 Lala, *The Creation of Wealth*, 23.
90 Griffiths, *The British Impact on India*, 447.
91 Morris, The Growth of Large Scale Industry.
92 They still do so even today. Recently, two large elephants, classified as rogues, entered the campus of one of India's premier educational establishments, the Indian Institute of Technology at Kharagpur, and created panic. They were subsequently chased out of the campus. One of them is supposed to have earlier killed a villager and injured a woman. Kharagpur is close to Jamshedpur, and it has the same vegetation and fauna but both are in different Indian states. See www.samachar.com/Rogue-elephants-enter-IITKharagpur-campus-trigger-panic-lchrNJaffej.html, accessed on February 7, 2011.
93 Lala, *The Creation of Wealth*, 26–27.
94 Lala, *The Creation of Wealth*, 27.
95 Das, *Industrial Enterprise in India*, 2.
96 Goswami, Sahibs, Babus and Banias.
97 Das, *Industrial Enterprise in India*, 5.
98 Das, *Industrial Enterprise in India*, 6.
99 Morris D. Morris, South Asian Entrepreneurship and the Rashomon Effect, 1800–1947, *Explorations in Economic History*, 16, 3 (1979), 341–361.
100 Goswami, Sahibs, Babus and Banias.
101 Sinha, Calcutta and the Currents of History.
102 Roy, *The Economic History of India*, 250.
103 Morris, South Asian Entrepreneurship and the Rashomon Effect.
104 Thomas Timberg, *The Marwaris: From Traders to Industrialists* (New Delhi: Vikas Publishing, 1978), 19.
105 Morris, South Asian Entrepreneurship and the Rashomon Effect.
106 Goswami, Sahibs, Babus and Banias.
107 Sinha, Calcutta and the Currents of History.
108 Goswami, Sahibs, Babus and Banias.
109 Sinha, Calcutta and the Currents of History.
110 Roy, *The Economic History of India*, 251.
111 Sinha, Calcutta and the Currents of History.
112 Tomlinson, *The Economy of Modern India*, 459.
113 Sinha, Calcutta and the Currents of History.
114 Goswami, Sahibs, Babus and Banias.
115 Sarkar, *Modern India*, 384.
116 Regrettably, the British did their best to discourage efforts by Walchand Hirachand and the Maharaja of Mysore to start production of automobiles and aircraft. See Sarkar, *Modern India*, 384.
117 Tomlinson, *The Economy of Modern India*, 136.
118 Das, *Industrial Enterprise in India*, 8.
119 Sarkar, *Modern India*, 384.
120 Das, *Industrial Enterprise in India*, 8.
121 Das, *Industrial Enterprise in India*, 9.
122 Sarkar, *Modern India*, 407.
123 Bagchi, Private Investment in India, 20.
124 Sarkar, *Modern India*, 40.

125 Managing agents dominated more than 85 percent of the companies listed on the Indian stock exchanges. There were three industries, coal, shipping, and cement, in which all companies were controlled by managing agents. In four others, jute, cotton, railways, and tea estates in north India, more than 90 percent of the companies were under the direction of managing agents. Four other industries in which managing agents controlled more than 80 percent of the producing units were engineering, electric power, vegetable oils, and plantations. See Andrew Brimmer, The Setting of Entrepreneurship in India, *Quarterly Journal of Economics*, 69, 4 (1955), 357–376.
126 Tomlinson, *The Economy of Modern India*, 117.
127 Maria Misra, *Business, Race and Politics in British India*, c. 1850–1960 (Oxford University Press, 1999), 4.
128 Tomlinson, *The Economy of Modern India*, 136.
129 Bagchi, *Private Investment in India*, 39.
130 Tomlinson, *The Economy of Modern India*, 100.
131 Rajni Palme Dutt, *India Today* (Bombay: People's Publishing House, 1949 [originally published 1940]), 148.
132 Tomlinson, *The Economy of Modern India*, 146.
133 Tomlinson, *The Economy of Modern India*, 145.
134 Mishra, *Business, Race and Politics in British India*, 112.
135 Brian R. Tomlinson, Colonial Firms and the Decline of Colonialism in Eastern India: 1914–47, *Modern Asian Studies*, 15, 3 (1981), 455–486.
136 Mishra, *Business, Race and Politics in British India*, 104.
137 Mishra, *Business, Race and Politics in British India*, 102.
138 Will Hutton, Interview, in Richard English and Martin Kenny (eds.), *Rethinking British Decline* (London: Macmillan, 2000), 50–60.
139 Mishra, *Business, Race and Politics in British India*, 28.
140 Tomlinson, Colonial Firms and the Decline of Colonialism in Eastern India.
141 Sinha, Calcutta and the Currents of History.
142 The story goes that a traveler and his camel were riding in the desert when night fell, and the traveler unfurled his tent to take shelter leaving the camel outside. Very soon, the camel piteously begged just to warm his poor little nose from the cold desert air in the tent. The traveler agreed, and a little while later the camel said could he enter just his ears as well, they were freezing! A little later the camel's entire head was in the tent, and then his neck. Meanwhile, the traveler had begun to make more and more space for his desert ship. Eventually, the camel nudged the traveler out of the tent with his nose, got his entire body into the tent and the traveler had to spend the entire night uncovered in the freezing desert. Similarly, the Marwaris, once they were in, slowly nudged the British out and acquired control over the companies that they had been financing.
143 Goswami, Sahibs, Babus and Banias.
144 Harish Damodaran, *India's New Capitalists: Caste, Business and Industry in a Modern Nation* (Ranikhet: Permanent Black, 2008), 21.
145 Roy, *The Economic History of India*, 251.
146 Tomlinson, *The Economy of Modern India*, 145.
147 Goswami, Sahibs, Babus and Banias.
148 Goswami, Sahibs, Babus and Banias.
149 Goswami, Sahibs, Babus and Banias.
150 Goswami, Sahibs, Babus and Banias.
151 Tandon, *Beyond Punjab*, 129.

152 In March 2011, the Enforcement Directorate of India's Ministry of Finance raided the Calcutta residence of Kashinath Tapuriah, pursuing a black money trail, alleging that Kashinath Tapuriah was a partner of a tax evader and money launderer named Hasan Ali, against whom the directorate was carrying out raids at premises in Poona, in connection with laundering $8 billion. See www.samachar.com/Black-money-case-ED-detains-Hasan-Ali-searches-Pune-home-ldhtLxgdjea.html, accessed March 7, 2011.
153 Goswami, Sahibs, Babus and Banias.
154 Goswami, Sahibs, Babus and Banias.
155 Bagchi, *Private Investment in India*, 50.
156 Cited in Clive Dewey, The Government of India's "New Industrial Policy," 1900–1925: Formation and Failure, in Kirti Narain Chaudhuri and Clive Dewey (eds.), *Economy and Society: Essays in Indian Economic and Social History* (New York: Oxford University Press, 1979), 215–257.
157 Quoted in Dutt, *India Today*, 139.
158 Dutt, *India Today*, 140.
159 Alfred Chatterton, *Industrial Evolution in India* (Madras: The Hindu, 1912), 6–7.
160 Dewey, The Government of India's "New Industrial Policy."
161 Dutt, *India Today*, 144.
162 Bagchi, *Private Investment in India*, 57.
163 James Berna, Patterns of Entrepreneurship in South India, *Economic Development and Cultural Change*, 7, 3 (1959), 349–354.

5   Asian late industrialization

1 Moses Abramovitz, Resource and Output Trends in the United States since 1870, *American Economic Review*, 46, 2 (1956), 5–23.
2 See the website www.theworldeconomy.org/, accessed February 13, 2011.
3 W. Mark Fruin, *The Japanese Enterprise System: Competitive Strategies and Cooperative Structures* (Oxford: Clarendon Press, 1992), 7.
4 Abramovitz, Resource and Output Trends in the United States since 1870.
5 Paul Bairoch, International Industrialization Levels from 1750 to 1980, *Journal of European Economic History*, 11, Fall (1982), 269–334. Morris D. Morris had also documented similar trends, though using the year 1913 as the base case of 100 for an index evaluating industrial performance for 25 years till 1938. By 1938, the industrial production index for the United States was 166.6, for the United Kingdom 121.5, for the Soviet Union 774.3, for Japan 528.9, and for India 250.7. Clearly, the industrialization levels of Japan and the Soviet Union, which were late industrializers, had outstripped the industrial revolution countries such as the United States and the United Kingdom, and even India was growing rapidly in industry, albeit from a very low base, relative to the United Kingdom. See Morris, The Growth of Large Scale Industry.
6 Richard R. Nelson and Howard Pack, The Asian Miracle and Modern Growth Theory, *Economic Journal*, 109 (1999), 416–436.
7 I thank Mr. Srinivas Rajgopal, the first Development Commissioner of Santa Cruz Export Processing Zone (SEEPZ), for his insights on the topic. See also http://crooksteven.blogspot.com/2011/01/taiwans-export-processing-zones.html; accessed on June 10, 2011.
8 Alexander Gerschenkron, *Economic Backwardness in Historical Perspective* (New York: Praeger, 1965), 8–11.
9 Nelson and Pack, The Asian Miracle and Modern Growth Theory.

10 Jan Fagerberg, Technology and International Differences in Growth Rates, *Journal of Economic Literature*, 32 (1994), 1147–1175.

11 Amsden, *Asia's Next Giant*, 9.

12 Gerschenkron, *Economic Backwardness in Historical Perspective*, 9–10.

13 Fruin, *The Japanese Enterprise System*, 38.

14 Moses Abramovitz, Catching Up, Forging Ahead and Falling Behind, *Journal of Economic History*, 46, 2 (1986), 385–406.

15 Hughes, *The Vital Few*, 122.

16 Fruin, *The Japanese Enterprise System*, 5.

17 Fruin, *The Japanese Enterprise System*, 38.

18 Kenneth Arrow, The Economic Implications of Learning by Doing, *Review of Economic Studies*, 29 (1962), 155–173.

19 Reinhard Bendix, *Work and Authority in Industry: Ideologies of Management in the Course of Industrialization* (New York: John Wiley, 1956), 206–207.

20 Holton, *The Scientific Imagination*, xi.

21 Amsden, *Asia's Next Giant*, 160.

22 Amsden, *Asia's Next Giant*, 5.

23 Alice Amsden, Diffusion of Development: The Late-Industrializing Model and Greater East Asia, *American Economic Review*, 81, 2 (1991), 282–286. Alice Amsden also states that "Of equal significance, the transition from light to heavy industry involves a transition from competing on the basis of cheap labor to competing on the basis of modern facilities and skills, given whatever labor costs made entry possible." See Amsden, *Asia's Next Giant*, 19.

24 William W. Lockwood, *The Economic Development of Japan: Growth and Structural Change 1868–1938* (Princeton University Press, 1954), 24.

25 See Ian Drummond, *British Economic Policy and the Empire, 1919–1939* (London: Allen and Unwin, 1972), 121–140, on how the Japanese textile firms acquired competitive advantages vis-à-vis Indian textile firms.

26 Deepak Nayyar, Introduction, in Deepak Nayyar (ed.), *Industrial Growth and Stagnation: The Debate in India* (New Delhi: Oxford University Press,1994), 1–17.

27 Ragnar Nurkse had, in his balanced growth framework, recommended the simultaneous investment of capital in a wide range of industries. Private investment would not be forthcoming or induced in a single area if the market was narrow. If there was overall market enlargement, via investment in many industries, the expansion of demand driven by increasing returns would guarantee success for all of the investments. See Ragnar Nurkse, *Problems of Capital Formation in Underdeveloped Countries* (Oxford: Blackwell, 1953), 14.

28 Fruin, *The Japanese Enterprise System*, 116.

29 Lockwood, *The Economic Development of Japan*, 27–32.

30 Amsden, Diffusion of Development; Gilbert E. Hubbard, *Eastern Industrialization and Its Effect on the West* (London: Oxford University Press, 1938), 3–182, had established quite early that Japanese industrial growth was based on productivity and capability enhancements, and not on wage arbitrage.

31 David Cannadine, *Class in Britain* (London: Penguin Books, 1998), 120.

32 Amsden, Diffusion of Development.

33 Amsden, *Asia's Next Giant*, 23.

34 Amsden, *Asia's Next Giant*, 172.

35 Amsden, *Asia's Next Giant*, 160.

36 The framework for analysis of capabilities has been widely used, and was popularized in Sanjaya Lall, Technological Capabilities and Industrialization, *World Development*, 20, 2 (1992), 165–186, and Amsden, *Asia's Next Giant*, 174.

37 Amsden, *Asia's Next Giant*, 233.

38 Abramovitz, Catching Up, Forging Ahead and Falling Behind.

39 David Dollar and Kenneth Sokoloff, Patterns of Productivity Growth in South Korean Manufacturing Industries, 1963–1979, *Journal of Development Economics*, 33, 2 (1990), 309–327.

40 Alice Amsden and Wan-Wen Chu, *Beyond Late Development: Taiwan's Upgrading Policies* (Cambridge, MA: MIT Press, 2003), 1.

41 Amsden, *Asia's Next Giant*, 117.

42 John Tang, Technological Leadership and Late Development: Evidence from Meiji Japan, 1868–1912, *Economic History Review*, 64, February (2011), 99–116.

43 Fruin, *The Japanese Enterprise System*, 59.

44 Amsden and Chu, *Second-Mover Advantage*, 2.

45 John A. Mathews, Competitive Advantages of the Latecomer Firm: A Resource-Based Account of Industrial Catch-Up Strategies, *Asia Pacific Journal of Management*, 19 (2002), 467–488; see also Michael Hobday, East Asian Latecomer Firms: Learning the Technology of Electronics, *World Development*, 23, 7 (1995), 1171–1193, and John A. Mathews, A Silicon Valley of the East: Creating Taiwan's Semiconductor Industry, *California Management Review*, 39, 4 (1997), 26–54, for detailed descriptions of the East Asian catch-up process in the field of electronics technology.

46 I am grateful to Professor Andrew Van de Ven, of the University of Minnesota, for pointing out Georg Simmel's initial identification and articulation of this inherent human sociological conflict.

47 See the separate works: Paul Lawrence and Jay Lorsch, *Organization and Environment: Managing Differentiation and Integration* (Boston: Division of Research, Graduate School of Business Administration, Harvard University, 1967); C. K. Prahalad and Yves Doz, *The Multinational Mission: Balancing Global Integration with Local Responsiveness* (New York: The Free Press, 1987); and Christopher Bartlett and Sumantra Ghoshal, *Managing across Borders: The Transnational Solution* (Boston: Harvard Business School Press, 1989).

48 Joseph Schumpeter, *Capitalism, Socialism and Democracy* (New York: Harper and Row, 1976), 87–106.

49 Abbott P. Usher, *A History of Mechanical Inventions* (Princeton University Press, 1955), 523–526.

50 Mansell Blackford, *A History of Small Business in America* (2nd edn., Chapel Hill: University of North Carolina Press, 2003), 1.

51 Michael J. Piore and Charles F. Sabel, *The Second Industrial Divide: Possibilities for Prosperity* (New York: Basic Books, 1984), 17.

52 See Paul Hirst and Jonathan Zeitlin, Flexible Specialization: Theory and Evidence in the Analysis of Industrial Change, in J. R. Hollingsworth and R. Boyer (eds.), *Contemporary Capitalism: The Embeddedness of Institutions* (Cambridge University Press, 1997), 220–239.

53 In order to acquire Western techniques, the non-European firms would have had to undergo a general process of "westernization"; see Cipolla, *Guns, Sails and Empires*, 147.

54 Monlin Chiang, *Tides from the West: A Chinese Autobiography* (New Haven, CT: Yale University Press, 1947), 147–148.

55 Nelson and Pack, The Asian Miracle and Modern Growth Theory.

56 Weightman, *The Industrial Revolutionaries*, 1–9.
57 Thorstein Veblen, *Imperial Germany and the Industrial Revolution* (Kitchener, Ont: Batoche Books, 2003 [first published, 1915]), 41–42.
58 Fruin, *The Japanese Enterprise System*, 59.
59 Fruin, *The Japanese Enterprise System*, 12.
60 Amsden, *Asia's Next Giant*, 233.
61 Linda Argote and Dennis Epple, Learning Curves in Manufacturing, *Science*, 247, February (1990), 20–24.
62 Ruttan, *Technology Growth and Development*, 94.
63 Amsden, *Asia's Next Giant*, 209.
64 Amsden has remarked that "Salaried engineers are a key figure in late industrialization because they are the gatekeepers of foreign technology transfers." See Amsden, *Asia's Next Giant*, 9.
65 Amsden, *Asia's Next Giant*, 10.
66 Amsden, *Asia's Next Giant*, 160.
67 Amsden, *Asia's Next Giant*, 209.
68 Jonathan S. Leonard, Carrots and Sticks: Pay, Supervision, and Turnover, *Journal of Labor Economics*, 5, 4 (1987), 136–152.
69 Amsden, *Asia's Next Giant*, 215.
70 Michio Morishima, *Why Has Japan "Succeeded"? Western Technology and the Japanese Ethos* (Cambridge University Press, 1982) 134.
71 Morishima, *Why Has Japan "Succeeded"?* 135.
72 Morishima, *Why Has Japan "Succeeded"?* 175.
73 Morishima, *Why Has Japan "Succeeded"?* 176.
74 Ira Magaziner and Mark Patinkin, Fast Heat: How Korea Won the Microwave War, *Harvard Business Review*, January–February (1989), 83–92.
75 Magaziner and Patinkin, Fast Heat.
76 Magaziner and Patinkin, Fast Heat.
77 Magaziner and Patinkin, Fast Heat.
78 Magaziner and Patinkin, Fast Heat.
79 Magaziner and Patinkin, Fast Heat.
80 Magaziner and Patinkin, Fast Heat.
81 John Stuart Mill, *Principles of Political Economy* (London: Longman, Green and Company, 1909 [first published, 1848]), 102–103.
82 Charles Babbage, *On the Economy of Machinery and Manufactures* (London: James Murray, 1832 [first published 1816]), 6.
83 Alfred Marshall, *Principles of Economics* (8th edn., London: Macmillan, 1920 [first published, 1890]), 250–266.
84 Nelson and Pack, The Asian Miracle and Modern Growth Theory.
85 Alexander Gerschenkron, *Europe in the Russian Mirror: Four Lectures in Economic History* (New York: Cambridge University Press, 1970), 72.
86 Gerschenkron, *Economic Backwardness in Historical Perspective*, 19.
87 Morishima, *Why Has Japan "Succeeded"?* 90.
88 Ian Inkster, *Japanese Industrialization: Historical and Cultural Perspectives* (New York: Routledge, 2001), 31.
89 Mathews, Competitive Advantages of the Latecomer Firm.
90 Chalmers Johnson, *MITI and the Japanese Miracle: The Growth of Industrial Policy, 1925–1975* (Stanford University Press, 1982).

91 Amsden, *Asia's Next Giant*, 27.
92 Dani Rodrik, Getting Interventions Right: How South Korea and Taiwan Grew Rich, *Economic Policy*, 20, April (1995), 53–107; Howard S. Ellis, Accelerated Investment as a Force in Economic Development, *Quarterly Journal of Economics*, 72, 4 (1958), 485–495.
93 Robert Wade, *Governing the Market: Economic Theory and the Role of Government in East Asian Industrialization* (Princeton University Press, 1990), 352.
94 Atul Kohli, *State-Directed Development: Political Power and Industrialization in the Global Periphery* (New York: Cambridge University Press, 2004), 13.
95 World Bank, *The East Asian Miracle: Economic Growth and Public Policy* (New York: Oxford University Press, 1993), 92–93.
96 Patel, *Glimpses of Indian Economic Policy*, 22.
97 Weightman, *The Industrial Revolutionaries*, 7.
98 Johannes Hirschmeier and Tsunehiko Yui, *The Development of Japanese Business* (Cambridge, MA: Harvard University Press, 1975), 95–103, 309–310.
99 Japan had been victorious in a war with China in 1895 and with Russia in 1905. Japan acquired Taiwan and the southern half of the Sakhalin Island as a result. Japan annexed Korea, previously a Chinese protectorate, in 1910.
100 Morishima, *Why Has Japan "Succeeded"?* 134; in 1942, a second engineering faculty, concentrating on the application of science to warfare, was started at Tokyo Imperial University; see Morishima, *Why Has Japan "Succeeded"?* 135.
101 William Easterly, *The Elusive Quest for Growth: Economists' Adventures and Misadventures in the Tropics* (Cambridge, MA: MIT Press, 2001), 183.
102 Weightman, *The Industrial Revolutionaries*, 390.
103 Morishima, *Why Has Japan "Succeeded"?* 83–84.
104 Mancur Olson, *The Rise and Decline of Nations* (New Haven, CT: Yale University Press, 1982), 2–3.
105 Everett E. Hagen, *On the Theory of Social Change: How Economic Growth Begins* (Homewood, IL: Dorsey, 1962), 185.
106 Philip Ball, *Critical Mass: How One Things Leads to Another* (London: Arrow Books, 2004), 101.
107 Malcolm Gladwell, *The Tipping Point: How Little Things Can Make a Big Difference* (Boston: Little, Brown, 2000), 9.
108 This possibility was suggested by the former American Secretary of State, Henry Kissinger, in the late 1980s to a group of senior executives at a closed-door seminar in Minneapolis. I was then a doctoral student and my adviser, W. Bruce Erickson, as a senior faculty member of the University of Minnesota, as well as a prominent local venture capitalist and antitrust consultant, had been invited to attend. The outcomes of that meeting were described to me later by Professor Erickson.
109 Felipe Fernandez-Armesto, *Civilizations* (London: Macmillan, 2000), 448.
110 Ashok Desai, *The Price of Onions* (New Delhi: Penguin, 1999), xii.
111 Bimal Jalan, *India's Economic Crisis: The Way Ahead* (New Delhi: Oxford University Press, 1991), 2–3.
112 About 47 tons of gold were shipped. The crisis occurred during a period when the Indian government was led by Chandra Shekhar, who was Prime Minister of India for a very short time. The P. V. Narasimha Rao government that took over then implemented the reforms against the backdrop of severe financial crisis. See Alan Wheatley, India's Next Challenge: Sustaining its Growth, *New York Times*, February 28, 2011,

www.nytimes.com/2011/03/01/business/global/01inside.html, accessed March 28, 2011, and S. Venkitaramanan, Return of India's Gold, *The Hindu Business Line*, November 16, 2009, www.thehindubusinessline.in/2009/11/16/stories/2009111650730900.htm, accessed March 28, 2011
113 Jalan, India's Economic Crisis, 2–3.
114 Buchanan, *The Development of Capitalist Enterprise in India*, 450.
115 Shashi Tharoor, *India: From Midnight to the Millennium* (New Delhi: Penguin Books, 1997), 159.

6 Democratizing entrepreneurship

1 This section is based in part on Walchand Hirachand's unpublished biography, by Dr. Swapan Dasgupta, which Walchand Hirachand's nephew, Ajit Gulabchand, let me look at.
2 A recent book details the life and activities of James McKay. See Mishra, *Business, Race and Politics in British India*, 149.
3 Jayavant M. Shrinagesh, *Between Two Stools: My Life in the ICS before and after Independence* (New Delhi: Rupa and Company, 2007), 121.
4 Sarkar, *Modern India*, 384.
5 Shrinagesh, *Between Two Stools*, 121.
6 Ruttan, *Technology Growth and Development*, 434.
7 Tomlinson, *The Economy of Modern India*, 167.
8 Albert H. Hanson, *The Process of Planning: A Study of India's Five-Year Plans, 1950–1964* (Oxford University Press, 1966), 37–38.
9 Tomlinson, *The Economy of Modern India*, 167.
10 Majumdar, Government Policies and Industrial Performance.
11 Patel, *Glimpses of Indian Economic Policy*, 38.
12 Patel, *Glimpses of Indian Economic Policy*, 38–39. Dr. Patel states that the planning for the First Five-Year Plan was an eclectic, discursive, tentative, and cautious comprehensive exercise. But, in the hands of practical men who shaped the plan, it contained much still-relevant wisdom. At that time, the memory of the disastrous Bengal famine of 1943–44, the dislocation of the Punjab peasantry, and the early food shortages emphasized the need for increasing food production. Hence, there were emphases on irrigation, large river-valley projects, community development projects, and fertilizer production.
13 Ahluwalia, *Industrial Growth in India*, 4; Majumdar, Government Policies and Industrial Performance.
14 Edward R. Luce, *In Spite of the Gods: The Strange Rise of Modern India* (London: Little, Brown, 2006), 27–28.
15 Patel, *Glimpses of Indian Economic Policy*, 44.
16 Milton Friedman and Rose Friedman, *Two Lucky People: Memoirs* (University of Chicago Press, 1998), 257.
17 Luce, *In Spite of the Gods*, 28.
18 Tomlinson, *The Economy of Modern India*, 175.
19 Paul Brass, *The Politics of India since Independence* (2nd edn., Cambridge University Press, 1990), 248; Majumdar, Government Policies and Industrial Performance.
20 Ahluwalia, *Industrial Growth in India*, 147.
21 Industries were allocated between the public and private sector. Basic and strategic industries were reserved for the public sector. In 17 strategic industries, such as heavy electrical plant, iron and steel, heavy castings, mineral extraction and processing, state-owned firms

were to be monopolies or have exclusive rights to new investments. Existing private firms were not guaranteed against nationalization. In 12 basic industries, investments were open to both private and public sector firms, but public firms were given the prerogative for additional investments. Private capital was allowed elsewhere, subject to plan targets and the provision of licensing and import controls. See Majumdar, Government Policies and Industrial Performance, for more details.

22 Patel *Glimpses of Indian Economic Policy*, 64.
23 Marathe, *Regulation and Development*, 57–58.
24 The late Subrahmanya Bhoothalingam was a distinguished ICS officer; he had been secretary to the Government of India in a number of crucial departments such as Steel, Economic and Defence Coordination, and Finance. He was closely associated with policy-making for industry, and the operation of the licensing system in the 1950s and 1960s. In the 1940s, he had been intimately associated with creating the system of controls that were put in place for the wartime Indian economy.
25 Subrahmanya Bhoothalingam, *Reflections on an Era: Memoirs of a Civil Servant* (Madras: Affiliated East-West Publishers, 1993), 188.
26 Marathe, *Regulation and Development*, 57–58.
27 Cited in Ramachandra Guha, *India after Gandhi: The History of the World's Largest Democracy* (London: Macmillan, 2007), 692.
28 Kohli, *State-Directed Development*, 8.
29 Lal, *Unfinished Business*, 39.
30 Tomlinson, *The Economy of Modern India*, 177.
31 Bhagwati, *India in Transition*, 56.
32 Sumit K. Majumdar, The Impact of Size and Age on Firm-Level Performance: Some Evidence from Indian Industry, *Review of Industrial Organization*, 12, 2 (1997), 231–241.
33 Raj, Growth and Stagnation, 53.
34 Patel, *Glimpses of Indian Economic Policy*, 66.
35 Marathe, *Regulation and Development*, 89.
36 Bhagwati, *India in Transition*, 60.
37 Government of India, *Report of the Industrial Licensing Policy Inquiry Committee*, Mr. S. Dutt, ICS, Chairman (New Delhi, Government of India, 1969) and Government of India, *Final Report on Industrial Planning and Licensing Policy*, Dr. R. K. Hazari, Chairman (New Delhi, Government of India, 1967).
38 Marathe, *Regulation and Development*, 57–58.
39 Ahluwalia, *Industrial Growth in India*, 4.
40 Ahluwalia, *Industrial Growth in India*, 4.
41 Guha, *India after Gandhi*, 693.
42 John Beames, *Memoirs of a Bengal Civilian* (London: Chatto and Windus, 1961; republished 1984 by Eland Publishing), 208.
43 Beames, *Memoirs*, 208–209.
44 Beames, *Memoirs*, 209.
45 Peter Evans, *Embedded Autonomy: States and Industrial Transformation* (Princeton University Press, 1995), 11.
46 Albert Hirschman, *The Rhetoric of Reaction: Perversity, Futility, Jeopardy* (Cambridge, MA: Harvard University Press, 1991), 7.
47 Bhagwati, *India in Transition*, 5; see Martin Weitzman, Prices versus Quantities, *Review of Economic Studies*, 41, 4 (1974), 477–491, on the merits of financial versus physical controls.

48 Thomas Schelling, *Micromotives and Macrobehavior* (New York: W. W. Norton, 1978), 118.

49 The word *babu* has been used to describe the mentality of relatively junior members of government departments who process much of the paperwork, and were popularly held to be the key impediments to human progress. John Masters remarked that: "The babu is not a person but an outlook … many blinkered men of his type … make references and cross references, check and recheck, refer and confer, and willingly spend their human energy in inhuman exactitude." See John Masters, *Bugles and a Tiger: My Life in the Gurkhas* (London: Cassell and Company, 1956), 296.

50 I thank Mr. L. Mansingh for conversations on the topic in 2010 and 2011. Since he was the person under whose signature the July 24, 1991 notification was issued, his insights on the process of industrial licensing in India have been important. I have also had several conversations on this topic with Dr. N. K. Sengupta. He was Controller of Capital Issues between 1979 and 1984. Before he passed away, the late Mr. P. D. Kasbekar, who between 1966 and 1972 had been first the Chief Controller of Imports and Exports and then the Controller of Capital Issues, two of the most important positions in the *License Raj*, described to me the logic of why such policies had been designed and how their implementation had been attempted.

51 Nitish K. Sengupta, *Unshackling Indian Industry: Towards Competitiveness through Deregulation* (New Delhi: Vision Books, 1992), 55.

52 Timothy Earle, *How Chiefs Come to Power: The Political Economy in Prehistory* (Stanford University Press, 1997), 68.

53 Earle, *How Chiefs Come to Power*, 70.

54 Earle, *How Chiefs Come to Power*, 67.

55 Friedrich Hayek, Socialist Calculation: The Competitive Solution, *Economica*, 7 (1940), 125–149.

56 Alan Ebenstein, *Friedrich Hayek: A Biography* (New York: Palgrave, 2001), 115.

57 George B. Sansom, *The Western World and Japan* (New York: Alfred A. Knopf, 1950), 68–69.

58 Cipolla, *Guns, Sails and Empires*, 19.

59 Earle, *How Chiefs Come to Power*, 70.

60 Hayek, Socialist Calculation.

61 Kusum Nair, *Blossoms in the Dust: The Human Factor in Indian Development* (New York: Praeger Publishers, 1961), xiii.

62 J. M. Shrinagesh had written that "the ability to fight one's own battles depends on the will to succeed." Shrinagesh, *Between Two Stools*, 18.

63 Nair, *Blossoms in the Dust*, 193.

64 Friedrich Hayek, *The Road to Serfdom* (50th anniversary edn., University of Chicago Press, 1994 [first published 1944]), 18.

65 Amartya Sen, *Development as Freedom* (New York: Anchor Books, 1999), 53.

66 Sen, *Development as Freedom*, 291.

67 Peter T. Bauer, *Economic Analysis and Policy in Underdeveloped Countries* (Cambridge University Press, 1957), 113–114.

68 Patel, *Glimpses of Indian Economic Policy*, 45.

69 Hiralal M. Patel, *Rites of Passage: A Civil Servant Remembers* (New Delhi: Rupa and Company, 2005), 158.

70 The literature on this topic is extensive. See Zoltan Acs, How Is Entrepreneurship Good for Economic Growth? *Innovations*, Winter (2006), 97–107; John McMillan and Christopher

Woodruff, The Central Role of Entrepreneurs in Transition Economies, *Journal of Economic Perspectives*, 16, 3 (2002), 153–170; Carl Schramm, Building Entrepreneurial Economies, *Foreign Affairs*, 83, 4 (2004), 104–115; André Van Stel, Martin Carree, and Roy Thurik, The Effect of Entrepreneurial Activity on National Economic Growth, *Small Business Economics*, 24 (2005), 311–321.

71 David McClelland, *Human Motivation* (New York: Cambridge University Press, 1987), 255.

72 Robert E. Kennedy, The Protestant Ethic and the Parsis, *American Journal of Sociology*, 68, July, 11–20 (1962); though, after independence the role of the Parsis in government employment vanished overnight.

73 Francis Fukuyama, *The Great Disruption: Human Nature and the Reconstitution of Social Order* (New York: The Free Press, 1999), 69.

74 Fukuyama, *The Great Disruption*, 69.

75 Holton, *The Scientific Imagination*, 162.

76 Dwijendra Tripathi, Occupational Mobility and Entrepreneurship in India: A Historical Analysis, *The Developing Economies*, 19, 1 (1981), 52–67.

77 David Audretsch, The Entrepreneurial Society, *Journal of Technology Transfer*, 34, 3 (2009), 245–254.

78 Nathaniel Leff, Entrepreneurship and Economic Development: The Problem Revisited, *Journal of Economic Literature*, 17, March (1979), 46–64.

79 William J. Baumol, *Entrepreneurship, Management and the Structure of Payoffs* (Cambridge, MA: MIT Press, 1993), 2.

80 Israel Kirzner, *Perception, Opportunity and Profit* (University of Chicago Press, 1979), 7–8.

81 Holton, *The Scientific Imagination*, 163.

82 Tripathi, Occupational Mobility and Entrepreneurship in India, 66.

83 See the fifth anniversary edition of C. K. Prahalad, *The Fortune at the Bottom of the Pyramid: Eradicating Poverty through Profits* (Philadelphia, PA: Wharton School Publishing, 2009), 20–23.

84 Prahalad, *The Fortune at the Bottom of the Pyramid*, preface.

85 I am grateful to Mr. M. S. Krishnamoorthy, a 40-plus-year veteran of corporate India, for extensive discussion of these ideas and his insights into the behavior of those operating at the grassroots of Indian industry.

86 Thorstein Veblen, Why is Economics not an Evolutionary Science? *Quarterly Journal of Economics*, 12, July (1898), 373–397.

87 Peter Lewin, *Capital in Disequilibrium: The Role of Capital in a Changing World* (New York: Routledge, 1999), 30–31.

88 Lewin, *Capital in Disequilibrium*, 34.

89 Brian Loasby, *Equilibrium and Evolution: An Exploration of Connecting Principles in Economics* (Manchester University Press, 1991), 59.

90 Loasby, *Equilibrium and Evolution*, 60.

91 Abhijit Banerjee and Esther Duflo, *Poor Economics: A Radical Rethinking of the Way to Fight Global Poverty* (New York: Public Affairs, 2011), 206.

92 Emerging markets are now used to developing novel products usable across the world, in a process termed reverse innovation by multinational companies. See Jeffrey Immelt, Vijay Govindarajan and Chris Trimble, How GE is Disrupting Itself, *Harvard Business Review*, 87, 10 (2009), 55–65.

93 Kamal Nath, *India's Century: The Age of Entrepreneurship in the World's Biggest Democracy* (New Delhi: Tata McGraw Hill, 2007), 3–5.

94 See the article I-M-Mobile, *Mumbai Mirror*, Sunday, January 2, 2011, 6.

95 Sen, *Development as Freedom*, 17.

96 Kenneth Clark, *Civilization* (London: BBC Books, 1969), 344–347, described the dark ages as times when isolation, lack of mobility and curiosity, and hopelessness destroyed the human spirit.

97 Venkatachar, *Witness to the Century*, 319.

98 Thorstein Veblen, *The Engineers and the Price System* (Kitchener, Ont: Batoche Books, 2001 [originally published, 1921]), 22.

99 Jawaharlal Nehru, *Toward Freedom: An Autobiography* (New York: John Day, 1941), 274–275.

100 The cathedral and the bazaar comparisons relate to two distinct modes of software development, as documented in an influential article by Eric Raymond. In the cathedral style of functioning, centralized and top-down development of software leads to releases, as and when destined, by a software development giant with a motivation to monopolize the market. In the bazaar model, specifically based around the case of the Linux operating system for computers, development is carried out by thousands of freelance coders and developers around the world, connected only by the Internet, who would voluntarily contribute to the common good by their efforts. See Eric Raymond, *The Cathedral and the Bazaar* (Thyrsus Enterprises [www.tuxedo.org/~esr/], 2000), 2–3.

101 Das, *India Unbound*, 91–92.

102 World Bank, *The East Asian Miracle: Economic Growth and Public Policy* (New York: Oxford University Press, 1993), 92–93.

103 Nandan Nilekani, *Imagining India: The Idea of a Renewed Nation* (New York, Penguin, 2008), 454.

104 Fyodor Dostoevsky, *Letters from the Underworld*, translated by C. J. Hogarth (London: J. M. Dent and Sons, 1913; first published 1864), 32.

105 Hughes, *The Vital Few*, 2.

106 Hughes, *The Vital Few*, 3.

107 Schelling, *Micromotives and Macrobehavior*, 14.

108 Friedrich Hayek, *Individualism and Economic Order* (University of Chicago Press, 1948), 6–7.

109 Samuel Bowles and Herbert Gintis, *Democracy and Capitalism: Property, Community, and the Contradictions of Modern Social Thought* (New York: Basic Books, 1987), 150.

110 Ball, *Critical Mass*, 36.

111 Government of India, *Entrepreneurship in India* (New Delhi: National Knowledge Commission, 2008).

112 Amar Bhide, *The Origin and Evolution of New Businesses* (New York: Oxford University Press, 2000), 90.

113 David Blanchflower and Andrew Oswald, What Makes an Entrepreneur? *Journal of Labor Economics*, 16, 1 (1998), 26–60.

114 Barton Hamilton, Does Entrepreneurship Pay? An Empirical Analysis of the Returns to Self-Employment, *Journal of Political Economy*, 108, 3 (2000), 604–631.

7   Contemporary India

1 Damodaran, *India's New Capitalists*, 110.

2 I owe the story of Videocon and the antecedents of its foray into the washing machines sector to Mr. L. Mansingh.

3 Kirzner, *Perception, Opportunity and Profit*, 148.

4 Vinod Nair, Sunil Mittal Speaking: I Started with a Dream, *Times of India*, December 22, 2002.
5 http://timesofindia.indiatimes.com/india/Reverse-brain-drain-in-India-has-begun-Khurshid-/articleshow/5762539.cms, accessed March 8, 2011.
6 www.sirisimpex.com, accessed March 8, 2011.
7 Damodaran, *India's New Capitalists*, 110.
8 www.divislabs.com/inside/aboutdivis.asp, accessed March 8, 2011.
9 Damodaran, *India's New Capitalists*, 111.
10 www.natcopharma.co.in/profile.html, accessed March 8, 2011.
11 www.bharatbiotech.com/cmd_prof.htm, accessed March 8, 2011.
12 Ashutosh Sheshabalaya, *Rising Elephant: The Growing Clash with India over White-Collar Jobs and Its Challenge to America and the World* (Monroe, ME: Common Courage Press, 2005), 68–69.
13 www.bharatbiotech.com/journey.htm, accessed March 8, 2011.
14 www.strandls.com/Company, accessed March 9, 2011.
15 www.shanthabiotech.com/history.htm, accessed March 9, 2011.
16 Sumit K. Majumdar, Innovation Capability and Globalization Propensity in India's Information Technology and Software Industry, *Information Technology and International Development*, 6, 4 (2010), 45–56.
17 http://en.wikipedia.org/wiki/Palani_G._Periyasamy, accessed March 8, 2011.
18 Damodaran, *India's New Capitalists*, 278.
19 www.agro-dutch.com/capability.htm, accessed March 8, 2011.
20 http://yourstory.in/entrepreneurs/youngturks-my-startup-story, accessed March 8, 2011.
21 See Todd H. Chiles, Christopher S. Tuggle, Jeffery S. McMullen, Leonard Bierman, and Daniel W. Greening, Dynamic Creation: Extending the Radical Austrian Approach to Entrepreneurship, *Organization Studies*, 31, 7 (2010), 7–46, for full details of the radical subjectivist approach to entrepreneurship.
22 George Shackle, *Time in Economics* (Amsterdam: North-Holland, 1958), 34.
23 Sumit K. Majumdar, Crowding Out! The Role of State Companies and the Dynamics of Industrial Competitiveness in India, *Industrial and Corporate Change*, 18, 1, 165–207 (2009).
24 Majumdar, Crowding Out!
25 The idea was developed by John Maynard Keynes, see *The General Theory of Employment, Interest and Money* (New York: Harcourt Brace, 1936); later extensions were developed by Milton Friedman, Comments on the Critics, *Journal of Political Economy*, 80 (1972), 906–950, and Benjamin Friedman, Crowding Out or Crowding In? Economic Consequences of Financing Government Deficits, *Brookings Papers on Economic Activity*, 3 (1978), 593–654.
26 Majumdar, Crowding Out!
27 Jean-Baptiste Say, *A Treatise on Political Economy or the Production, Distribution and Consumption of Wealth* (New York: Augustus M. Kelley, 1971; [first published 1803]).
28 In separate work I have also found that new firm entry has led to productivity growth in the manufacturing sector as a whole. See Sumit K. Majumdar, Private Enterprise Growth and Human Capital Productivity in India, *Entrepreneurship Theory and Practice*, 31, 6 (2007), 853–872.
29 Deane, *The First Industrial Revolution*, 1.
30 Sumit K. Majumdar, India Astride a Supply Side Revolution, *Hindu Business Line*, August 23, 2005; www.thehindubusinessline.in/2005/08/23/stories/2005082300271000.htm

31 Patel, *Rites of Passage*, 159.
32 Ian M. D. Little, Dipak Mazumdar and John M. Page, Jr., *Small Manufacturing Enterprises: A Comparative Analysis of India and Other Economies* (New York: Oxford University Press, 1987), 5.
33 This was the classification of micro, small and medium enterprises promulgated in the Micro, Small and Medium Enterprises Development Act, 2006, notified by a *Gazette of India* notification dated September 29, 2006, by the Ministry of Micro, Small and Medium Enterprises, Government of India.
34 The late Narasimha Raghunathan was the Development Commissioner for Small Sscale Industries, and wrote extensively on the subject in his memoirs; see N. Raghunathan, *Memories, Men and Matters* (Bombay: Bharatiya Vidya Bhavan, 1999), 294.
35 Patel, *Glimpses of Indian Economic Policy*, 64.
36 Raghunathan, *Memories, Men and Matters*, 295.
37 Raghunathan, *Memories, Men and Matters*, 295.
38 I owe insights on this topic to Mr. S. Rajgopal. Mr. Rajgopal, who retired as India's Cabinet Secretary, had earlier in his career been MSSIDC's Managing Director.
39 Mr. S. Rajgopal provided detailed insights on the company. See www.lupinworld.com/about_index.htm, accessed June 28, 2011.
40 Raghunathan, *Memories, Men and Matters*, 300; Government of India, *Report of the Expert Committee on Small Enterprises*, Mr. Abid Hussain, Chairman (New Delhi: Ministry of Micro, Small and Medium Enterprises, 1997).
41 The practice originated with the American mass-manufacturing system, so that managers would understand all of the technological functionalities, though the accidental by-product was to reduce workers to the status of interchangeable parts. See William Lazonick, *Competitive Advantage on the Shop Floor* (Cambridge, MA: Harvard University Press, 1990), 229.
42 Details of the Bharat Forge story were provided by Messrs. S. Mukherji and L. Mansingh.
43 Dipak Mazumdar and Sandip Sarkar, *Globalization, Labor Markets, and Inequality in India* (New York: Routledge, 2008), 223.
44 Gary Herrigel, *Industrial Constructions: The Sources of German Industrial Power* (Cambridge University Press, 1996), 1.
45 There are similar clusters in Germany. In the Remscheid and Slingen area of the Bergland there is a cutlery cluster; textiles, machinery, mechanical and optical equipment manufacturers are found in Württemberg, and toys, fine machinery, and weapons manufacturers are located at Thüringen. See Herrigel, *Industrial Constructions*, 15.
46 See the website: www.jaipurbearingcluster.com/report2.asp, accessed March 29, 2011.
47 www.jaipurbearingcluster.com/industrydetail.asp?mode=company&id=27&name=Manu Yantralaya (P) Ltd., accessed March 29, 2011.

8 The services sector debate

1 Devesh Kapur and Ravi Ramamurti, India's Emerging Competitive Advantage in Services, *Academy of Management Executive*, 15, 2 (2001), 20–33
2 India's first modern political economist, Justice Mahadev Govind Ranade, at one time a judge of the Bombay High Court, believed that the primary cause of poverty in India was the over-dependence of the economy on agriculture. See Ajit K. Dasgupta, *History of Indian Economic Thought* (London: Routledge, 1993), 11.

3 Hollis B. Chenery, Patterns of Industrial Growth, *American Economic Review*, 50, 4 (1960), 624–654.

4 Ejaz Ghani and Homi Kharas, The Service Revolution in South Asia: An Overview, in Ejaz Ghani (ed.), *The Service Revolution in South Asia* (New Delhi: Oxford University Press, 2010), 1–32.

5 A recent analysis of India's growth performance does not find that the services sector is significantly superior in contributing to overall growth, and that all sectors, agriculture, manufacturing and services, equally matter in influencing growth. See Nirvikar Singh, Services-Led Industrialization in India: Assessment and Lessons, in David O'Connor (ed.), *Industrial Development for the Twenty-First Century: Sustainable Development Perspectives* (New York: Orient Longman, 2008), 235–291.

6 Sukti Dasgupta and Ajit Singh, Will Services be the New Engine of Indian Economic Growth? *Development and* Change, 36, 6 (2005), 1035–1057.

7 William Baumol, The Macroeconomics of Unbalanced Growth: The Anatomy of Urban Crisis, *American Economic Review*, 57, 3 (1967), 415–426.

8 Sumit K. Majumdar, Hsihui Chang and Octavian Carare, General Purpose Technology Adoption and Firm Productivity: Evaluating Broadband Impact in the United States Telecommunications Industry, *Industrial and Corporate Change*, 19, 3 (2010), 641–674.

9 Andrew Liveris, *Make It in America: The Case for Re-inventing the Economy* (Hoboken, NJ: Wiley, 2011), 24–25.

10 Sumit K. Majumdar, Kenneth Simons, and Ashok Nag, Bodyshopping versus Offshoring Among Indian Software and Information Technology Firms, *Information Technology and Management*, 12, 1 (2011), 17–34; Sumit K. Majumdar, Bodyshopping versus Capability Leverage: On the Relationship between Foreign Trade and Wages for Pharmaceutical and Service Sector Firms in India, *Analytique*, 6, 6 (2010), 3–7.

11 Chanda, *Bound Together*, 293.

12 Majumdar, Innovation Capability and Globalization Propensity.

13 Paul Samuelson, International Trade and the Equalisation of Factor Prices, *Economic Journal*, June (1948), 163–184.

14 The literature on the distinction between goods and services is, surprisingly, slim. This is an anomaly that ought to be corrected since the issue of the role of services in an economy is so important. See Ravi Sarathy, Global Strategy in Service Industries, *Long Range Planning*, 27, 6 (1994), 115–124, still the most apposite piece on the subject.

15 See Rajiv D. Banker, Abraham Charnes, and William W. Cooper, Some Models for Estimating Technical and Scale Efficiencies in Data Envelopment Analysis, *Management Science*, 30, 9 (1984) 1078–1092, and Abraham Charnes, William W. Cooper, and Eduardo Rhodes, Measuring the Efficiency of Decision Making Units, *European Journal of Operations Research*, 2, 6 (1978), 429–444, for the original algorithms.

16 The foundations of DEA lie in two major algorithms. Using only observed output and input data, and without making any assumptions as to the nature of underlying technology or functional form, the DEA algorithm calculates an ex-post measure of the efficiency of each observation. This is accomplished by constructing an empirically based frontier, and by evaluating each observation against all others included in the data set. DEA has two properties relevant for the present study. First, it is a technique for comparative efficiency measurement. Each observation is evaluated against itself and all other observations. Thus, the efficiency of each observation, relative to all others in the data-set, can be estimated. Second, for each observation, a single efficiency statistic is calculated. This is a ratio measure of performance as to how efficient each observation was with regard to

converting a set of inputs jointly and simultaneously into a set of outputs. Readers wishing to learn more should see Peter W. Bauer, Recent Developments in the Econometric Estimation of Frontiers, *Journal of Econometrics*, 46 (1990), 39–56; Abraham Charnes, William W. Cooper, Arie Y. Lewin, and Lawrence M. Seiford, *Data Envelopment Analysis: Theory, Methodology and Applications* (Boston: Kluwer Academic Publishers, 1995); and Lawrence M. Seiford and Robert M. Thrall, Recent Developments in DEA: The Mathematical Programming Approach to Frontier Analysis, *Journal of Econometrics*, 46 (1990), 7–38. The DEA literature is now massive.

17 DEA has been very extensively used for macroeconomic comparisons, including those based on aggregate Indian data. The important thing is that the data be comparable whatever the item of analysis is. That, of course, depends on what is being compared. Then, conclusions drawn on those analyses are acceptable.

18 I obtained the values of these variables from the Reserve Bank of India Database on the Indian Economy.

19 Charnes *et al.*, *Data Envelopment Analysis*; Seiford and Thrall, Recent Developments in DEA.

20 Stephen Parente and Edward Prescott have also remarked that differences in international incomes are the consequences of differences in the knowledge that individual societies have applied to the production of goods and services, specifically with reference to the embodying of knowledge in production processes; Stephen Parente and Edward Prescott, *Barriers to Riches* (Cambridge, MA: MIT Press, 2002), 2.

21 These shares are still too high because if a large country with an extensive population is to succeed economically, a much larger part of the working force must eventually be employed outside agriculture where value additions are far greater. This is a theme of development economics since the late 1950s and had been articulated for India by Gunnar Myrdal; see Myrdal, *Asian Drama*, 164.

22 Adam Szirmai, *The Dynamics of Socio-economic Development* (Cambridge University Press, 2007), Table 3.8.

23 Ghani and Kharas, The Service Revolution in South Asia.

24 Census Bureau: http://dx.doi.org/10.1787/data-00048-en, Table 1351, Index of Industrial Production by Country; Bureau of Labor Statistics: www.bls.gov/fls/, Table 1348, Real Gross Domestic Product per Capita and per Employed Persons by Country.

25 These are strong results, since one is actually calculating the strength of the relationship between changes in one variable and changes in the other variable, and not estimating the relationship just between the levels of the variables. Very similar results are established in a more broad-based analysis of the inter-connections among several service activities and employment. Manufacturing, construction, and community, social, and personal services are the most important drivers of employment; see Sangeeta Chakravarty and Arup Mitra, Is Industry still the Engine of Growth? An Econometric Study of the Organized Sector Employment in India, *Journal of Policy Modeling*, 31 (2009), 22–35.

26 Amsden, *Asia's Next Giant*.

27 Larry Westphal, Industrial Policy in an Export-Propelled Economy: Lessons from South Korea's Experience, *Journal of Economic Perspectives*, 4, 3 (1990), 41–59.

28 Amsden, *Asia's Next Giant*, 172.

29 Amsden *Asia's Next Giant*, 159.

30 Prescott and Parente, *Barriers to Riches*, 4.

31 Yanrui Wu, Service Sector Growth in India and China: A Comparison, *China: An International Journal*, 5, 1 (2007), 137–154.

32 http://economictimes.indiatimes.com/news/international-business/
china-end-september-forex-reserves-top-3-2-trillion/articleshow/
10352712.cms
33 Szirmai, *The Dynamics of Socio-Economic Development*, Table 9.2.
34 The impact of China's manufacturing sector growth on other economies can be gauged by
the fact that between 2001 and 2010 the United States lost over 5 million manufacturing
jobs and shut 42,000 factories. See comments by Andrew Liveris, Chief Executive Officer
of Dow Chemical, highlighting contemporary corporate America's concerns; Liveris, *Make
It in America*, 11.
35 The gross national income per capita is the gross national income, converted to United States
$ using the World Bank Atlas method, divided by the mid-year population. Gross national
income is the sum of value-added by all resident producers, plus any product taxes, less subsidies, not included in the valuation of output, plus net receipts of primary income, compen-
sation of employees, and property income, from abroad. Gross national income, calculated in
national currency, is converted to United States $ at official exchange rates for comparisons
across economies, although an alternative rate is used when the official exchange rate is judged
to diverge by an exceptionally large margin from the rate actually applied in international
transactions. To smooth fluctuations in prices and exchange rates, a special method of conversion is used by the World Bank. This applies a conversion factor averaging the exchange
rate for a given year and the two preceding years, adjusted for differences in rates of inflation
between the country and through the year 2000 France, Germany, Japan, the United Kingdom
and the United States. From 2001, these countries include the euro area, Japan, the United
Kingdom, and the United States.
36 Rahul Jacob, Cheap China Goods Era Over – Li & Fung, *Financial Times*, March 24, 2011;
www.samachar.com/Cheap-China-goods-era-over – Li – Fung-ldyvLPdbgbg.html, accessed
24 March, 2011.
37 India's Export Surges 37.5 Percent to $246 Bn in 2010–11, www.samachar.com/Indias-
export-surges-375-percent-to-246-bn-in-201011-letwNrhdghg.html?source=recommended_
news, accessed April 19, 2011.
38 Jadunath Sarkar, *Economics of British India* (4th edn., Calcutta: M. C. Sarkar and Sons
(1917), 179.

9   A paean for manufacturing

1 Eamon Fingleton, *In Praise of Hard Industries: Why Manufacturing, not the Information
Economy, Is the Key to Economic Prosperity* (Boston: Houghton Mifflin, 1999), 5.
2 Rostow, *Theorists of Economic Growth*, 22.
3 Erik Reinert, *How Rich Countries Got Rich and Poor Countries Stay Poor* (New York:
Public Affairs, 2007), 74.
4 Chandler, *Scale and Scope*, 29.
5 Gavin Wright, The Origins of American Industrial Success, 1879–1940, *American Economic
Review*, 80 (1990), 651–668.
6 Hounshell, *From the American System to Mass Production*, 1.
7 Wright, The Origins of American Industrial Success.
8 Wright, The Origins of American Industrial Success.
9 Chandler, *The Visible Hand*, 3.
10 Tomlinson, *The Economy of Modern India*, 10.

11 Amsden defines capital widening as small and divisible additions embodying the same technology and capital-to-labor ratio, while capital deepening involves large and indivisible additions embodying new technology and a higher capital-to-labor ratio; See Amsden, *Asia's Next Giant*, 303–304.

12 Zinkin, *Development for a Free Asia*, 8.

13 Babbage, *On the Economy of Machinery*, 354.

14 Babbage, *On the Economy of Machinery*, 4.

15 Zinkin, *Development for a Free Asia*, 17.

16 Cipolla, *Guns, Sails and Empires*, 146.

17 Cameron, *A Concise Economic History of the World*, 167; Prasanta Chandra Mahalanobis had also noted that the industrial revolution in the Western countries and Japan was the outcome of social transformation and the scientific revolutions; see Rudra, *Prasanta Chandra Mahalanobis*, 226.

18 Veblen,*The Engineers and the Price System*, 22.

19 Patel, *Rites of Passage*, 169.

20 The empirical literature on this topic is equally supportive. Some of the pieces in support are: G. Andrew Bernat, Does Manufacturing Matter? A Spatial Econometric View of Kaldor's Laws, *Journal of Regional Science*, 36 (1996), 463–477; Bernard Fingleton and John S. L. McCombie, Increasing Returns and Economic Growth: Some New Evidence from Manufacturing from the European Union Regions, *Oxford Economic Papers*, 50, 89–105(1998).

21 Murray Weitzman, Recombinant Growth, *Quarterly Journal of Economics*, 113, 2 (1998), 331–360.

22 This key insight was formulated and popularized five decades ago by Wilfred Salter, *Productivity and Technical Change* (Cambridge University Press, 1960), 43–44; see Charles Kennedy and Anthony Thirlwall, Surveys in Applied Economics: Technical Change, *Economic Journal*, 82, 325 (1972), 12–72.

23 Lewin, *Capital in Disequilibrium* 111–112.

24 Albert Hirschman, *The Strategy of Economic Development* (New Haven, CT: Yale University Press, 1958), 5.

25 These ideas were developed by numerous individuals, starting with the work of John Maurice Clark, *Studies in the Economics of Overhead Costs* (University of Chicago Press, 1923), and in the modern literature have gained currency with the work of Paul Romer, Increasing Returns and Long Run Growth, *Journal of Political Economy*, 94, 5, 1002–1037 (1986) and Robert E. Lucas, On the Mechanics of Economic Development, *Journal of Monetary Economics*, 22 (1988), 3–42.

26 Marathe, *Regulation and Development*, 103–104.

27 Thorstein Veblen, *The Theory of Business Enterprise* (New York: Charles Scribner's Sons, 1904), 5–20.

28 Nayyar, Introduction.

29 Rudra, *Prasanta Chandra Mahalanobis*, 227.

30 Mokshagundam Visvesvaraya, *Reconstructing India* (London: P. S. King and Sons, 1920), 153.

31 Reinert, *How Rich Countries Got Rich*, 315.

32 John R. Hicks, *Essays in World Economics* (Oxford: Clarendon Press, 1959), 183–185.

33 Allyn Young, Increasing Returns and Economic Progress, *Economic Journal*, 38, 152 (1928), 527–542.

34 Arrow, The Economic Implications of Learning by Doing; Paul. A. David, *Technical Choice, Innovation and Economic Growth: Essays on American and British Experience in the Nineteenth Century* (New York: Cambridge University Press, 1975), 15.

35 Amsden, *Asia's Next Giant*, 153; a vigorous statement of the position was advanced by Nicholas Kaldor, *Causes of the Slow Rate of Economic Growth of the United Kingdom: An Inaugural Lecture* (Cambridge University Press, 1966), 289.

36 Kevin Murphy, Andrei Shleifer and Robert Vishny, Industrialization and the Big Push, *Journal of Political Economy*, 97, 5 (1989), 1003–1026; P. C. Mahalanobis thought that a big push was necessary to move society forward as a whole; the mechanism of such a big push could be the process of industrialization; that would be the key to a scientific and social revolution and for sustainable growth. See Rudra, *Prasanta Chandra Mahalanobis*, 226; I. G. Patel stated that "the central idea was that you needed to infuse modernity, technological change and efficiency all along the line and not just in a few export industries." See Patel, *Glimpses of Indian Economic Policy*, 21.

37 Lucas, On the Mechanics of Economic Development.

38 On this topic, Bhagwati has written: "By contrast, Rosenstein-Rodan focused on balanced growth in an ingenious argument for coordination of decentralized investment decisions, each held up in a Nash equilibrium but made feasible through governmentally contrived co-operative equilibrium: an idea that has now been elegantly formalized in a multiple-equilibrium framework by the economists Kevin Murphy, Andre Schleifer, and Robert Vishny." See Bhagwati, *India in Transition*, 52–53.

39 Paul N. Rosenstein-Rodan, The Problems of Industrialisation of Eastern and South-Eastern Europe, *Economic Journal*, 53, 2 (1943), 202–211.

40 Kennedy, *The Rise and Fall of the Great Powers*, 146.

41 Owen, *From Empire to Europe*, 14.

42 Owen, *From Empire to Europe*, 14.

43 Hughes, *The Vital Few*, 294.

44 Babbage, *On the Economy of Machinery*, 8.

45 Using a data set of United States manufacturers, Zvi Griliches studied the substitutability of physical capital and skilled labor versus that of physical capital and unskilled labor, finding that the latter was substitutable while the former was not; see Zvi Griliches, Capital–Skill Complementarity, *Review of Economics and Statistics*, 51, November (1969), 465–468; several other analyses support the hypotheses that capital and skills, and technology and skills, are complements. As an example, see Ann P. Bartel and Frank Lichtenberg, The Comparative Advantage of Educated Workers in Implementing New Technology, *Review of Economics and Statistics*, 69, February (1987), 1–11.

46 Claudia Goldin and Lawrence F. Katz, The Origins of Technology–Skill Complementarity, *Quarterly Journal of Economics*, 113 (1998), 693–732.

47 Goldin and Katz, The Origins of Technology–Skill Complementarity.

48 Timothy F. Bresnahan and Manuel Trajtenberg, General Purpose Technologies: "Engines of Growth"? *Journal of Econometrics*, 65, 1 (1995), 83–108.

49 Elnahan Helpman and Manuel Trajtenberg, Diffusion of General Purpose Technologies, in E. Helpman (ed.), *General Purpose Technologies and Economic Growth* (Cambridge MA: MIT Press, 1998), 85–119.

50 Lawrence F. Katz, Technological Change, Computerization and the Wage Structure, in Eric Brynjolfsson and Brian Kahin (eds.), *Understanding the Digital Economy* (Cambridge, MA: MIT Press, 2000), 217–244.

51 Walter W. Powell and Kaisa Snellman (2004): The Knowledge Economy, *Annual Review of Sociology*, 30, August (2004), 199–220.

52 Reinert, *How Rich Countries Got Rich*, 78.
53 Reinert, *How Rich Countries Got Rich*, 79.
54 Reinert, *How Rich Countries Got Rich*, 81.
55 Weightman, *The Industrial Revolutionaries*, 389–390.
56 Weightman, *The Industrial Revolutionaries*, 390.
57 Vere Gordon Childe, *Man Makes Himself* (London: Watts and Company, 1936), 234.
58 Childe, *Man Makes Himself*, 134.
59 Morishima, *Why Has Japan "Succeeded"?*, 83–84.
60 Gadgil and Guha, *Ecology and Equity*, 29.
61 Friedrich List also described the stages an economy must pass through, which were hunting, agriculture, agriculture plus manufacturing, and manufacturing plus commerce; see Dasgupta, *History of Indian Economic Thought*, 91.
62 Friedrich List, *The National System of Political Economy*, translated by Sampson S. Lloyd (London: Longmans, Green and Company, 1909 [first published 1841]), 108–110.
63 Liah Greenfeld, *The Spirit of Capitalism: Nationalism and Economic Growth* (Cambridge, MA: Harvard University Press, 2001), 203.
64 Weightman, *The Industrial Revolutionaries*, 387.
65 Weightman, *The Industrial Revolutionaries*, 7.
66 Dasgupta, *History of Indian Economic Thought*, 90.
67 Ranade, *Essays on Indian Economics*, 106.
68 Dasgupta, *History of Indian Economic Thought*, 91.
69 Geoffrey F. Hudson, *Europe and China: A Survey of Their Relations from the Earliest Times to 1800* (Boston: Beacon Press 1961 [originally published 1931]), 268.
70 David Glantz and Jonathan House, *When Titans Clashed: How the Red Army Stopped Hitler* (Lawrence: University Press of Kansas, 1995), 2.
71 Glantz and House, *When Titans Clashed*, 151.
72 Glantz and House, *When Titans Clashed*, 150.
73 Glantz and House, *When Titans Clashed*, 306.
74 Morishima, *Why Has Japan "Succeeded"?*, 135.
75 Brass, *The Politics of India since Independence*, 249.
76 Emile Benoit, Growth Effects of Defense in Developing Countries, *International Development Review*, 14, 1 (1972), 2–10.
77 Emile Benoit, Growth and Defense in Developing Countries, *Economic Development and Cultural Change*, 26 (1978), 271–280.
78 The literature is large and only a few items are listed. An item that suggests a negative finding is Jeffrey Kentor and Edward Kick, Bringing the Military Back In: Military Expenditures and Economic Growth, 1990 to 2003, *Journal of World-Systems Research*, 15, 2 (2008), 142–172; some items that suggest an equivocal finding or relationship, with causality going both from defense spending to positive economic growth, and positive economic growth spurring defense spending, are Abdur R. Chowdhury, Defense Spending and Economic Growth: A Causal Analysis, *Journal of Conflict Resolution*, 35 (1991), 80–97; Basudeb Biswas and Rati Ram, Military Expenditures and Economic Growth in Less Developed Countries: An Augmented Model and Further Evidence, *Economic Development and Cultural Change*, 34, 2 (1986), 361–372; Saadet Deger and Somnath Sen, Military Expenditures, Spin-Off and Economic Development, *Journal of Development Economics*, 13, August–October (1983), 67–83; and Jasen Castillo, Julia Lowell, Ashley J. Tellis, Jorge Munoz, and Benjamin Zycher, *Military Expenditures and Economic Growth* (Santa Monica, CA: Rand Corporation, 2001). A generally positive finding for richer countries was established by Peter C. Frederiksen and Robert E. Looney, Defense Expenditures

372 Notes to pages 255 to 262

and Economic Growth in Developing Countries, *Armed Forces and Society*, 9, Summer (1983), 633–645; Castillo *et al.*, *Military Expenditures and Economic Growth*, 95, state that large and fast-growing economies are likely to devote a larger share of their growing pool of resources to defense activities.

79 Emile Benoit has also suggested that the military system introduced both military personnel and civilians to important industrial and urban skills and attitudes. These included following and transmitting precise instructions, living and working by the clock, noticing and reading signs, spending and saving money, using transportation such as bicycles, motorcycles, cars, buses, boats, and planes, working with, repairing, and maintaining machinery, listening to radios and becoming interested in national and international news; see Emile Benoit, *Defense and Economic Growth in Developing Countries* (Lexington, MA: Lexington Books, 1973), 17.

80 Vernon W. Ruttan, *Is War Necessary for Economic Growth?* (New York: Oxford University Press, 2006) is a comprehensive statement of the positive outcomes of military research and procurement activities on civil sector development.

81 Ruttan, *Technology Growth and Development*, 547.

82 Waldemar Kaempffert, War and Technology, *American Journal of Sociology*, 46 (1941), 431–444.

83 Howard Rheingold, *Virtual Reality* (New York: Summit Books, 1991), 79–80.

84 Maryellen Kelley and Todd A. Watkins, In from the Cold: Prospects for the Conversion of the Defense Industrial Base, *Science*, 268, April 28, (1995), 525–532.

85 Kelley and Watkins, In from the Cold.

86 Hounshell, *From the American System to Mass Production*, 331–336.

87 Nathan Rosenberg, *Technology and American Economic Growth* (New York: Harper and Row, 1972), 92.

88 Ruttan, *Technology Growth and Development*, 426.

89 Joel Mokyr, *The Lever of Riches: Technological Creativity and Economic Progress* (New York: Oxford University Press, 1990), 136–137.

90 Ruttan, *Technology Growth and Development*, 432.

91 Hounshell, *From the American System to Mass Production*, 38.

92 Ruttan, *Technology Growth and Development*, 440.

93 Richard J. Samuels, *Rich Nation, Strong Army: National Security and the Technological Transformation of Japan* (Ithaca, NY: Cornell University Press, 1994), 79–83.

94 Ruttan, *Technology Growth and Development*, 549.

95 Samuels, *Rich Nation, Strong Army*, 18.

96 Ruttan, *Technology Growth and Development*, 549.

97 Ruttan, *Is War Necessary for Economic Growth?*, 114–129.

98 Morris, The Growth of Large Scale Industry.

99 Pacey, *Technology in World Civilization*, 144–145.

100 Pacey, *Technology in World Civilization*, 131.

101 Pacey, *Technology in World Civilization*, 125.

102 Pacey, *Technology in World Civilization*, 130.

103 The literature on spillovers is extremely large. See Susan Feinberg and Sumit K. Majumdar, Technology Spillovers from Foreign Direct Investment in the Indian Pharmaceutical Industry, *Journal of International Business Studies*, 32, 3 (2001), 421–438, for an assessment of why spillovers occur or do not occur in India.

104 Shrinagesh, *Between Two Stools*, 122.

105 Shrinagesh, *Between Two Stools*, 122.

106 Shrinagesh, *Between Two Stools*, 123.
107 Shrinagesh, *Between Two Stools*, 123.
108 Shrinagesh, *Between Two Stools*, 126.

10   Reindustrializing India

1 Braudel, *A History of Civilizations*, 374.
2 Ruttan, *Technology Growth and Development*, 247.
3 David E. Nye, *Electrifying America: Social Meanings of a New Technology, 1880–1940* (Cambridge, MA: MIT Press, 1990), 193–194.
4 Sam H. Schurr, Energy, Technological Change and Productive Efficiency: An Economic-Historical Interpretation, *Annual Review of Energy*, 9 (1984), 409–425; Ruttan, *Technology Growth and Development*, 253.
5 Ruttan, *Technology Growth and Development*, 254.
6 Some of the items in the literature finding the positive correlations are: Alfred E. Musson, Industrial Motive Power in the United Kingdom, 1800–70, *Economic History Review*, 29, 3 (1976), 415–439; John A. Mathews, Energizing Industrial Development, *Transnational Corporations*, 17, 3 (2008), 59–84; Ernst Worrell, Lynn Price, Nathan Martin, Jacco Farla, and Roberto Schaeffer, Energy Intensity in the Iron and Steel Industry: A Comparison of Physical and Economic Indicators, *Energy Policy*, 25, 7–9 (1997), 727–744; B. Sudhakara Reddy and Binay Kumar Ray, Decomposition of Energy Consumption and Energy Intensity in Indian Manufacturing Industries, *Energy for Sustainable Development*, 14, 1 (2010), 35–47; Renuka Mahadevan and John Asafu-Adjaye, Energy Consumption, Economic Growth and Prices: A Reassessment Using Panel VECM for Developed and Developing Countries, *Energy Policy*, 35, 4 (2007), 2481–2490; Odile Blanchard, Energy Consumption and Modes of Industrialization: Four Developing Countries, *Energy Policy*, 20, 12 (1992), 1174–1185; Gregory Clark and David Jacks, Coal and the Industrial Revolution, 1700–1869, *European Review of Economic History*, 11, 1 (2007), 39–72.
7 Government of India, *The National Strategy for Manufacturing* (New Delhi: National Manufacturing Competitiveness Council, 2006), 33.
8 Sidney Pollard and Paul Robertson, *The British Shipbuilding Industry: 1870–1914* (Cambridge, MA: Harvard University Press, 1979), 129.
9 Pollard and Robertson, *The British Shipbuilding Industry*, 121.
10 Morris, The Growth of Large Scale Industry.
11 I thank Mr. S. Rajgopal, who was also India's Power Secretary, for his insights.
12 Chiles *et al.*, Dynamic Creation.
13 I am grateful to Jagdish Khattar for long conversations in May 2010 and May 2011.
14 Our family's 1972 model Premier President, the renamed Fiat 1100D, was once extensively treated at one of these workshops, and my grandmother's 1951 Austin A40 Devon regularly used to have its gearbox remanufactured at another similar establishment. Since parts from Britain had ceased coming to India in the 1950s, between the 1960s and the mid 1990s, when the car was in the family, numerous Austin A40 mechanical parts had been made and remade in Romesh Mitter Road in Calcutta.
15 John Hamm, Why Entrepreneurs Don't Scale, *Harvard Business Review*, 80, 12 (2002), 110–115.
16 Costas Markides and Paul Geroski, Colonizers and Consolidators: The Two Cultures of Corporate Strategy, *Strategy+Business*, 32, autumn (2003), 1–11.

17 Gary Loveman and Werner Sengenberger, The Re-emergence of Small-scale Production: An International Comparison, *Small Business Economics*, 3, 1 (1991), 1–37.

18 The first full analysis of the phenomenon was by Rayaproulu Nagaraj, Sub-contracting in Indian Manufacturing Industries: Analysis, Evidence and Issues, *Economic and Political Weekly*, 19, August (1984), 1435–1453.

19 Inge Ivarsson and Claes G. Alvstam, International Technology Transfer through Local Business Linkages: The Case of Volvo Trucks and their Domestic Suppliers in India, *Oxford Development Studies*, 32, 2 (2004), 241–260.

20 I thank Mr. Subramaniam Ramamoorthi, a former Chief Secretary to the Government of Maharashtra, who was Textiles Commissioner of the Government of India during the time when industry restructuring occurred, for his textiles sector insights.

21 Luce, *In Spite of the Gods*, 51–53.

22 Luce, *In Spite of the Gods*, 53.

23 Luce, *In Spite of the Gods*, 54.

24 Pranab Bardhan, *Awakening Giants, Feet of Clay: Assessing the Economic Rise of India and China* (Princeton University Press, 2010), 7.

25 Karl Marx, *Capital*, vol. 1 (Harmondsworth: Penguin, 1976 [first published 1867]), 928.

26 Arthur Okun, *Equality and Efficiency: The Big Tradeoff* (Washington, DC: The Brookings Institution, 1975), 4.

27 See the website www.spxindia.org/index.htm, accessed March 29, 2011.

28 The SPX has physical facilities which are co-located with other industry-promoting bodies. In Madras, the SPX is located within the MSME offices. In Poona, the SPX is located within the premises of the Confederation of Indian Industry (CII) and in national capital region the SPX center is located within the CII premises in Gurgaon.

29 Daniel Spulber, *Market Microstructure: Intermediaries and the Theory of the Firm* (New York: Cambridge University Press, 1999), 4.

30 Morris, The Growth of Large Scale Industry.

31 I thank two of India's information technology sector's pioneers, Mr. S. Rajgopal and Mr. F. C. Kohli, for detailed insights. Mr. Faqir Chand Kohli was the founder of Tata Consultancy Services, the company that spearheaded India's drive to be a world supplier of software services.

32 See the website www.softwaretop100.org/global-software-top-100-edition-2010. I am indebted to my co-author, Dr. Ashok Nag, for these facts. Also see his blog on the topic, www.blog.ashoknag.com.

33 Majumdar *et al.*, Bodyshopping versus Offshoring.

34 There is an extensive ecosystem of agents based overseas, in locations such as Australia, Britain, and the United States, who physically import individuals from India as economic migrants. These migrants carry out low-wage tasks in foreign locations. Bodyshopping also refers to this process. For a full description, see Biao Xiang, *Global "Body Shopping": An Indian Labor System in the Information Technology Industry* (Princeton University Press, 2007), 4. Our analysis involved the assessment of the activities of Indian information technology companies, and not of these Indian information technology labor contractors.

35 Jagdish Bhagwati, Splintering and Disembodiment of Services and Developing Nations, *World Economy*, 7, 2 (1984), 133–143.

36 Fernand Braudel, *The Perspective of the World* (Berkeley: University of California Press, 1984), 520–521.

37 A company like Infosys, which in 1989 had annual revenues of $1 million, has current annual revenues of over $5 billion today. See Michael Schuman, *The Miracle: The Epic Story of Asia's Quest for Wealth* (New York: HarperCollins, 2009), 33.

38 Gabriel Bitran and Maureen Lojo, A Framework for Analyzing Service Operations, *European Management Journal*, 11, 3 (1993), 271–282.

39 Sarathy, Global Strategy in Service Industries.

40 Michael Cusumano, *The Business of Software: What Every Manager, Programmer, and Entrepreneur Must Know to Thrive and Survive in Good Times and Bad* (New York: The Free Press, 2004), 29.

41 Ashish Arora, V. S. Arunachalam, Jai Asundi, and Ronald Fernandes, The Indian Software Services Industry, *Research Policy*, 30, (2001), 1267–1287.

42 The useful definition of information goods is by Hal Varian and Carl Shapiro, *Information Rules* (Boston: Harvard Business School Press, 1999), 5.

43 Cusumano, *The Business of Software*, 36.

44 Howard Baetjer, *Software as Capital: An Economic Perspective on Software Engineering* (Piscataway, NJ: Wiley-IEEE, 1997), 11.

45 John Zysman, Transforming Production in a Digital Era, in William Dutton, Brian Kahin, Ramon O'Callaghan and Andrew Wyckoff (eds.), *Transforming Enterprise* (Cambridge, MA: MIT Press, 2004), 257–282.

46 The list is available at www.softwaretop100.org/global-software-top-100-edition-2010

47 Anthony P. D'Costa, Uneven and Combined Development: Understanding India's Software Exports, *World Development*, 13, 1 (2003), 211–226.

48 Comments made by Sudipto Deb at a meeting in New Delhi, May 2011.

49 Michael Hobday, East versus Southeast Asian Innovation Systems: Comparing OEM- and TNC-led Growth in Electronics, in Linsu Kim and Richard Nelson (eds.), *Technology, Learning and Innovation: Experiences of Newly Industrializing Economies* (Cambridge University Press, 2000), 129–169.

50 Sheshabalaya, *Rising Elephant*, 88; see the websites www.tallysolutions.com/website/html/products.php and www.puncom.com/Aboutus.htm; accessed May 24, 2011.

51 Sheshabalaya, *Rising Elephant*, 89–90; see the websites www.sankhya.net/, and www.geometricglobal.com/Services+and+Products/index.aspx; accessed May 24, 2011.

52 IBM had also tried developing a similar application but failed to then implement it because of high bandwidth requirements, which limited deployment in the Indian environment.

53 I am grateful to Dr. Ashok Nag for details of the FT and MCX story.

54 Vibha Pingle, *Rethinking the Developmental State: India's Industry in Comparative Perspective* (New Delhi: Oxford University Press, 2000), 173.

55 Cusumano, *The Business of Software*, 10.

56 Wickham Skinner, Manufacturing: Missing Link in Corporate Strategy, *Harvard Business Review*, May–June (1969), 136–145.

57 Wickham Skinner, Three Yards and a Cloud of Dust: Industrial Management at Century End, *Production and Operations Management*, 5, 1 (1996), 15–24.

58 Some of these advanced manufacturing concepts or techniques listed by Wickham Skinner in Three Yards and a Cloud of Dust, were activity based costing, agile manufacturing, benchmarking, computer aided design, computer aided manufacturing, cellular manufacturing, computer integrated manufacturing, concurrent engineering, design for manufacturability, doctrine of continuous empowerment, flexible manufacturing, flexible machining system, group technology, just in time inventory and flow management, lean manufacturing,

product realization management, quality circles, re-engineering, time based management, total quality management, value analysis, and zero defects program.

59 Andrew McAfee, Mastering the Three Worlds of Information Technology, *Harvard Business Review*, November (2006), 141–149.
60 Robert Skidelsky, *The World after Communism: A Polemic for Our Times* (London: Papermac, 1995), 125.
61 Richard Florida, The New Industrial Revolution, *Futures*, July–August (1991), 559–576.
62 Carliss Y. Baldwin and Kim B. Clark, Managing in the Age of Modularity, *Harvard Business Review*, 75, 5, September–October (1997), 84–93.
63 Nicholas Crafts, Steam as a General Purpose Technology: A Growth Accounting Perspective, *Economic Journal* 114, 495 (2004), 338–351; Majumdar *et al.*, General Purpose Technology Adoption and Firm Productivity.
64 Timothy F. Bresnahan, Computerization and Wage Dispersion: An Analytical Interpretation, *Economic Journal*, 109, 456 (1999), 390–415.
65 Thomas Malone and Robert Laubacher, The Dawn of the E-Lance Economy, *Harvard Business Review*, September–October, 145–152 (1998).
66 Meier, *Biography of a Subject*, 70.
67 The use of detailed pre-production planning and specifications sheets has a long history in mass manufacturing. In the sewing machine industry, several companies instituted operations sheets in which all operations were listed along with the equipment required so that work could be followed and materials moved faster; see Hounshell, *From the American System to Mass Production*, 82. Similarly, Singer Sewing Machine Company instituted a system called the Blue Book which laid out all the machining operations and work-flow routes; see Ruttan, *Technology Growth and Development*, 433.
68 Ashish Nandy, *Traditions, Tyranny and Utopias: Essays in the Politics of Awareness* (New Delhi: Oxford University Press, 1992), 23.
69 John Strachey, *India: Its Administration and Progress* (3rd edn., London: Macmillan, 1903), 5.
70 Government of India, *Automotive Mission Plan, 2006–2016: A Mission for Development of Indian Automotive Industry* (New Delhi: Ministry of Heavy Industry and Public Enterprises, 2006).
71 The large number of cars on India's roads have created considerable congestion. On a recent trip to Bombay, I counted 30 models of car on Bombay's roads in the course of a 20-minute journey. I did not note a single Ambassador, though I did note one Fiat 1100 of 1961 vintage. India's giant roads and infrastructure deficit issues, however, deserve a separate book.
72 Government of India, *Automotive Mission Plan*.
73 Setright, *Drive On*, 226.
74 Thakurdas *et al.*, *A Plan of Economic Development for India*, 9.
75 Robert Fogel, *Railroads and American Economic Growth* (Baltimore, MD: Johns Hopkins University Press, 1964), 234–236.
76 Cited in Sarkar, *Modern India*, 407.
77 Bendix, *Work and Authority in Industry*, 206–207.

Bibliography

Abramovitz, M., Resource and Output Trends in the United States since 1870, *American Economic Review*, 46, 2 (1956), 5–23
    Catching Up, Forging Ahead, and Falling Behind, *Journal of Economic History*, 46, 2 (1986), 385–406
Acs, Z., How Is Entrepreneurship Good for Economic Growth? *Innovations*, Winter (2006), 97–107
Adams, B., *The Law of Civilization and Decay*, London: S. Sonnenschein and Company (1895)
Ahluwalia, I. J., *Industrial Growth in India: Stagnation since the Mid-Sixties*, New Delhi: Oxford University Press (1985)
Akerlof, G. and R. Shiller, *Animal Spirits*, Princeton University Press (2009)
Allen, C., *In Search of the Buddha: The Men Who Discovered India's Lost Religion*, New York: Carroll and Graf (2002)
Allen, R. C., Why the Industrial Revolution Was British: Commerce, Induced Invention, and the Scientific Revolution, *Economic History Review*, 64, 2 (2011), 357–384
Amable, B., *The Diversity of Capitalism*, New York: Oxford University Press (2003)
Amsden, A. H., *Asia's Next Giant: South Korea and Late Industrialization*, New York: Oxford University Press (1989)
    Diffusion of Development: The Late-Industrializing Model and Greater East Asia, *American Economic Review*, 81, 2 (1991), 282–286
Amsden, A. H. and W.-W. Chu, *Beyond Late Development: Taiwan's Upgrading Policies*, Cambridge, MA: MIT Press (2003)
Argote, L. and D. Epple, Learning Curves in Manufacturing, *Science*, 247, February (1990), 20–24
Arora, A., V. S. Arunachalam, J. Asundi, and R. Fernandes, The Indian Software Services Industry, *Research Policy*, 30 (2001), 1267–1287
Arrow, K., The Economic Implications of Learning by Doing, *Review of Economic Studies*, 29 (1962), 155–173
Ashton, T. S., *The Industrial Revolution, 1760–1830*, Oxford University Press (1948)

Audretsch, D., The Entrepreneurial Society, *Journal of Technology Transfer*, 34, 3 (2009), 245–254

Babbage, C., *On the Economy of Machinery and Manufactures*, London: James Murray (1832 [first published 1816])

Baetjer, H., *Software as Capital: An Economic Perspective on Software Engineering*, Piscataway, NJ: Wiley-IEEE (1997)

Bagchi, A. K., *Private Investment in India: 1900–1939*, Cambridge University Press (1972)

The Political Economy of Underdevelopment, Cambridge University Press (1982)

Colonialism and Indian Economy, New Delhi: Oxford University Press (2010)

Bairoch, P., International Industrialization Levels from 1750 to 1980, *Journal of European Economic History*, 11 (1982), 269–334

Baldwin, C. Y. and K. B. Clark, Managing in the Age of Modularity, *Harvard Business Review*, 75, 5, September–October (1997), 84–93

Ball, P., *Critical Mass: How One Thing Leads to Another*, London: Arrow Books (2004)

Banerjee, A. and E. Duflo, *Poor Economics: A Radical Rethinking of the Way to Fight Global Poverty*, New York: Public Affairs (2011)

Banker, R. D., A. Charnes, and W. W. Cooper, Some Models for Estimating Technical and Scale Efficiencies in Data Envelopment Analysis, *Management Science*, 30, 9 (1984), 1078–1092

Bardhan, P. K., *Awakening Giants, Feet of Clay: Assessing the Economic Rise of India and China*, Princeton University Press (2010)

Barnett, C. *The Lost Victory: British Dreams, British Realities, 1945–1950*, London: Pan Books (1995)

Barro, R., *The Determinants of Economic Growth: A Cross-Country Empirical Study*, Cambridge, MA: MIT Press (1997)

Bartel, A. P. and F. Lichtenberg, The Comparative Advantage of Educated Workers in Implementing New Technology, *Review of Economics and Statistics*, 69, February (1987), 1–11

Bartlett, C. and S. Ghoshal, *Managing across Borders: The Transnational Solution*, Boston: Harvard Business School Press (1989)

Bauer, P. T., *Economic Analysis and Policy in Underdeveloped Countries*, Cambridge University Press (1957)

Bauer, P. W., Recent Developments in the Econometric Estimation of Frontiers, *Journal of Econometrics*, 46 (1990), 39–56

Baumol, W. J., The Macroeconomics of Unbalanced Growth: The Anatomy of Urban Crisis, *American Economic Review*, 57, 3 (1967), 415–426

Entrepreneurship, Management and the Structure of Payoffs, Cambridge, MA: MIT Press (1993)

Bayly, C. A., *Indian Society and the Making of the British Empire*, Cambridge University Press (1988)

Beames, J., *Memoirs of a Bengal Civilian*, London: Chatto and Windus (1961; republished 1984 by Eland Publishing)

Bendix, R., *Work and Authority in Industry: Ideologies of Management in the Course of Industrialization*, New York: John Wiley (1956)

Benoit, E., Growth Effects of Defense in Developing Countries, *International Development Review*, 14, 1 (1972), 2–10

Defense and Economic Growth in Developing Countries, Lexington, MA: Lexington Books (1973)

Growth and Defense in Developing Countries, *Economic Development and Cultural Change*, 26 (1978), 271–280

Berna, J., Patterns of Entrepreneurship in South India, *Economic Development and Cultural Change*, 7, 3 (1959), 349–354

Bernat, G. A., Does Manufacturing Matter? A Spatial Econometric View of Kaldor's Laws, *Journal of Regional Science*, 36 (1996), 463–477

Betta, C., From Orientals to Imagined Britons: Baghdadi Jews in Shanghai, *Modern Asian Studies*, 37, 4 (2003), 999–1023

Bhagwati, J. N., Splintering and Disembodiment of Services and Developing Nations, *World Economy*, 7, 2 (1984), 133–143

Poverty and Public Policy, *World Development*, 14, 5 (1988), 538–555

India in Transition: Freeing the Economy, New York: Oxford University Press (1993)

Bhide, A., *The Origin and Evolution of New Businesses*, New York: Oxford University Press (2000)

Bhoothalingam, S., *Reflections on an Era: Memoirs of a Civil Servant*, Madras: Affiliated East–West Publishers (1993)

Blackford, M. G., *A History of Small Business in America*, 2nd edn., Chapel Hill: University of North Carolina Press (2003)

Biswas, B. and R. Ram, Military Expenditures and Economic Growth in Less Developed Countries: An Augmented Model and Further Evidence, *Economic Development and Cultural Change*, 34, 2, 361–372 (1986)

Bitran, G. and M. Lojo, A Framework for Analyzing Service Operations, *European Management Journal*, 11, 3 (1993), 271–282

Blanchard, O., Energy Consumption and Modes of Industrialization: Four Developing Countries, *Energy Policy*, 20, 12 (1992), 1174–1185

Blanchflower, D. and A. J. Oswald, What Makes an Entrepreneur? *Journal of Labor Economics*, 16, 1 (1998), 26–60

Bowen, H. V., *The Business of Empire: The East India Company and Imperial Britain*, Cambridge University Press (2006)

Bowles, S. and H. Gintis, *Democracy and Capitalism: Property, Community, and the Contradictions of Modern Social Thought*, New York: Basic Books (1987)

Brass, P., *The Politics of India since Independence*, Cambridge University Press (1990)

Braudel, F., *The Wheels of Commerce*, New York: Harper and Row (1979)

The Perspective of the World, Berkeley: University of California Press (1984)

A History of Civilizations, London: Penguin Books (1993 [first published 1963])

Brendon, P., *The Decline and Fall of the British Empire, 1781–1997*, London: Vintage Books (2007)

Brenner, R., *Betting on Ideas: Wars, Invention, Inflation*, University of Chicago Press (1985)

Bresnahan, T. F., Computerization and Wage Dispersion: An Analytical Interpretation, *Economic Journal*, 109, 456 (1999), 390–415

Bresnahan, T. F. and M. Trajtenberg, General Purpose Technologies: "Engines of Growth"? *Journal of Econometrics*, 65, 1 (1995), 83–108

Brimmer, A. F., The Setting of Entrepreneurship in India, *Quarterly Journal of Economics*, 69, 4 (1955), 357–376

Buchanan, D. H., *The Development of Capitalist Enterprise in India*, New York: Macmillan (1934)

Burke, S. M. and S. A. Quraishi, *The British Raj in India: An Historical Review*, Karachi: Oxford University Press (1995)

Cameron, R., *A Concise Economic History of the World: From Paleolithic Times to the Present*, 3rd edn., New York: Oxford University Press (1997)

Cannadine, D., *Class in Britain*, London: Penguin Books (1998)

Casson, M., *Enterprise and Competitiveness*, Oxford: Clarendon Press (1990)

Castillo, J., J. Lowell, A. J. Tellis, J. Munoz, and B. Zycher, *Military Expenditures and Economic Growth*, Santa Monica, CA: Rand Corporation (2001)

Chakravarty, S. and A. Mitra, Is Industry still the Engine of Growth? An Econometric Study of the Organized Sector Employment in India, *Journal of Policy Modeling*, 31 (2009), 22–35

Chanda, N., *Bound Together: How Traders, Preachers, Adventurers and Warriors Shaped Civilization*, New Delhi: Penguin (2007)

Chandavarkar, R., Industrialization in India before 1947: Conventional Approaches and Alternative Perspectives, *Modern Asian Studies*, 19, 3 (1985), 623–668

The Origins of Industrial Capitalism in India: Business Strategies and the Working Classes in Bombay, 1900–1940, Cambridge University Press (1994)

Chandler, A. D. Jr., *The Visible Hand: The Managerial Revolution in American Business*, Cambridge, MA: Harvard University Press (1977) *Scale and Scope: The Dynamics of Industrial Capitalism*, Cambridge, MA: The Belknap Press of Harvard University Press (1990)

Chandra, B., M. Mukherjee, A. Mukherjee, K. N. Panikkar, and S. Mahajan, *India's Struggle for Independence*, New Delhi: Penguin (1987)

Chang, H.-J., *Kicking Away the Ladder: Development Strategy in Historical Perspective*, London: Anthem Press (2002)

Chapman, S., *Merchant Enterprise in Britain: From the Industrial Revolution to World War I*, Cambridge University Press (1992)

Charnes, A., W. W. Cooper, and E. Rhodes, Measuring the Efficiency of Decision Making Units, *European Journal of Operations Research*, 2, 6 (1978), 429–444

Charnes, A., W. W. Cooper, A. Y. Lewin, and L. M. Seiford, *Data Envelopment Analysis: Theory, Methodology and Applications*, Boston: Kluwer Academic Publishers (1995)

Chatterjee, P., *A Princely Impostor: The Strange and Universal History of the Kumar of Bhawal*, Princeton University Press (2002)

Chatterton, A., *Industrial Evolution in India*, Madras: The Hindu (1912)

Chaudhuri, K. N., Markets and Traders in India during the Seventeenth and Eighteenth Centuries, in K. N. Chaudhuri and C. J. Dewey (eds.), *Economy and Society: Studies in Indian Economic and Social History*, New York: Oxford University Press (1979), 143–162 *Asia before Europe*, Cambridge University Press (1990)

Chen, E. K. Y., *Hyper-growth in Asian Economies: A Comparative Study of Hong Kong, Japan, Korea, Singapore and Taiwan*, London: Macmillan (1979)

Chenery, H. B., Patterns of Industrial Growth, *American Economic Review*, 50, 4 (1960), 624–654

Chiang, M., *Tides from the West: A Chinese Autobiography*, New Haven, CT: Yale University Press (1947)

Childe, V. G., *Man Makes Himself*, London: Watts and Company (1936) Archaeological Ages as Technological Stages, *Journal of the Royal Anthropological Institute*, 74 (1944), 7–24

Chiles, T. H., C. S. Tuggle, J. S. McMullen, L. Bierman, and D. W. Greening, Dynamic Creation: Extending the Radical Austrian Approach to Entrepreneurship, *Organization Studies*, 31, 7 (2010), 7–46

Chowdhury, A. R., Defense Spending and Economic Growth: A Causal Analysis, *Journal of Conflict Resolution*, 35 (1991), 80–97

Cipolla, C., *Guns, Sails and Empires: Technological Innovation and the Early Phases of European Expansion, 1400–1700*, Manhattan, KS: Sunflower University Press (1965)

Clark, G., *A Farewell to Alms: A Brief Economic History of the World*, Princeton University Press (2007)

Clark, G. and D. Jacks, Coal and the Industrial Revolution, 1700–1869, *European Review of Economic History*, 11, 1 (2007), 39–72

Clark, J. M., *Studies in the Economics of Overhead Costs*, University of Chicago Press (1923)

Clark, K., *Civilization*, London: BBC Books (1969)

Crafts, N., Steam as a General Purpose Technology: A Growth Accounting Perspective, *Economic Journal*, 114, 495 (2004), 338–351

Cusumano, M., *The Business of Software: What Every Manager, Programmer, and Entrepreneur Must Know to Thrive and Survive in Good Times and Bad*, New York: The Free Press (2004)

Damodaran, H., *India's New Capitalists: Caste, Business, and Industry in a Modern Nation*, Ranikhet: Permanent Black (2008)

Das, G., *India Unbound: The Social and Economic Revolution from Independence to the Global Information Age*, London: Profile Books (2002)

Das, N., *Industrial Enterprise in India*, 2nd edn., Calcutta, Orient Longmans (1956)

Dasgupta, A. K., *History of Indian Economic Thought*, London: Routledge (1993)

Dasgupta, S., *The Bengal Renaissance: Identity and Creativity from Rammohun Roy to Rabindranath Tagore*, New Delhi: Permanent Black (2007)

Dasgupta, S. and A. Singh, Will Services Be the New Engine of Indian Economic Growth? *Development and Change*, 36, 6 (2005), 1035–1057

Datta, B., The Teaching of Economics in India, in C. T. Kurien, E. R. Prabhakar, and S. Gopal (eds.), *Economy, Society and Development*, New Delhi: Sage Publications (1991), 293–301.

David, P. A., *Technical Choice, Innovation and Economic Growth: Essays on American and British Experience in the Nineteenth Century*, New York: Cambridge University Press (1975)

Dayal, R., *A Life of Our Times*, London: Sangam Books (1998)

D'Costa, A. P., Uneven and Combined Development: Understanding India's Software Exports, *World Development*, 13, 1 (2003), 211–226

Deane, P., *The First Industrial Revolution*, 2nd edn., Cambridge University Press (1979)

Deger, S. and S. Sen, Military Expenditures, Spin-Off and Economic Development, *Journal of Development Economics*, 13, August–October (1983), 67–83

Desai, A. V., *The Price of Onions*, New Delhi: Penguin (1999)

Dewey, C. J., The Government of India's "New Industrial Policy," 1900–1925: Formation and Failure, in K. N. Chaudhuri and C. J. Dewey (eds.), *Economy and Society: Essays in Indian Economic and Social History*, New York: Oxford University Press (1979)

Digby, W., *"Prosperous" British India: A Revelation from Official Records*, London: Unwin (1901)

Dirks, N. B., *The Scandal of Empire: India and the Creation of Imperial Britain*, Cambridge, MA: Harvard University Press (2006)

Dollar, D. and K. Sokoloff, Patterns of Productivity Growth in South Korean Manufacturing, 1963–1979, *Journal of Development Economics*, 33, 2 (1990), 309–327

Dostoevsky, F., *Letters from the Underworld*, translated by C. J. Hogarth, London: J. M. Dent and Sons, (1913 [first published 1864])

Drummond, I., *British Economic Policy and the Empire, 1919–1939*, London: Allen and Unwin (1972)

Dutt, R. P., *India Today*, Bombay: People's Publishing House (1949 [first published 1940])

Dutt, R. C., *The Economic History of India*, vol. 1, *Under Early British Rule*, New Delhi: Publications Division (1960 [first published 1901])

   The Economic History of India, vol. 2, *In the Victorian Age, 1837–1900*, New Delhi: Publications Division (1960 [first published 1903])

Dutton, H. I., *The Patent System and Inventive Activity during the Industrial Revolution, 1750–1852*, Manchester University Press (1984)

Earle, T., *How Chiefs Come to Power: The Political Economy in Prehistory*, Stanford University Press (1997)

Easterly, W., *The Elusive Quest for Growth: Economists' Adventures and Misadventures in the Tropics*, Cambridge, MA: MIT Press (2001)

Ebenstein, A., *Friedrich Hayek: A Biography*, New York: Palgrave Macmillan (2001)

Ellis, H. S., Accelerated Investment as a Force in Economic Development, *Quarterly Journal of Economics*, 72, 4 (1958), 485–495

Eraly, A., *The Gem in the Lotus: The Seeding of Indian Civilization*, London: Phoenix (2000)

Eswaran, M. and A. Kotwal, *Why Poverty Persists in India: An Analytical Framework for Understanding the Indian Economy*, New Delhi: Oxford University Press (1994)

Evans, P., *Embedded Autonomy: States and Industrial Transformation*, Princeton University Press (1995)

Fagerberg, J., Technology and International Differences in Growth Rates, *Journal of Economic Literature*, 32 (1994), 1147–1175

Feinberg, S. and S. K. Majumdar, Technology Spillovers from Foreign Direct Investment in the Indian Pharmaceutical Industry, *Journal of International Business Studies*, 32, 3 (2001), 421–438

Fernandes, L., *India's New Middle Classes: Democratic Politics in an Era of Economic Reform*, Minneapolis: University of Minnesota Press (2006)

Fernandez-Armesto, F., *Civilizations*, London: Macmillan (2000)

Fingleton, B. and J. S. L. McCombie, Increasing Returns and Economic Growth: Some New Evidence from Manufacturing from the European Union Regions, *Oxford Economic Papers*, 50 (1998), 89–105

Fingleton, E., *In Praise of Hard Industries: Why Manufacturing, not the Information Economy, is the Key to Economic Prosperity*, Boston: Houghton Mifflin (1999)

Florida, R., The New Industrial Revolution, *Futures*, July–August (1991), 559–576

Fogel, R. W., *Railroads and American Economic Growth*, Baltimore, MD: Johns Hopkins University Press (1964)

Forbes, N., Doing Business in India: What Has Liberalization Changed? in A. O. Krueger (ed.), *Economic Policy Reforms and the Indian Economy*, New Delhi: Oxford University Press (2002), 129–167

Fraser, A. H. L., *Among Indian Rajahs and Ryots*, Philadelphia: J. B. Lippincott Company (1911)

Frederiksen, P. C. and R. E. Looney, Defense Expenditures and Economic Growth in Developing Countries, *Armed Forces and Society*, 9, Summer (1983), 633–645

French, P., *Liberty or Death: India's Journey to Independence and Division*, London: HarperCollins (1997)

Friedman, B., Crowding Out or Crowding In? Economic Consequences of Financing Government Deficits, *Brookings Papers on Economic Activity*, 3 (1978), 593–654

Friedman, M., Comments on the Critics, *Journal of Political Economy*, 80 (1972), 906–950

Friedman, M. and R. Friedman, *Two Lucky People: Memoirs*, University of Chicago Press (1998)

Fukuyama, F., *The Great Disruption: Human Nature and the Reconstitution of Social Order*, New York: The Free Press (1999)

Fruin, W. M., *The Japanese Enterprise System: Competitive Strategies and Cooperative Structures*, Oxford: Clarendon Press (1992)

Gadgil, D. R., *The Industrial Evolution of India in Recent Times*, 4th edn., Oxford University Press (1944)

Gadgil, M. and R. Guha, *Ecology and Equity: The Use and Abuse of Nature in Contemporary India*, New Delhi: Penguin Books (1995)

Gee, E. R., The History of Coal Mining in India, *Mining Engineer*, 6, 3 (1940), 313–318

Gerschenkron, A., *Economic Backwardness in Historical Perspective*, New York: Praeger (1965)

Europe in the Russian Mirror: Four Lectures in Economic History, New York: Cambridge University Press (1970)

Ghani, E. and H. Kharas, The Service Revolution in South Asia: An Overview, in E. Ghani (ed.), *The Service Revolution in South Asia*, New Delhi: Oxford University Press (2010), 1–32

Ghosh, S., Calcutta's Industrial Archaeology, in S. Chaudhuri (ed.), *Calcutta, The Living City*, vol. 1, *The Past*, New Delhi, Oxford University Press (1990), 246–255

Gladwell, M., *The Tipping Point: How Little Things Can Make a Big Difference*, Boston: Little, Brown (2000)

Glantz, D. and J. House, *When Titans Clashed: How the Red Army Stopped Hitler*, Lawrence: University Press of Kansas (1995)

Goldin, C. and L. F. Katz, The Origins of Technology–Skill Complementarity, *Quarterly Journal of Economics*, 113 (1998), 693–732

Gopal, S., *Modern India*, London: Historical Association (1967)

Goswami, O., Sahibs, Babus and Banias: Changes in Industrial Control in Eastern India, 1918–50, *Journal of Asian Studies*, 48, 2 (1989), 289–309

Government of India, *Report of the Monopolies Inquiry Commission*, Justice K. C. Dasgupta, ICS, Chairman, New Delhi: Ministry of Finance (1965)

Final Report on Industrial Planning and Licensing Policy, Dr. R. K. Hazari, Chairman, New Delhi: Planning Commission (1967)

Report of the Industrial Licensing Policy Inquiry Committee, Mr. S. Dutt, ICS, Chairman, New Delhi: Ministry of Industrial Development (1969)

Report of the Expert Committee on Small Enterprises, Mr. Abid Husain, Chairman, New Delhi: Ministry of Micro, Small and Medium Enterprises (1997)

Automotive Mission Plan, 2006–2016: A Mission for Development of Indian Automotive Industry, New Delhi: Ministry of Heavy Industry and Public Enterprises (2006)

The National Strategy for Manufacturing, New Delhi: National Manufacturing Competitiveness Council (2006)

Entrepreneurship in India, New Delhi: National Knowledge Commission (2008)

Handbook of Industrial Policy and Statistics, New Delhi: Department of Industrial Policy and Promotion, Ministry of Commerce and Industry (2009)

Handbook of Indian Statistics (New Delhi: Ministry of Statistics and Programme Implementation, 2011)

Greenfeld, L., *The Spirit of Capitalism: Nationalism and Economic Growth*, Cambridge, MA: Harvard University Press (2001)

Griffiths, P. J., *The British Impact on India*, London: Macdonald (1952)

Griliches, Z., Capital–Skill Complementarity, *Review of Economics and Statistics*, 51, November (1969), 465–468

Guha, A., The Comprador Role of Parsi Seths, 1750–1850, *Economic and Political Weekly*, November 28 (1970), 1933–1936

Guha, R., *India after Gandhi: The History of the World's Largest Democracy*. London: Macmillan (2007)

Hagen, E. E., *On the Theory of Social Change: How Economic Growth Begins*, Homewood, IL: Dorsey Press (1962)

Hall, B. H., The Financing of Research and Development, *Oxford Review of Economic Policy*, 18, 1 (2002), 35–51

Hamilton, B., Does Entrepreneurship Pay? An Empirical Analysis of the Returns to Self-Employment, *Journal of Political Economy*, 108, 3 (2000), 604–631

Hamm, J. Why Entrepreneurs Don't Scale, *Harvard Business Review*, 80, 12 (2002), 110–115

Hanson, A. H., *The Process of Planning: A Study of India's Five Year Plans, 1950–1964*, Oxford University Press (1966)

Hayami, Y. and V. W. Ruttan, *Agricultural Development: An International Perspective*, 2nd edn., Baltimore: Johns Hopkins University Press (1985)

Hayek, F. A., Socialist Calculation: The Competitive Solution, *Economica*, 7 (1940), 125–149

The Use of Knowledge in Society, *American Economic Review*, 35, 4 (1945), 519–530

Individualism and Economic Order, University of Chicago Press (1948)

The Road to Serfdom, 50th anniversary edn., University of Chicago Press (1994 [first published 1944])

Helpman, E. and M. Trajtenberg, Diffusion of General Purpose Technologies, in E. Helpman (ed.), *General Purpose Technologies and Economic Growth*, Cambridge MA: MIT Press (1998), 85–119

Herrigel, G., *Industrial Constructions: The Sources of German Industrial Power*, Cambridge University Press (1996)

Hicks, J. R., *The Theory of Wages*, London: Macmillan (1932)

Essays in World Economics, Oxford: Clarendon Press (1959)

Hikino, T. and A. H. Amsden, Staying Behind, Stumbling Back, Sneaking Up, Soaring Ahead: Late Industrialization in Historical Perspective, in W. J. Baumol, R. R. Nelson, and E. N. Wolff (eds.), *Convergence of Productivity: Cross-National Studies and Historical Evidence*, New York: Oxford University Press (1994), 285–315

Hirschman, A. O., *The Strategy of Economic Development*, New Haven, CT: Yale University Press (1958)

The Rhetoric of Reaction: Perversity, Futility, Jeopardy, Cambridge, MA: Harvard University Press (1991)

Hirschmeier, J. and T. Yui, *The Development of Japanese Business*, Cambridge, MA: Harvard University Press (1975)

Hirst, P. and J. Zeitlin, Flexible Specialization: Theory and Evidence in the Analysis of Industrial Change, in J. R. Hollingsworth and R. Boyer (eds.), *Contemporary Capitalism: The Embeddedness of Institutions*, Cambridge University Press, (1997), 220–239

Hobday, M., East Asian Latecomer Firms: Learning the Technology of Electronics, *World Development*, 23, 7 (1995), 1171–1193

East versus Southeast Asian Innovation Systems: Comparing OEM- and TNC-led Growth in Electronics, in L. Kim and R. Nelson (eds.), *Technology, Learning and Innovation: Experiences of Newly Industrializing Economies*, Cambridge University Press (2000), 129–169

Hobsbawm, E., *The Age of Revolution: 1789–1848*, London: Abacus (1962)

Industry and Empire: From 1750 to the Present Day, London: Pelican Books (1969)

The Age of Capital: 1848–1875, London: Abacus (1975)

The Age of Extremes: A History of the World, 1914–1991, New York: Vintage Books (1994)

Holton, G., *The Scientific Imagination*, Cambridge, MA: Harvard University Press (1998)

Hounshell, D., *From the American System to Mass Production, 1800–1932*, Baltimore: Johns Hopkins University Press (1984)

Hubbard, G. E., *Eastern Industrialization and Its Effect on the West*, London: Oxford University Press (1938)

Hudson, G. F., *Europe and China: A Survey of Their Relations from the Earliest Times to 1800*, Boston: Beacon Press (1961 [first published 1931])

Hughes, J. R. T., *The Vital Few: The Entrepreneur and American Economic Progress*, New York: Oxford University Press (1966)

Hutton, W., Interview, in R. English and M. Kenny (eds.), *Rethinking British Decline*, London: Macmillan (2000), 50–60

Immelt, J. R., V. Govindarajan, and C. Trimble, How GE is Disrupting Itself, *Harvard Business Review*, 87, 10 (2009), 55–65

Inkster, I., *Japanese Industrialization: Historical and Cultural Perspectives*, New York: Routledge (2001)

Ivarsson, I. and C. G. Alvstam, International Technology Transfer through Local Business Linkages: The Case of Volvo Trucks and their Domestic

Suppliers in India, *Oxford Development Studies*, 32, 2 (2004), 241–260

Jacob, M. C., *Scientific Culture and the Making of the Industrial West*, New York: Oxford University Press (1997)

The Cultural Foundations of Early Industrialization, in M. Berg and K. Bruland (eds.), *Technological Revolutions in Europe: Historical Perspectives*, Cheltenham: Edward Elgar (1998), 67–85

Jacobs, J., *The Nature of Economies*, New York: The Modern Library (2000)

Jalan, B., *India's Economic Crisis: The Way Ahead*, New Delhi: Oxford University Press (1991)

Jardine, L., *Worldly Goods: A New History of the Renaissance*, London: Macmillan (1996)

Johnson, C., *MITI and the Japanese Miracle*, Stanford University Press (1982)

Kaempffert, W., War and Technology, *American Journal of Sociology*, 46 (1941), 431–444

Kaldor, N., *Causes of the Slow Rate of Economic Growth of the United Kingdom: An Inaugural Lecture*, Cambridge University Press (1966)

Kamdar, M., *Planet India: The Turbulent Rise of the World's Largest Democracy*, New York: Pocket Books (2007)

Kapur, D. and R. Ramamurti, India's Emerging Competitive Advantage in Services, *Academy of Management Executive*, 15, 2 (2001), 20–33

Katz, L. F., Technological Change, Computerization and the Wage Structure, in E. Brynjolfsson and B. Kahin (eds.), *Understanding the Digital Economy*, Cambridge, MA: MIT Press (2000), 217–244

Keay, J., *India: A History*, New York: Grove Press (2000)

Kelley, M. and T. A. Watkins, In from the Cold: Prospects for the Conversion of the Defense Industrial Base, *Science*, 268, April 28 (1995), 525–532

Kennedy, C. and A. P. Thirlwall, Surveys in Applied Economics: Technical Change, *Economic Journal*, 82, 325 (1972), 12–72

Kennedy, P., *The Rise and Fall of the Great Powers: Economic Change and Military Conflict from 1500 to 2000*, New York: Random House (1987)

Kennedy, R. E., The Protestant Ethic and the Parsees, *American Journal of Sociology*, 68, July (1962), 11–20

Kentor, J. and E. Kick, Bringing the Military Back In: Military Expenditures and Economic Growth, 1990 to 2003, *Journal of World-Systems Research*, 15, 2 (2008), 142–172

Keynes, J. M., *The General Theory of Employment, Interest and Money*, New York: Harcourt Brace (1936)

Khan, B. Z. and K. L. Sokoloff, The Early Development of Intellectual Property Institutions in the United States, *Journal of Economic Perspectives*, 15, 3 (2001), 233–246

Institutions and Democratic Invention in Nineteenth-Century America, *American Economic Review*, 94, May (2004), 395–401

Kirzner, I., *Perception, Opportunity and Profit*, University of Chicago Press (1979)

Kohli, A., *State-Directed Development: Political Power and Industrialization in the Global Periphery*, New York: Cambridge University Press (2004)

Kohli, F. C., *The IT Revolution in India*, New Delhi: Rupa and Company (2005)

Kuznets, S., *Modern Economic Growth*, New Haven, CT: Yale University Press (1966)

Lal, D., *Unfinished Business: India in the World Economy*, New Delhi: Oxford University Press (1999)

Lala, R. M. *The Creation of Wealth*, New Delhi: Penguin Portfolio (2004)

Lall, S., Technological Capabilities and Industrialization, *World Development*, 20, 2 (1992), 165–186

Landes, D., *The Unbound Prometheus: Technological Change and Industrial Development in Western Europe from 1750 to the Present*, Cambridge, MA: Harvard University Press (1969)

The Wealth and Poverty of Nations: Why Some Are So Rich and Some So Poor, New York: W. W. Norton (1998)

Lawrence, P. R. and J. Lorsch, *Organization and Environment: Managing Differentiation and Integration*, Boston: Division of Research, Graduate School of Business Administration, Harvard University (1967)

Lazonick, W., *Competitive Advantage on the Shop Floor*, Cambridge, MA: Harvard University Press (1990)

Leff, N., Entrepreneurship and Economic Development: The Problem Revisited, *Journal of Economic Literature*, 17, March (1979), 46–64

Leonard, J. S., Carrots and Sticks: Pay, Supervision, and Turnover, *Journal of Labor Economics*, 5, 4 (1987), 136–152

Lewin, P., *Capital in Disequilibrium: The Role of Capital in a Changing World*, New York: Routledge (1999)

Lewis, J. P., *Quiet Crisis in India: Economic Development and American Policy*, Garden City, NY: Anchor Books (1964)

Lipset, S. M., The Social Requisites of Democracy Revisited, *American Sociological Review*, 59 (1994), 1–22

Lipson, E., *The Economic History of England*, vol. 3, London: A. & C. Black (1931)

List, F., *The National System of Political Economy*, translated by Sampson S. Lloyd, London: Longmans, Green and Company (1909 [first published 1841])

Little, I. M. D., D. Mazumdar, and J. M. Page, Jr., *Small Manufacturing Enterprises: A Comparative Analysis of India and Other Economies*, New York: Oxford University Press (1987)

Liveris, A., *Make It in America: The Case for Re-inventing the Economy*, Hoboken, NJ: Wiley (2011)

Loasby, B., *Equilibrium and Evolution: An Exploration of Connecting Principles in Economics*, Manchester University Press (1991)

Lockwood, W. W., *The Economic Development of Japan: Growth and Structural Change, 1868–1938*, Princeton University Press (1954)

Loveman, G. and W. Sengenberger, The Re-emergence of Small-scale Production: An International Comparison, *Small Business Economics*, 3, 1 (1991), 1–37

Lucas, R. E., On the Mechanics of Economic Development, *Journal of Monetary Economics*, 22 (1988), 3–42

Luce, E., *In Spite of the Gods: The Strange Rise of Modern India*. London: Little, Brown (2006)

Maddison, A., *Class Structure and Economic Growth: India and Pakistan since the Moghuls*, New York: Norton (1971)

　　Explaining the Economic Performance of Nations, 1820–1989, in W. J. Baumol, R. R. Nelson and E. N. Wolff (eds.), *Convergence of Productivity: Cross-National Studies and Historical Evidence*, New York: Oxford University Press (1994), 20–61

Magaziner, I. and M. Patinkin, Fast Heat: How Korea Won the Microwave War, *Harvard Business Review*, January–February (1989), 83–92

Mahadevan, R. and J. Asafu-Adjaye, Energy Consumption, Economic Growth and Prices: A Reassessment using Panel VECM for Developed and Developing Countries, *Energy Policy*, 35, 4 (2007), 2481–2490

Maitra, S. N., *A Collector's Piece*, Calcutta: Writer's Workshop (1997)

Majumdar, S. K., Government Policies and Industrial Performance: An Institutional Analysis of the Indian Experience, *Journal of Institutional and Theoretical Economics*, 152, 2 (1996), 380–411

　　The Impact of Size and Age on Firm-Level Performance: Some Evidence from Indian Industry. *Review of Industrial Organization*, 12, 2 (1997), 231–241

　　Private Enterprise Growth and Human Capital Productivity in India, *Entrepreneurship Theory and Practice*, 31, 6 (2007), 853–872

　　Crowding Out! The Role of State Companies and the Dynamics of Industrial Competitiveness in India, *Industrial and Corporate Change*, 18, 1 (2009), 165–207

Bodyshopping versus Capability Leverage: On the Relationship between Foreign Trade and Wages for Pharmaceutical and Service Sector Firms in India, *Analytique*, 6, 6 (2010), 3–7

Innovation Capability and Globalization Propensity in India's Information Technology and Software Industry, *Information Technology and International Development*, 6, 4 (2010), 45–56

Retentions, Relationships and Innovations: The Financing of R&D in India, *Economics of Innovation and New Technology*, 20, 3 (2011), 233–257

Majumdar, S. K., H. Chang, and O. Carare, General Purpose Technology Adoption and Firm Productivity: Evaluating Broadband Impact in the United States Telecommunications Industry, *Industrial and Corporate Change*, 19, 3 (2010), 641–674

Majumdar, S. K., K. Simons, and A. Nag, Bodyshopping versus Offshoring among Indian Software and Information Technology Firms, *Information Technology and Management*, 12, 1 (2011), 17–34

Malone, T. and R. Laubacher, The Dawn of the E-Lance Economy, *Harvard Business Review*, September–October (1998), 145–152

Marathe, S. S., *Regulation and Development: India's Policy Experience of Controls over Industry*, 2nd edn., New Delhi: Sage Publications (1989)

Markides, C. and P. Geroski, Colonizers and Consolidators: The Two Cultures of Corporate Strategy, *Strategy+Business*, 32, Autumn (2003), 1–11

Markovitz, C., *The Global World of Indian Merchants: Traders of Sind from Bukhara to Panama*, Cambridge University Press (2000)

Marshall, A., *Principles of Economics*, 8th edn., London: Macmillan (1920 [first published, 1890])

Marx, K., *Capital*, vol. 1, Harmondsworth: Penguin (1976 [first published, 1867])

Masters, J., *Bugles and a Tiger: My Life in the Gurkhas*, London: Cassell and Company (1956)

Mathews, J. A., A Silicon Valley of the East: Creating Taiwan's Semiconductor Industry, *California Management Review*, 39, 4 (1997), 26–54

Competitive Advantages of the Latecomer Firm: A Resource-Based Account of Industrial Catch-Up Strategies, *Asia Pacific Journal of Management*, 19 (2002), 467–488

Energizing Industrial Development, *Transnational Corporations*, 17, 3, (2008), 59–84

Mazumdar, D. and S. Sarkar, *Globalization, Labor Markets, and Inequality in India*, New York: Routledge (2008)

McAfee, A., Mastering the Three Worlds of Information Technology, *Harvard Business Review*, November (2006), 141–149

McClelland, D., *Human Motivation*, New York: Cambridge University Press (1987)

McKendrick, N., The Consumer Revolution of Eighteenth-Century England, in N. McKendrick, J. Brewer, and J. H. Plumb (eds.), *The Birth of a Consumer Society: The Commercialization of Eighteenth Century England*, Bloomington: Indiana University Press (1982), 9–33

McMillan, J. and C. Woodruff, The Central Role of Entrepreneurs in Transition Economies, *Journal of Economic Perspectives*, 16, 3 (2002), 153–170

Meier, G. M., *Biography of a Subject: An Evolution of Development Economics*, New York: Oxford University Press (2005)

Meredith, R., *The Elephant and the Dragon: The Rise of India and China and What it Means for All of Us*, New York: W. W. Norton and Company (2007)

Metcalf, T. R., *Ideologies of the Raj*, New Delhi, Foundation Books (1998)

Mill, J. S., *Principles of Political Economy*, London: Longman, Green and Company (1909 [first published, 1848])

Misra, M., *Business, Race and Politics in British India, c. 1850–1960*, Oxford University Press (1999)

Mokyr, J., *The Lever of Riches: Technological Creativity and Economic Progress*, New York: Oxford University Press (1990)

Intellectual Property Rights, the Industrial Revolution, and the Beginnings of Modern Economic Growth, *American Economic Review*, 99, 2 (2009), 349–355

The Enlightenment Economy: An Economic History of Britain, 1700–1850, New Haven, CT: Yale University Press (2010)

Moorhouse, G., *India Britannica*, Chicago: Academy Chicago Publishers (1983)

Morishima, M., *Why Has Japan "Succeeded"? Western Technology and the Japanese Ethos*, Cambridge University Press (1982)

Morris, M. D., South Asian Entrepreneurship and the Rashomon Effect, 1800–1947, *Explorations in Economic History*, 16, 3 (1979), 341–361

The Growth of Large Scale Industry, in D. Kumar and M. Desai (eds.), *The Cambridge Economic History of India, Volume 2, c.1757–c.1970*, Cambridge University Press (1983), 553–669

Mukherjee, H., The Swadeshi Movement of 1905: A Turning-Point in India's Struggle for National Liberation, lecture delivered June 30, 2006, Ramakrishna Mission Institute of Culture, Calcutta

Mukherjee, M., *An Indian for All Seasons: The Many Lives of R. C. Dutt*, New Delhi: Penguin Books (2009)

Murphy, K., A. Shleifer, and R. Vishny, Industrialization and the Big Push, *Journal of Political Economy*, 97, 5 (1989), 1003–1026

Musson, A. E., Industrial Motive Power in the United Kingdom, 1800–70, *Economic History Review*, 29, 3 (1976), 415–439

Musson, A. E. and E. Robinson, *Science and Technology in the Industrial Revolution*, Reading: Gordon and Breach (1969)

Myrdal, G., *Asian Drama: An Inquiry into the Poverty of Nations*, New York: Vintage Books (1971)

Nagaraj, R., Sub-contracting in Indian Manufacturing Industries: Analysis, Evidence and Issues, *Economic and Political Weekly*, 19, August (1984), 1435–1453

Nair, K., *Blossoms in the Dust: The Human Factor in Indian Development*, New York: Praeger Publishers (1961)

Nandy, A., *Traditions, Tyranny and Utopias: Essays in the Politics of Awareness*, New Delhi: Oxford University Press (1992)

Naoroji, D., *Poverty and Un-British Rule*, London: S. Sonnenschein and Company (1901)

Nath, K., *India's Century: The Age of Entrepreneurship in the World's Biggest Democracy*, New Delhi: Tata McGraw-Hill (2007)

Nayyar, D., Introduction, in D. Nayyar (ed.), *Industrial Growth and Stagnation: The Debate in India*, New Delhi: Oxford University Press (1994), 1–17

Nehru, B. K., *Nice Guys Finish Second*. New Delhi: Viking (1997)

Nehru, J., *Toward Freedom: An Autobiography*, New York: John Day (1941)

Nelson, R. R. and H. Pack, The Asian Miracle and Modern Growth Theory, *Economic Journal*, 109 (1999), 416–436

Nilekani, N., *Imagining India: The Idea of a Renewed Nation*, New York: Penguin (2008)

North, D. and R. P. Thomas, *The Rise of the Western World: A New Economic History*, Cambridge University Press (1973)

Nurkse, R., *Problems of Capital Formation in Underdeveloped Countries*, Oxford: Blackwell (1953)

Nye, D. E., *Electrifying America: Social Meanings of a New Technology, 1880–1940*, Cambridge, MA: MIT Press (1990)

O'Brien, P., Modern Conceptions of the Industrial Revolution, in P. O'Brien and R. Quinault (eds.), *The Industrial Revolution and British Society*, Cambridge University Press (1997), 1–30

Okun, A., *Equality and Efficiency: The Big Tradeoff*, Washington, DC: The Brookings Institution (1975)

Olson, M., *The Rise and Decline of Nations*, New Haven, CT: Yale University Press (1982)

Owen, G., *From Empire to Europe: The Decline and Revival of British Industry since the Second World War*, London: HarperCollins (1999)

Pacey, A., *Technology in World Civilization: A Thousand-Year History*, Cambridge, MA: MIT Press (1990)

Parente, S. L. and E. C. Prescott, *Barriers to Riches*, Cambridge, MA: MIT Press (2002)

Parry, B., *Delusions and Discoveries: India in the British Imagination, 1880–1930*, London: Verso Press (1998)

Patel, H. M., *Rites of Passage: A Civil Servant Remembers*, New Delhi: Rupa and Company (2005)

Patel, I. G., *Glimpses of Indian Economic Policy: An Insider's View*, New Delhi: Oxford University Press (2002)

Pavlov, V. I., *Historical Premises for India's Transition to Capitalism: Late Eighteenth to Mid Nineteenth Century*, Moscow: Nauka Publishing House Central Department of Oriental Literature (1978)

Paz, O., *In Light of India*, New York: Harcourt Brace (1995)

Pingle, V., *Rethinking the Developmental State: India's Industry in Comparative Perspective*. New Delhi: Oxford University Press (2000)

Piore, M. J. and C. F. Sabel, *The Second Industrial Divide: Possibilities for Prosperity*, New York: Basic Books (1984)

Piramal, G. and M. Hedreck, *India's Industrialists*, vol. 1, Boulder, CO: Lynne Rienner Publishers (1985)

Pollard, S. and P. Robertson, *The British Shipbuilding Industry: 1870–1914*, Cambridge, MA: Harvard University Press (1979)

Pomeranz, K. and S. Topik, *The World that Trade Created: Culture, Society and the World Economy, 1400 to the Present*, Armonk, NY: M. E. Sharpe (1997)

Powell, W. W. and K. Snellman, The Knowledge Economy, *Annual Review of Sociology*, 30, August (2004), 199–220

Prahalad, C. K., *The Fortune at the Bottom of the Pyramid: Eradicating Poverty through Profits*, Philadelphia, PA: Wharton School Publishing (2009)

Prahalad, C. K. and Y. Doz, *The Multinational Mission: Balancing Global Integration with Local Responsiveness*, New York: The Free Press (1987)

Raghunathan, N., *Memories, Men and Matters*, Bombay: Bharatiya Vidya Bhavan (1999)

Raj, K. N., Growth and Stagnation in Industrial Development, in D. Nayyar (ed.), *Industrial Growth and Stagnation: The Debate in India*, New Delhi: Oxford University Press (1994), 51–77

Ranade, M. G., *Essays on Indian Economics*, 2nd edn., Madras: G. A. Natesan and Company (1906)

Rangarajan, C., Industrial Growth: Another Look, in D. Nayyar, *Industrial Growth and Stagnation: The Debate in India*, New Delhi: Oxford University Press (1994), 289–317

Ratnagar, S., Harappan Trade in Its World Context, in R. Samaddar (ed.), *Trade in Early India*, New Delhi: Oxford University Press (2001), 102–127

Ray, H. P., *The Winds of Change: Buddhism and the Maritime Links of Early South Asia*, New Delhi: Oxford University Press (1994)

Ray, R. K., *Industrialization in India: Growth and Conflict in the Private Corporate Sector, 1914–1947*, New Delhi: Oxford University Press (1979)

Raychaudhuri, T., *Perceptions, Emotions, Sensibilities: Essays on India's Colonial and Post-Colonial Experiences*, New Delhi: Oxford University Press (1999)

Raymond, E., *The Cathedral and the Bazaar*, Thyrsus Enterprises [www.tuxedo.org/~esr/] (2000)

Reddy, B. S. and B. K. Ray, Decomposition of Energy Consumption and Energy Intensity in Indian Manufacturing Industries, *Energy for Sustainable Development*, 14, 1 (2010), 35–47

Reinert, E., *How Rich Countries Got Rich and Poor Countries Stay Poor*, New York: Public Affairs (2007)

Reynolds, L. G., *Economic Growth in the Third World, 1850–1980: An Introduction*, New Haven, CT: Yale University Press (1985)

Rheingold, H., *Virtual Reality*, New York: Summit Books (1991)

Riencourt, A. de, *The Soul of India*, London: Honeyglen Publishing (1986 [first published 1960])

Robins, N., *The Corporation that Changed the World: How the East India Company Shaped the Modern Multinational*, Hyderabad: Orient Longman (2006)

Rodrik, D., Getting Interventions Right: How South Korea and Taiwan Grew Rich, *Economic Policy*, 20, April (1995), 53–107

Roland, J. G., Baghdadi Jews in India and China in the Nineteenth Century: A Comparison of Economic Roles, in J. Goldstein (ed.), *The Jews of China, Volume 1, Historical and Cultural Perspectives*, New York: M. E. Sharpe (1999), 141–156

Romer, P., Increasing Returns and Long Run Growth, *Journal of Political Economy*, 94, 5 (1986), 1002–1037

Rosen, G., *Contrasting Styles of Industrial Reform: China and India in the 1980s*, University of Chicago Press (1992)

Rosenberg, N., *Technology and American Economic Growth*, New York: Harper and Row (1972)

Inside the Black Box: Technology and Economics, New York: Cambridge University Press (1982)

Exploring the Black Box: Technology, Economics and History, New York: Cambridge University Press (1994)

Rosenberg, N. and L. E. Birdzell, *How the West Grew Rich: The Economic Transformation of the Industrial World*, New York: Basic Books (1986)

Rosenstein-Rodan, P., Problems of Industrialization of Eastern and Southeastern Europe, *Economic Journal*, 53 (1943), 202–211

Rostow, W. W. Jr., *Theorists of Economic Growth from David Hume to the Present*, New York: Oxford University Press (1990)

Roy, T., *The Economic History of India, 1857–1947*, Oxford University Press (2006)

Rudolph, L. I. and S. H. Rudolph, *The Pursuit of Lakshmi: The Political Economy of the Indian State*, University of Chicago Press (1987)

Rudra, A., *Prasanta Chandra Mahalanobis: A Biography*, New Delhi: Oxford University Press (1999)

Rungta, R. S., *The Rise of Business Corporations in India, 1851–1900*, Cambridge University Press (1970)

Ruttan, V. W., *Technology, Growth, and Development: An Induced Innovation Perspective*, New York: Oxford University Press (2001)

Is War Necessary for Economic Growth?, New York: Oxford University Press (2006)

Said, E., *Culture and Imperialism*, London: Vintage Books (1993)

Salter, W. E. G., *Productivity and Technical Change*, Cambridge University Press (1960)

Samuels, R. J., *Rich Nation, Strong Army: National Security and the Technological Transformation of Japan*, Ithaca, NY: Cornell University Press (1994)

Samuelson, P. A., International Trade and the Equalisation of Factor Prices, *Economic Journal*, June (1948), 163–184

Sansom, G. B., *The Western World and Japan*, New York: Alfred A. Knopf (1950)

Sarathy, R., Global Strategy in Service Industries, *Long Range Planning*, 27, 6 (1994), 115–124

Sarkar, J., *Economics of British India*, 4th edn., Calcutta: M. C. Sarkar and Sons (1917)

Sarkar, S., *Modern India: 1885–1947*, New Delhi: Macmillan (1983)

Say, J.-B., *A Treatise on Political Economy or the Production, Distribution and Consumption of Wealth*, New York: A. M. Kelley (1971 [first published 1803])

Schelling, T., *Micromotives and Macrobehavior*, New York: W. W. Norton (1978)

Schuman, M., *The Miracle: The Epic Story of Asia's Quest for Wealth*, New York: HarperCollins (2009)

Schumpeter, J., *Capitalism, Socialism and Democracy*, New York: Harper and Row (1976)

Schurr, S. H., Energy, Technological Change and Productive Efficiency: An Economic-Historical Interpretation, *Annual Review of Energy*, 9 (1984), 409–425

Schramm, C., Building Entrepreneurial Economies, *Foreign Affairs*, 83, 4 (2004), 104–115

Seiford, L. M. and R. M. Thrall, Recent Developments in DEA: The Mathematical Programming Approach to Frontier Analysis, *Journal of Econometrics*, 46 (1990), 7–38

Sen, A., *Development as Freedom*, New York, Anchor Books (1999)

Sen, S., *Distant Sovereignty: Nationalist Imperialism and the Origins of British India*, New York: Routledge (2002)

Sen, S. K., Economic Transition in Bengal, in *Renascent Bengal (1817–1857): Proceedings of a Seminar Organized by the Asiatic Society*, Calcutta: The Asiatic Society (1972)

Sengupta, N. K., *Unshackling Indian Industry: Towards Competitiveness through Deregulation*, New Delhi: Vision Books (1992)

Setright, L. J. K., *Drive On: The Social History of the Motor Car*, London: Granta Books (2002)

Shackle, G. L. S., *Time in Economics*, Amsterdam: North-Holland (1958)

Sheshabalaya, A., *Rising Elephant: The Growing Clash with India over White-Collar Jobs and Its Challenge to America and the World*, Monroe, ME: Common Courage Press (2005)

Shrinagesh, J. M., *Between Two Stools: My Life in the ICS before and after Independence*, New Delhi: Rupa and Company (2007)

Singh, N., Services-Led Industrialization in India: Assessment and Lessons, in D. O'Connor (ed.), *Industrial Development for the Twenty-First Century: Sustainable Development Perspectives*, New York: Orient Longman (2008), 235–291

Sinha, P., Calcutta and the Currents of History, 1690–1912, in S. Chaudhuri (ed.), *Calcutta: The Living City, Volume 1, The Past*, New Delhi: Oxford University Press (1990), 31–44

Skidelsky, R., *The World After Communism: A Polemic for Our Times*, London: Papermac (1995)

Skinner, W., Manufacturing: Missing Link in Corporate Strategy, *Harvard Business Review*, May–June (1969), 136–145

Three Yards and a Cloud of Dust: Industrial Management at Century End, *Production and Operations Management*, 5, 1 (1996), 15–24

Sokoloff, K. L. and B. Z. Khan, The Democratization of Invention during Early Industrialization: Evidence from the United States, 1790–1846, *Journal of Economic History*, 50, 2 (1990), 363–378

Spence, M., *The Next Convergence: The Future of Economic Growth in a Multiconnected World*, New York: Farrar, Straus and Giroux (2011)

Spulber, D., *Market Microstructure: Intermediaries and the Theory of the Firm*, New York: Cambridge University Press (1999)

Strachey, J., *India: Its Administration and Progress*, 3rd edn., London: Macmillan (1903)

Subramanian, C., *Hand of Destiny: Memoirs, Volume 2, The Green Revolution*, Bombay: Bharatiya Vidya Bhavan (1995)

Subrahmanyam, S., Introduction, in S. Subrahmanyam (ed.), *Merchants, Markets and the State in Early Modern India*, New Delhi: Oxford University Press (1990), 1–17

Subrahmanyam, S. and C. A. Bayly, Portfolio Capitalists and the Political Economy of Early Modern India, in S. Subrahmanyam (ed.), *Merchants, Markets and the State in Early Modern India*, New Delhi: Oxford University Press (1990), 242–265

Szirmai, A., *The Dynamics of Socio-economic Development*, Cambridge University Press (2007)

Tandon, P. L., *Beyond Punjab*, New Delhi: Thompson Press (1971)

Tang, J., Technological Leadership and Late Development: Evidence from Meiji Japan, 1868–1912, *Economic History Review*, 64, February (2011), 99–116

Teece, D. J., The Dynamics of Industrial Capitalism: Perspective on Alfred Chandler's *Scale and Scope, Journal of Economic Literature*, 31, 1 (1993), 199–225

Thakurdas, P., J. R. D. Tata, G. D. Birla, A. Dalal, Shri Ram, K. Lalbhai, A. D. Shroff, and J. Mathai, *A Plan of Economic Development for India: Parts I and II*, Harmondsworth: Penguin (1945)

Tharoor, S., *India: From Midnight to the Millennium*, New Delhi: Penguin Books (1997)

Thomas, K., History and Anthropology, *Past and Present*, 24 (1963), 3–24

Timberg, T. A., *The Marwaris: From Traders to Industrialists*, New Delhi: Vikas Publishing House (1978)

Tocqueville, A. de, *Democracy in America*, edited, translated, and with an introduction by H. C. Mansfield and D. Winthrop, University of Chicago Press (2000 [first published 1835])

Tomlinson, B. R., Colonial Firms and the Decline of Colonialism in Eastern India: 1914–47, *Modern Asian Studies*, 15, 3 (1981), 455–486

The Economy of Modern India, 1860–1970, Cambridge University Press (1993)

Tripathi, D., Occupational Mobility and Entrepreneurship in India: A Historical Analysis, *The Developing Economies*, 19, 1 (1981), 52–67

Tully, M., *The Heart of India*, London: Penguin Books (1995)

Usher, A. P., *A History of Mechanical Inventions*, Princeton University Press (1955)

Van Stel, A., M. Carree, and R. Thurik, The Effect of Entrepreneurial Activity on National Economic Growth, *Small Business Economics*, 24 (2005), 311–321

Varian, H. and C. Shapiro, *Information Rules*, Boston: Harvard Business School Press (1999)

Veblen, T., Why is Economics not an Evolutionary Science? *Quarterly Journal of Economics*, 12, July (1898), 373–397

The Theory of Business Enterprise, New York: Charles Scribner's Sons (1904)

The Engineers and the Price System, Kitchener, Ont: Batoche Books (2001 [first published, 1921])

Imperial Germany and the Industrial Revolution, Kitchener, Ont: Batoche Books (2003 [first published, 1915])

Venkatachar, C. S., *Witness to the Century: Writings of C. S. Venkatachar, ICS*, ed. S. Sapru and K. M. Acharya, Bangalore: published privately (1999)

Vicziany, M., Bombay Merchants and Structural Changes in the Export Community: 1850 to 1880, in K. N. Chaudhuri and C. J. Dewey (eds.), *Economy and Society: Essays in Indian Economic and Social History*, New York: Oxford University Press (1979)

Visvesvaraya, M., *Reconstructing India*, London: P. S. King and Son (1920)

Vries, J. de, *The Industrious Revolution: Consumer Behavior and the Household Economy, 1650 to the Present*, Cambridge University Press (2008)

Wacha, D. E., *The Life and Life Work of J. N. Tata*, 2nd edn., Madras: Ganesh and Company (1915)

Wade, R., *Governing the Market: Economic Theory and the Role of Government in East Asian Industrialization*, Princeton University Press (1990)

Wadia, P. A. and K. T. Merchant, *Our Economic Problem*, 6th edn., Bombay, Vora and Company, (1959)

Weightman, G., *The Industrial Revolutionaries: The Creation of the Modern World, 1776–1919*, London: Atlantic Books (2007)

Weitzman, M., Prices versus Quantities, *Review of Economic Studies*, 41, 4 (1974), 477–491

Recombinant Growth, *Quarterly Journal of Economics*, 113, 2 (1998), 331–360

Westphal, L., Industrial Policy in an Export-Propelled Economy: Lessons from South Korea's Experience, *Journal of Economic Perspectives*, 4, 3 (1990), 41–59

World Bank, *The East Asian Miracle: Economic Growth and Public Policy*, New York: Oxford University Press (1993)

Worrell, E., L. Price, N. Martin, J. Farla, and R. Schaeffer, Energy Intensity in the Iron and Steel Industry: A Comparison of Physical and Economic Indicators, *Energy Policy*, 25, 7–9 (1997), 727–744

Wright, G., The Origins of American Industrial Success, 1879–1940, *American Economic Review*, 80 (1990), 651–658

Wu, Y., Service Sector Growth in India and China: A Comparison, *China: An International Journal*, 5, 1 (2007), 137–154

Xiang, B., *Global "Body Shopping": An Indian Labor System in the Information Technology Industry*, Princeton University Press (2007)

Yergin, D. and J. Stanislaw, *Commanding Heights*, New York: Touchstone (1998)

Young, A., Increasing Returns and Economic Progress, *Economic Journal*, 38, 152 (1928), 527–542

Zinkin, M., *Development for a Free Asia*, London: Chatto and Windus (1963)

Zysman, J., Transforming Production in a Digital Era, in W. Dutton, B. Kahin, R. O'Callaghan, and A. Wyckoff (eds.), *Transforming Enterprise*, Cambridge, MA: MIT Press (2004), 257–282

Index

Achaemenid Empire, 71
Ackland, George, 90, 91
Adams, Brooks, 85
administrative controls
 capacity pre-emption, 161
 unused manufacturing capacity, 161
 centralization of power, 160
 constrictive not constructive, 160
 creation of an administrative monster, 160
 entrepreneurs pirates not patriots, 160
 judgment of planners on firms' operational matters, 160
 licensing and regulations as entry barriers, 161
 protecting domestic markets, 161
 rent-seeking by firms, 161
Aeronautical Development Agency, 259
Agricultural development
 lack of, 62
Agro-Dutch Industries, 191
Alexandria, 71
Ali, Haidar, 77
Allen, Robert, 339
Ambassador car, 162, 225
 as Calcutta taxis, 174
 retired cars re-manufactured, 277
American Civil War 1861 to 1865, 59, 97
 opportunities for supply of Indian cotton, 108
American mass production items, 48
American Revolution, 48
American system of manufactures, 51
American system of manufacturing
 role of firearms production, 256
Amrita Bazar Group, 104

Amsden, Alice
 on role of government in industrialization, 148
 role of capital goods, 136
Amul cooperative model, 106
Ananda Bazar Group, 104
animal spirits, 175
Annual Survey of Industries (ASI), 198
application of science to industry, 40
Arcelor-Mittal Group, 20, 92, 186
 origins in eastern India engineering and metals eco-system, 117
Arkwright, Richard, 42, 44, 85
Arvind Mills, 98
Ashton, Thomas, xxiv, 40, 41, 242
assembly lines, 54
 used in meat packing and manufacture of automobiles, 48
Associated Cement Companies, 20
Auchinleck, Field Marshal Claude, 114
Aurangazeb
 brutal fascist regime of, 80
 dies in 1707, 78, 171
automobiles, 53, 54
 impact on human economy and society, 53

B-24 Liberator, 262, 263
 flying survivor an Indian Air Force aircraft, 262
 further service in India, 231, 262
 remanufactured in India, 262
Babbage, Charles, 146, 241, 248
 role of techniques, 146
 views on India, 241
Bacon, Francis, 40
Bagchi, Amiya, 338
Bairoch, Paul, 63, 128
Ball, Philip, 150

Curzon, George, (*cont.*)
 impact on Bengali entrepreneurship,
  101
Cusumano, Michael, 290

Dacca muslins, 84
Dalal, Ardeshir ICS, 19, 158
 later Director of Tata Sons, 334
Dallas, Texas, 53
Damascene swords, 258
 originally forged in Hyderabad, 92
Damodaran, Harish, 186
Dandekar, Narayan ICS, 335
Darjeeling, 270
Darwinian competition, 21
Das, Gurcharan, 30
Das, Nabagopal ICS, 114
Dasgupta, Justice Kulada Charan ICS,
  20
data envelopment analysis (DEA), 226,
  367
Davar, Cowasjee N., 45, 97
Davy, Humphrey, 52
Dayal, Rajeshwar ICS, 329
DC-3 Dakota, 262
 remanufactured in India, 262
de Jouy, Brillon
 Parisian merchant, 43
de Tocqueville, Alexis, xx, 168
Deane, Phyllis, xxiv, 41
Deb, Sudipto, 288
Deccan, 17, 74, 78, 85
Defence Research and Development
  Organization (DRDO), 258,
  259, 261
Defoe, Daniel, 44
deindustrialization, xxiii, 11, 45, 224,
  241, 284
Delhi, 3, 88, 92
 2,000 year old rust-proof iron pillar,
  92
delicensing industrial entry
 big bang preceded by piecemeal
  reforms, 188
 D-Day 24th July 1991, 166
 institutional discontinuity, 168
 reacquiring freedom, 168
 re-entry into an age of autonomous
  thinking, 170
 removal of institutional entry
  barriers, 166, 170

 removal of mental entry barriers,
  170
demand aggregation, 60
demand for technically-competent
  managers, 58
democratic society
 role of individual choices, 168
democratization of commerce, 171
 changes in entrepreneurs' qualities,
  171
democratization of enterprise, xx
 followed political democracy, xx
democratization of entrepreneurship,
  179, 210, 278
 arising from an institutional
  discontinuity, 168
 burden of strategic choice on
  businessman, 169
 capital scarcity and no occurrence in
  nineteenth century, 98
 decentralized disequilibrium, 192
 economic self-determination and
  moral responsibility, 169
 financial conditions impeding
  occurrence, 98
 first initiative in Asia by Taiwan at
  KEPZ, 132
 response by micro and small
  entrepreneurs, 210
 role of export processing zone (EPZ)
  and SEZ model, 132
 role of SFCs and SIDCs, 164
 start of the process in Madras, 125
 world's largest episode, 171
democratization of financing, 106, 107
 birth of idea, 106
 impact on democratization of
  entrepreneurship, 107
 launch of Gujarat's industrial
  revolution, 106
 nationalization of major Indian
  banks in 1969 and 1980, 107
democratization of invention, 56, 62,
  302
 access to economic opportunities, 57
 stimulation of inventors' efforts, 56
democratization of markets, 61, 62,
  248
 consumer revolution, 61
Department of Industrial Policy and
  Promotion, 23, 27

Printed in the United States
by Baker & Taylor Publisher Services